NAOKI URASAWA'S

20th CENTURY BOYS

Naoki Urasawa's
20th Century Boys
Volume 09

VIZ Signature Edition

STORY AND ART BY NAOKI URASAWA

20 SEIKI SHONEN 9 by Naoki URASAWA/Studio Nuts
© 2002 Naoki URASAWA/Studio Nuts
With the cooperation of Takashi NAGASAKI
All rights reserved. Original Japanese
edition published in 2002 by Shogakukan Inc., Tokyo.

English Adaptation/Akemi Wegmüller
Touch-up Art & Lettering/Freeman Wong
Cover & Interior Design/Sam Elzway
Editor/Kit Fox

VP, Production/Alvin Lu
VP, Sales & Product Marketing/Gonzalo Ferreyra
VP, Creative/Linda Espinosa
Publisher/Hyoe Narita

Printed in the U.S.A.

Published by VIZ Media, LLC
P.O. Box 77010
San Francisco, CA 94107

10 9 8 7 6 5 4 3 2 1
First printing, June 2010

VIZ SIGNATURE
www.vizsignature.com

VIZ
media
www.viz.com

NAOKI URASAWA'S
20th CENTURY BOYS

VOL 09
RABBIT NABOKOV

Story & Art by
NAOKI URASAWA

With the cooperation of
Takashi NAGASAKI

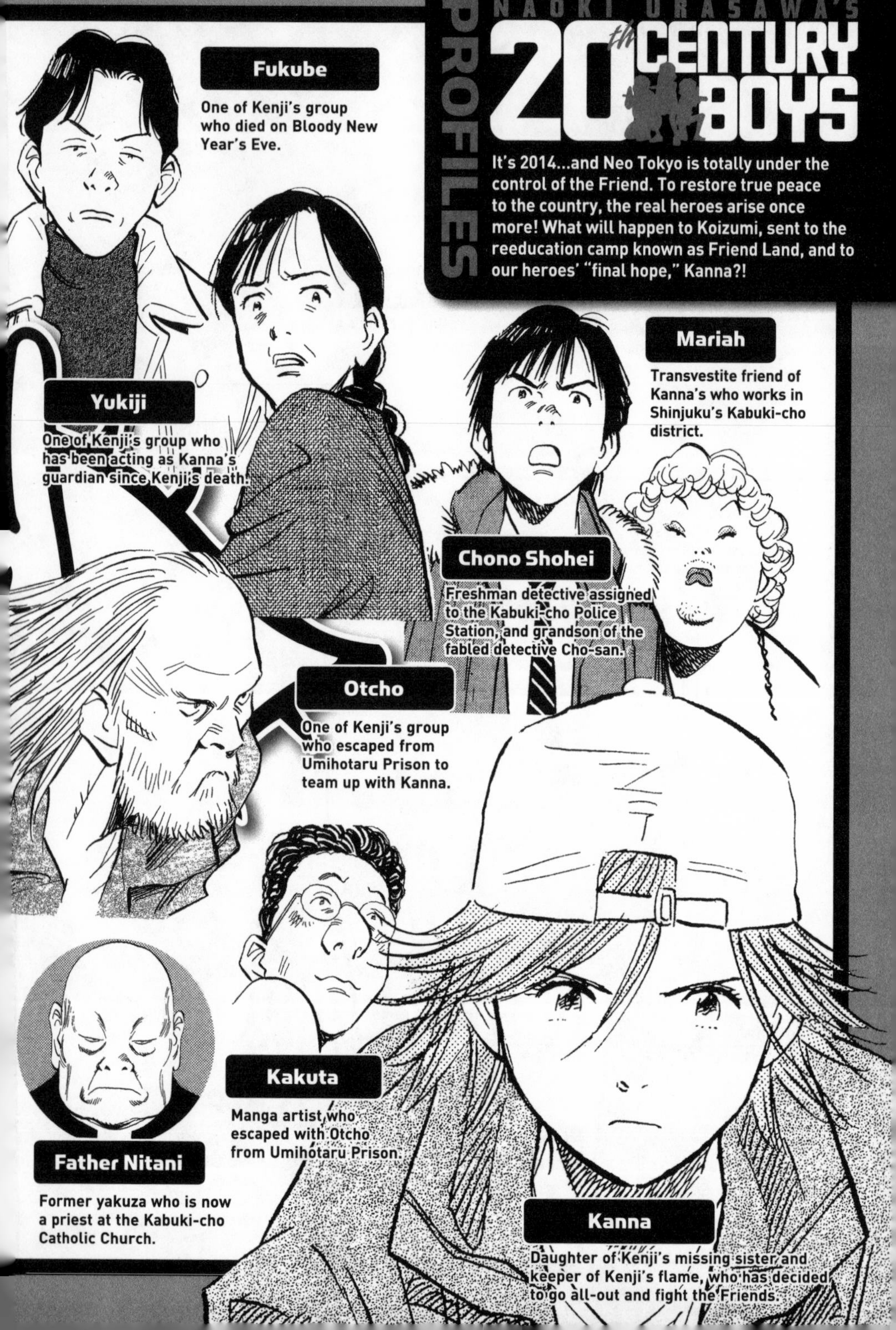

PROFILES

NAOKI URASAWA'S

20th CENTURY BOYS

It's 2014...and Neo Tokyo is totally under the control of the Friend. To restore true peace to the country, the real heroes arise once more! What will happen to Koizumi, sent to the reeducation camp known as Friend Land, and to our heroes' "final hope," Kanna?!

Fukube

One of Kenji's group who died on Bloody New Year's Eve.

Mariah

Transvestite friend of Kanna's who works in Shinjuku's Kabuki-cho district.

Yukiji

One of Kenji's group who has been acting as Kanna's guardian since Kenji's death.

Chono Shohei

Freshman detective assigned to the Kabuki-cho Police Station, and grandson of the fabled detective Cho-san.

Otcho

One of Kenji's group who escaped from Umihotaru Prison to team up with Kanna.

Kakuta

Manga artist who escaped with Otcho from Umihotaru Prison.

Father Nitani

Former yakuza who is now a priest at the Kabuki-cho Catholic Church.

Kanna

Daughter of Kenji's missing sister and keeper of Kenji's flame, who has decided to go all-out and fight the Friends.

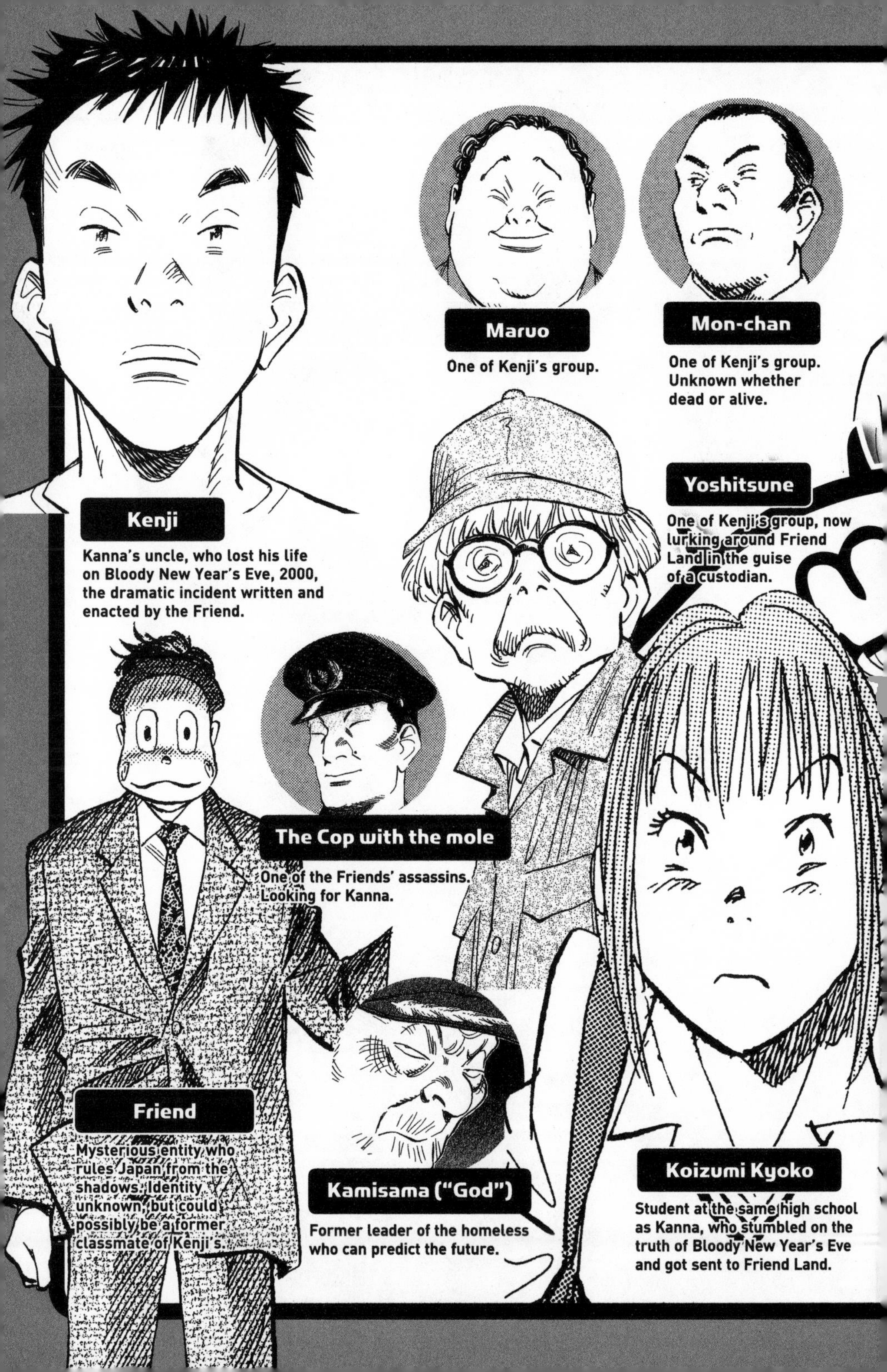
Kenji
Kanna's uncle, who lost his life on Bloody New Year's Eve, 2000, the dramatic incident written and enacted by the Friend.
Maruo
One of Kenji's group.
Mon-chan
One of Kenji's group. Unknown whether dead or alive.
Yoshitsune
One of Kenji's group, now lurking around Friend Land in the guise of a custodian.
The Cop with the mole
One of the Friends' assassins. Looking for Kanna.
Friend
Mysterious entity who rules Japan from the shadows. Identity unknown, but could possibly be a former classmate of Kenji's.
Kamisama ("God")
Former leader of the homeless who can predict the future.
Koizumi Kyoko
Student at the same high school as Kanna, who stumbled on the truth of Bloody New Year's Eve and got sent to Friend Land.

CONTENTS

VOL 09
RABBIT NABOKOV

NAOKI
URASAWA'S

20 CENTURY BOYS

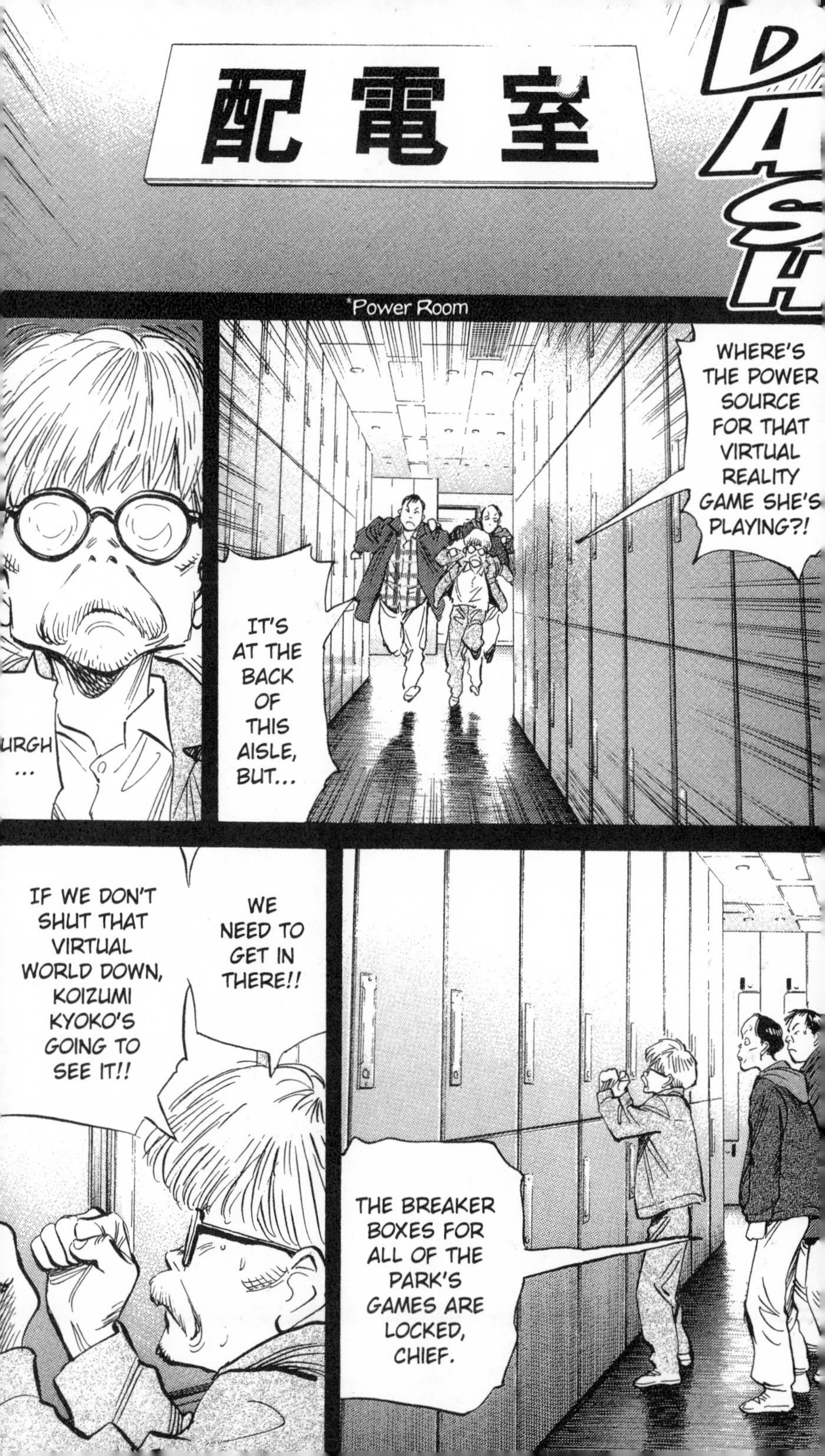
配電室
DASH
*Power Room
WHERE'S THE POWER SOURCE FOR THAT VIRTUAL REALITY GAME SHE'S PLAYING?!
IT'S AT THE BACK OF THIS AISLE, BUT...
URGH ...
THE BREAKER BOXES FOR ALL OF THE PARK'S GAMES ARE LOCKED, CHIEF.
WE NEED TO GET IN THERE!!
IF WE DON'T SHUT THAT VIRTUAL WORLD DOWN, KOIZUMI KYOKO'S GOING TO SEE IT!!

IF YOU TELL EVEN ONE PERSON...

SHE'S GOING TO SEE THE *FRIEND'S* FACE WHILE SHE'S IN THERE!!

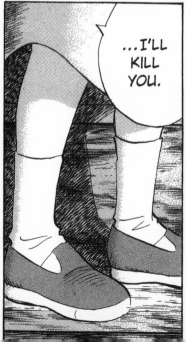

...I'LL KILL YOU.

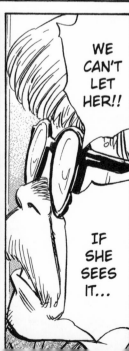

WE CAN'T LET HER!!

IF SHE SEES IT...

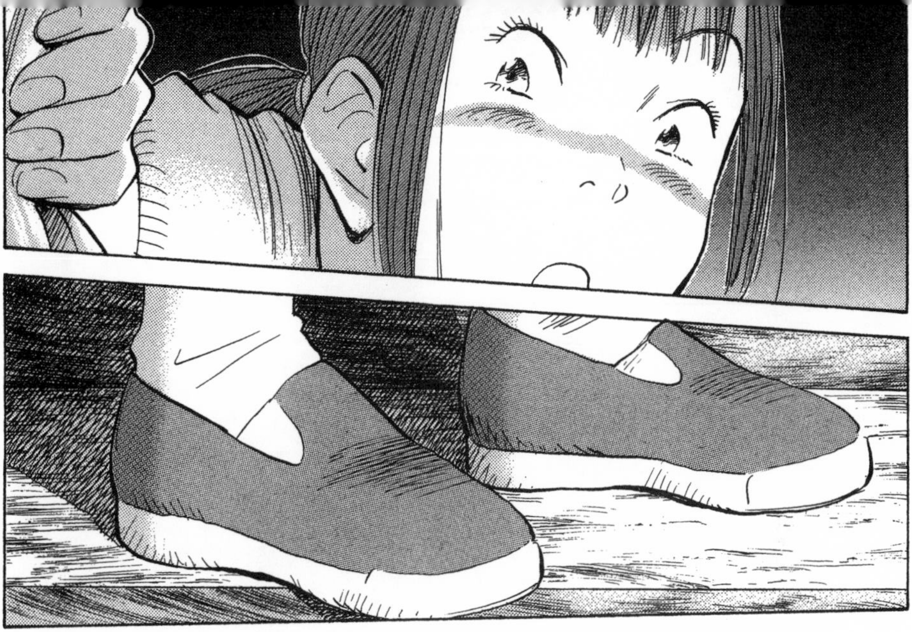

Chapter 1
Don't Look

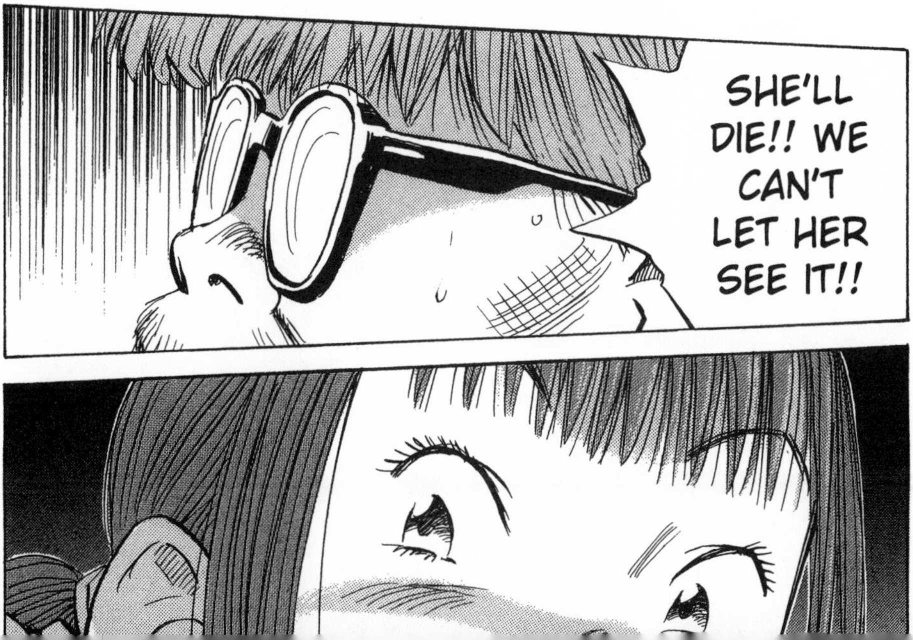
SHE'LL DIE!! WE CAN'T LET HER SEE IT!!

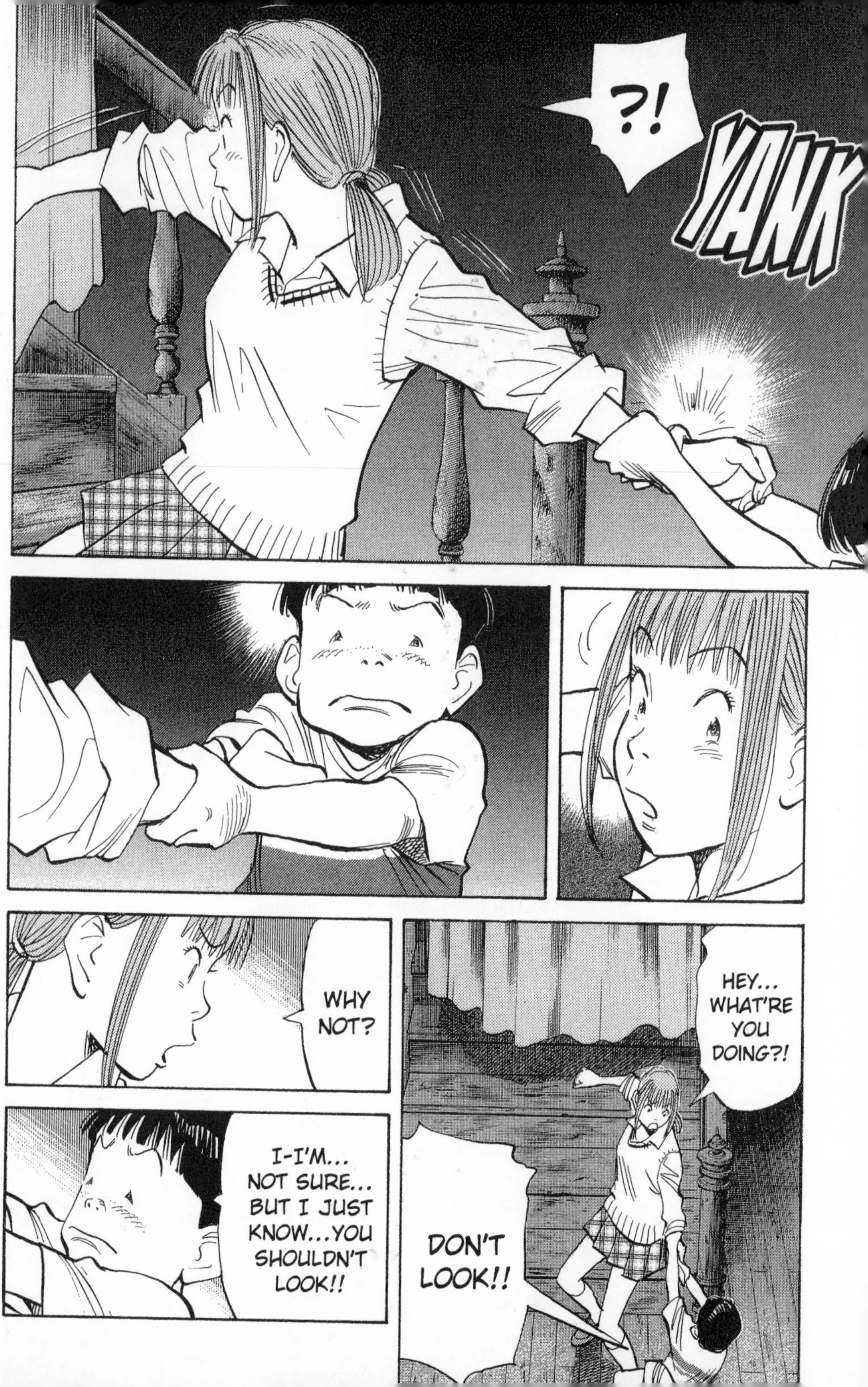
?!
YANK
HEY... WHAT'RE YOU DOING?!
DON'T LOOK!!
WHY NOT?
I-I'M... NOT SURE... BUT I JUST KNOW...YOU SHOULDN'T LOOK!!

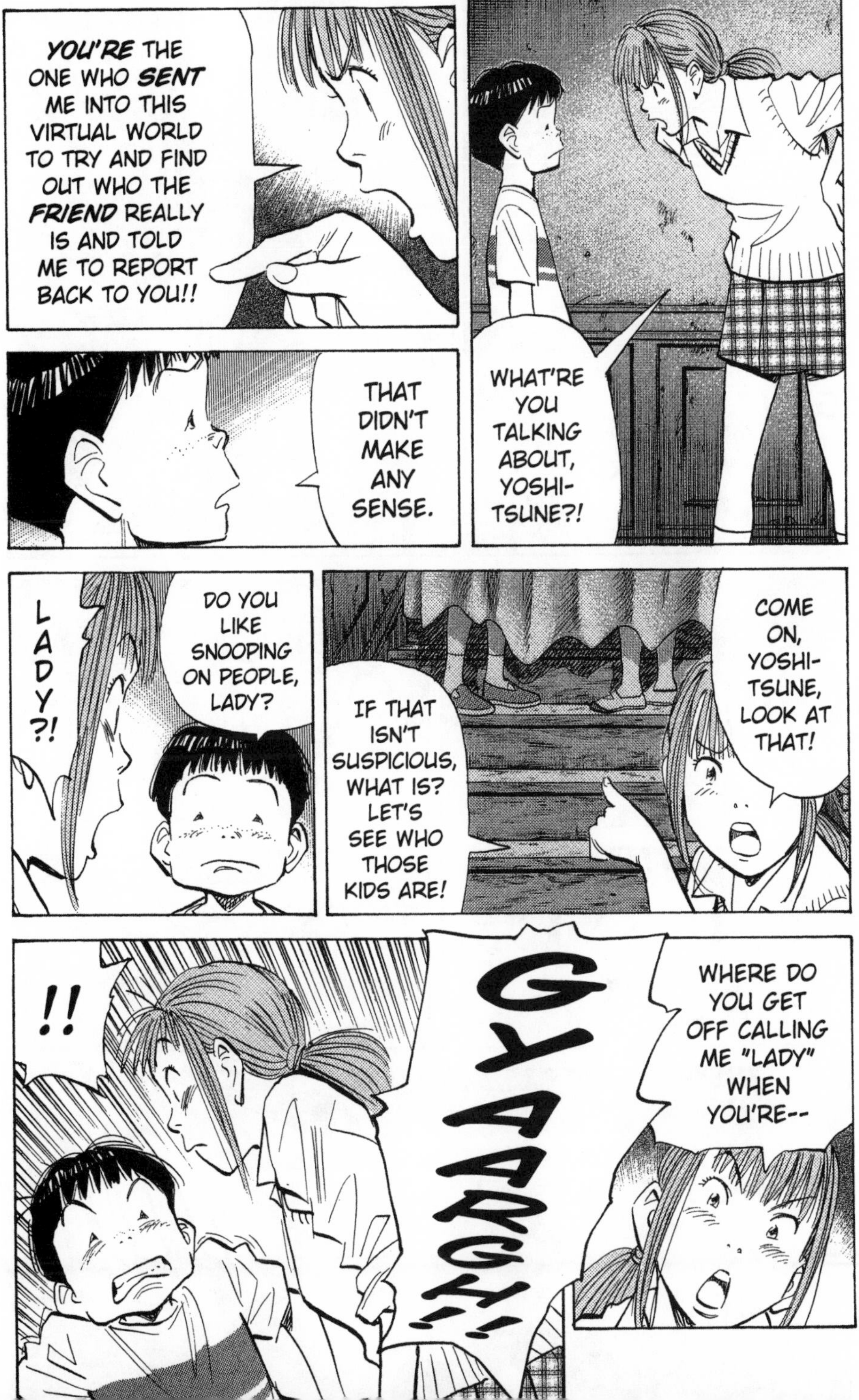
WHAT'RE YOU TALKING ABOUT, YOSHI-TSUNE?!
YOU'RE THE ONE WHO SENT ME INTO THIS VIRTUAL WORLD TO TRY AND FIND OUT WHO THE FRIEND REALLY IS AND TOLD ME TO REPORT BACK TO YOU!!
THAT DIDN'T MAKE ANY SENSE.
COME ON, YOSHI-TSUNE, LOOK AT THAT!
IF THAT ISN'T SUSPICIOUS, WHAT IS? LET'S SEE WHO THOSE KIDS ARE!
DO YOU LIKE SNOOPING ON PEOPLE, LADY?
LADY?!
WHERE DO YOU GET OFF CALLING ME "LADY" WHEN YOU'RE--
GYAARGH!!
!!

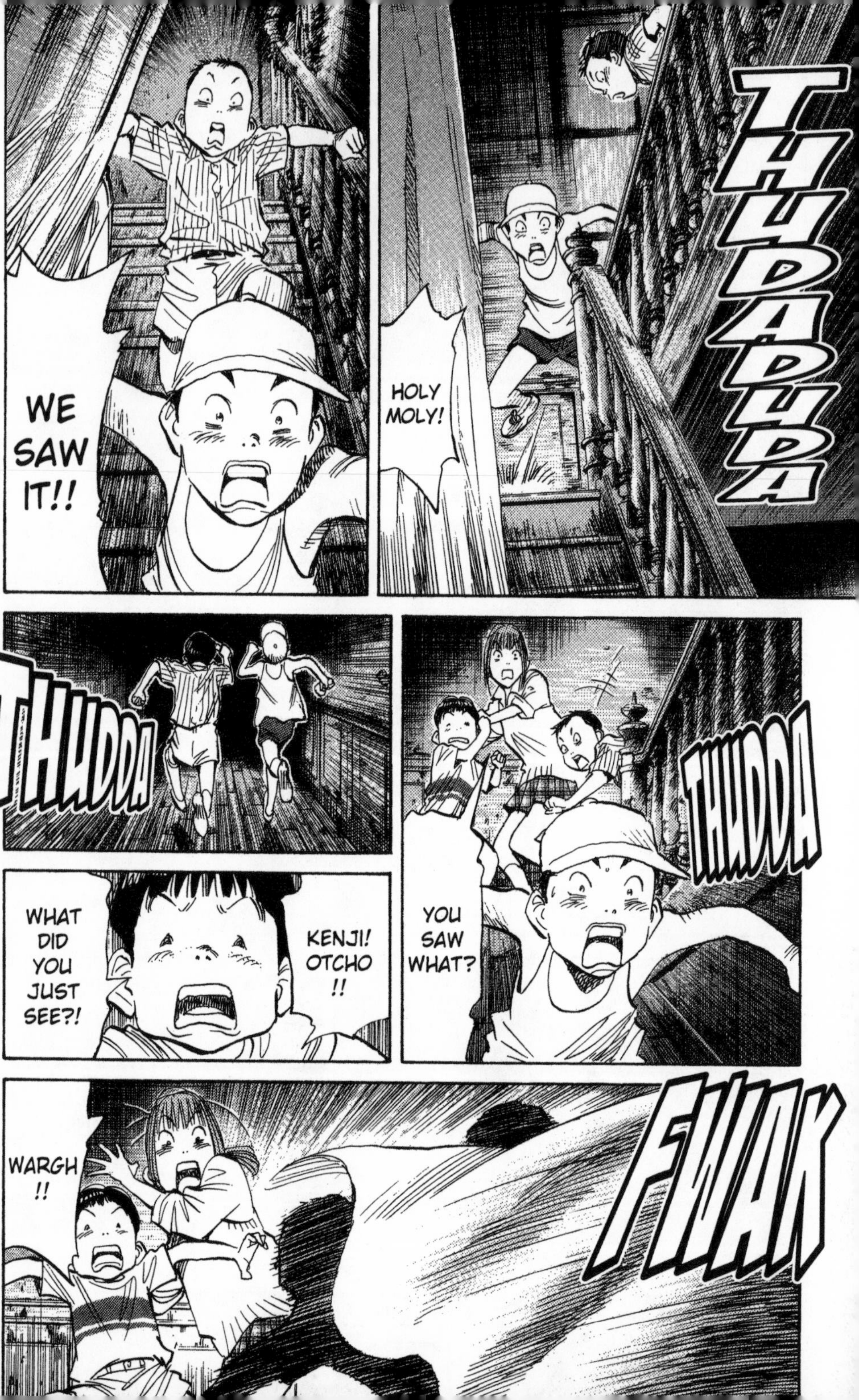
THUDADUDA
HOLY MOLY!
WE SAW IT!!
THUDDA
YOU SAW WHAT?
THUDDA
KENJI! OTCHO!!
WHAT DID YOU JUST SEE?!
FWAK
WARGH!!

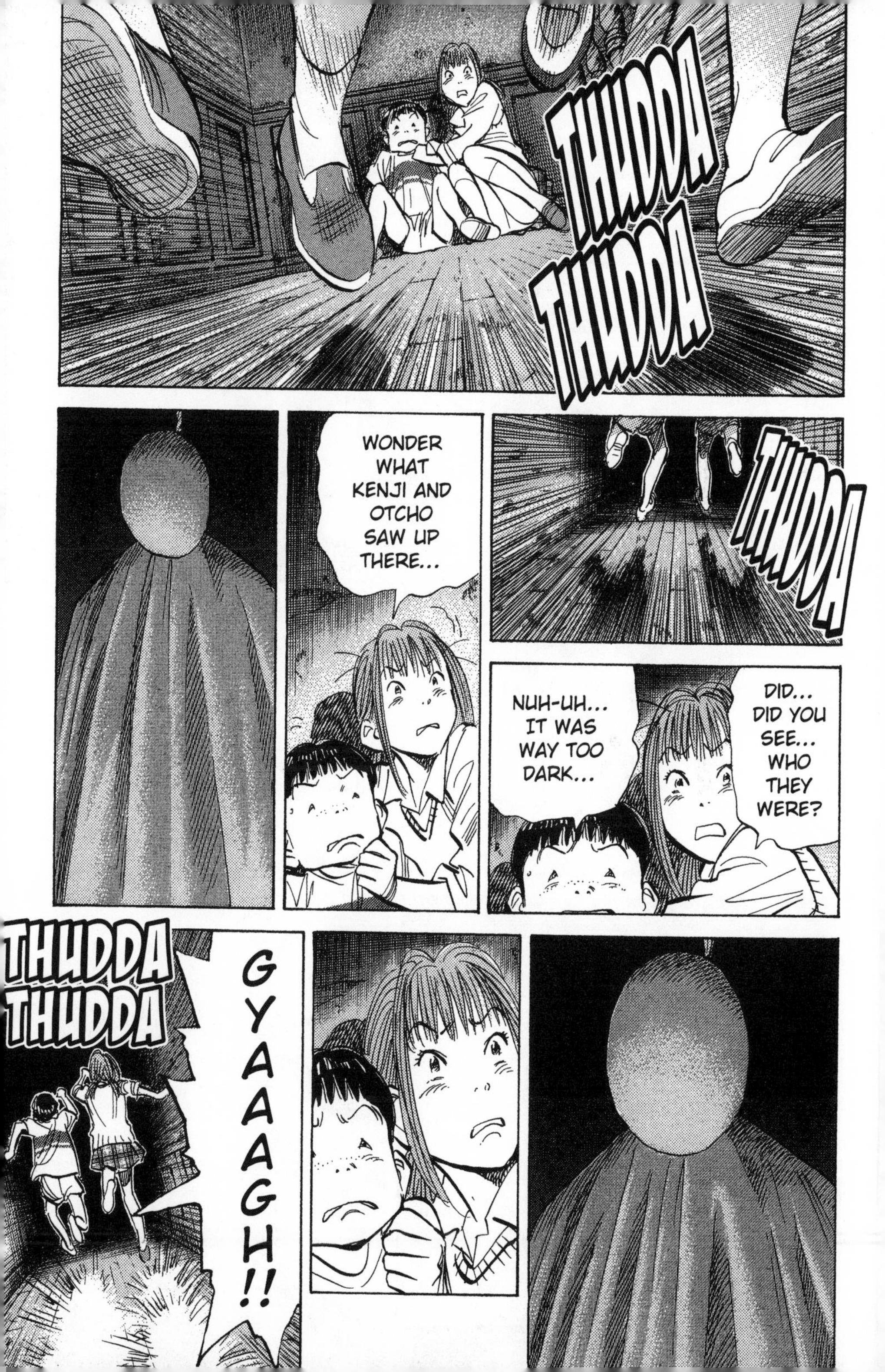
THUDDA THUDDA
THUDDA
DID... DID YOU SEE... WHO THEY WERE?
NUH-UH... IT WAS WAY TOO DARK...
WONDER WHAT KENJI AND OTCHO SAW UP THERE...
GYAAAAGH!!
THUDDA THUDDA

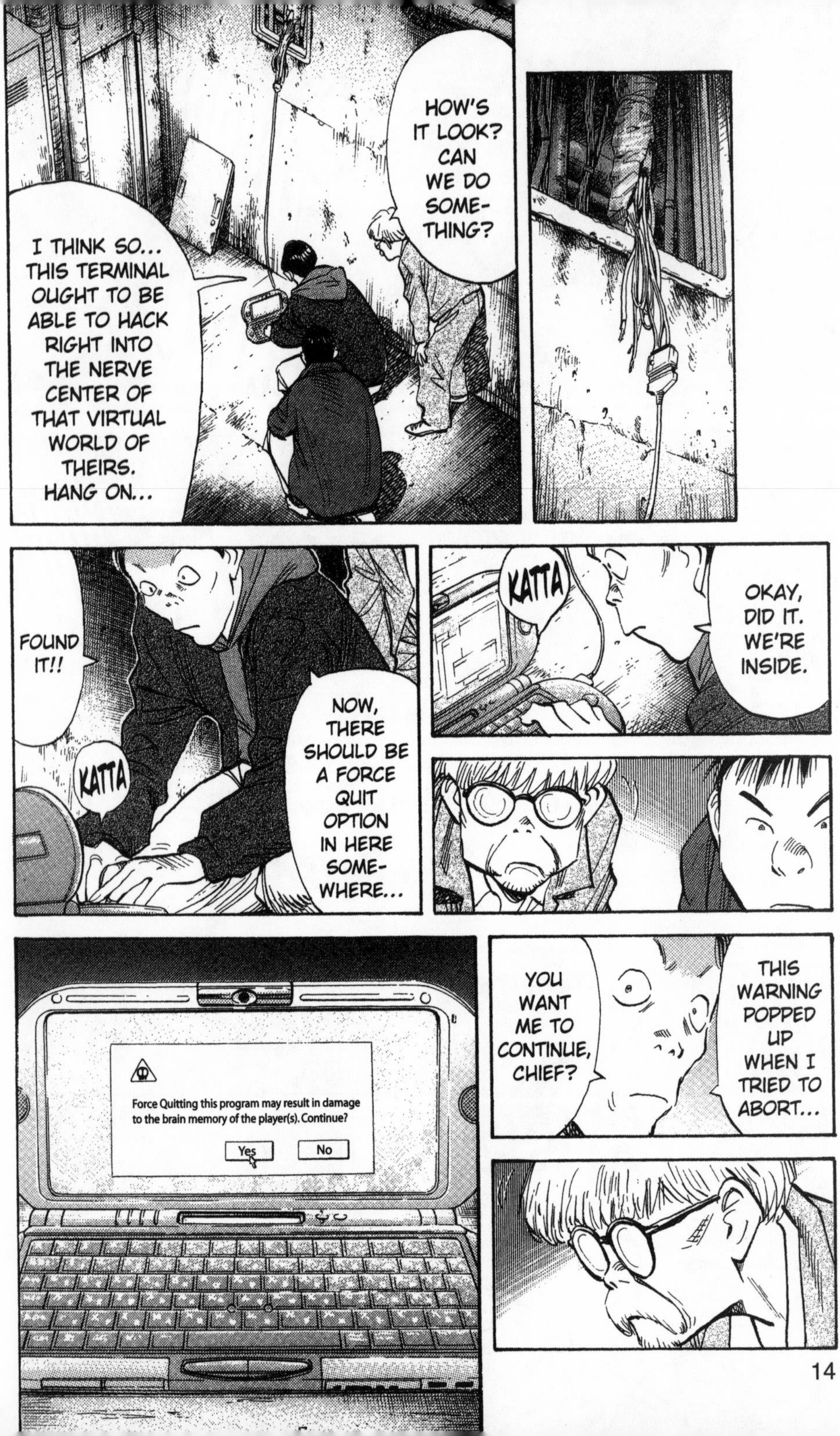
HOW'S IT LOOK? CAN WE DO SOME-THING?
I THINK SO... THIS TERMINAL OUGHT TO BE ABLE TO HACK RIGHT INTO THE NERVE CENTER OF THAT VIRTUAL WORLD OF THEIRS. HANG ON...
OKAY, DID IT. WE'RE INSIDE.
KATTA
NOW, THERE SHOULD BE A FORCE QUIT OPTION IN HERE SOME-WHERE...
FOUND IT!!
KATTA
THIS WARNING POPPED UP WHEN I TRIED TO ABORT...
YOU WANT ME TO CONTINUE, CHIEF?
Force Quitting this program may result in damage to the brain memory of the player(s). Continue?
Yes
No

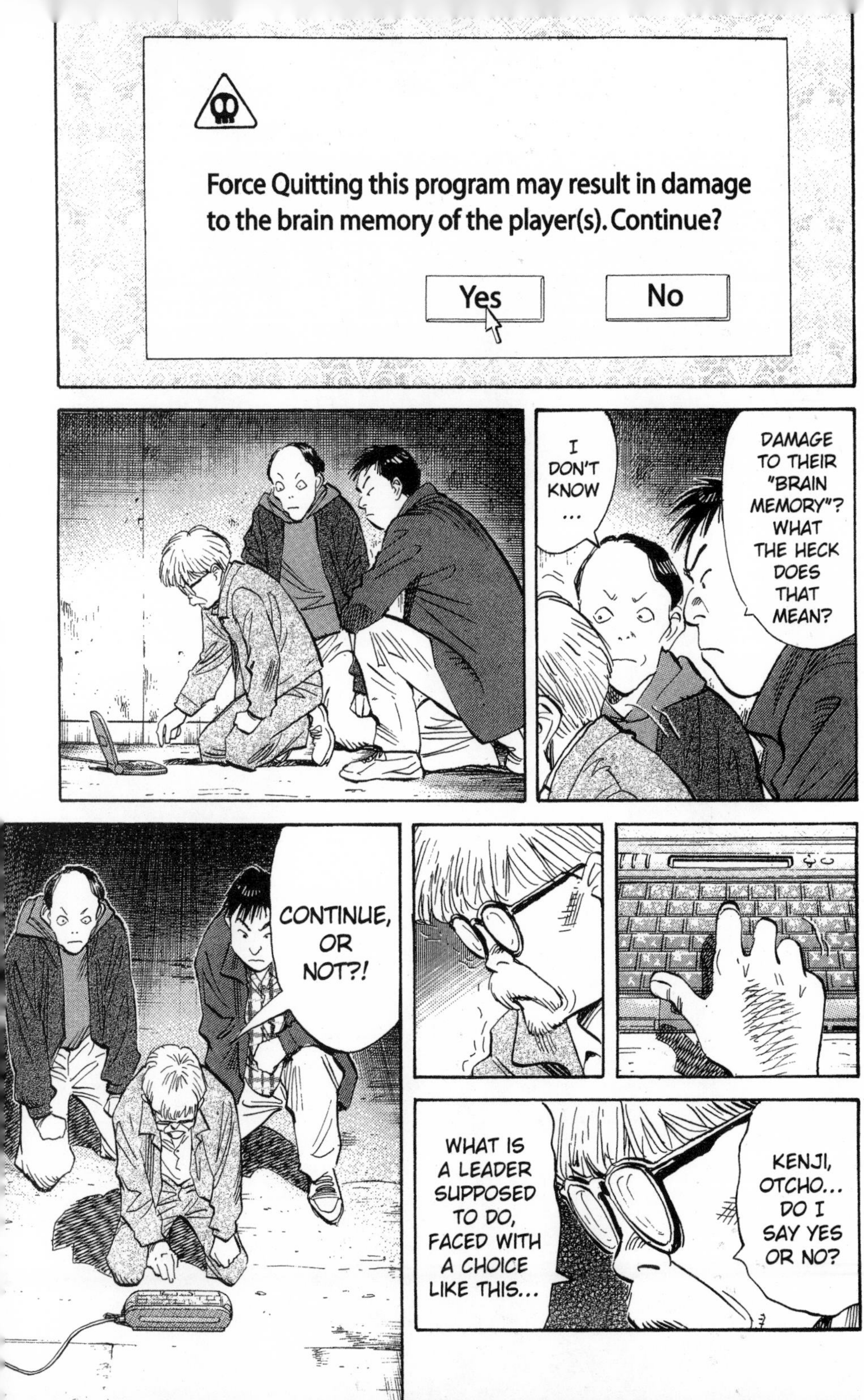
Force Quitting this program may result in damage to the brain memory of the player(s). Continue?
Yes
No
DAMAGE TO THEIR "BRAIN MEMORY"? WHAT THE HECK DOES THAT MEAN?
I DON'T KNOW...
KENJI, OTCHO... DO I SAY YES OR NO?
WHAT IS A LEADER SUPPOSED TO DO, FACED WITH A CHOICE LIKE THIS...
CONTINUE, OR NOT?!

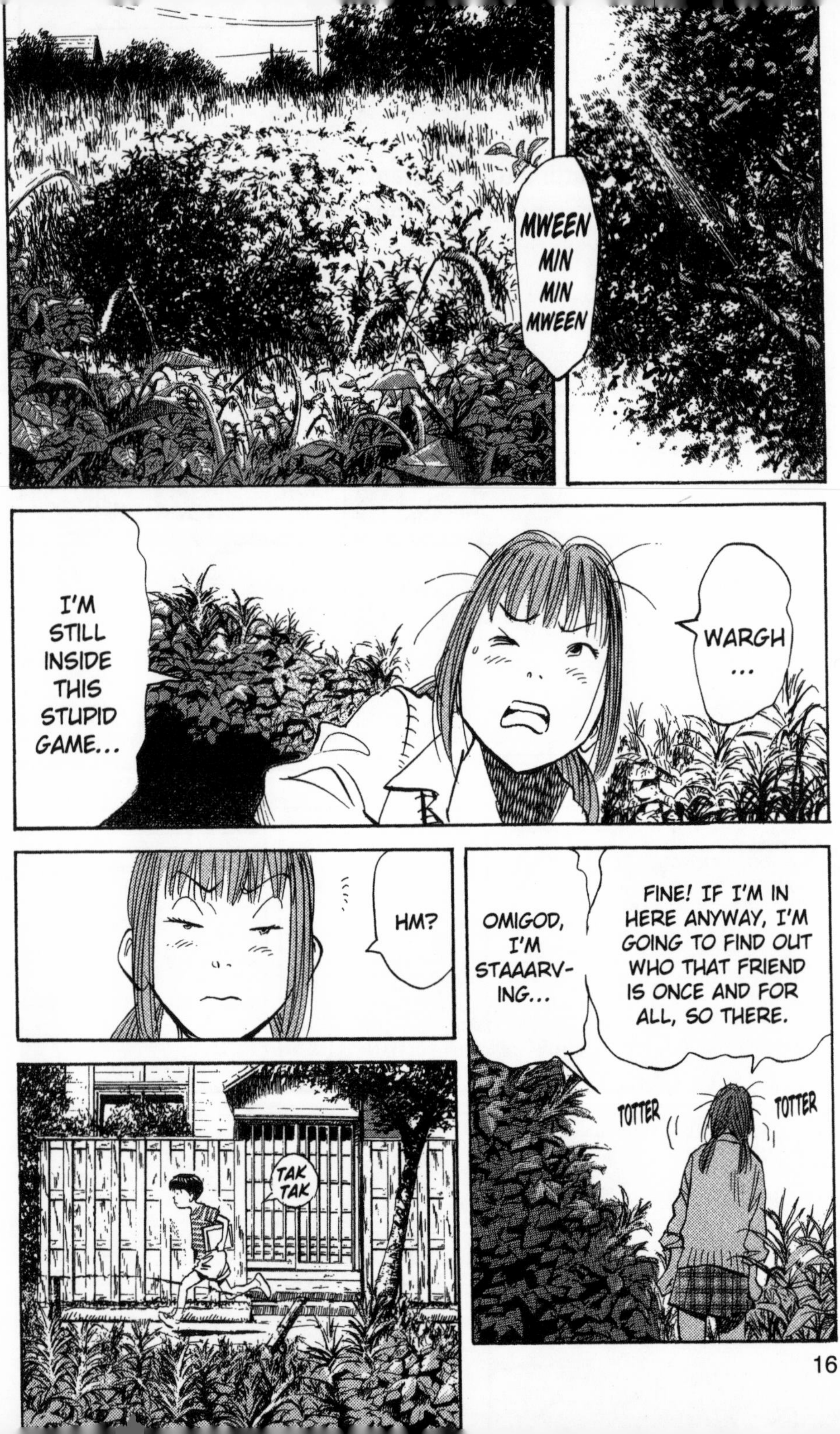

MWEEN MIN MIN MWEEN
WARGH ...
I'M STILL INSIDE THIS STUPID GAME...
FINE! IF I'M IN HERE ANYWAY, I'M GOING TO FIND OUT WHO THAT FRIEND IS ONCE AND FOR ALL, SO THERE.
OMIGOD, I'M STAAARV-ING...
TOTTER
TOTTER
HM?
TAK TAK

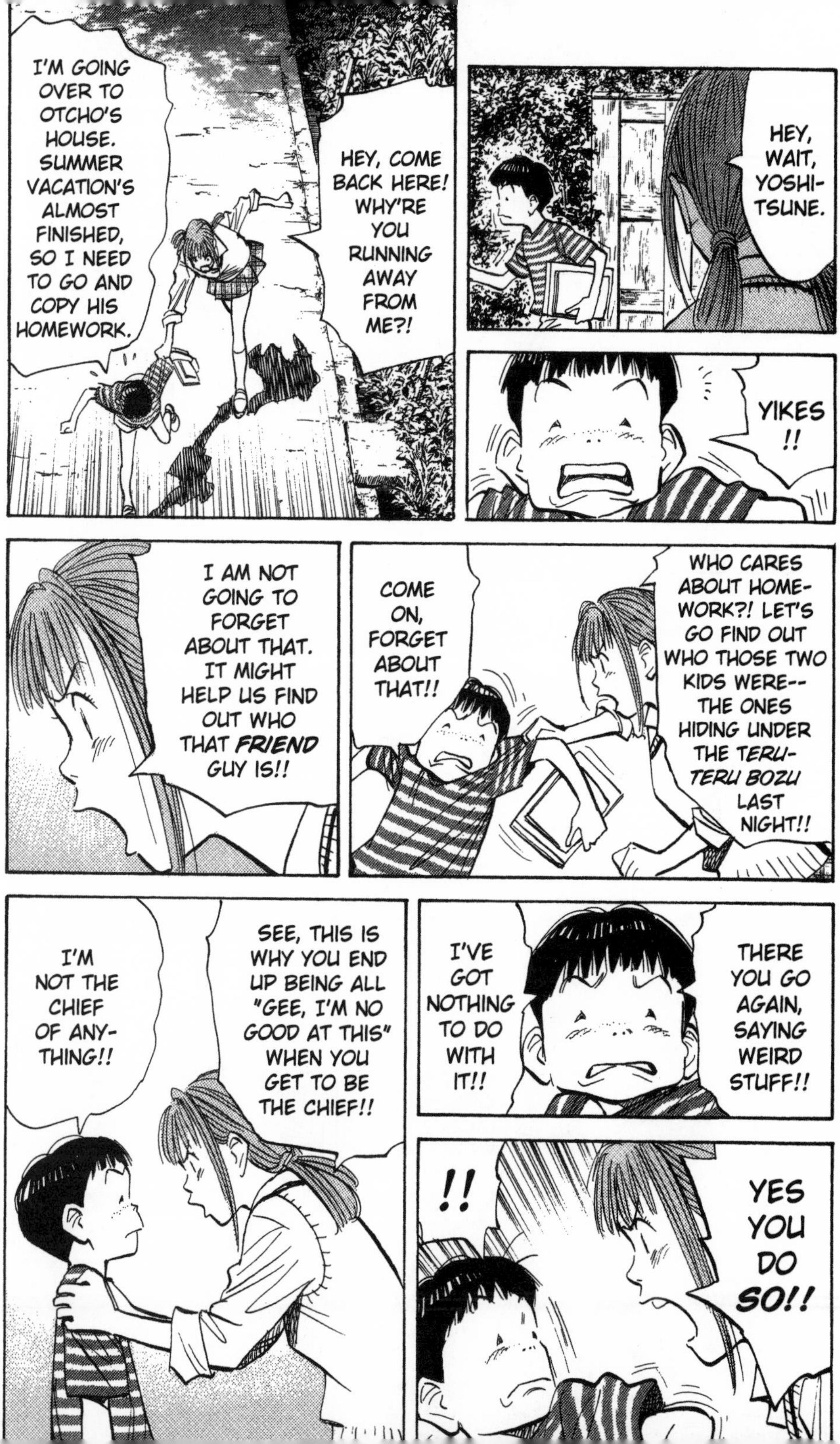
HEY, WAIT, YOSHI-TSUNE.
YIKES!!
HEY, COME BACK HERE! WHY'RE YOU RUNNING AWAY FROM ME?!
I'M GOING OVER TO OTCHO'S HOUSE. SUMMER VACATION'S ALMOST FINISHED, SO I NEED TO GO AND COPY HIS HOMEWORK.
WHO CARES ABOUT HOME-WORK?! LET'S GO FIND OUT WHO THOSE TWO KIDS WERE-- THE ONES HIDING UNDER THE TERU-TERU BOZU LAST NIGHT!!
COME ON, FORGET ABOUT THAT!!
I AM NOT GOING TO FORGET ABOUT THAT. IT MIGHT HELP US FIND OUT WHO THAT FRIEND GUY IS!!
THERE YOU GO AGAIN, SAYING WEIRD STUFF!!
I'VE GOT NOTHING TO DO WITH IT!!
YES YOU DO SO!!
!!
SEE, THIS IS WHY YOU END UP BEING ALL "GEE, I'M NO GOOD AT THIS" WHEN YOU GET TO BE THE CHIEF!!
I'M NOT THE CHIEF OF ANY-THING!!

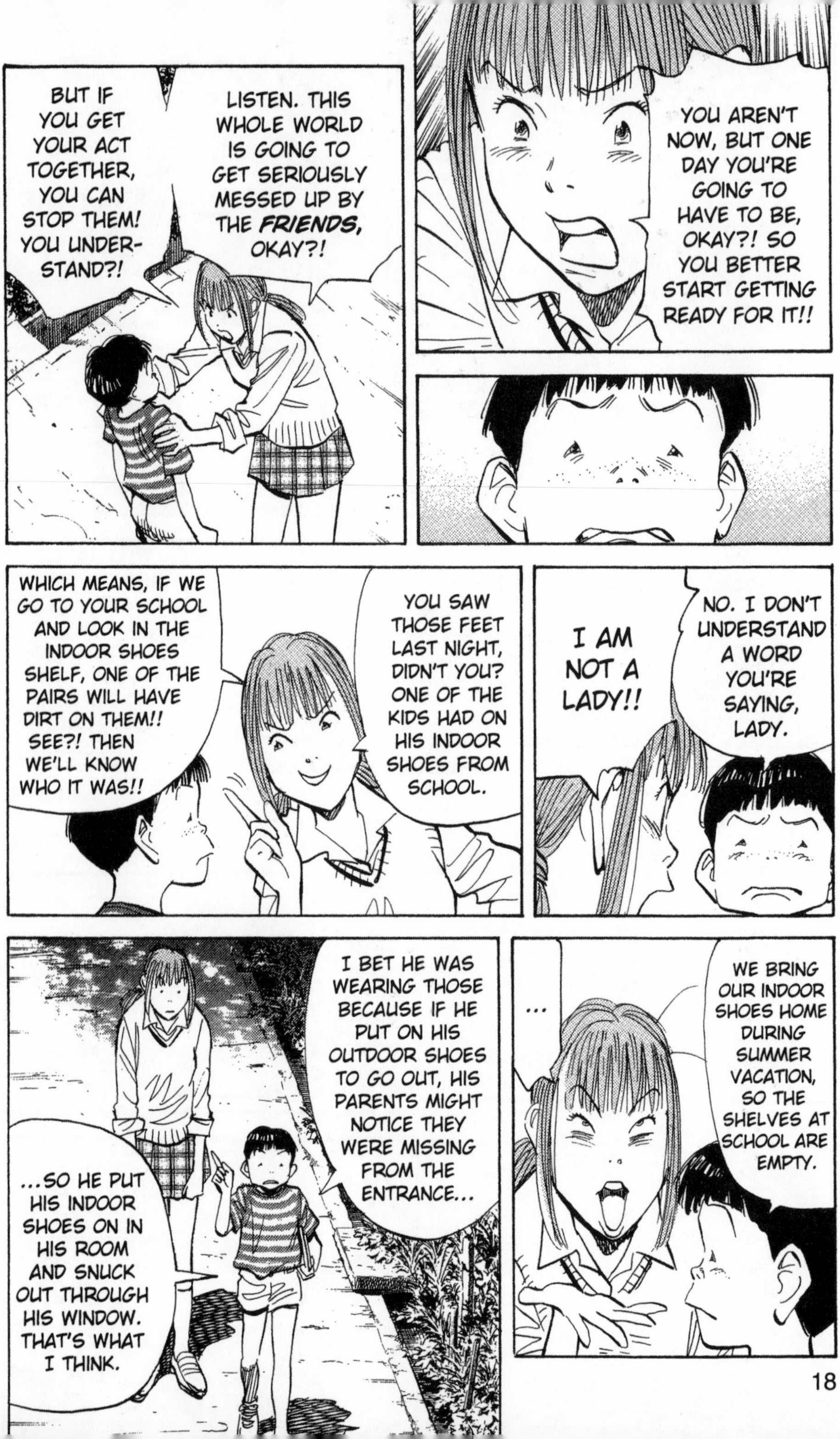
YOU AREN'T NOW, BUT ONE DAY YOU'RE GOING TO HAVE TO BE, OKAY?! SO YOU BETTER START GETTING READY FOR IT!!
LISTEN. THIS WHOLE WORLD IS GOING TO GET SERIOUSLY MESSED UP BY THE *FRIENDS,* OKAY?!
BUT IF YOU GET YOUR ACT TOGETHER, YOU CAN STOP THEM! YOU UNDER-STAND?!
NO. I DON'T UNDERSTAND A WORD YOU'RE SAYING, LADY.
I AM NOT A LADY!!
YOU SAW THOSE FEET LAST NIGHT, DIDN'T YOU? ONE OF THE KIDS HAD ON HIS INDOOR SHOES FROM SCHOOL.
WHICH MEANS, IF WE GO TO YOUR SCHOOL AND LOOK IN THE INDOOR SHOES SHELF, ONE OF THE PAIRS WILL HAVE DIRT ON THEM!! SEE?! THEN WE'LL KNOW WHO IT WAS!!
WE BRING OUR INDOOR SHOES HOME DURING SUMMER VACATION, SO THE SHELVES AT SCHOOL ARE EMPTY.
...
I BET HE WAS WEARING THOSE BECAUSE IF HE PUT ON HIS OUTDOOR SHOES TO GO OUT, HIS PARENTS MIGHT NOTICE THEY WERE MISSING FROM THE ENTRANCE...
...SO HE PUT HIS INDOOR SHOES ON IN HIS ROOM AND SNUCK OUT THROUGH HIS WINDOW. THAT'S WHAT I THINK.

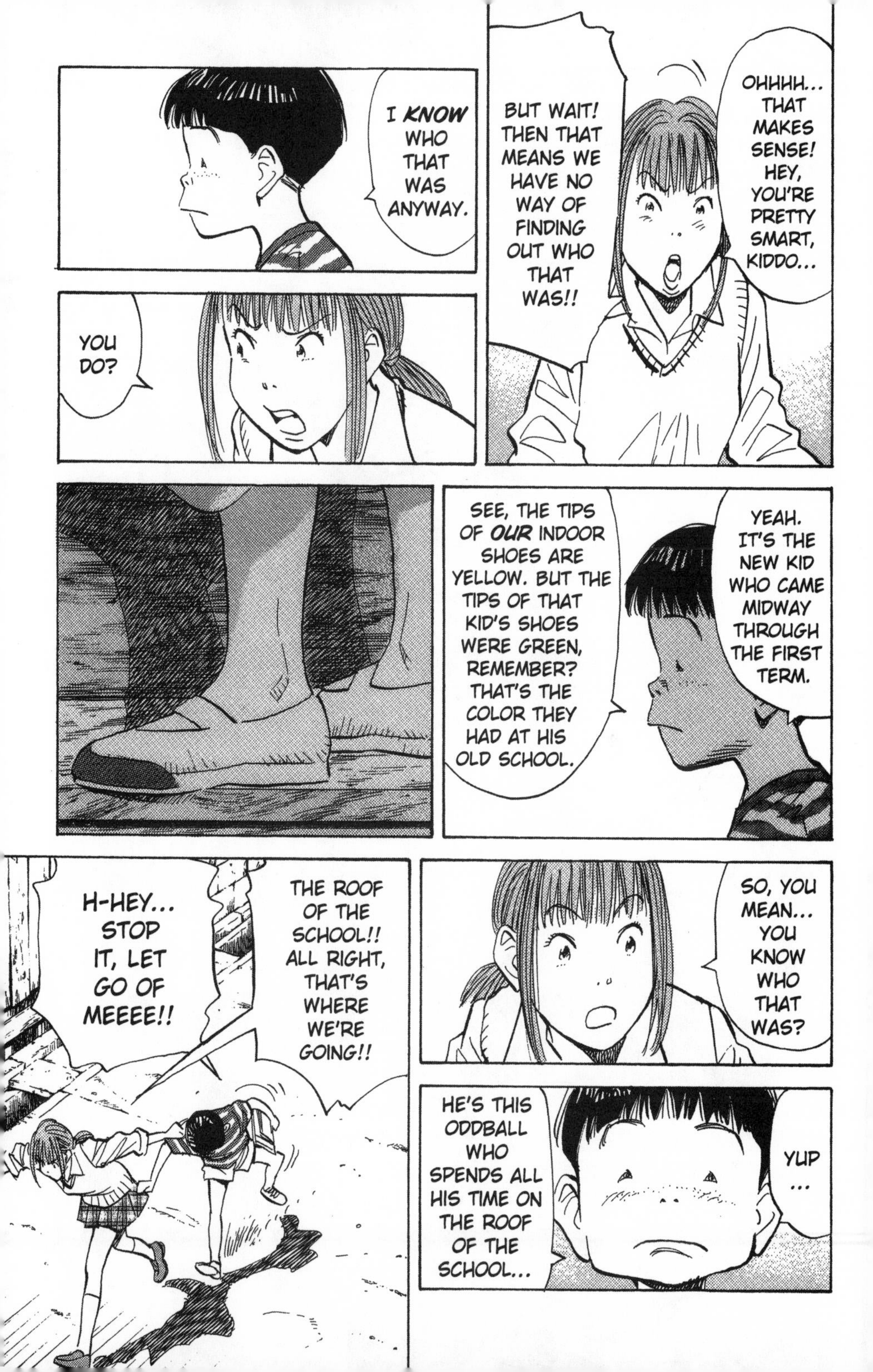
OHHHH... THAT MAKES SENSE! HEY, YOU'RE PRETTY SMART, KIDDO...
BUT WAIT! THEN THAT MEANS WE HAVE NO WAY OF FINDING OUT WHO THAT WAS!!
I *KNOW* WHO THAT WAS ANYWAY.
YOU DO?
YEAH. IT'S THE NEW KID WHO CAME MIDWAY THROUGH THE FIRST TERM.
SEE, THE TIPS OF *OUR* INDOOR SHOES ARE YELLOW. BUT THE TIPS OF THAT KID'S SHOES WERE GREEN, REMEMBER? THAT'S THE COLOR THEY HAD AT HIS OLD SCHOOL.
SO, YOU MEAN... YOU KNOW WHO THAT WAS?
YUP...
HE'S THIS ODDBALL WHO SPENDS ALL HIS TIME ON THE ROOF OF THE SCHOOL...
THE ROOF OF THE SCHOOL!! ALL RIGHT, THAT'S WHERE WE'RE GOING!!
H-HEY... STOP IT, LET GO OF MEEEE!!

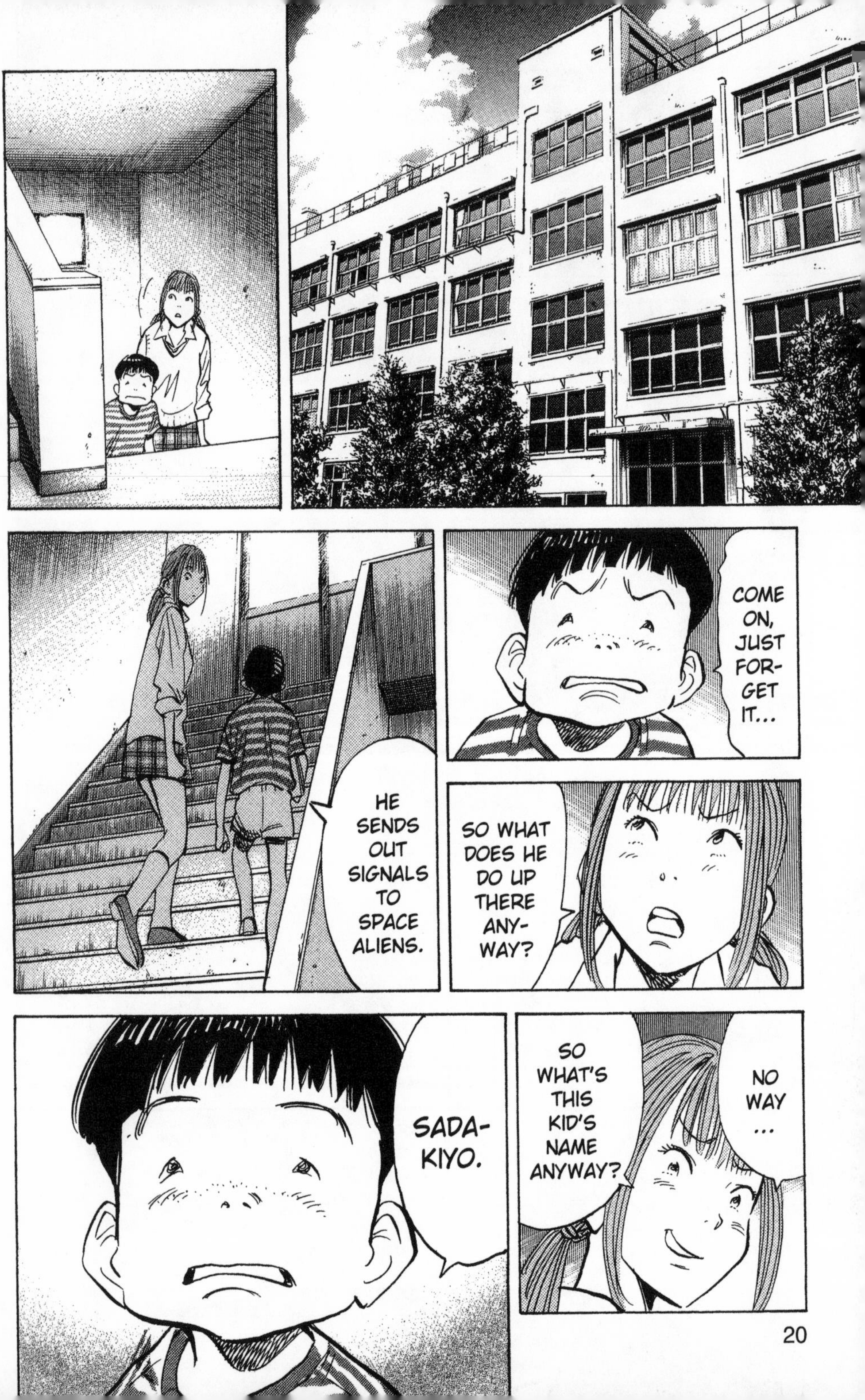
COME ON, JUST FOR-GET IT...
SO WHAT DOES HE DO UP THERE ANY-WAY?
HE SENDS OUT SIGNALS TO SPACE ALIENS.
NO WAY...
SO WHAT'S THIS KID'S NAME ANYWAY?
SADA-KIYO.

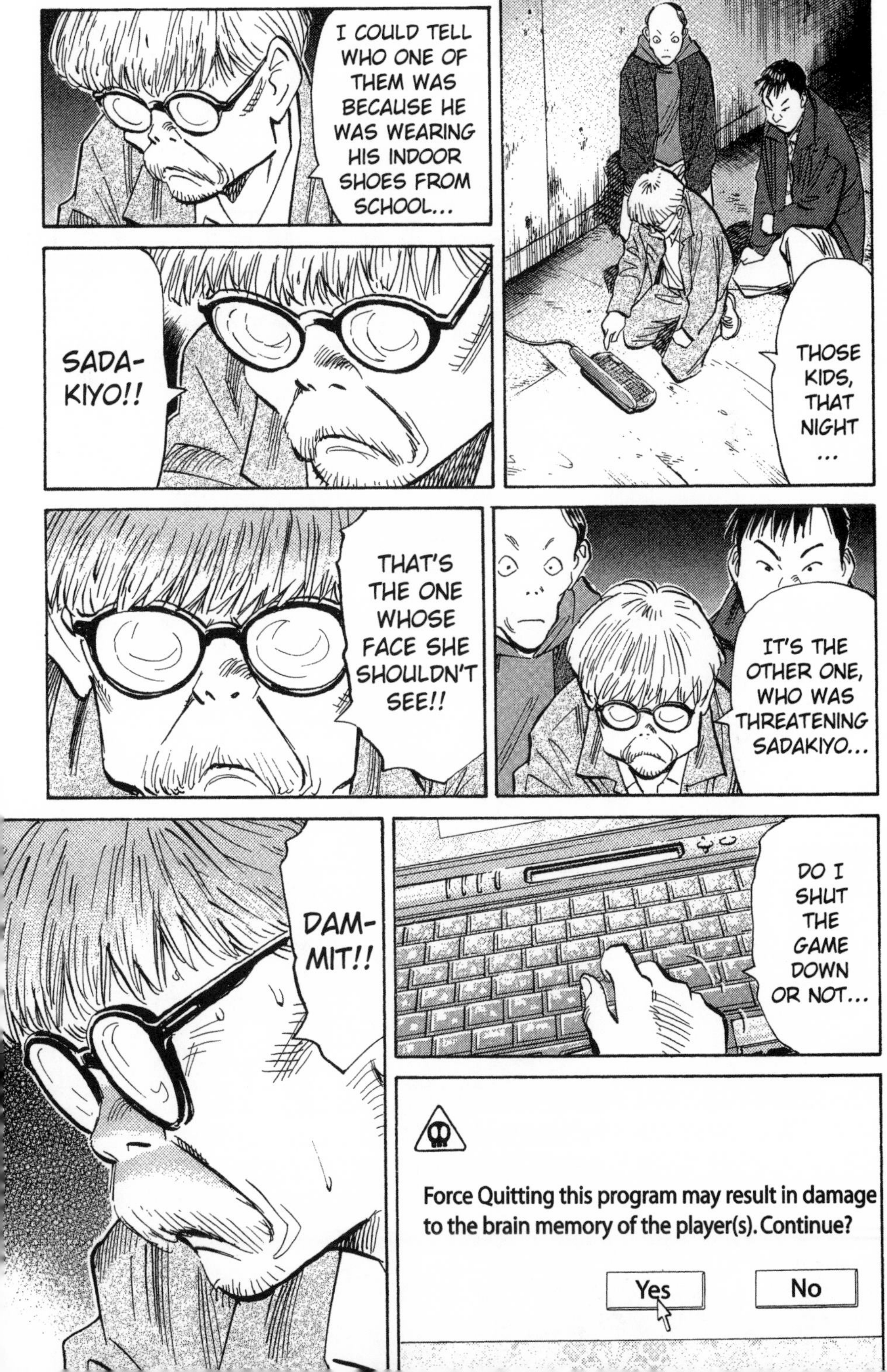
THOSE KIDS, THAT NIGHT...
I COULD TELL WHO ONE OF THEM WAS BECAUSE HE WAS WEARING HIS INDOOR SHOES FROM SCHOOL...
SADA-KIYO!!
IT'S THE OTHER ONE, WHO WAS THREATENING SADAKIYO...
THAT'S THE ONE WHOSE FACE SHE SHOULDN'T SEE!!
DO I SHUT THE GAME DOWN OR NOT...
Force Quitting this program may result in damage to the brain memory of the player(s). Continue?
Yes
No
DAM-MIT!!

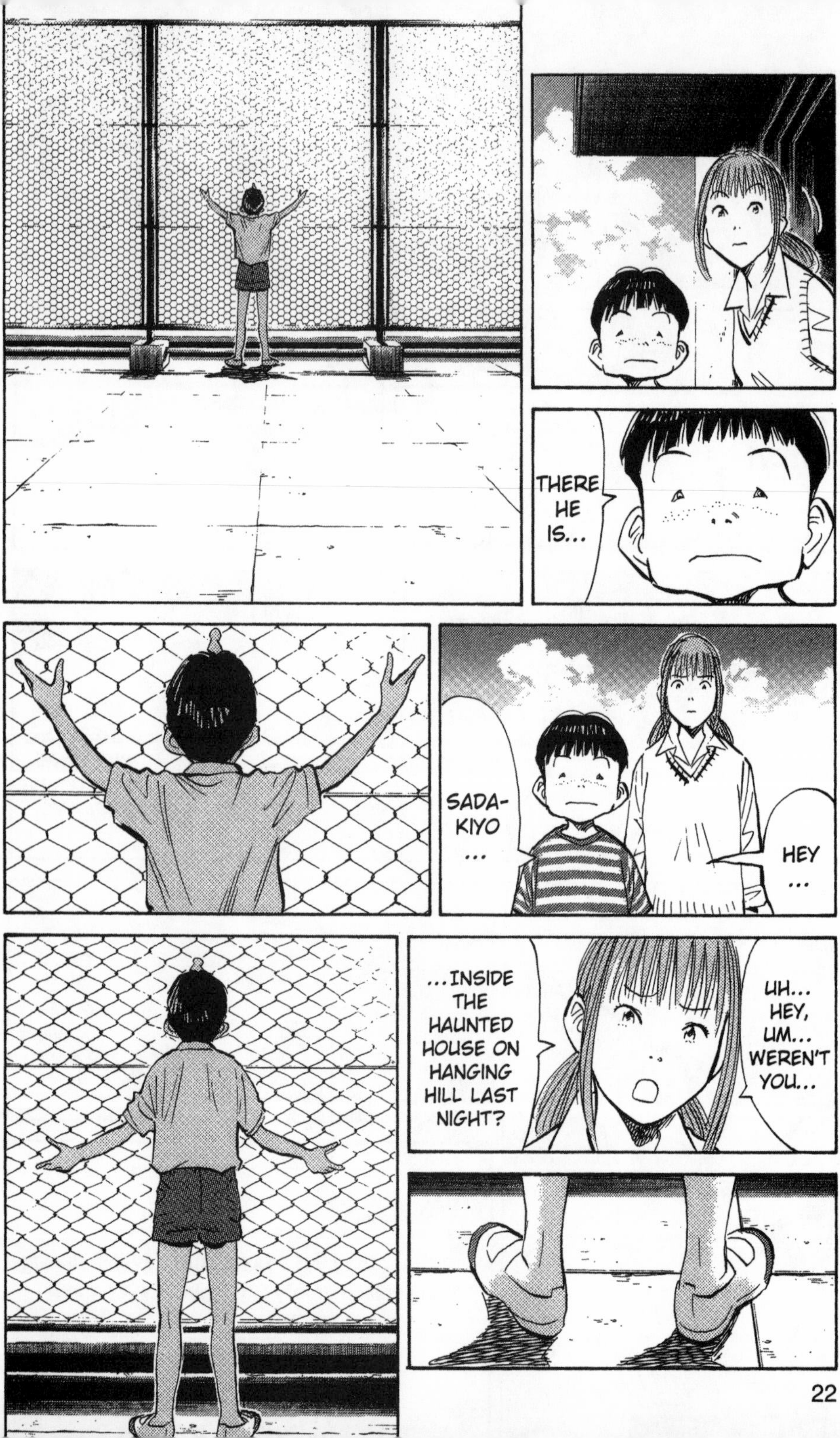
THERE HE IS...
HEY...
SADA-KIYO...
UH... HEY, UM... WEREN'T YOU...
...INSIDE THE HAUNTED HOUSE ON HANGING HILL LAST NIGHT?

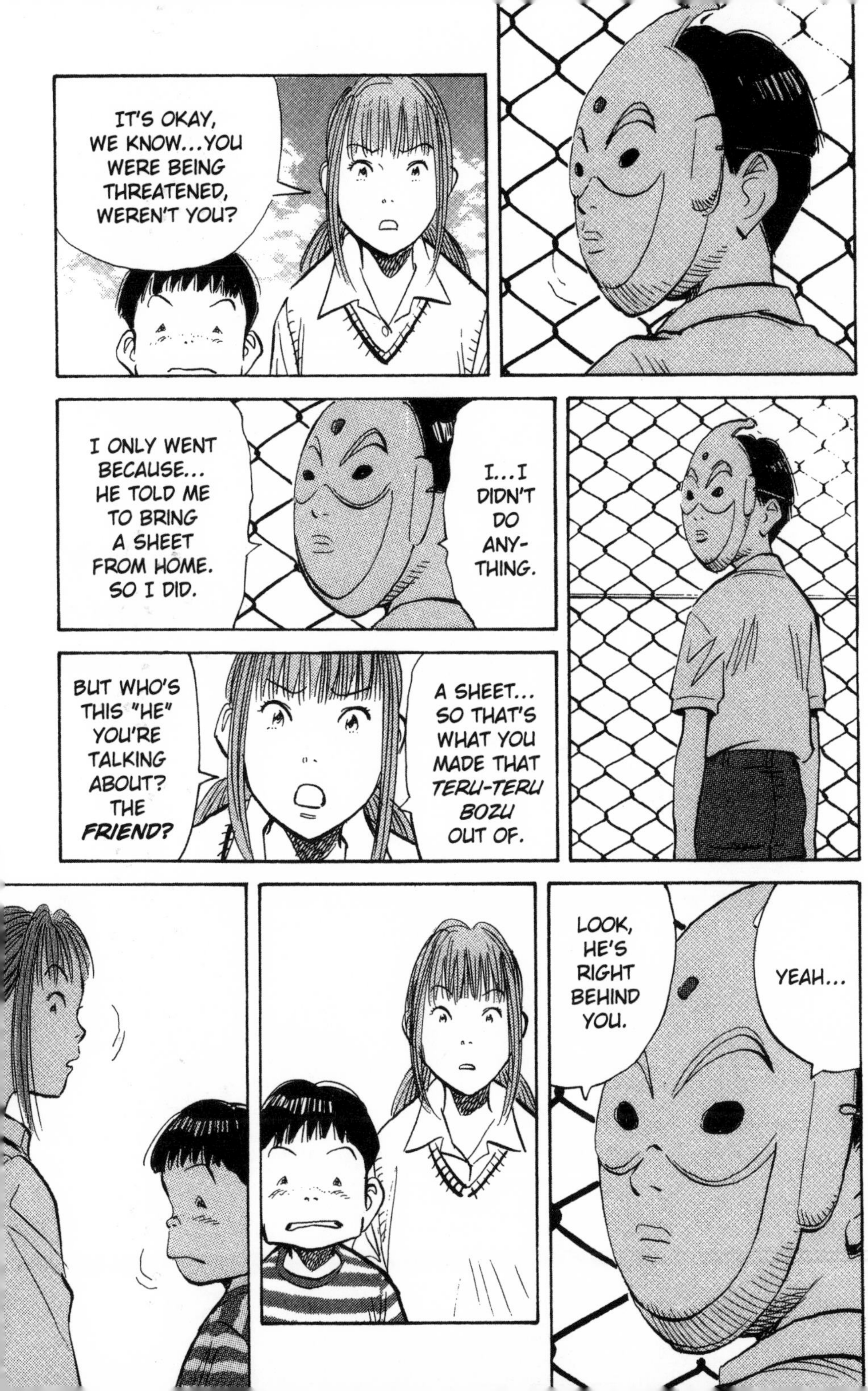
IT'S OKAY, WE KNOW...YOU WERE BEING THREATENED, WEREN'T YOU?
I...I DIDN'T DO ANY-THING.
I ONLY WENT BECAUSE... HE TOLD ME TO BRING A SHEET FROM HOME. SO I DID.
A SHEET... SO THAT'S WHAT YOU MADE THAT *TERU-TERU BOZU* OUT OF.
BUT WHO'S THIS "HE" YOU'RE TALKING ABOUT? THE ***FRIEND?***
YEAH...
LOOK, HE'S RIGHT BEHIND YOU.

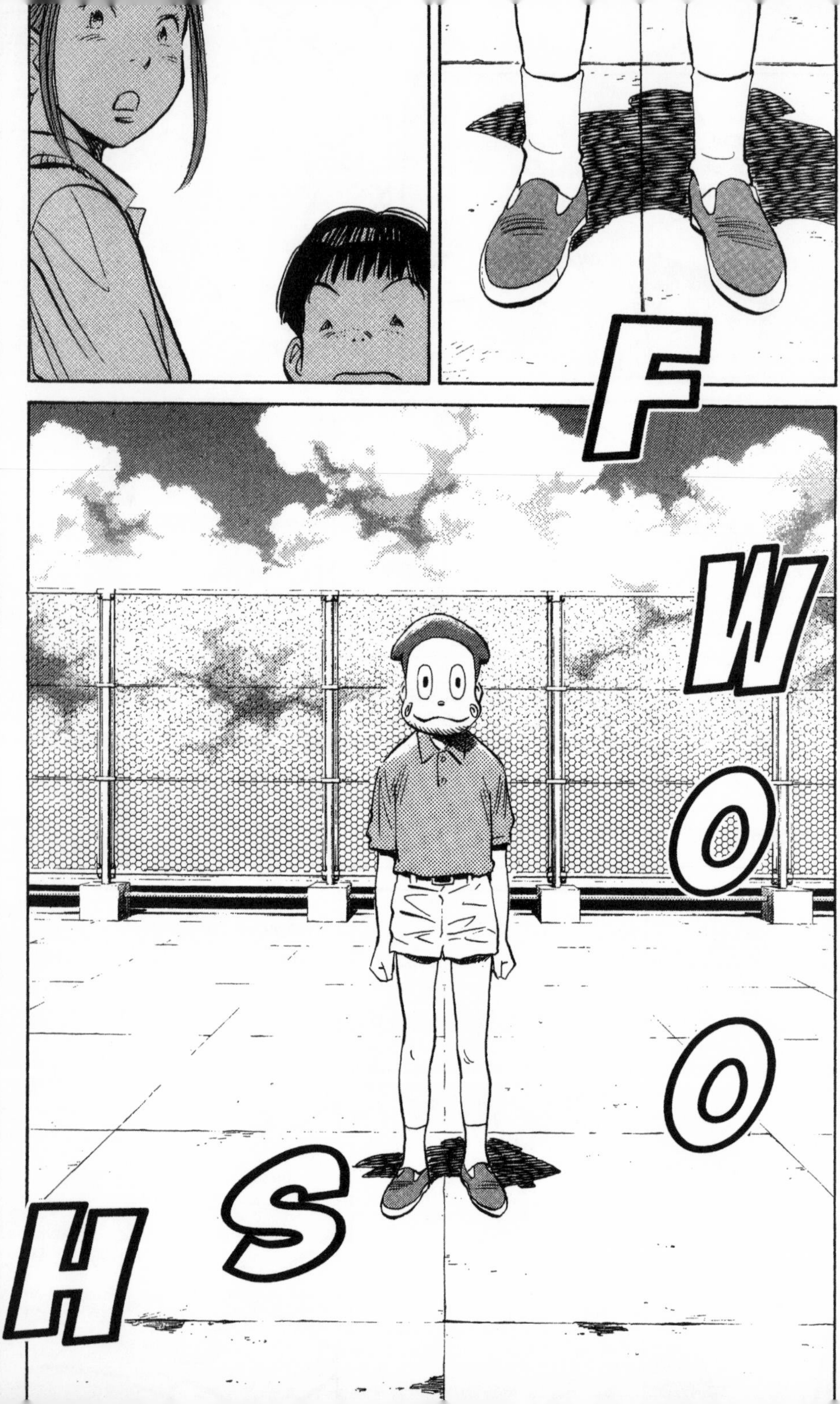
FWOOSH

Chapter 2 Nightmare

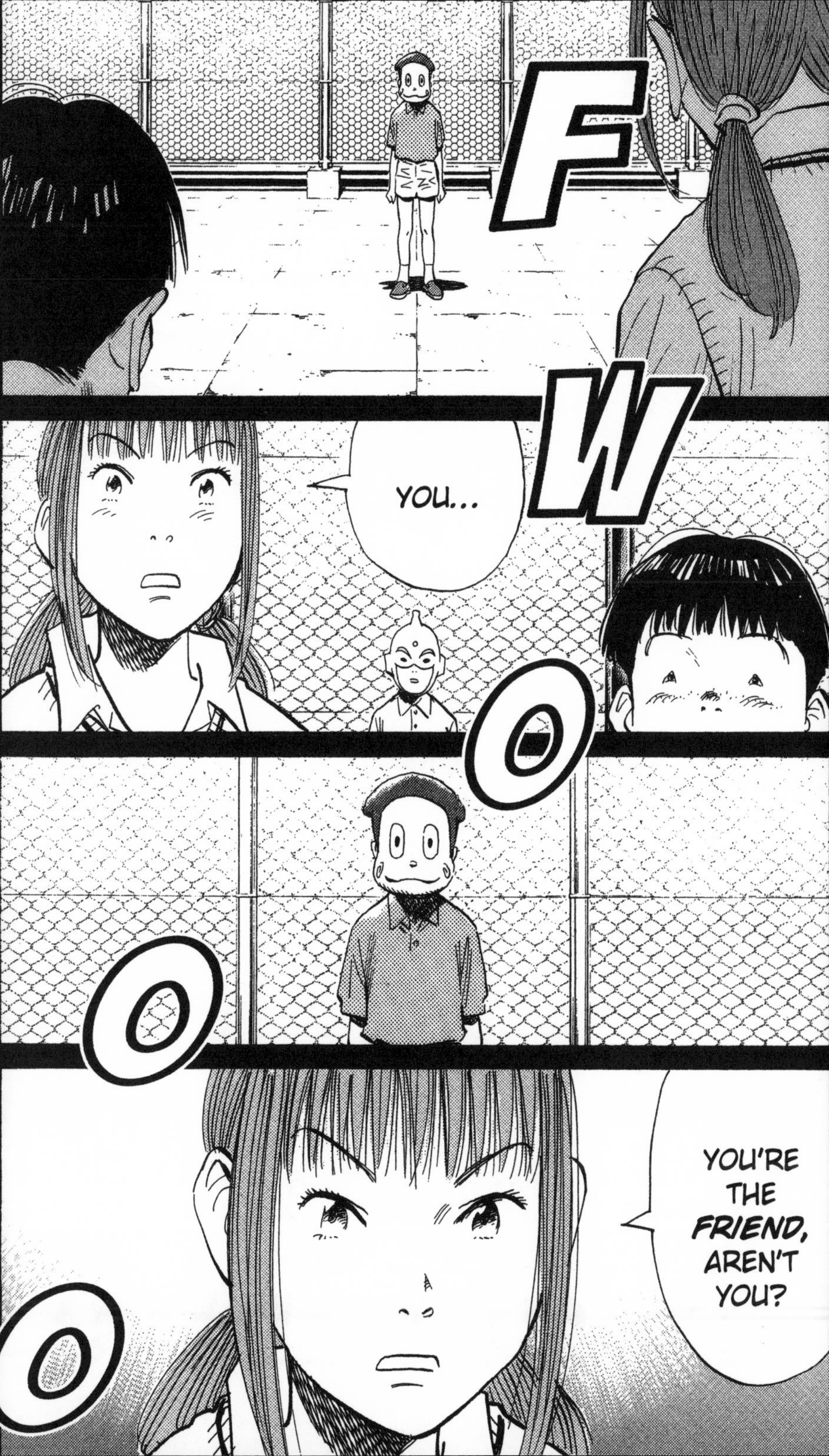
FWOOO
YOU...
YOU'RE THE *FRIEND,* AREN'T YOU?

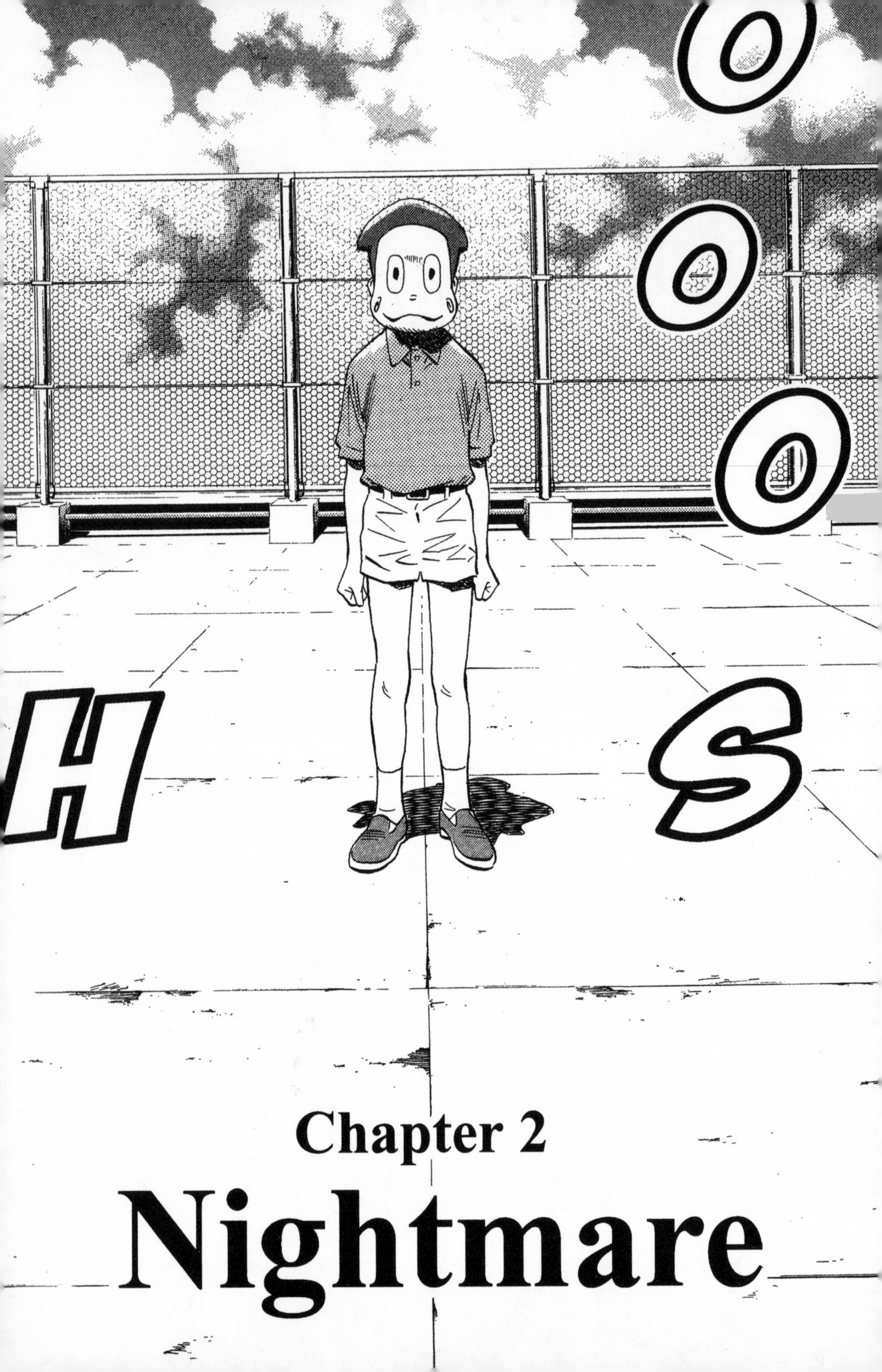

O
O
O
S
H

Chapter 2
Nightmare

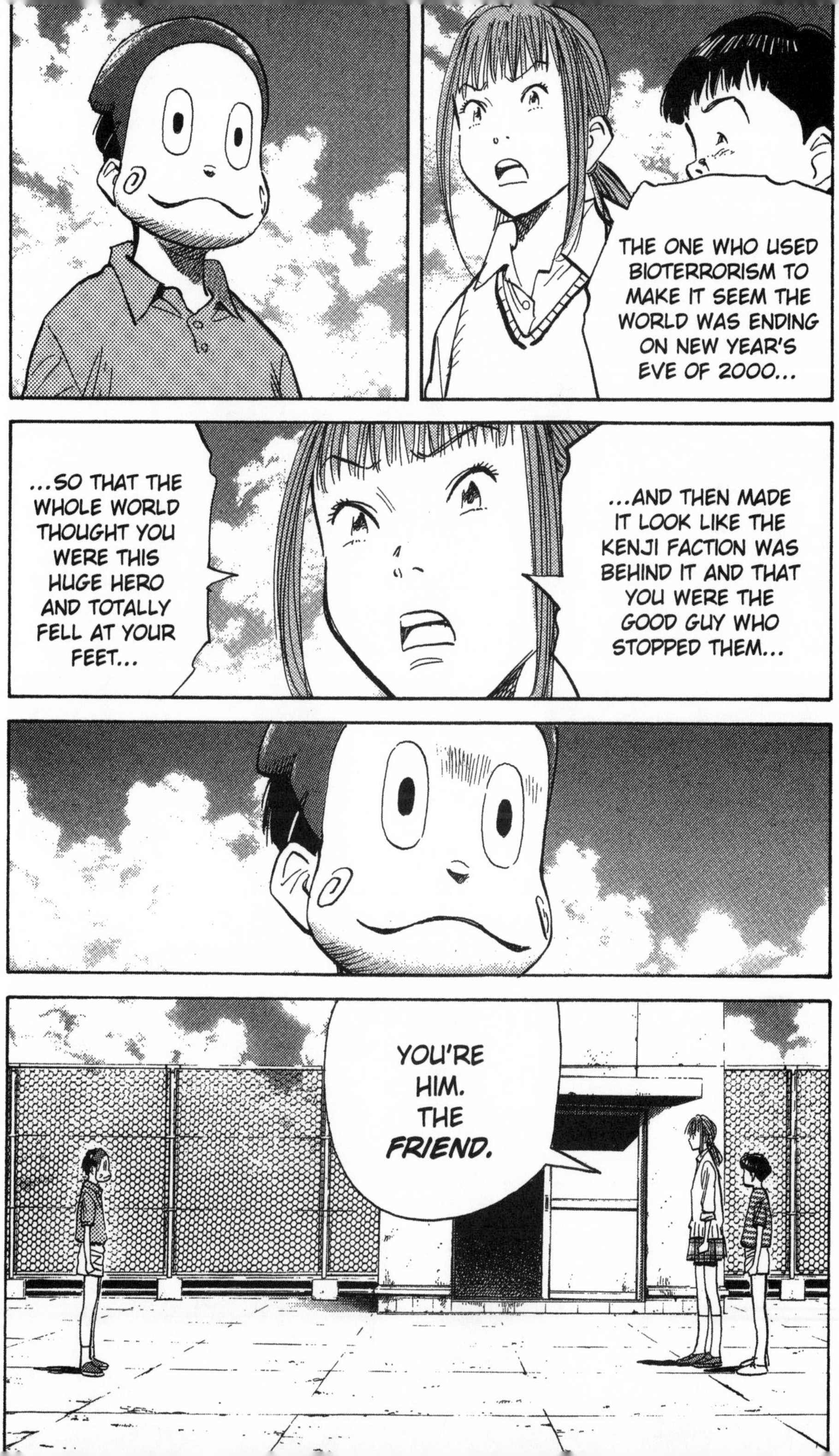
THE ONE WHO USED BIOTERRORISM TO MAKE IT SEEM THE WORLD WAS ENDING ON NEW YEAR'S EVE OF 2000...
...AND THEN MADE IT LOOK LIKE THE KENJI FACTION WAS BEHIND IT AND THAT YOU WERE THE GOOD GUY WHO STOPPED THEM...
...SO THAT THE WHOLE WORLD THOUGHT YOU WERE THIS HUGE HERO AND TOTALLY FELL AT YOUR FEET...
YOU'RE HIM. THE *FRIEND.*

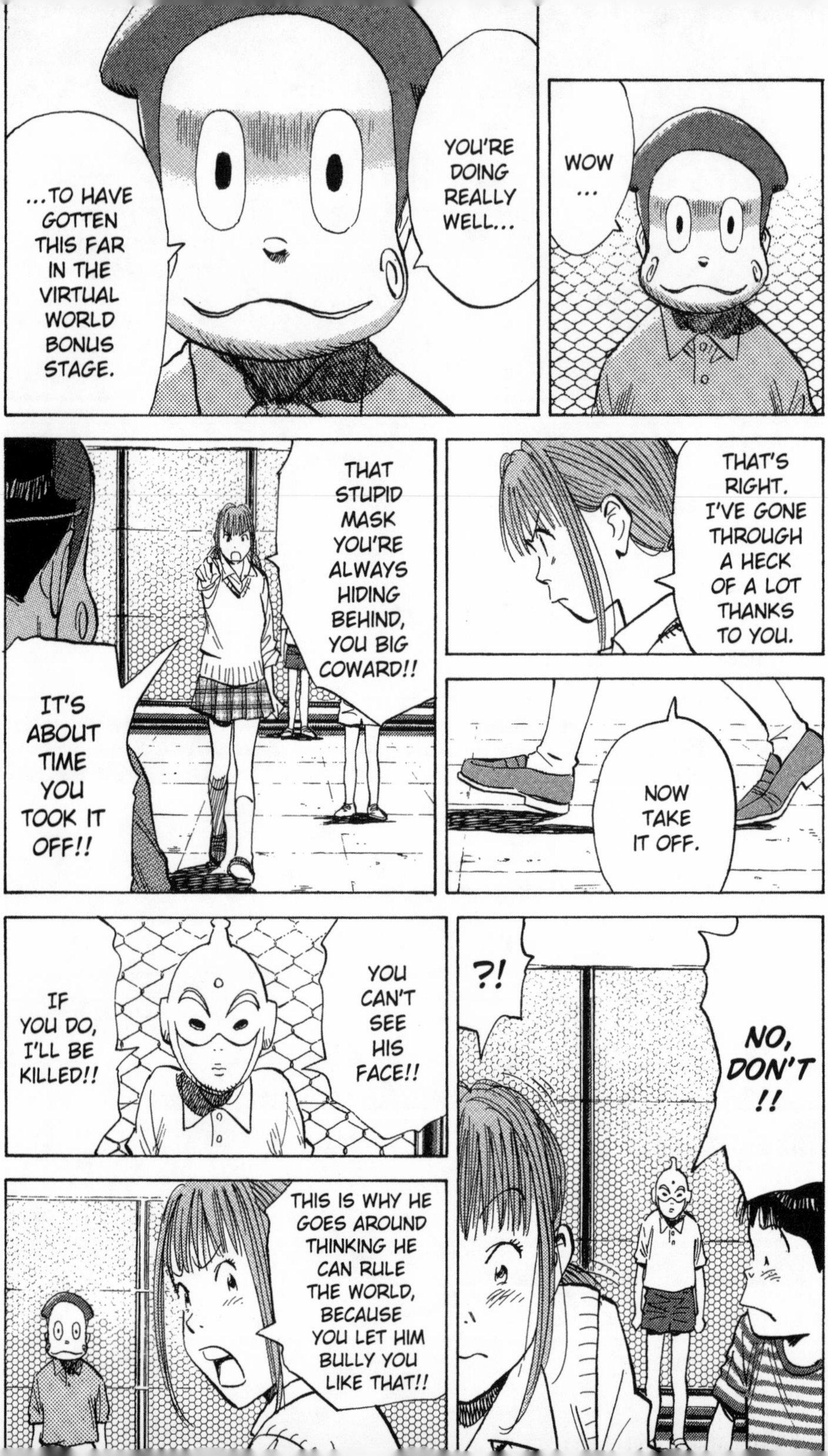
WOW ...
YOU'RE DOING REALLY WELL...
...TO HAVE GOTTEN THIS FAR IN THE VIRTUAL WORLD BONUS STAGE.
THAT'S RIGHT. I'VE GONE THROUGH A HECK OF A LOT THANKS TO YOU.
NOW TAKE IT OFF.
THAT STUPID MASK YOU'RE ALWAYS HIDING BEHIND, YOU BIG COWARD!!
IT'S ABOUT TIME YOU TOOK IT OFF!!
NO, DON'T !!
?!
YOU CAN'T SEE HIS FACE!!
IF YOU DO, I'LL BE KILLED!!
THIS IS WHY HE GOES AROUND THINKING HE CAN RULE THE WORLD, BECAUSE YOU LET HIM BULLY YOU LIKE THAT!!

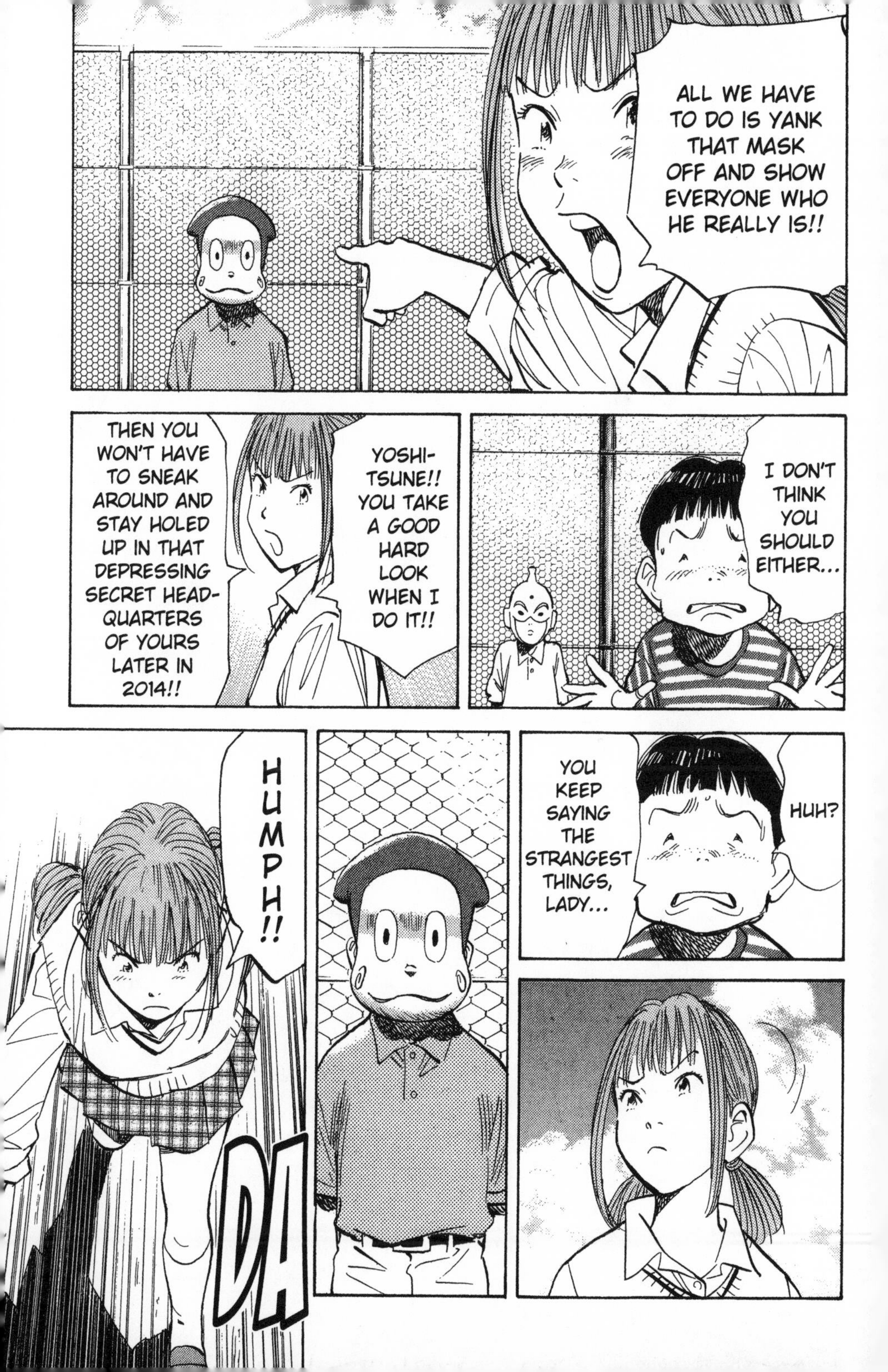
ALL WE HAVE TO DO IS YANK THAT MASK OFF AND SHOW EVERYONE WHO HE REALLY IS!!
I DON'T THINK YOU SHOULD EITHER...
YOSHI-TSUNE!! YOU TAKE A GOOD HARD LOOK WHEN I DO IT!!
THEN YOU WON'T HAVE TO SNEAK AROUND AND STAY HOLED UP IN THAT DEPRESSING SECRET HEAD-QUARTERS OF YOURS LATER IN 2014!!
HUH?
YOU KEEP SAYING THE STRANGEST THINGS, LADY...
HUMPH!!
DA

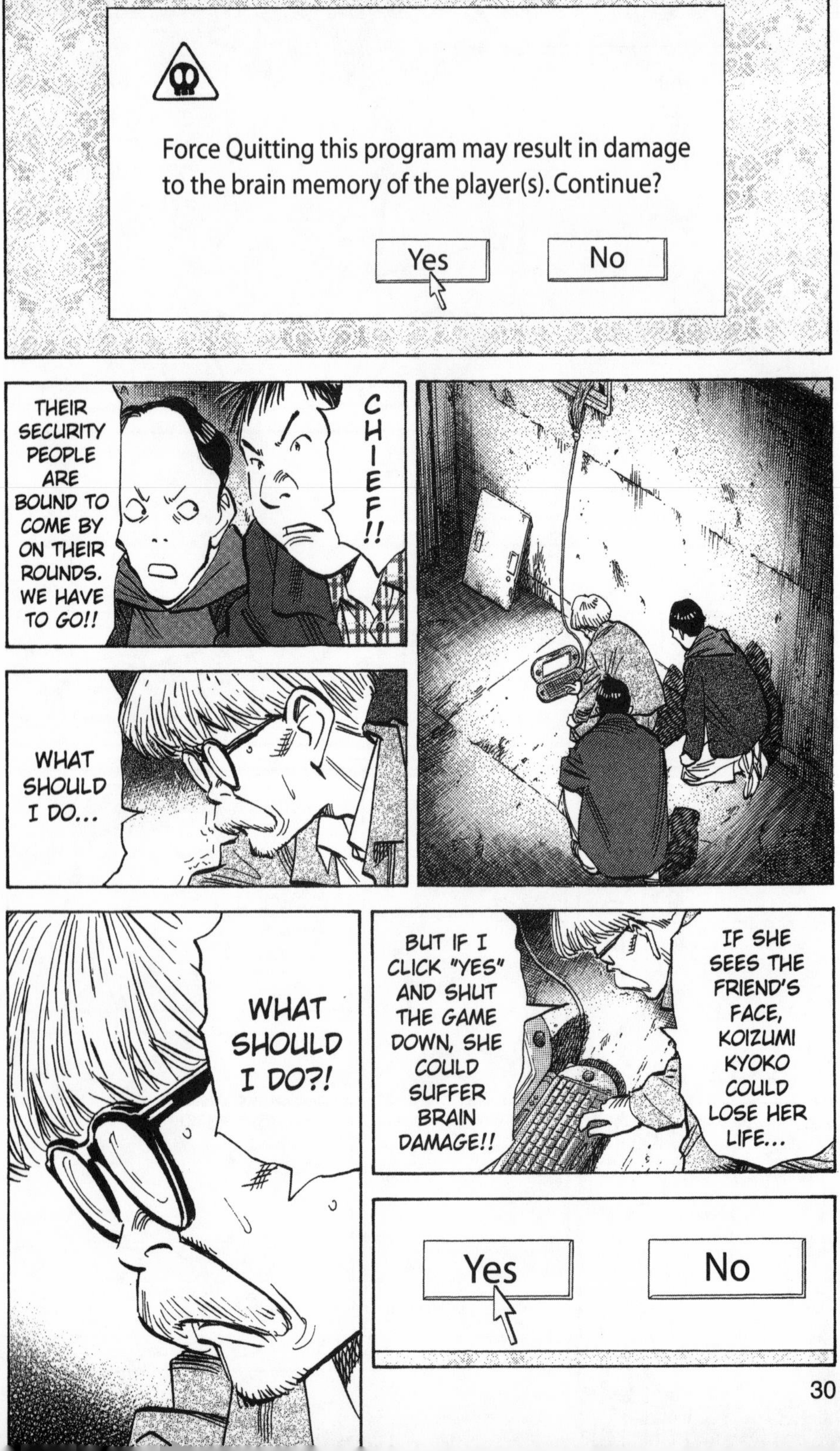
Force Quitting this program may result in damage to the brain memory of the player(s). Continue?
Yes
No
CHIEF!!
THEIR SECURITY PEOPLE ARE BOUND TO COME BY ON THEIR ROUNDS. WE HAVE TO GO!!
WHAT SHOULD I DO...
IF SHE SEES THE FRIEND'S FACE, KOIZUMI KYOKO COULD LOSE HER LIFE...
BUT IF I CLICK "YES" AND SHUT THE GAME DOWN, SHE COULD SUFFER BRAIN DAMAGE!!
Yes
No
WHAT SHOULD I DO?!

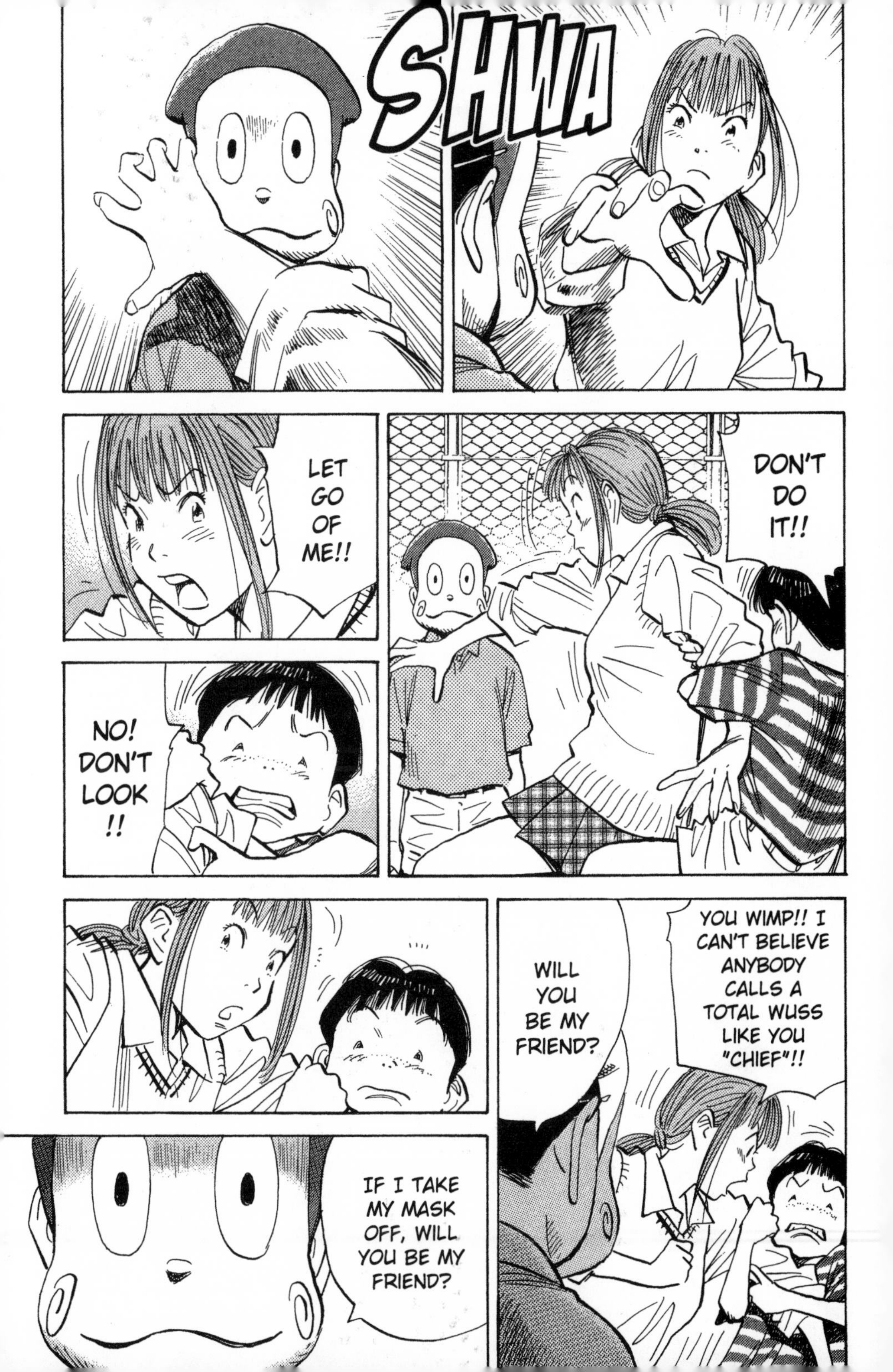
SHWA
DON'T DO IT!!
LET GO OF ME!!
NO! DON'T LOOK!!
YOU WIMP!! I CAN'T BELIEVE ANYBODY CALLS A TOTAL WUSS LIKE YOU "CHIEF"!!
WILL YOU BE MY FRIEND?
IF I TAKE MY MASK OFF, WILL YOU BE MY FRIEND?

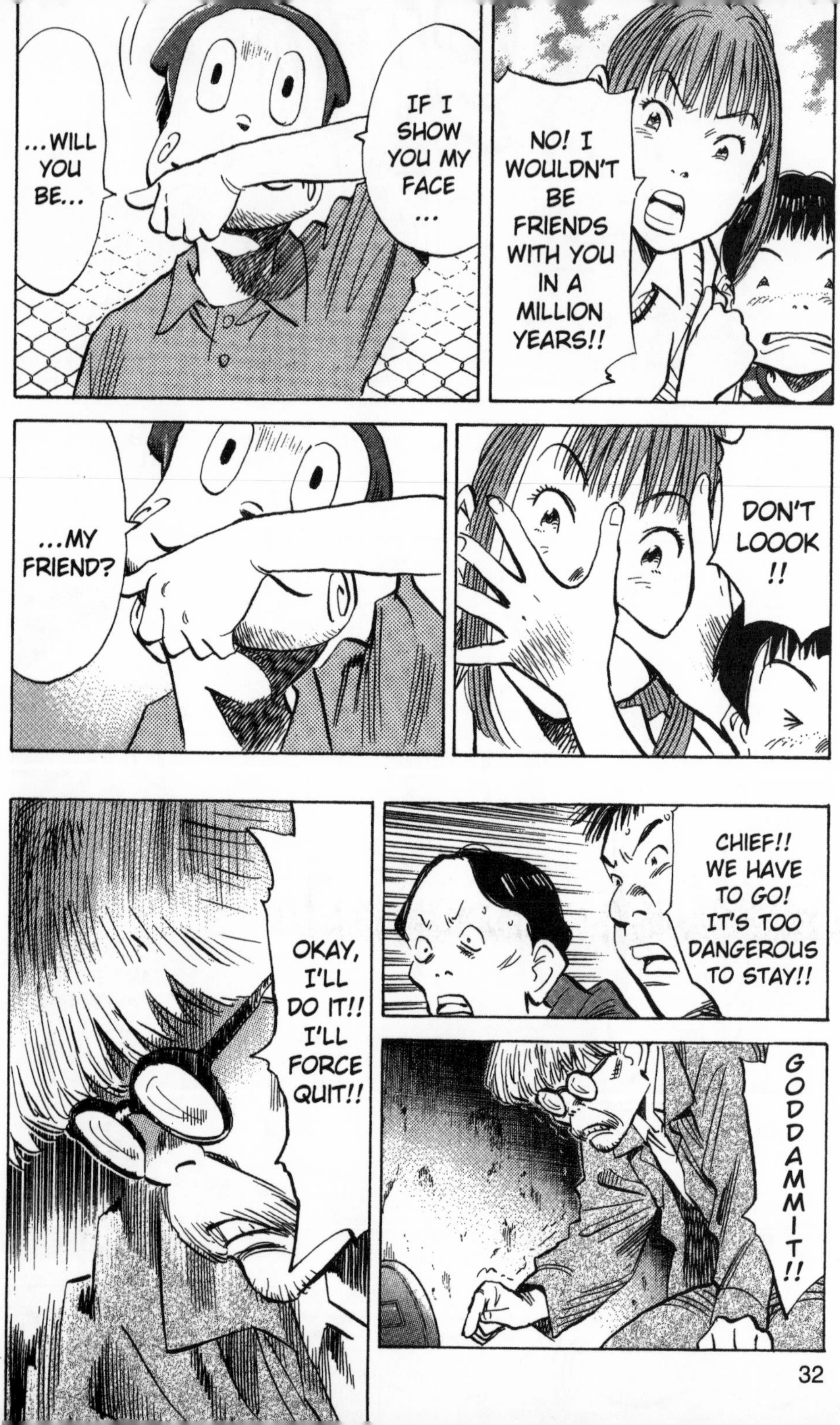
NO! I WOULDN'T BE FRIENDS WITH YOU IN A MILLION YEARS!!
IF I SHOW YOU MY FACE ...
...WILL YOU BE...
DON'T LOOOK !!
...MY FRIEND?
CHIEF!! WE HAVE TO GO! IT'S TOO DANGEROUS TO STAY!!
GODDAMMIT!!
OKAY, I'LL DO IT!! I'LL FORCE QUIT!!

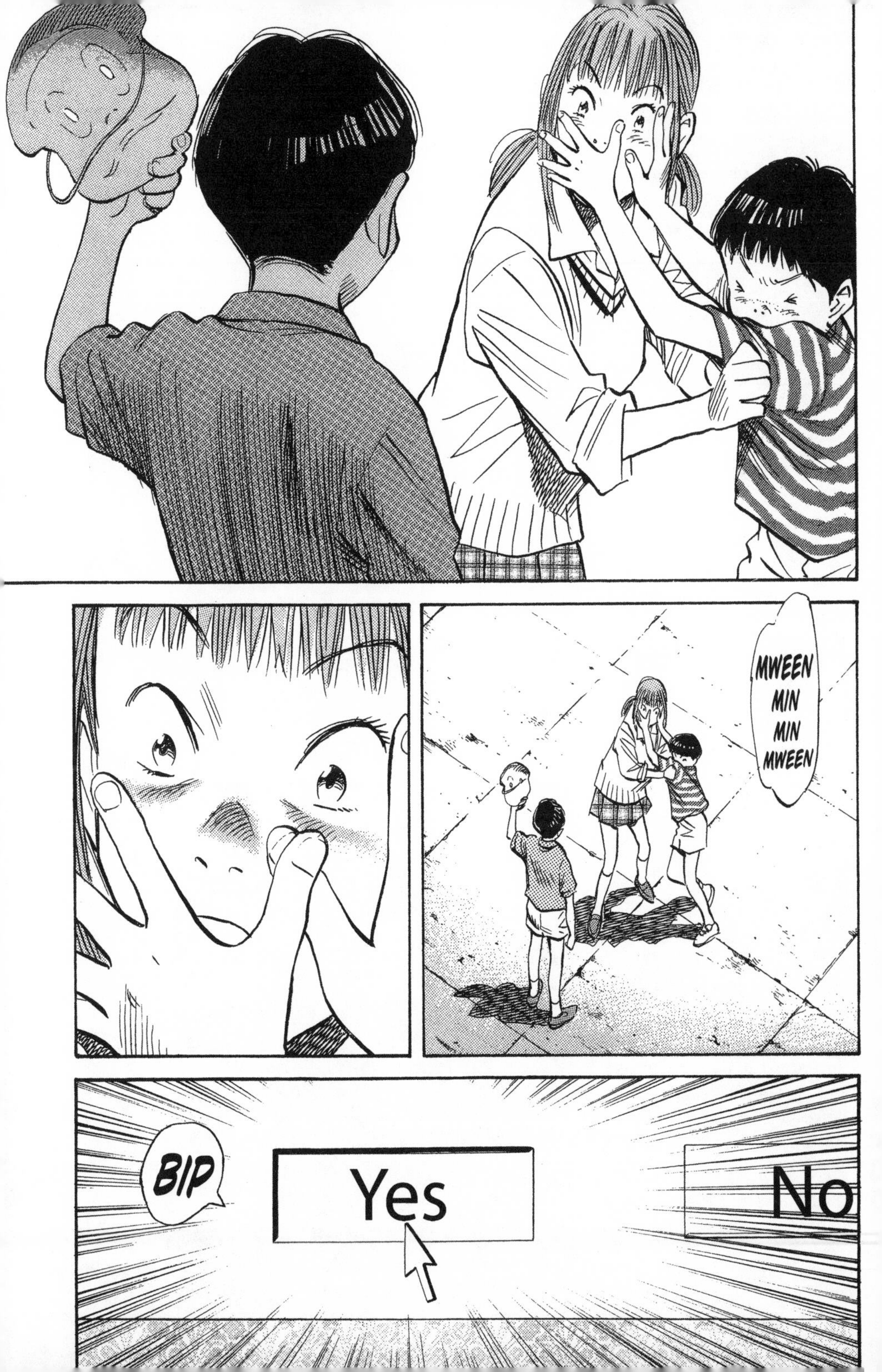
MWEEN MIN MIN MWEEN
BIP
Yes
No

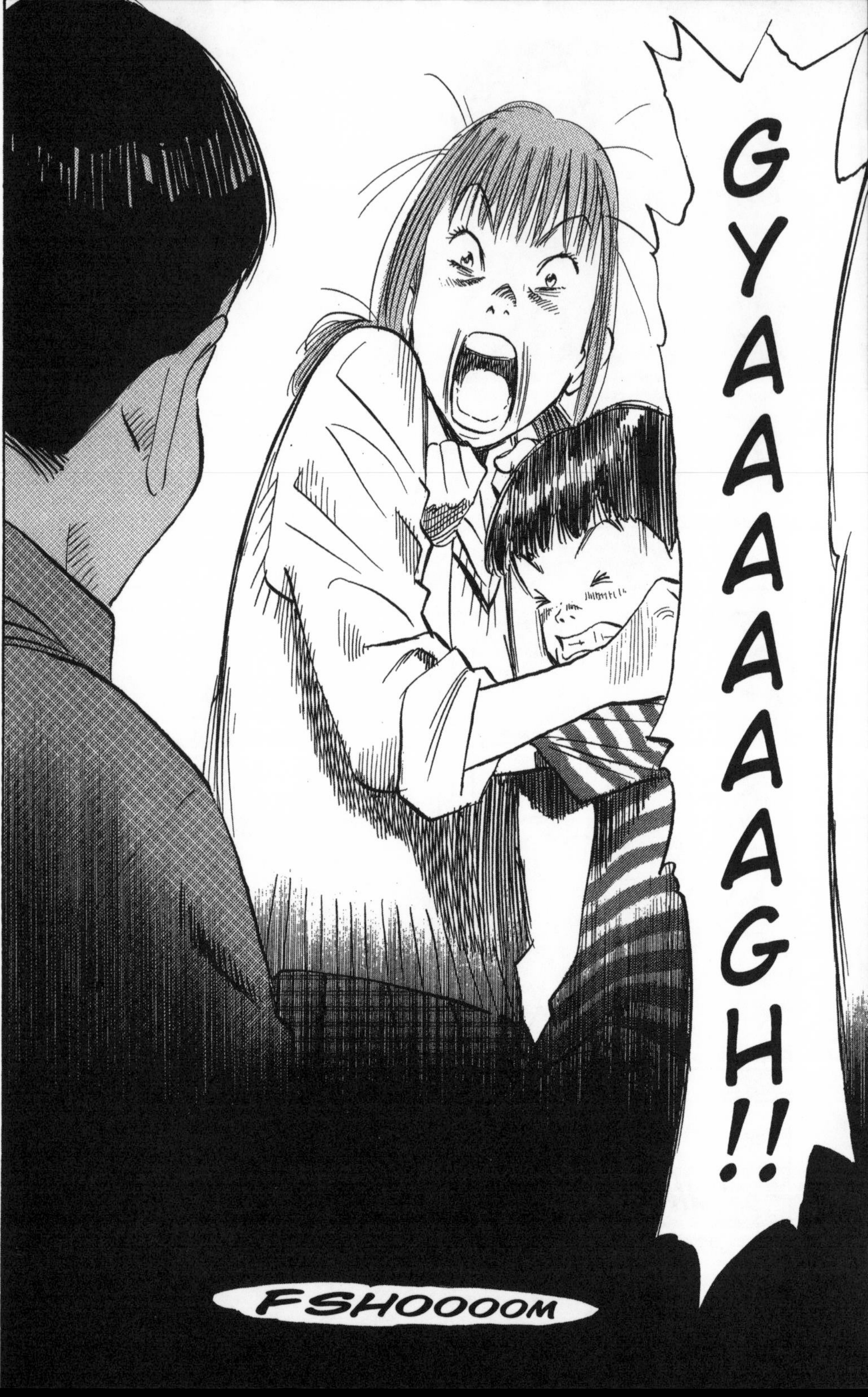
GYAAAAAAAGH!!
FSHOOOOM

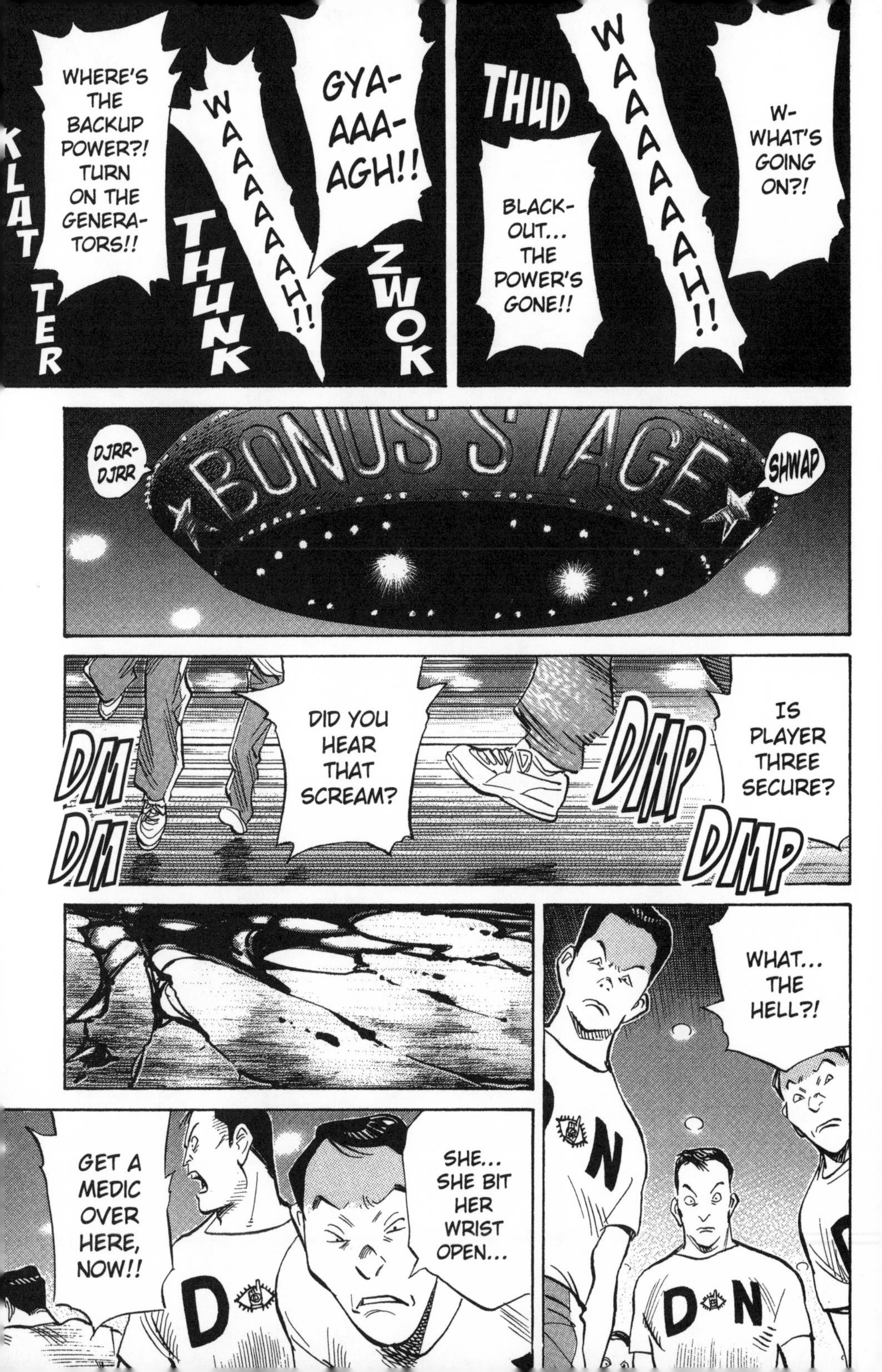
W-
WHAT'S
GOING
ON?!
WAAAAAAAAH!!
THUD
BLACK-
OUT...
THE
POWER'S
GONE!!
GYA-
AAA-
AGH!!
WAAAAAAAH!!
ZWOK
WHERE'S
THE
BACKUP
POWER?!
TURN
ON THE
GENERA-
TORS!!
THUNK
KLATTER
BONUS STAGE
SHWAP
DJRR-
DJRR
IS
PLAYER
THREE
SECURE?
DMP
DMP
DID YOU
HEAR
THAT
SCREAM?
DM
DM
WHAT...
THE
HELL?!
SHE...
SHE BIT
HER
WRIST
OPEN...
GET A
MEDIC
OVER
HERE,
NOW!!

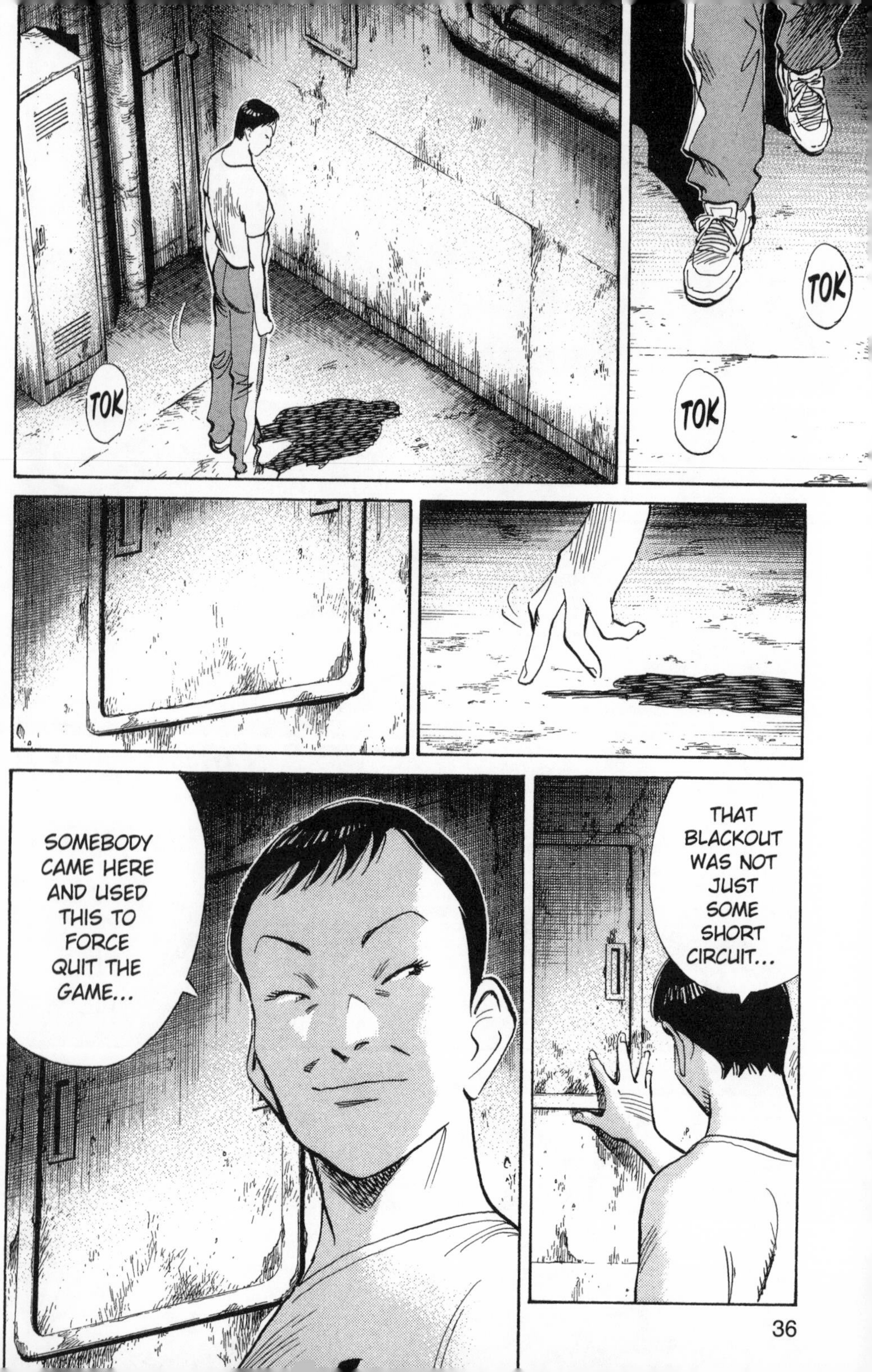
TOK
TOK
TOK
THAT BLACKOUT WAS NOT JUST SOME SHORT CIRCUIT...
SOMEBODY CAME HERE AND USED THIS TO FORCE QUIT THE GAME...

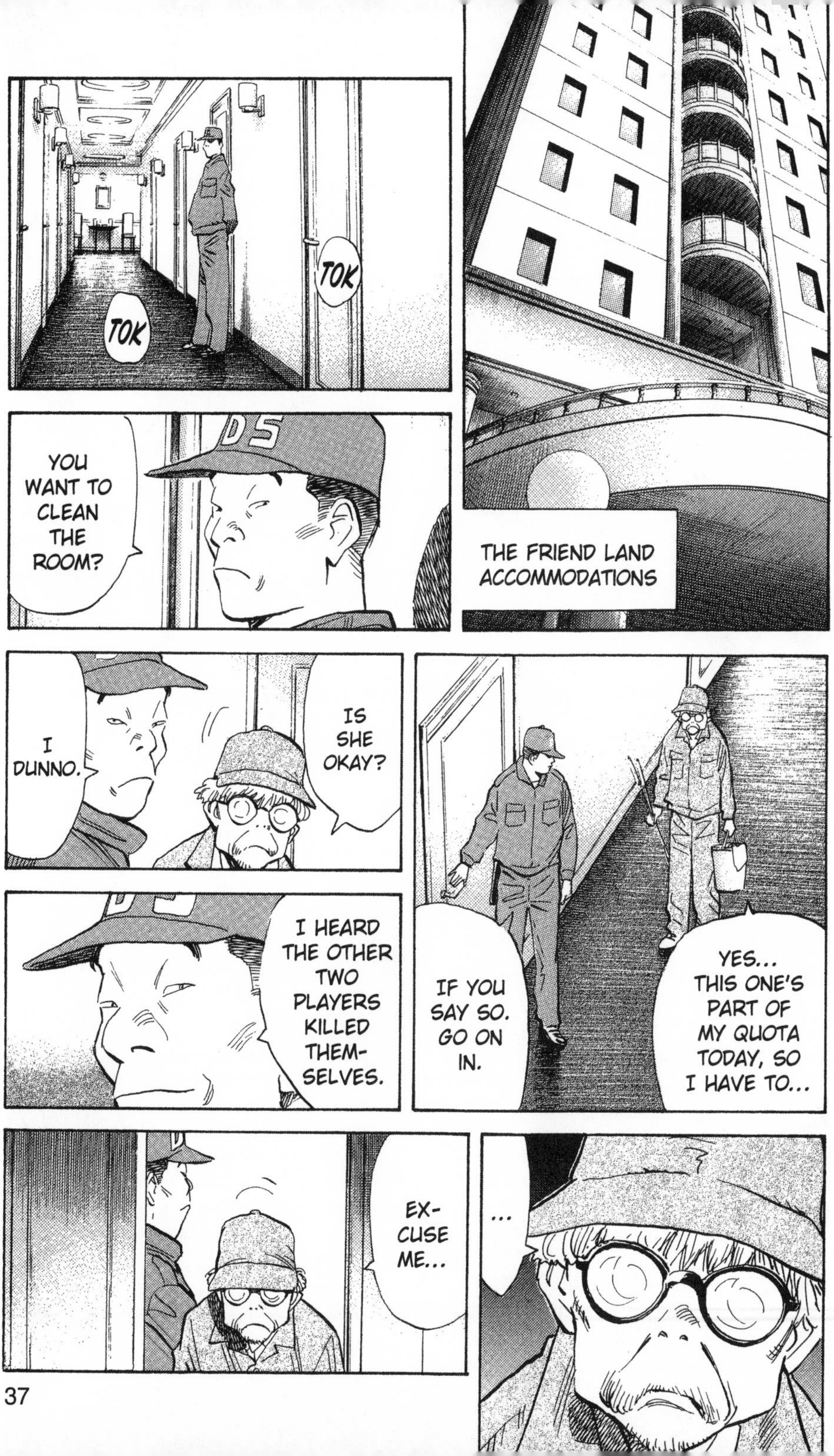
THE FRIEND LAND ACCOMMODATIONS
TOK
TOK
YOU WANT TO CLEAN THE ROOM?
YES... THIS ONE'S PART OF MY QUOTA TODAY, SO I HAVE TO...
IF YOU SAY SO. GO ON IN.
IS SHE OKAY?
I DUNNO.
I HEARD THE OTHER TWO PLAYERS KILLED THEM-SELVES.
...
EX-CUSE ME...

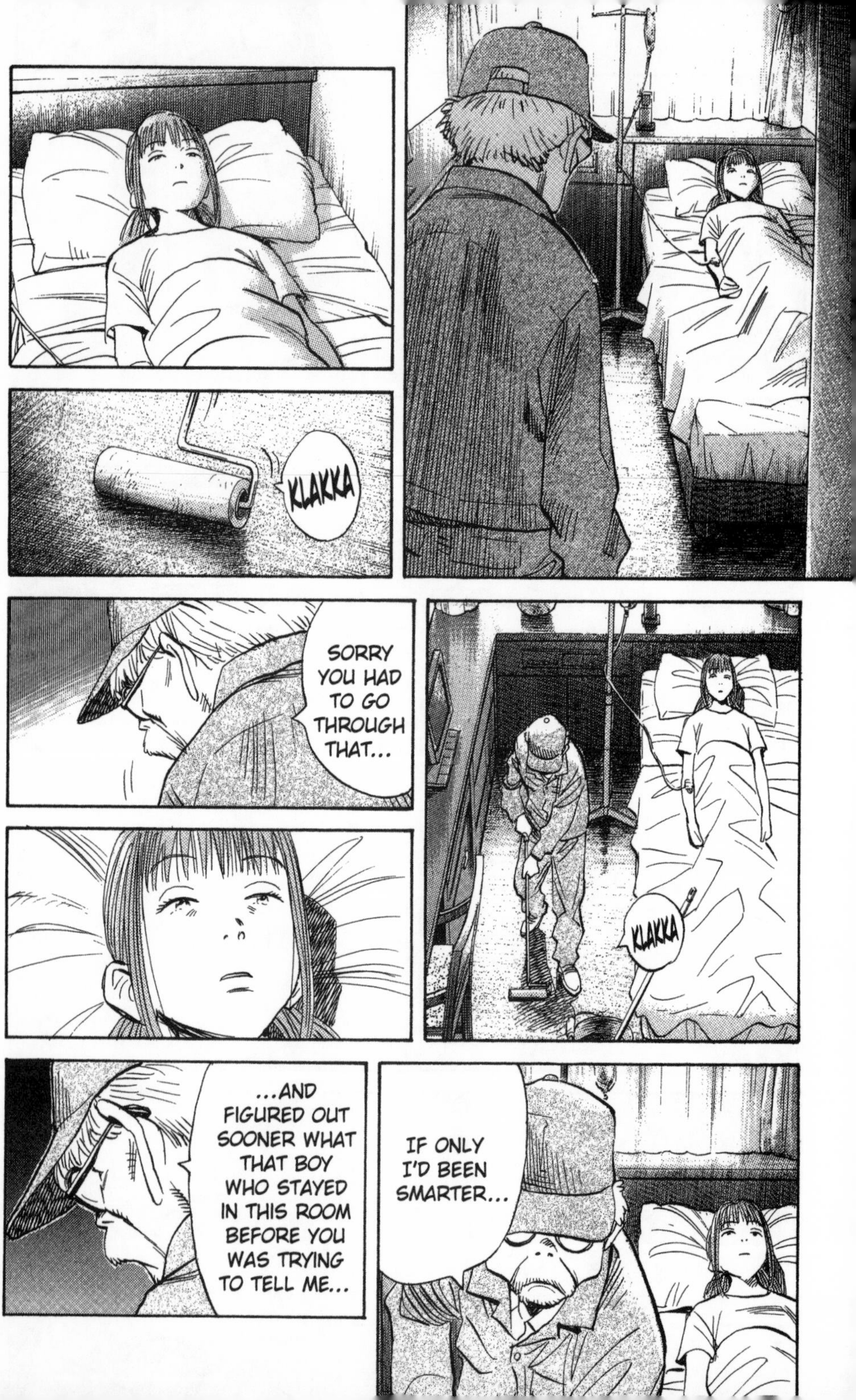
KLAKKA
KLAKKA
SORRY YOU HAD TO GO THROUGH THAT...
IF ONLY I'D BEEN SMARTER...
...AND FIGURED OUT SOONER WHAT THAT BOY WHO STAYED IN THIS ROOM BEFORE YOU WAS TRYING TO TELL ME...

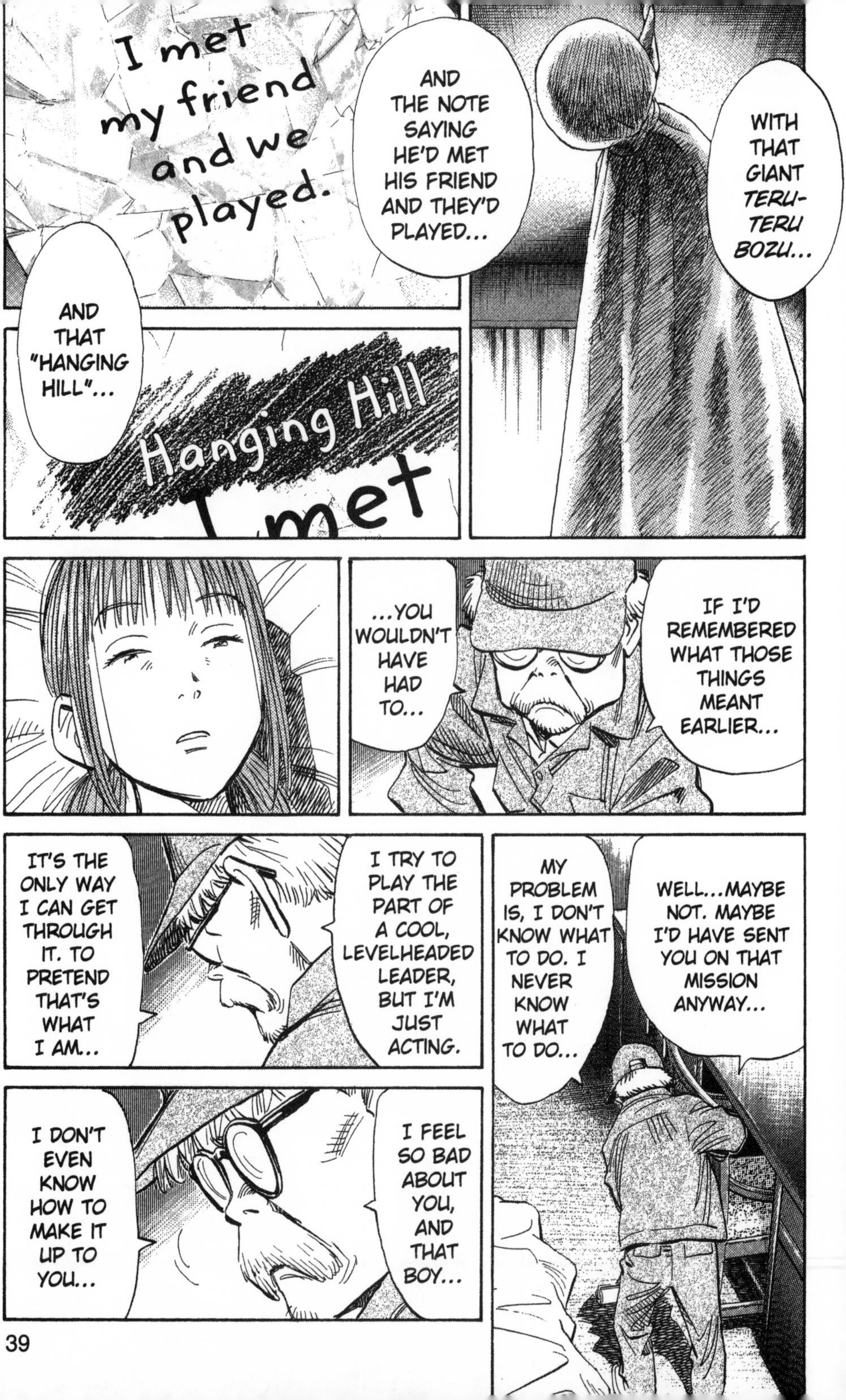
WITH THAT GIANT TERU-TERU BOZU...
AND THE NOTE SAYING HE'D MET HIS FRIEND AND THEY'D PLAYED...
I met my friend and we played.
AND THAT "HANGING HILL"...
Hanging Hill
I met
IF I'D REMEMBERED WHAT THOSE THINGS MEANT EARLIER...
...YOU WOULDN'T HAVE HAD TO...
WELL...MAYBE NOT. MAYBE I'D HAVE SENT YOU ON THAT MISSION ANYWAY...
MY PROBLEM IS, I DON'T KNOW WHAT TO DO. I NEVER KNOW WHAT TO DO...
I TRY TO PLAY THE PART OF A COOL, LEVELHEADED LEADER, BUT I'M JUST ACTING.
IT'S THE ONLY WAY I CAN GET THROUGH IT. TO PRETEND THAT'S WHAT I AM...
I FEEL SO BAD ABOUT YOU, AND THAT BOY...
I DON'T EVEN KNOW HOW TO MAKE IT UP TO YOU...

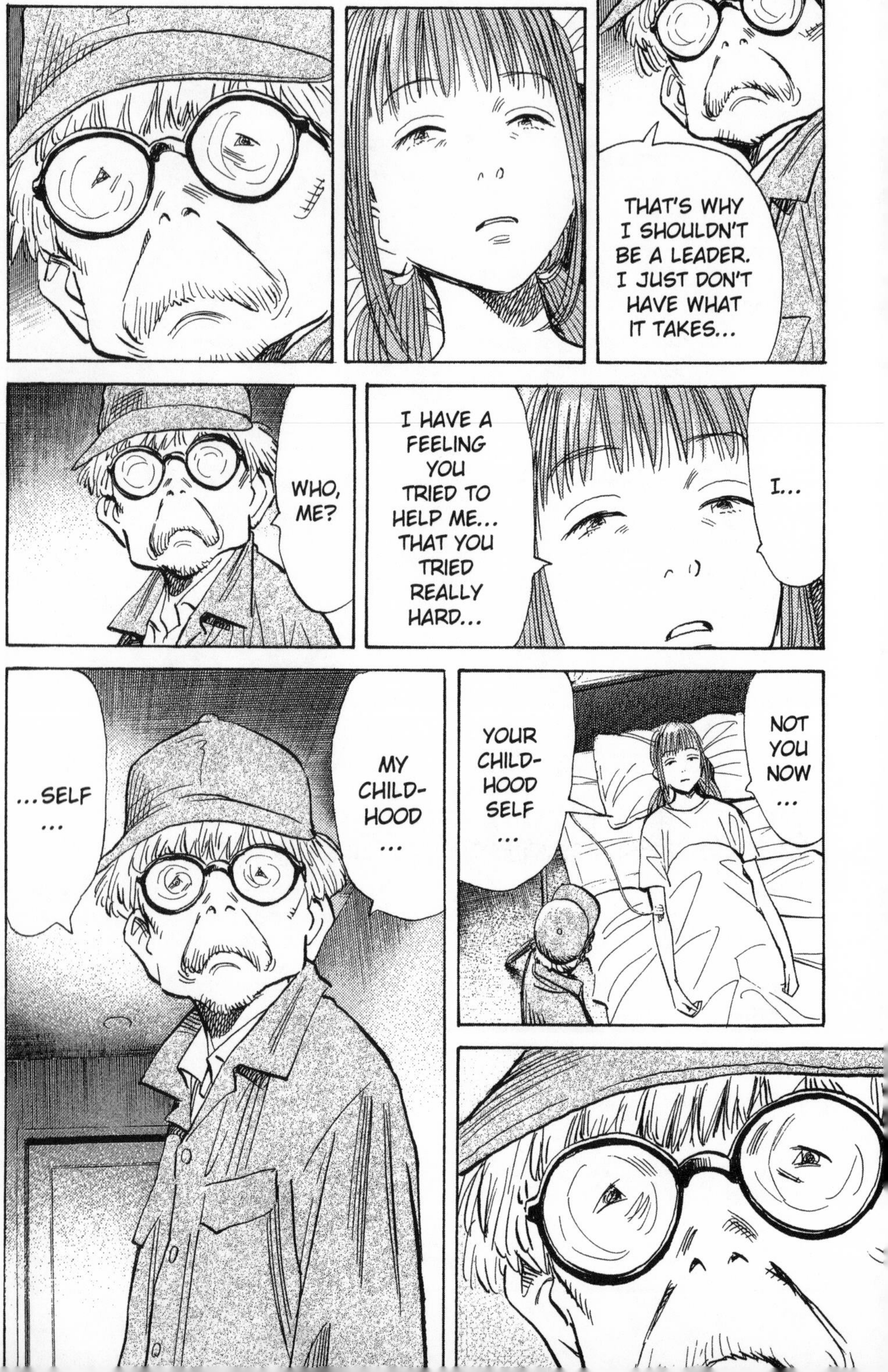
THAT'S WHY I SHOULDN'T BE A LEADER. I JUST DON'T HAVE WHAT IT TAKES...
I...
I HAVE A FEELING YOU TRIED TO HELP ME... THAT YOU TRIED REALLY HARD...
WHO, ME?
NOT YOU NOW...
YOUR CHILD-HOOD SELF...
MY CHILD-HOOD...
...SELF...

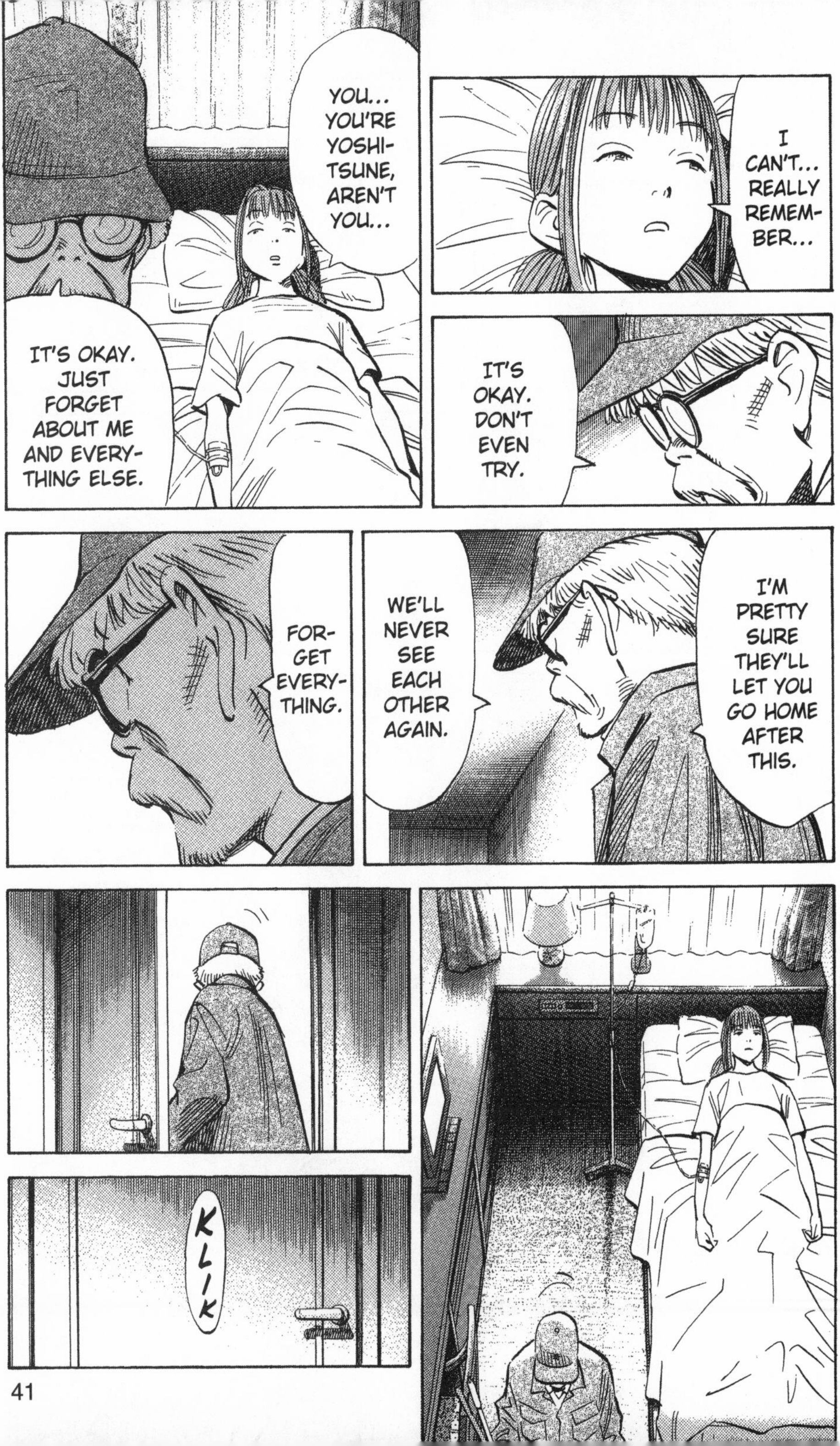
I CAN'T... REALLY REMEMBER...
IT'S OKAY. DON'T EVEN TRY.
YOU... YOU'RE YOSHITSUNE, AREN'T YOU...
IT'S OKAY. JUST FORGET ABOUT ME AND EVERYTHING ELSE.
I'M PRETTY SURE THEY'LL LET YOU GO HOME AFTER THIS.
WE'LL NEVER SEE EACH OTHER AGAIN.
FORGET EVERYTHING.
KLIK

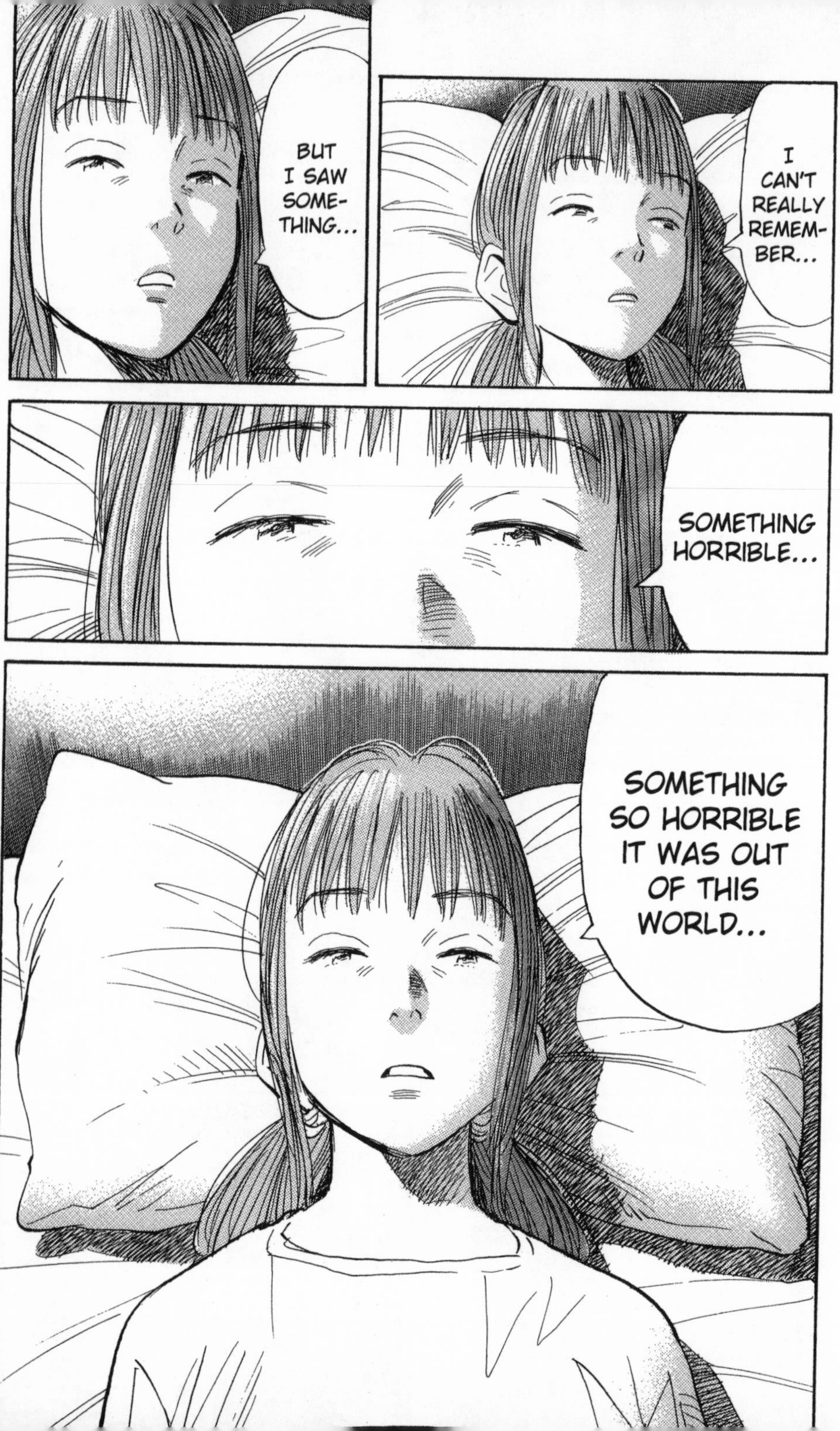
I CAN'T REALLY REMEMBER...
BUT I SAW SOMETHING...
SOMETHING HORRIBLE...
SOMETHING SO HORRIBLE IT WAS OUT OF THIS WORLD...

Chapter 3 Playing for Real

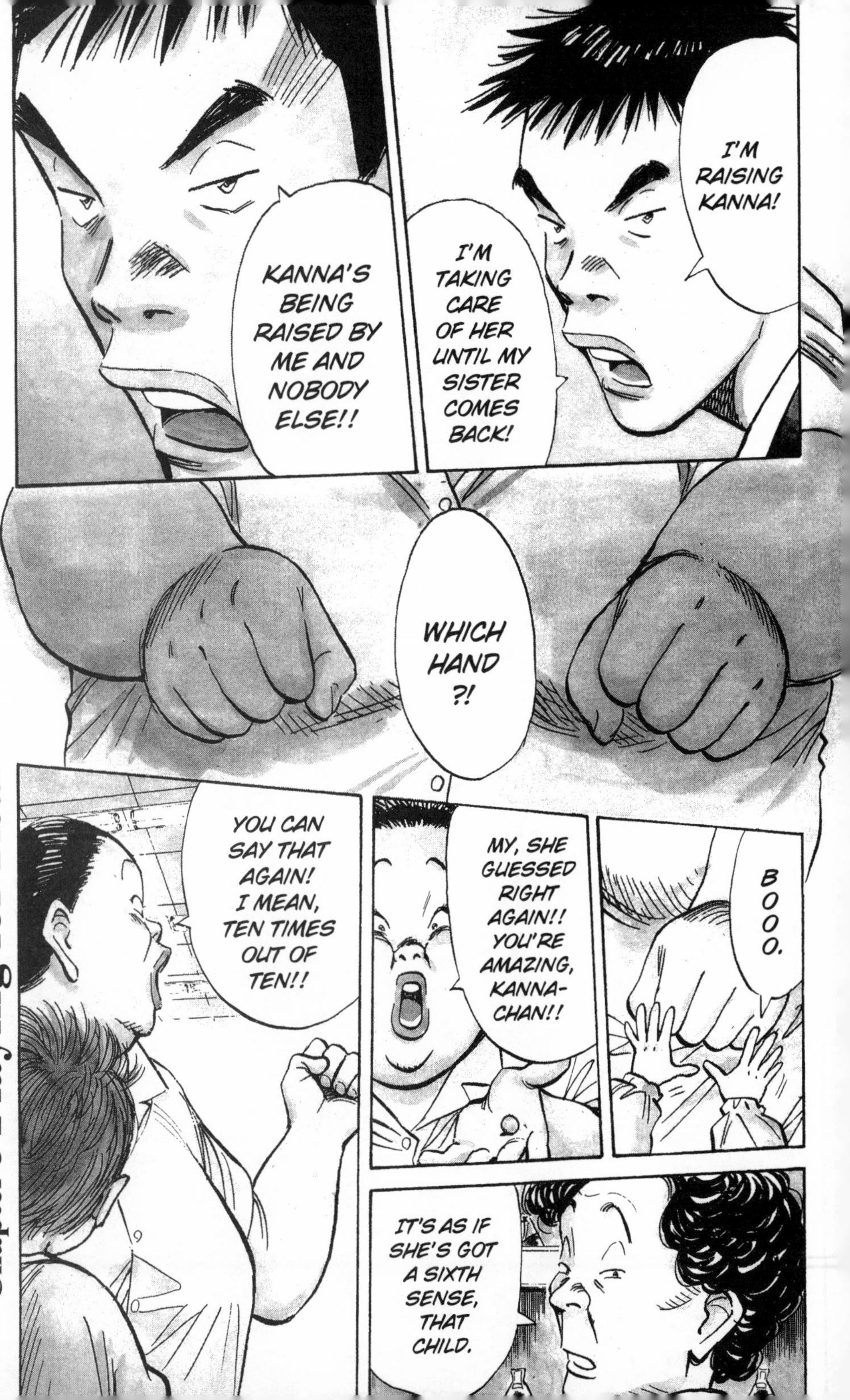
I'M RAISING KANNA!
I'M TAKING CARE OF HER UNTIL MY SISTER COMES BACK!
KANNA'S BEING RAISED BY ME AND NOBODY ELSE!!
WHICH HAND ?!
BOOO.
MY, SHE GUESSED RIGHT AGAIN!! YOU'RE AMAZING, KANNA-CHAN!!
IT'S AS IF SHE'S GOT A SIXTH SENSE, THAT CHILD.
YOU CAN SAY THAT AGAIN! I MEAN, TEN TIMES OUT OF TEN!!

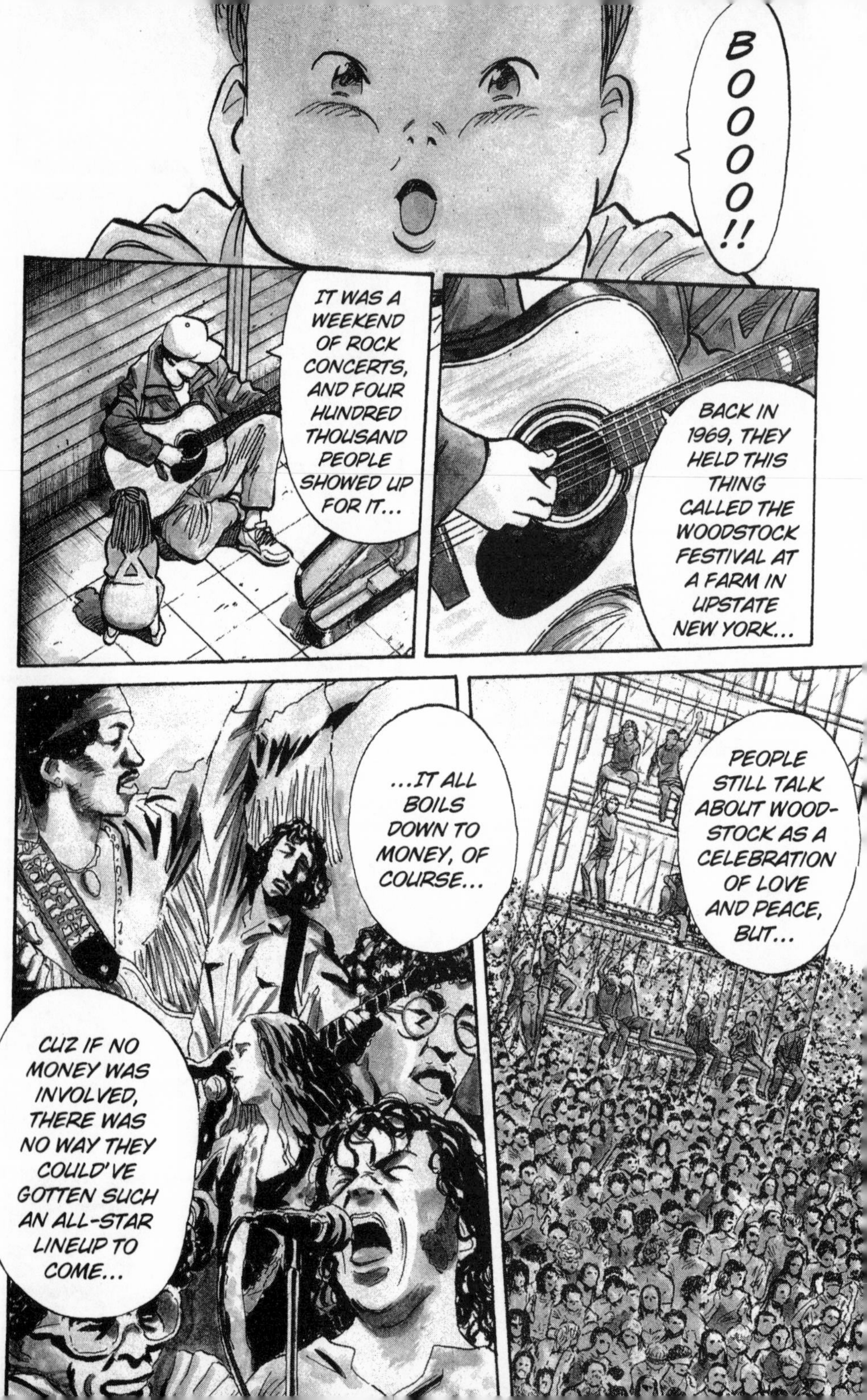
BOOOOO!!
BACK IN 1969, THEY HELD THIS THING CALLED THE WOODSTOCK FESTIVAL AT A FARM IN UPSTATE NEW YORK...
IT WAS A WEEKEND OF ROCK CONCERTS, AND FOUR HUNDRED THOUSAND PEOPLE SHOWED UP FOR IT...
PEOPLE STILL TALK ABOUT WOOD-STOCK AS A CELEBRATION OF LOVE AND PEACE, BUT...
...IT ALL BOILS DOWN TO MONEY, OF COURSE...
CUZ IF NO MONEY WAS INVOLVED, THERE WAS NO WAY THEY COULD'VE GOTTEN SUCH AN ALL-STAR LINEUP TO COME...

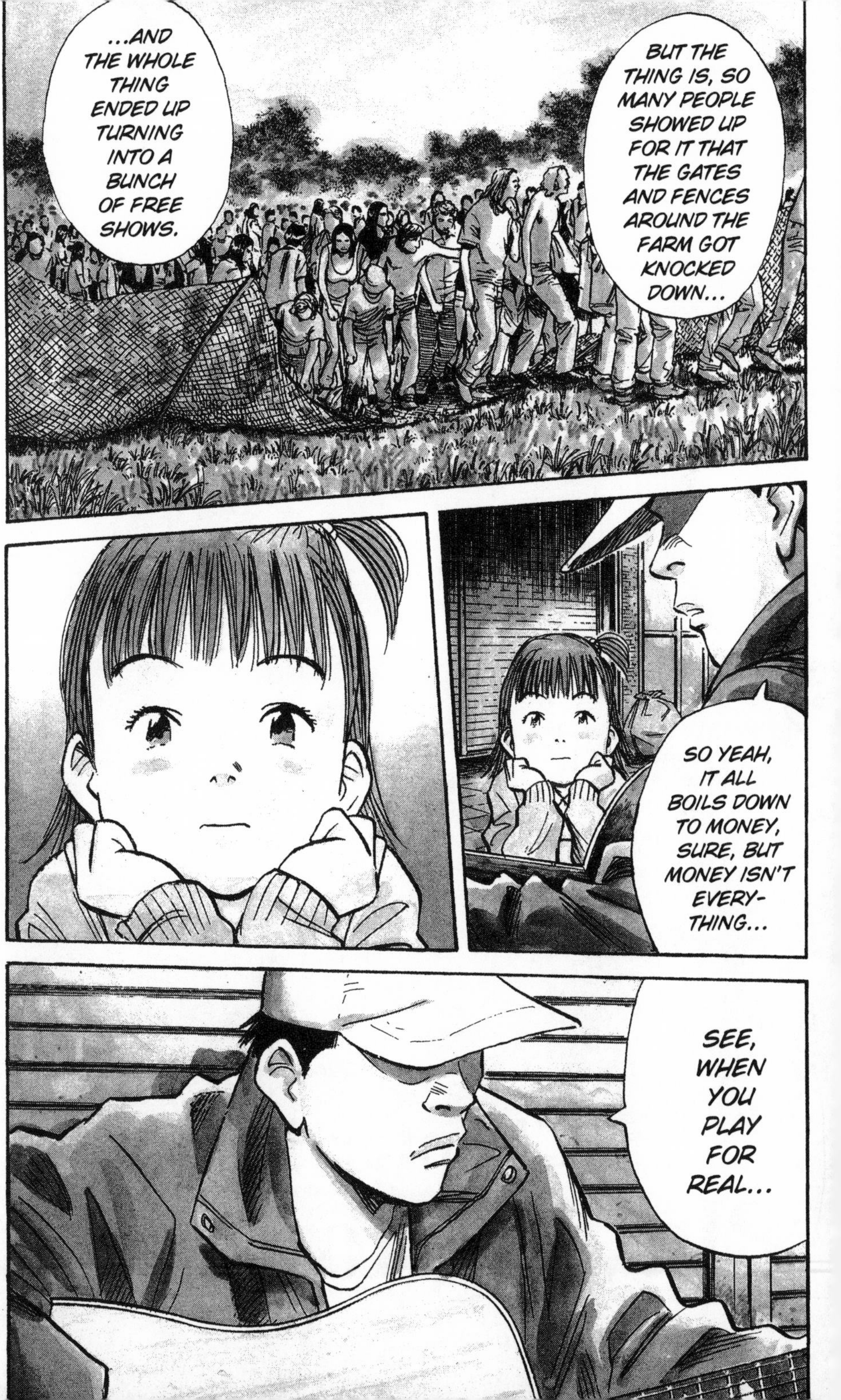
BUT THE THING IS, SO MANY PEOPLE SHOWED UP FOR IT THAT THE GATES AND FENCES AROUND THE FARM GOT KNOCKED DOWN...
...AND THE WHOLE THING ENDED UP TURNING INTO A BUNCH OF FREE SHOWS.
SO YEAH, IT ALL BOILS DOWN TO MONEY, SURE, BUT MONEY ISN'T EVERY-THING...
SEE, WHEN YOU PLAY FOR REAL...

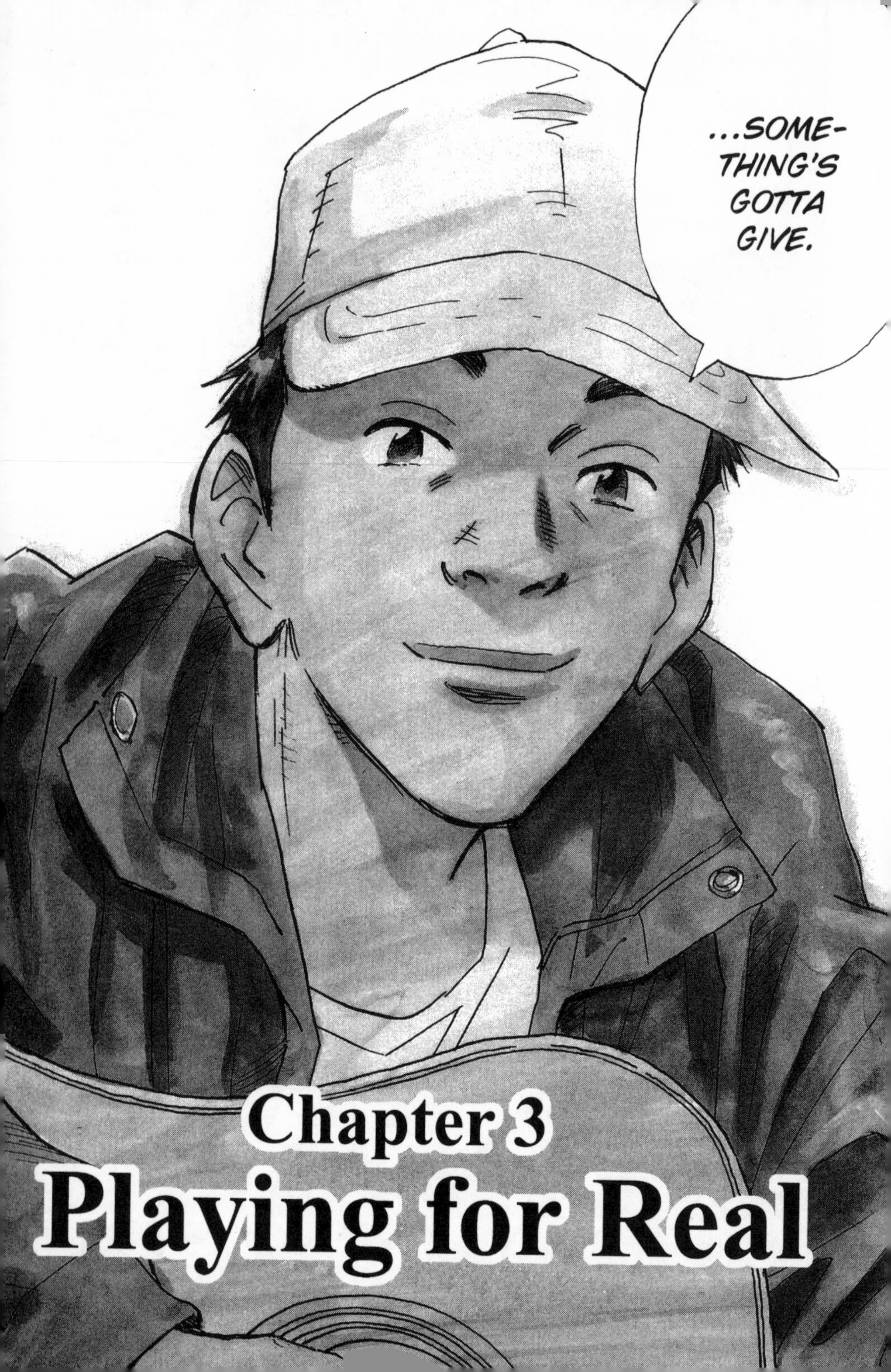
...SOME-THING'S GOTTA GIVE.
Chapter 3
Playing for Real

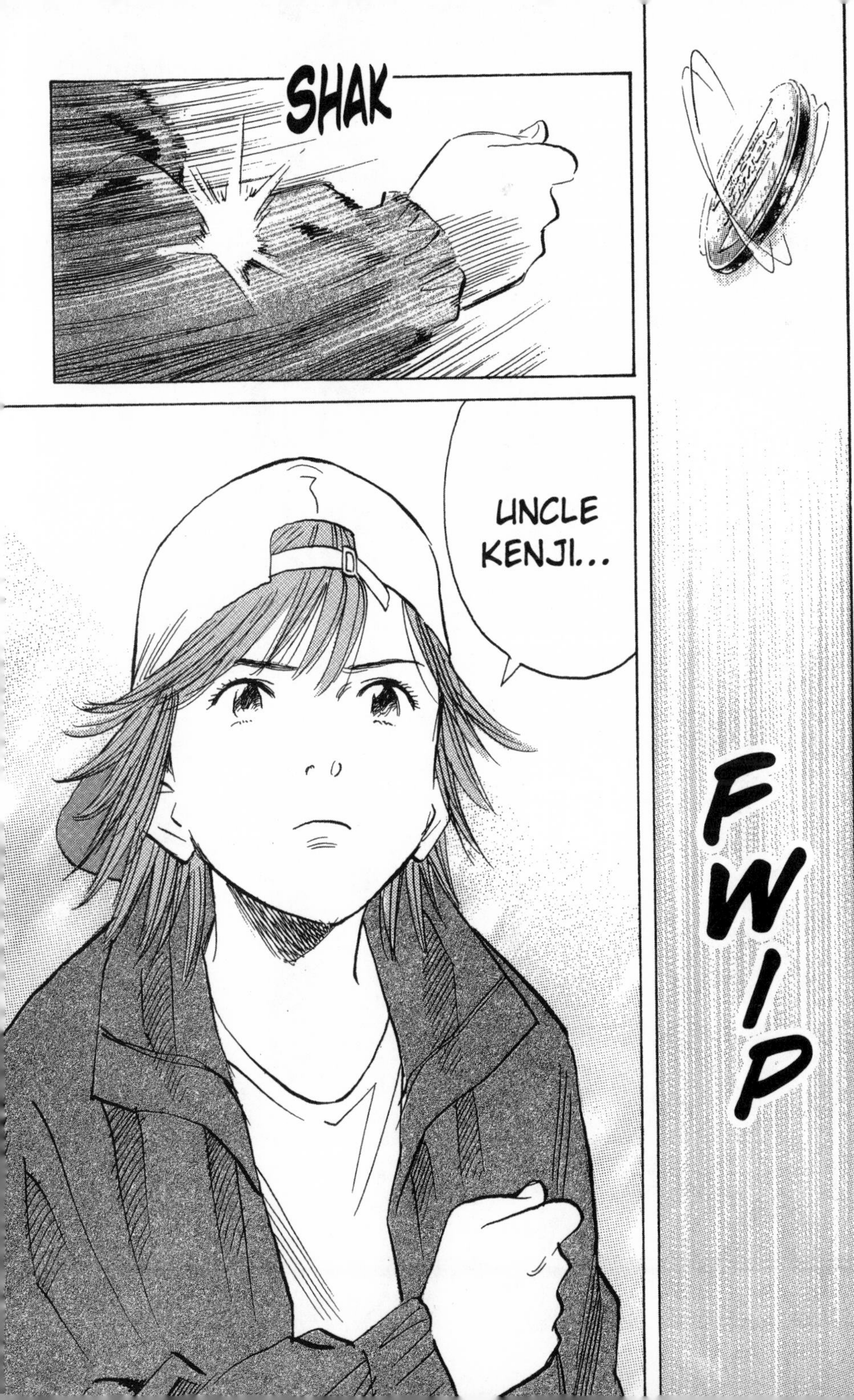
FWIP
SHAK
UNCLE KENJI...

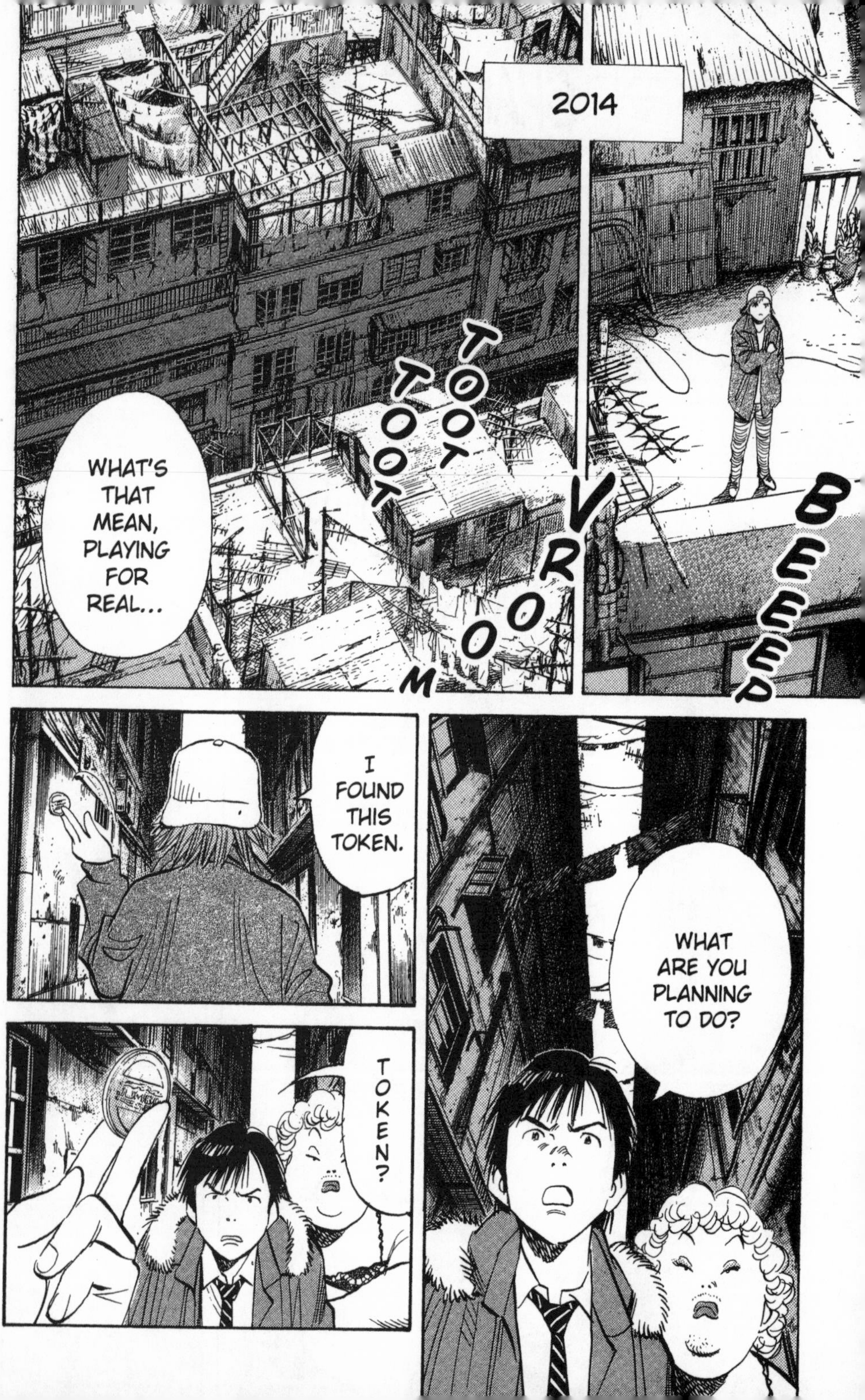
2014
BEEEP
TOOT TOOT
VROOOM
WHAT'S THAT MEAN, PLAYING FOR REAL...
WHAT ARE YOU PLANNING TO DO?
I FOUND THIS TOKEN.
TOKEN?

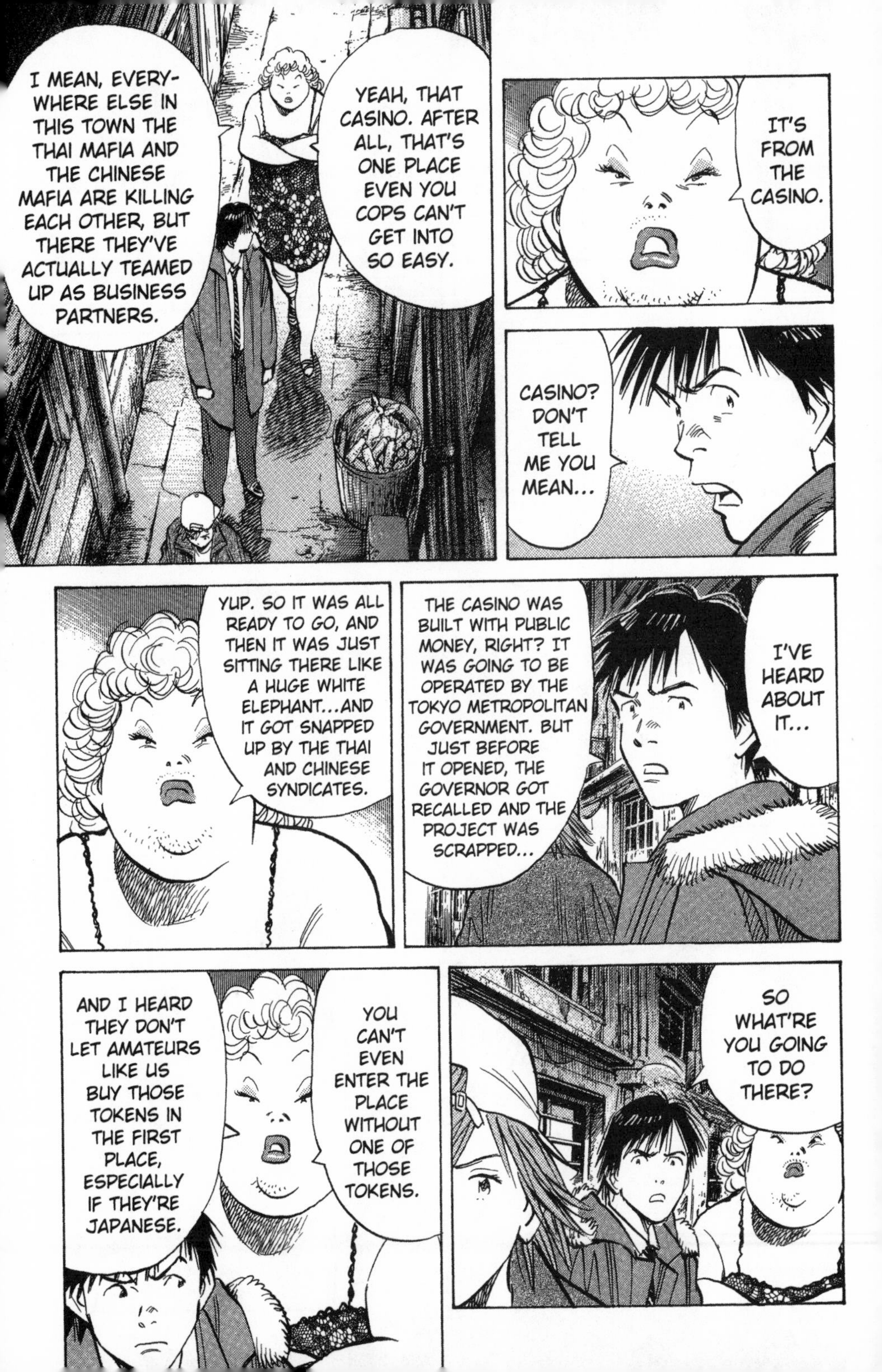
IT'S FROM THE CASINO.
CASINO? DON'T TELL ME YOU MEAN...
YEAH, THAT CASINO. AFTER ALL, THAT'S ONE PLACE EVEN YOU COPS CAN'T GET INTO SO EASY.
I MEAN, EVERY-WHERE ELSE IN THIS TOWN THE THAI MAFIA AND THE CHINESE MAFIA ARE KILLING EACH OTHER, BUT THERE THEY'VE ACTUALLY TEAMED UP AS BUSINESS PARTNERS.
I'VE HEARD ABOUT IT...
THE CASINO WAS BUILT WITH PUBLIC MONEY, RIGHT? IT WAS GOING TO BE OPERATED BY THE TOKYO METROPOLITAN GOVERNMENT. BUT JUST BEFORE IT OPENED, THE GOVERNOR GOT RECALLED AND THE PROJECT WAS SCRAPPED...
YUP. SO IT WAS ALL READY TO GO, AND THEN IT WAS JUST SITTING THERE LIKE A HUGE WHITE ELEPHANT...AND IT GOT SNAPPED UP BY THE THAI AND CHINESE SYNDICATES.
SO WHAT'RE YOU GOING TO DO THERE?
YOU CAN'T EVEN ENTER THE PLACE WITHOUT ONE OF THOSE TOKENS.
AND I HEARD THEY DON'T LET AMATEURS LIKE US BUY THOSE TOKENS IN THE FIRST PLACE, ESPECIALLY IF THEY'RE JAPANESE.

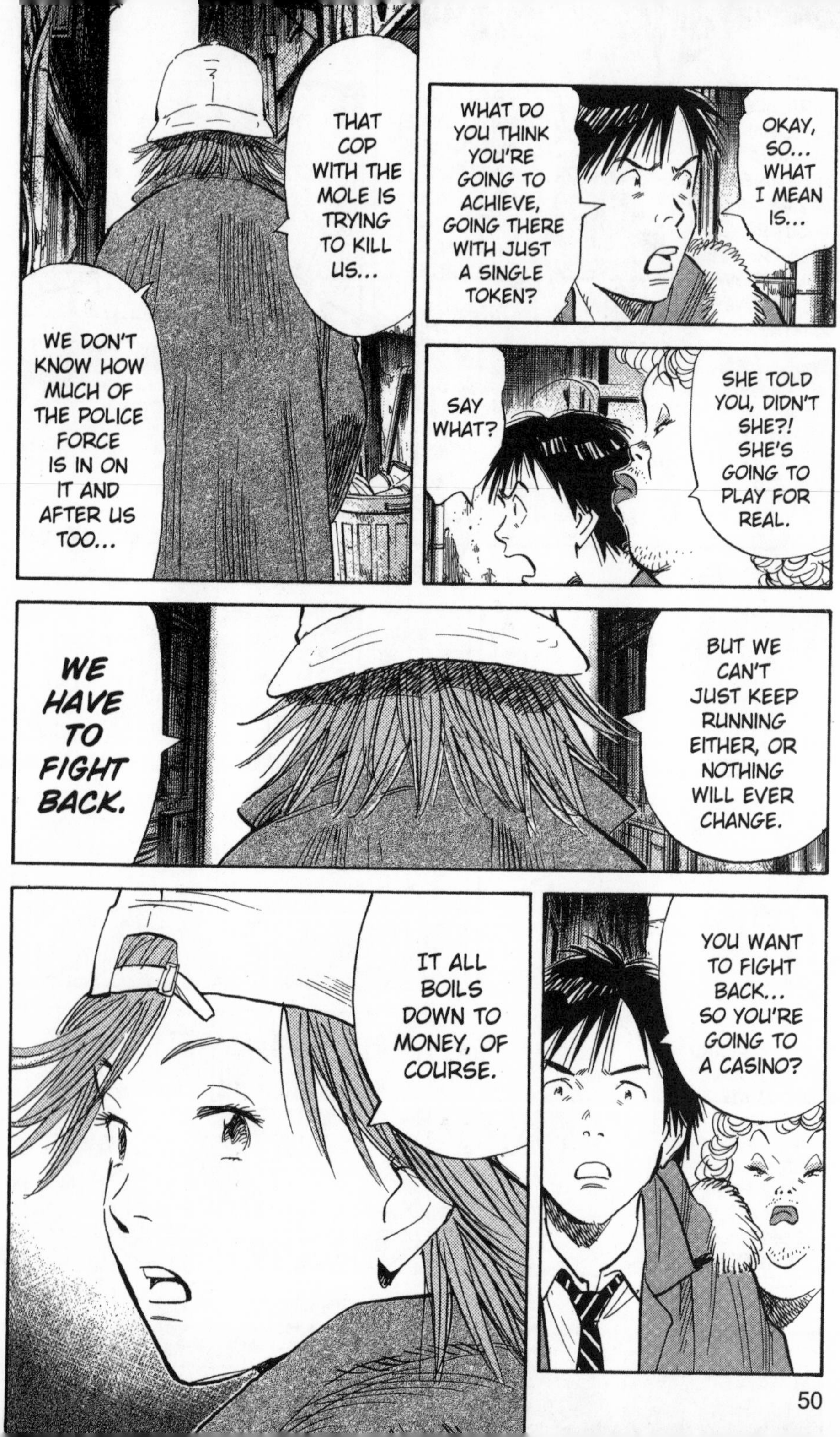

OKAY, SO... WHAT I MEAN IS...
WHAT DO YOU THINK YOU'RE GOING TO ACHIEVE, GOING THERE WITH JUST A SINGLE TOKEN?
SHE TOLD YOU, DIDN'T SHE?! SHE'S GOING TO PLAY FOR REAL.
SAY WHAT?
THAT COP WITH THE MOLE IS TRYING TO KILL US...
WE DON'T KNOW HOW MUCH OF THE POLICE FORCE IS IN ON IT AND AFTER US TOO...
BUT WE CAN'T JUST KEEP RUNNING EITHER, OR NOTHING WILL EVER CHANGE.
WE HAVE TO FIGHT BACK.
YOU WANT TO FIGHT BACK... SO YOU'RE GOING TO A CASINO?
IT ALL BOILS DOWN TO MONEY, OF COURSE.

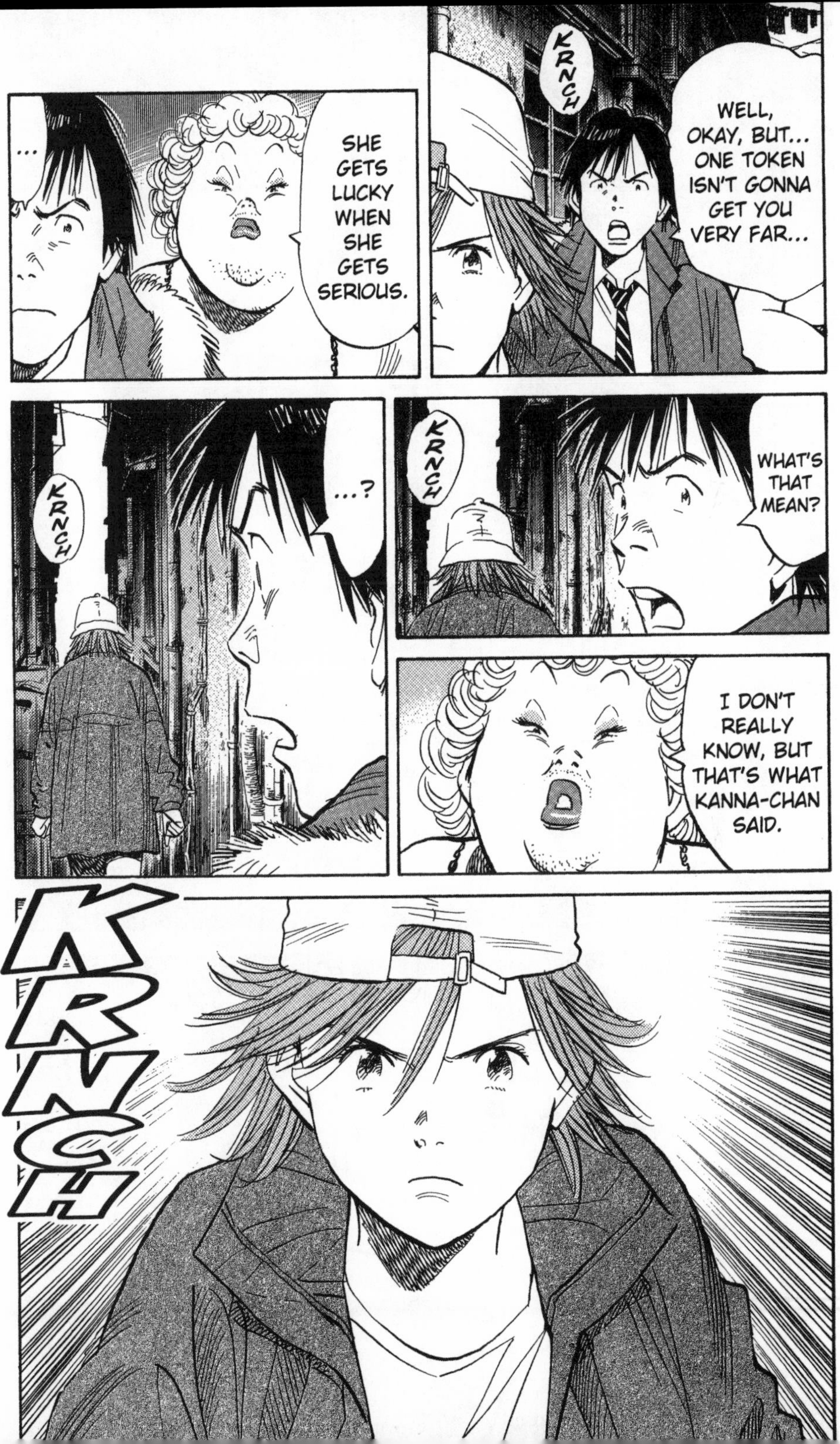
WELL, OKAY, BUT... ONE TOKEN ISN'T GONNA GET YOU VERY FAR...
KRNCH
SHE GETS LUCKY WHEN SHE GETS SERIOUS.
...
WHAT'S THAT MEAN?
KRNCH
I DON'T REALLY KNOW, BUT THAT'S WHAT KANNA-CHAN SAID.
...?
KRNCH
KRNCH

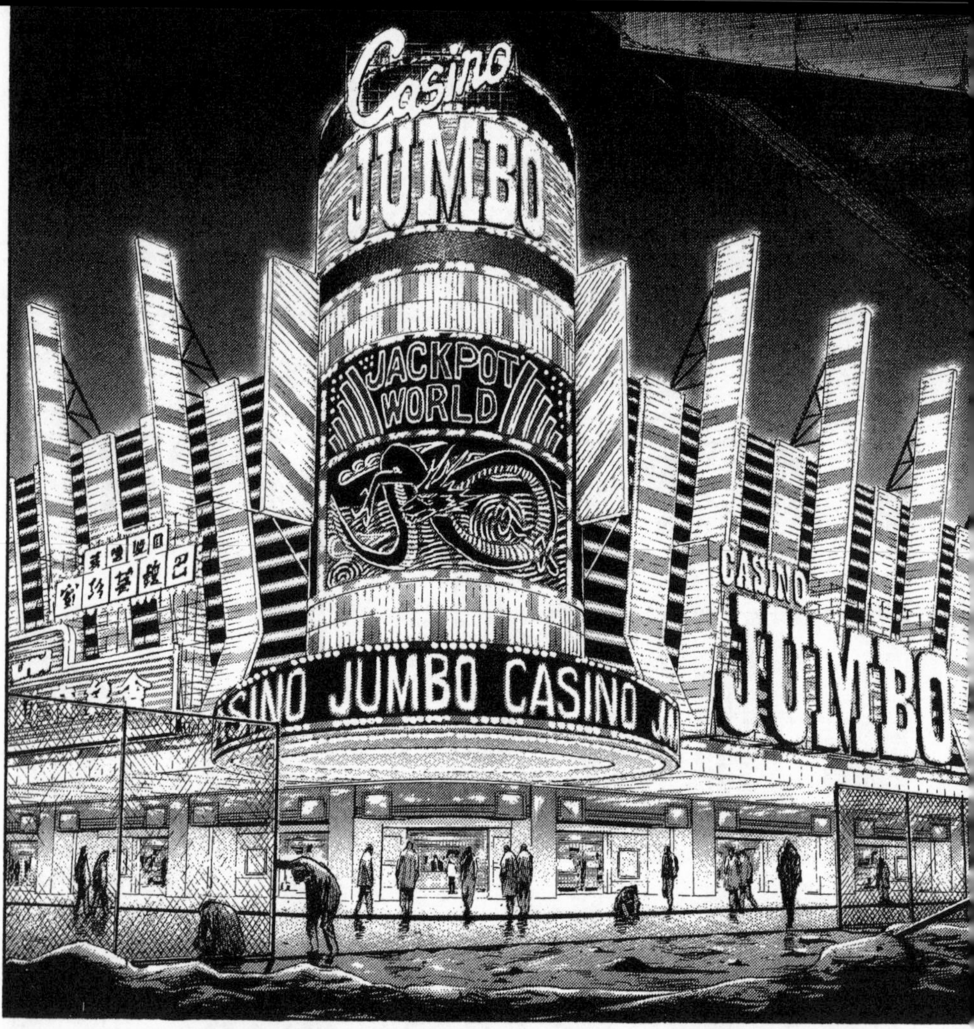
Casino
JUMBO
JACKPOT WORLD
CASINO JUMBO CASINO
CASINO
JUMBO
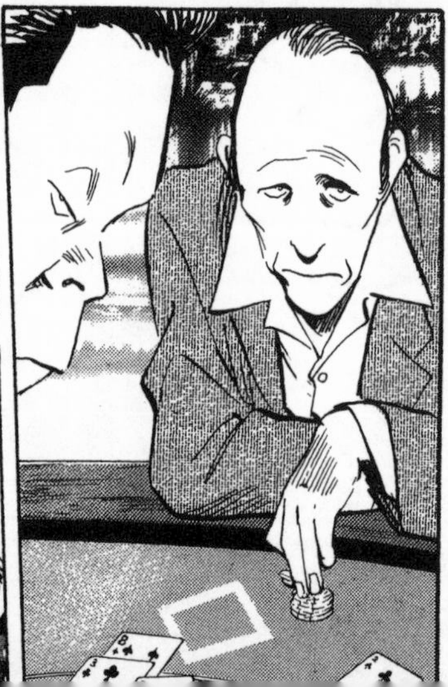
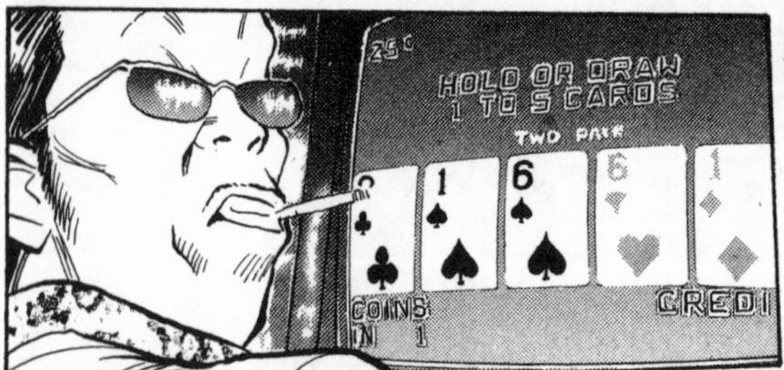
HOLD OR DRAW
1 TO 5 CARDS
TWO PAIR
COINS
IN 1
CREDI
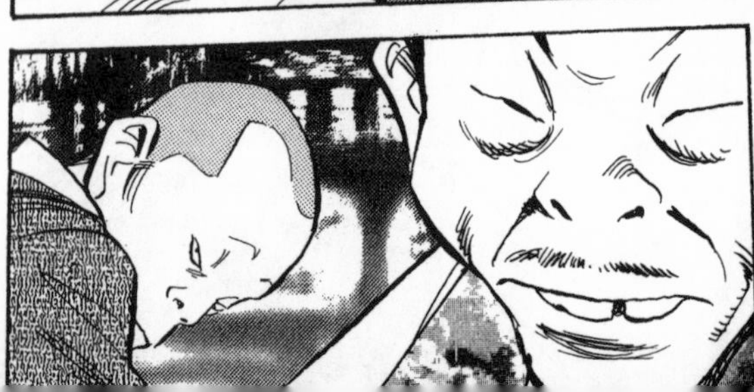

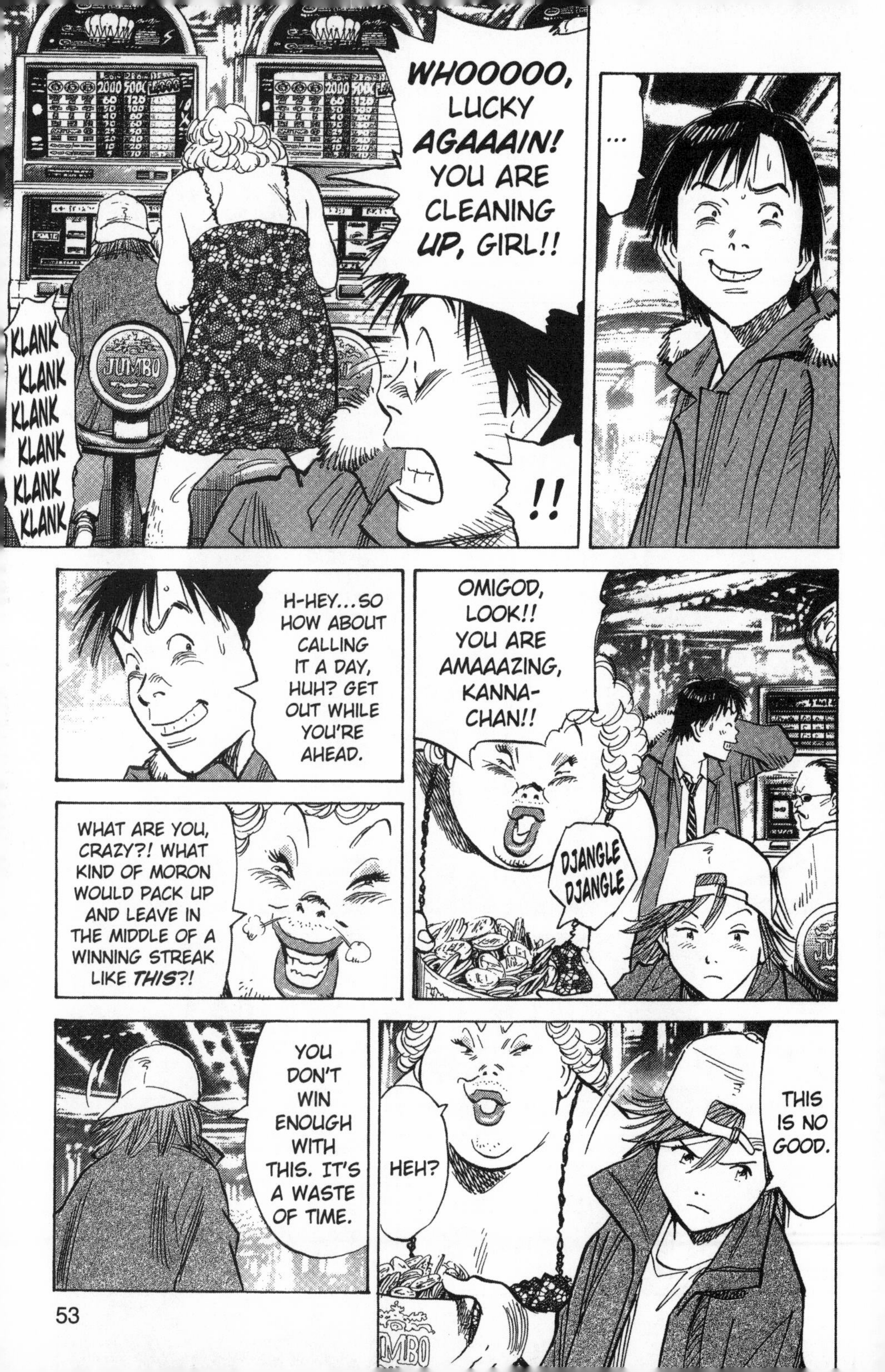
...
WHOOOOO, LUCKY AGAAAIN! YOU ARE CLEANING UP, GIRL!!
!!
KLANK KLANK KLANK KLANK KLANK KLANK
OMIGOD, LOOK!! YOU ARE AMAAAZING, KANNA-CHAN!!
DJANGLE DJANGLE
H-HEY...SO HOW ABOUT CALLING IT A DAY, HUH? GET OUT WHILE YOU'RE AHEAD.
WHAT ARE YOU, CRAZY?! WHAT KIND OF MORON WOULD PACK UP AND LEAVE IN THE MIDDLE OF A WINNING STREAK LIKE THIS?!
THIS IS NO GOOD.
HEH?
YOU DON'T WIN ENOUGH WITH THIS. IT'S A WASTE OF TIME.

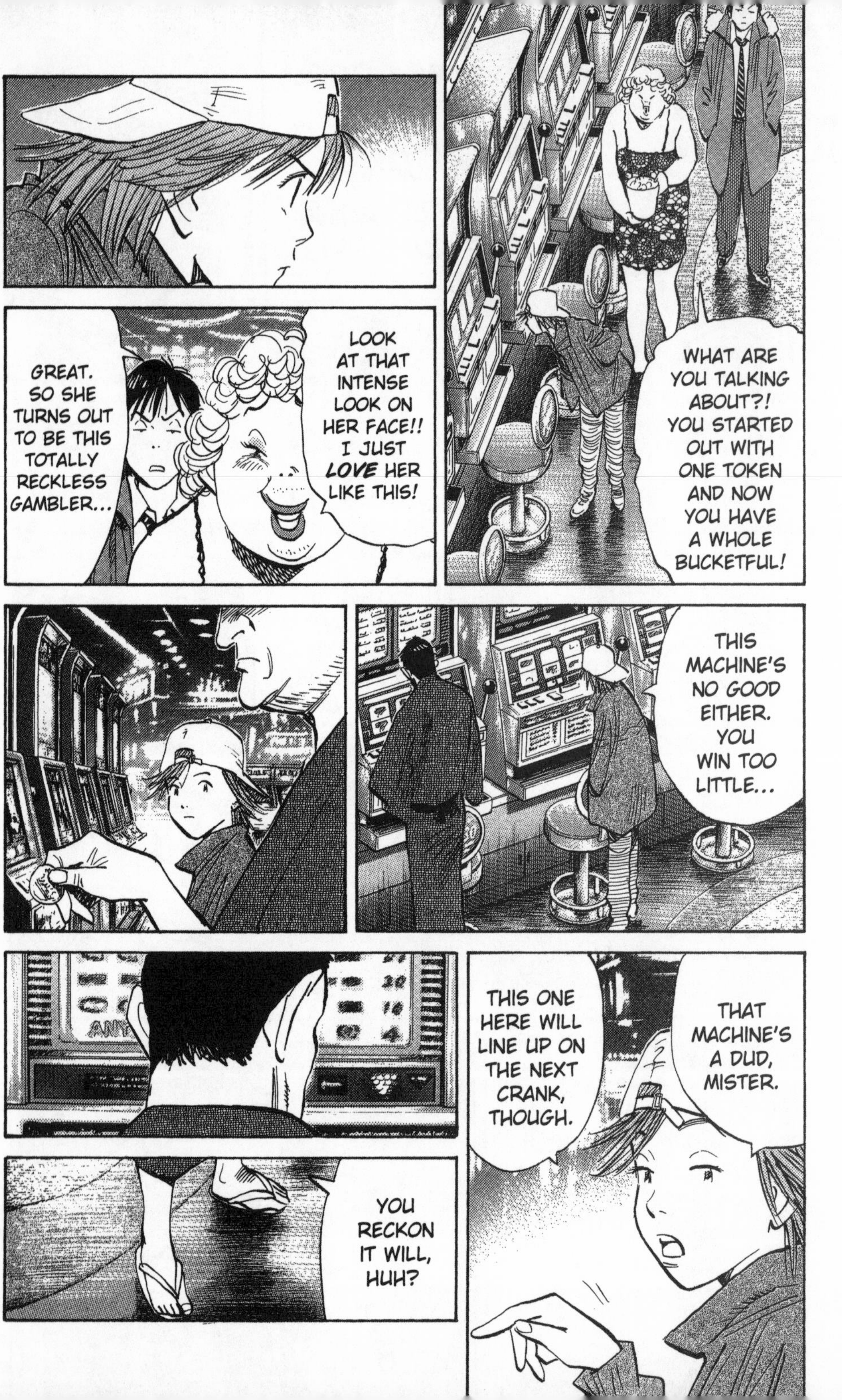
WHAT ARE YOU TALKING ABOUT?! YOU STARTED OUT WITH ONE TOKEN AND NOW YOU HAVE A WHOLE BUCKETFUL!
LOOK AT THAT INTENSE LOOK ON HER FACE!! I JUST *LOVE* HER LIKE THIS!
GREAT. SO SHE TURNS OUT TO BE THIS TOTALLY RECKLESS GAMBLER...
THIS MACHINE'S NO GOOD EITHER. YOU WIN TOO LITTLE...
THAT MACHINE'S A DUD, MISTER.
THIS ONE HERE WILL LINE UP ON THE NEXT CRANK, THOUGH.
YOU RECKON IT WILL, HUH?

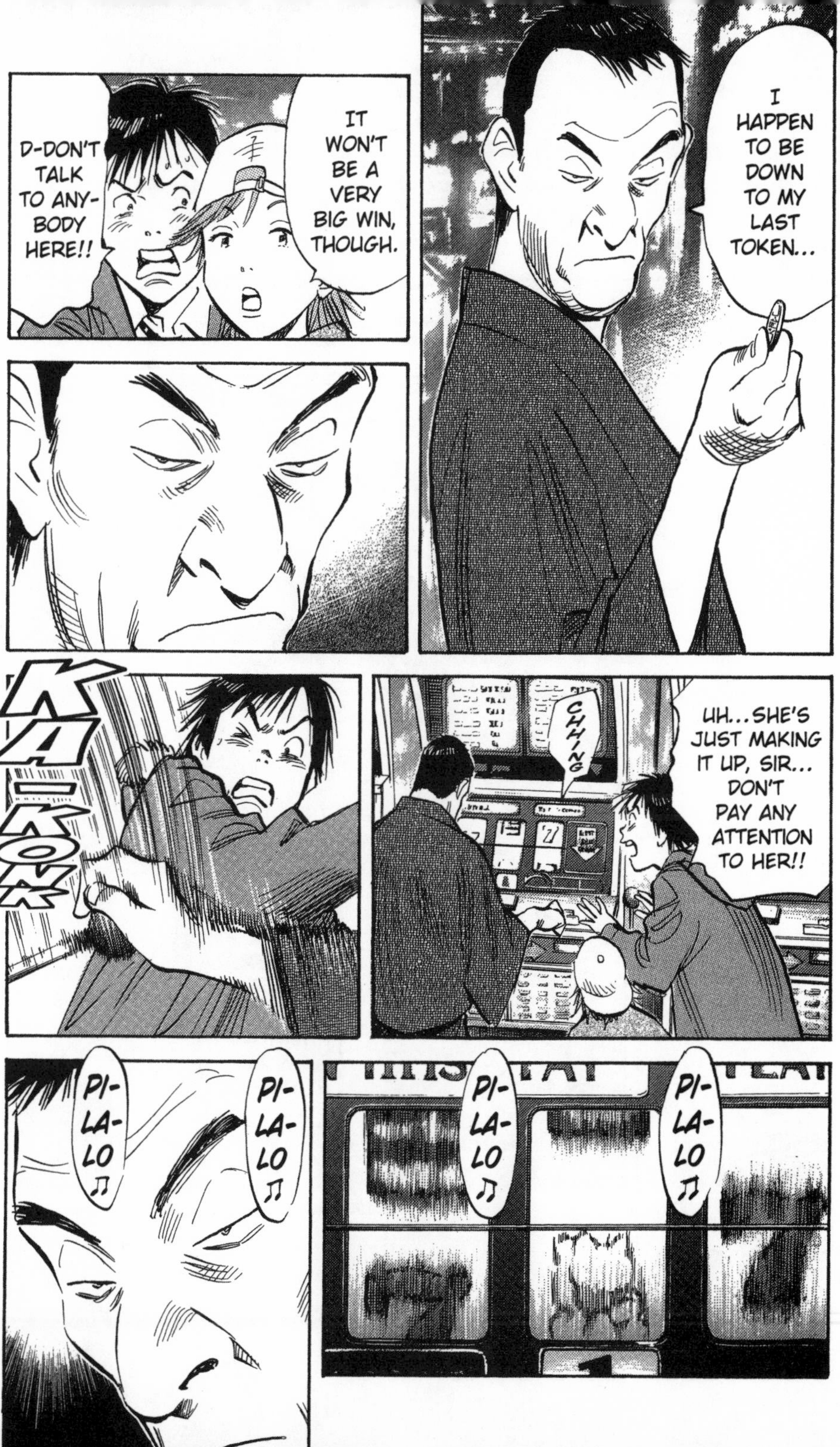
I HAPPEN TO BE DOWN TO MY LAST TOKEN...
IT WON'T BE A VERY BIG WIN, THOUGH.
D-DON'T TALK TO ANY-BODY HERE!!
UH...SHE'S JUST MAKING IT UP, SIR... DON'T PAY ANY ATTENTION TO HER!!
CHHING
KA-KONK
PI-LA-LO♫
PI-LA-LO♫
PI-LA-LO♫
PI-LA-LO♫

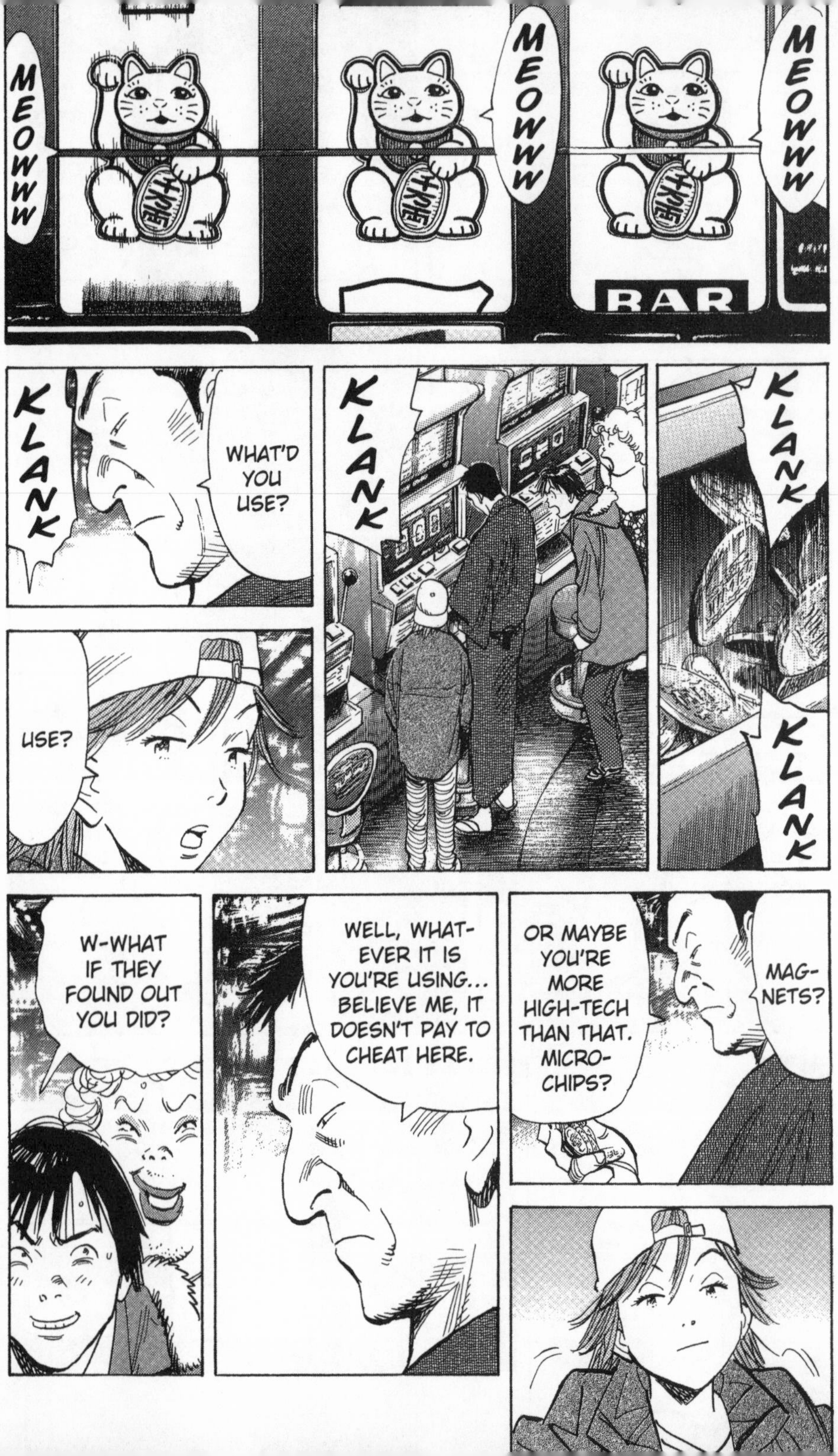
MEOWWW
MEOWWW
MEOWWW
BAR
KLANK
KLANK
KLANK
WHAT'D YOU USE?
KLANK
USE?
MAG-NETS?
OR MAYBE YOU'RE MORE HIGH-TECH THAN THAT. MICRO-CHIPS?
WELL, WHAT-EVER IT IS YOU'RE USING... BELIEVE ME, IT DOESN'T PAY TO CHEAT HERE.
W-WHAT IF THEY FOUND OUT YOU DID?

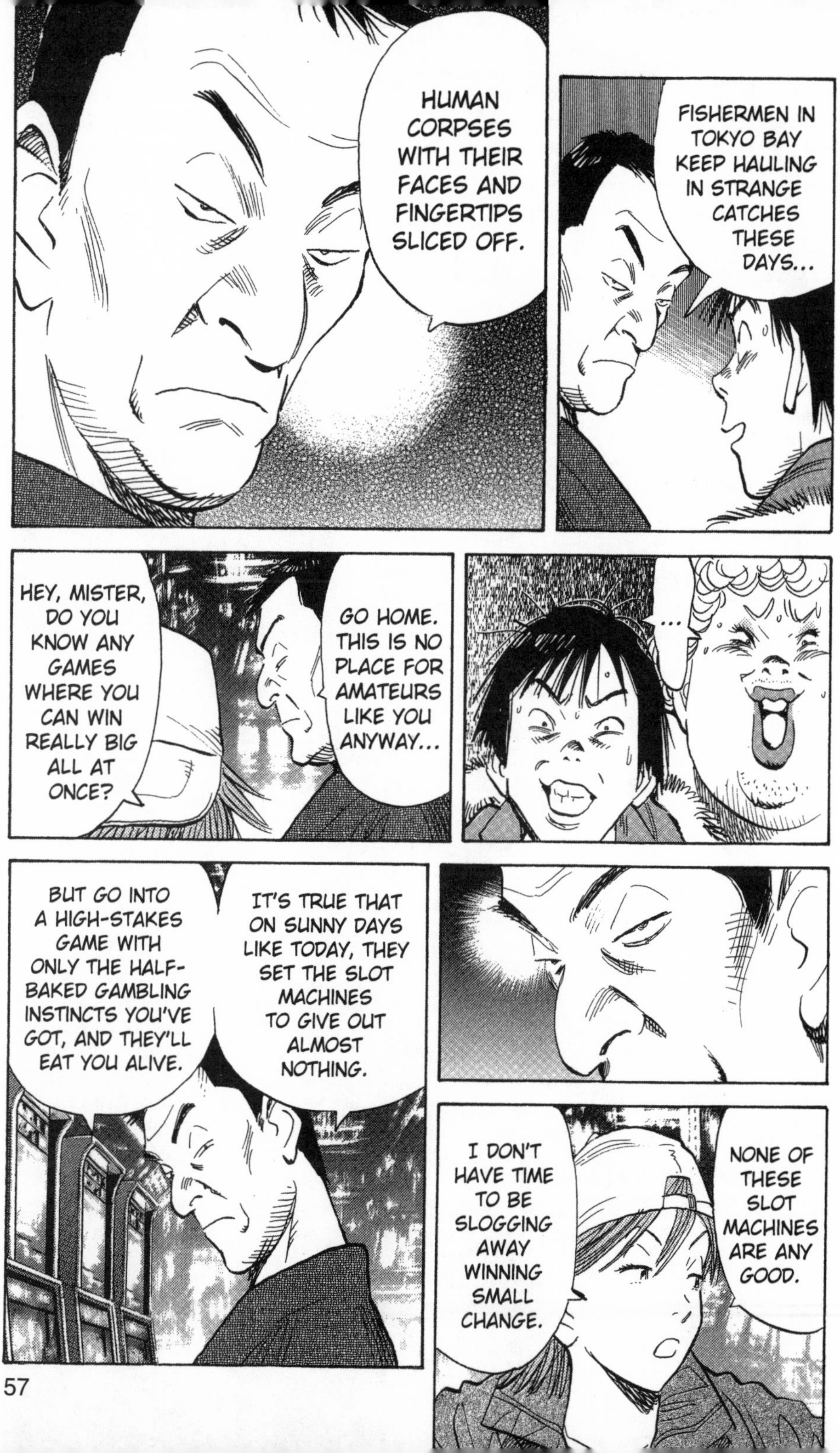
FISHERMEN IN TOKYO BAY KEEP HAULING IN STRANGE CATCHES THESE DAYS...
HUMAN CORPSES WITH THEIR FACES AND FINGERTIPS SLICED OFF.
...
GO HOME. THIS IS NO PLACE FOR AMATEURS LIKE YOU ANYWAY...
HEY, MISTER, DO YOU KNOW ANY GAMES WHERE YOU CAN WIN REALLY BIG ALL AT ONCE?
NONE OF THESE SLOT MACHINES ARE ANY GOOD.
I DON'T HAVE TIME TO BE SLOGGING AWAY WINNING SMALL CHANGE.
IT'S TRUE THAT ON SUNNY DAYS LIKE TODAY, THEY SET THE SLOT MACHINES TO GIVE OUT ALMOST NOTHING.
BUT GO INTO A HIGH-STAKES GAME WITH ONLY THE HALF-BAKED GAMBLING INSTINCTS YOU'VE GOT, AND THEY'LL EAT YOU ALIVE.

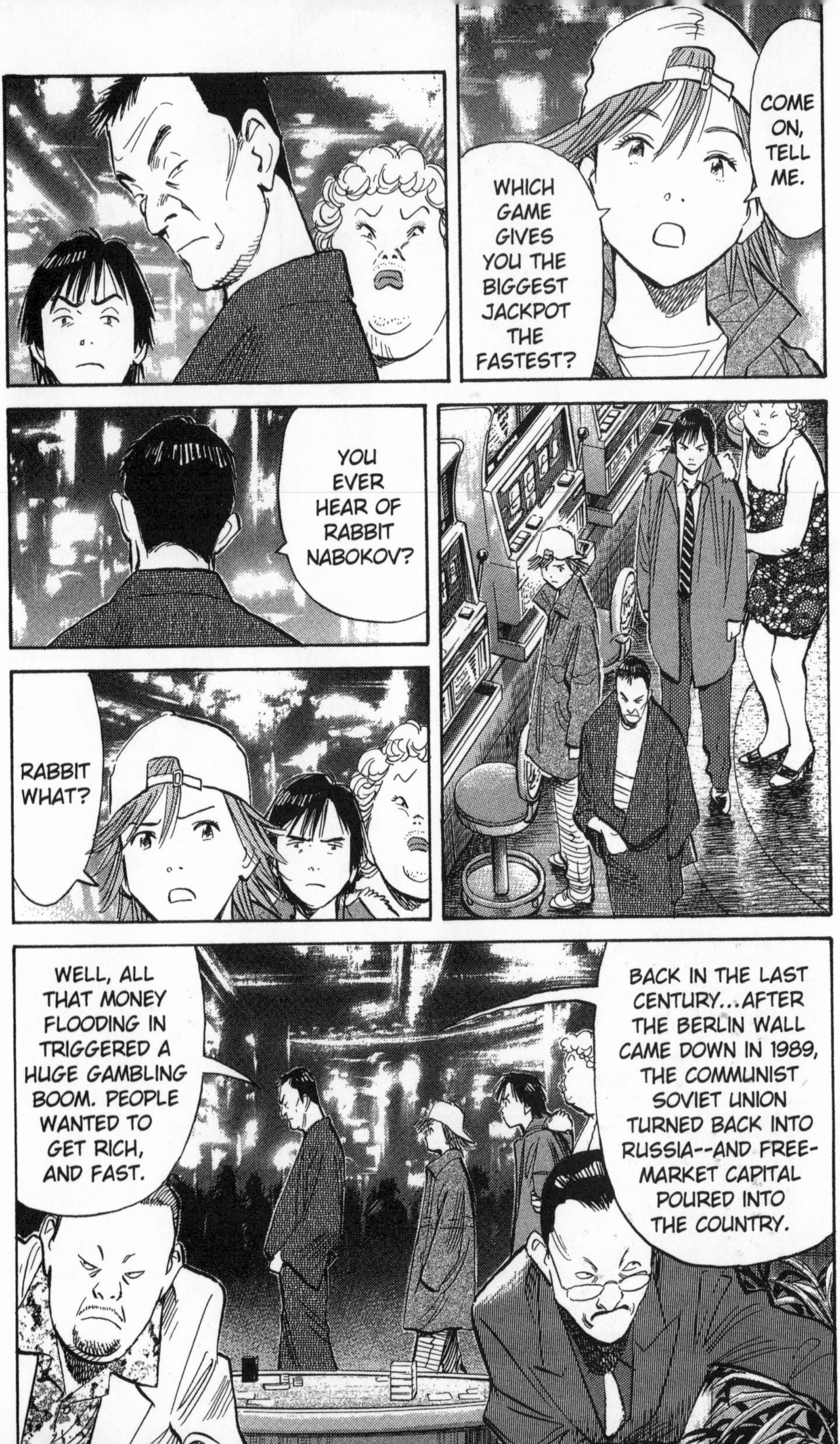
COME ON, TELL ME.
WHICH GAME GIVES YOU THE BIGGEST JACKPOT THE FASTEST?
YOU EVER HEAR OF RABBIT NABOKOV?
RABBIT WHAT?
BACK IN THE LAST CENTURY...AFTER THE BERLIN WALL CAME DOWN IN 1989, THE COMMUNIST SOVIET UNION TURNED BACK INTO RUSSIA--AND FREE-MARKET CAPITAL POURED INTO THE COUNTRY.
WELL, ALL THAT MONEY FLOODING IN TRIGGERED A HUGE GAMBLING BOOM. PEOPLE WANTED TO GET RICH, AND FAST.

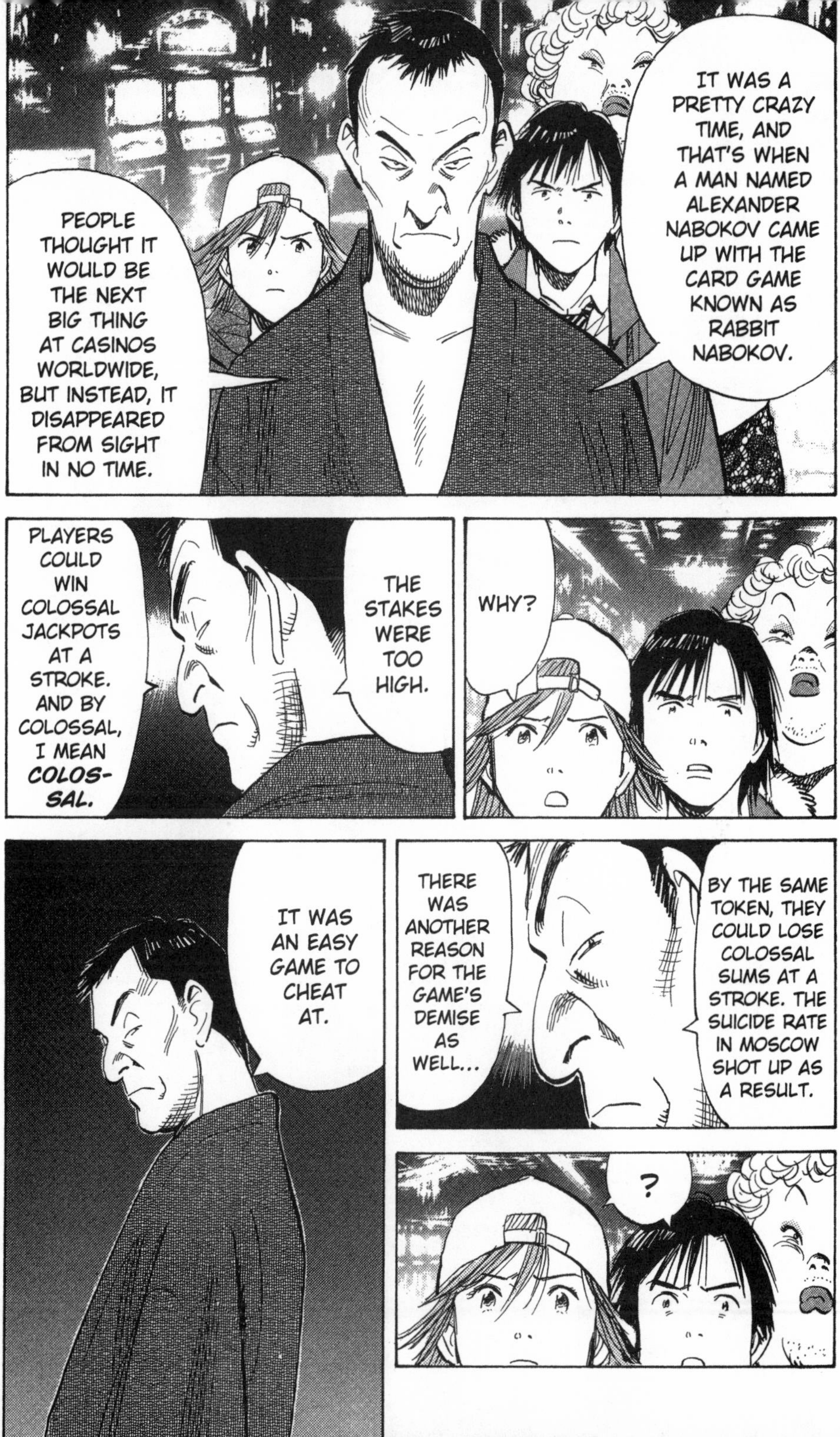
IT WAS A PRETTY CRAZY TIME, AND THAT'S WHEN A MAN NAMED ALEXANDER NABOKOV CAME UP WITH THE CARD GAME KNOWN AS RABBIT NABOKOV.
PEOPLE THOUGHT IT WOULD BE THE NEXT BIG THING AT CASINOS WORLDWIDE, BUT INSTEAD, IT DISAPPEARED FROM SIGHT IN NO TIME.
WHY?
THE STAKES WERE TOO HIGH.
PLAYERS COULD WIN COLOSSAL JACKPOTS AT A STROKE. AND BY COLOSSAL, I MEAN ***COLOS-SAL.***
BY THE SAME TOKEN, THEY COULD LOSE COLOSSAL SUMS AT A STROKE. THE SUICIDE RATE IN MOSCOW SHOT UP AS A RESULT.
THERE WAS ANOTHER REASON FOR THE GAME'S DEMISE AS WELL...
?
IT WAS AN EASY GAME TO CHEAT AT.

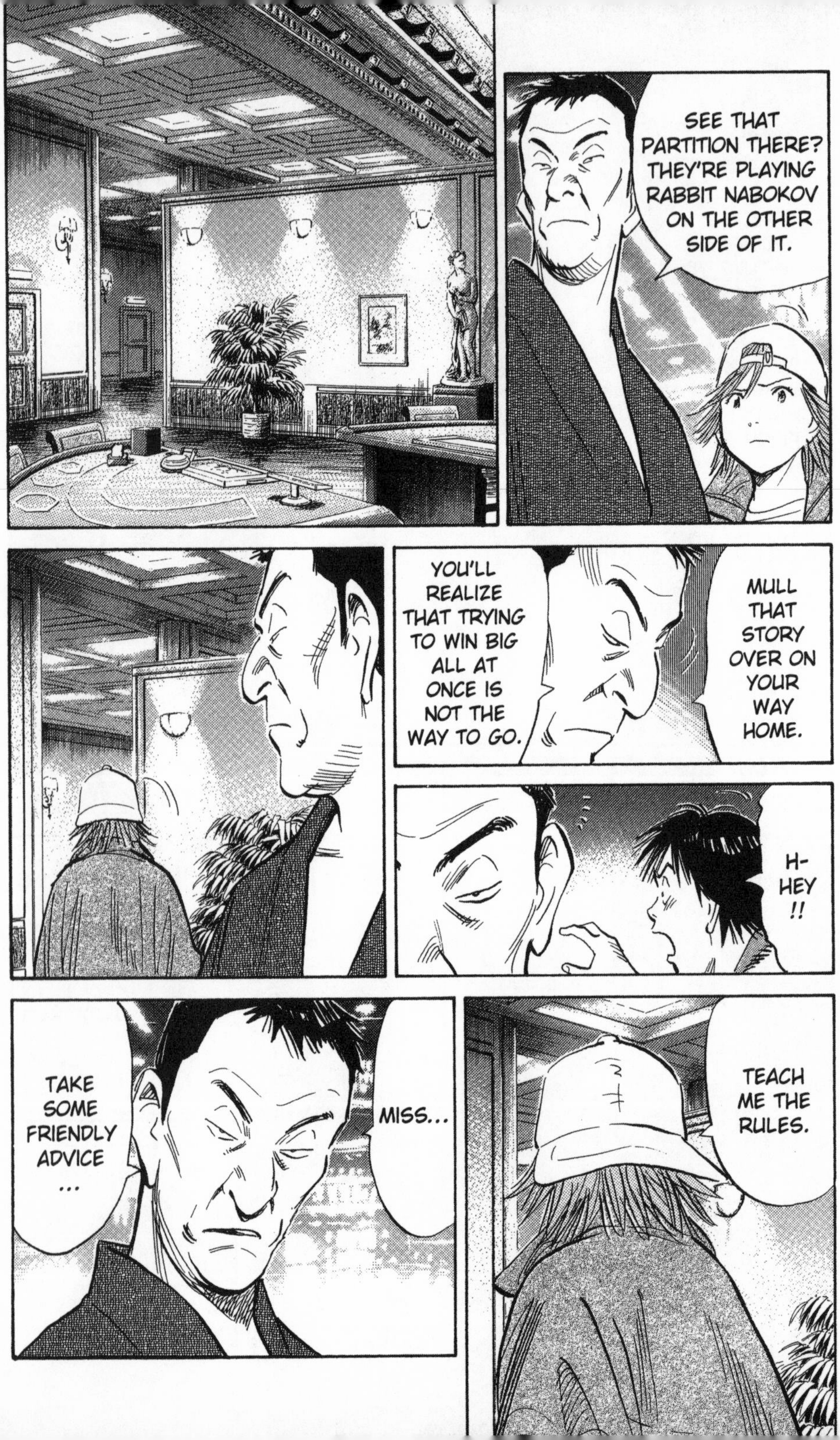
SEE THAT PARTITION THERE? THEY'RE PLAYING RABBIT NABOKOV ON THE OTHER SIDE OF IT.
MULL THAT STORY OVER ON YOUR WAY HOME.
YOU'LL REALIZE THAT TRYING TO WIN BIG ALL AT ONCE IS NOT THE WAY TO GO.
H-HEY!!
TEACH ME THE RULES.
MISS...
TAKE SOME FRIENDLY ADVICE...

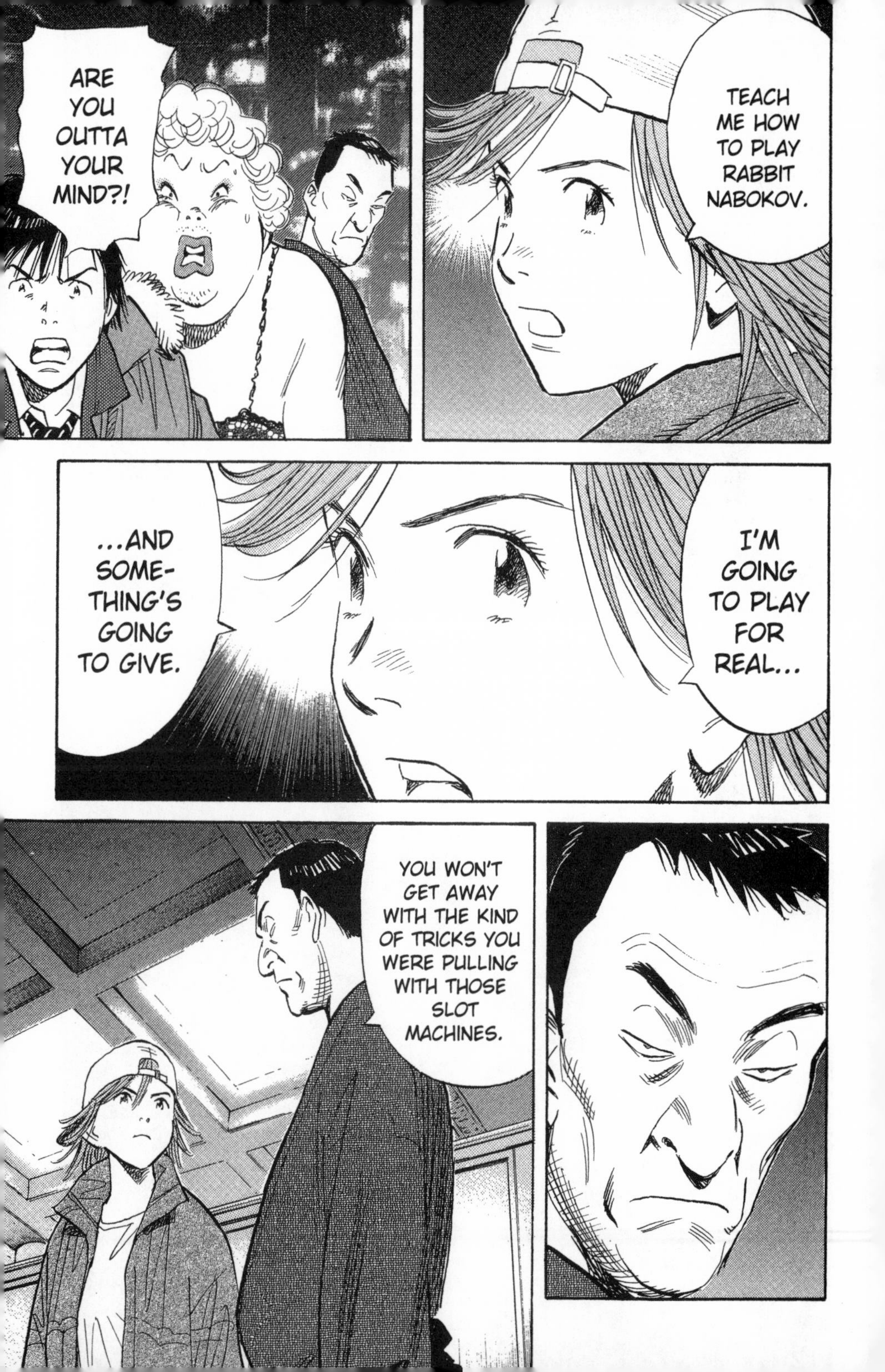
TEACH ME HOW TO PLAY RABBIT NABOKOV.
ARE YOU OUTTA YOUR MIND?!
I'M GOING TO PLAY FOR REAL...
...AND SOME-THING'S GOING TO GIVE.
YOU WON'T GET AWAY WITH THE KIND OF TRICKS YOU WERE PULLING WITH THOSE SLOT MACHINES.

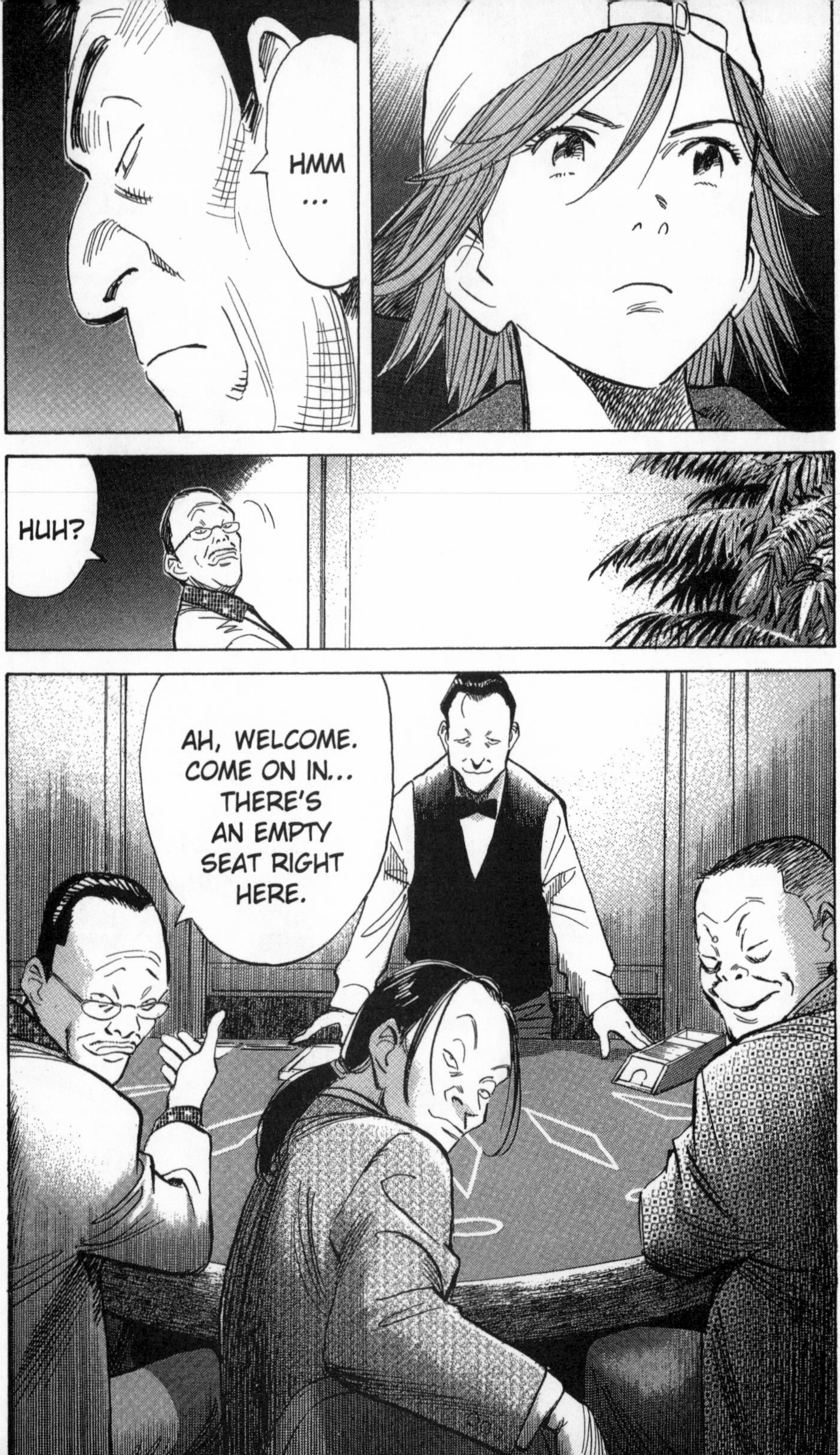
HMM ...
HUH?
AH, WELCOME. COME ON IN... THERE'S AN EMPTY SEAT RIGHT HERE.

Chapter 4 Rabbit Nabokov

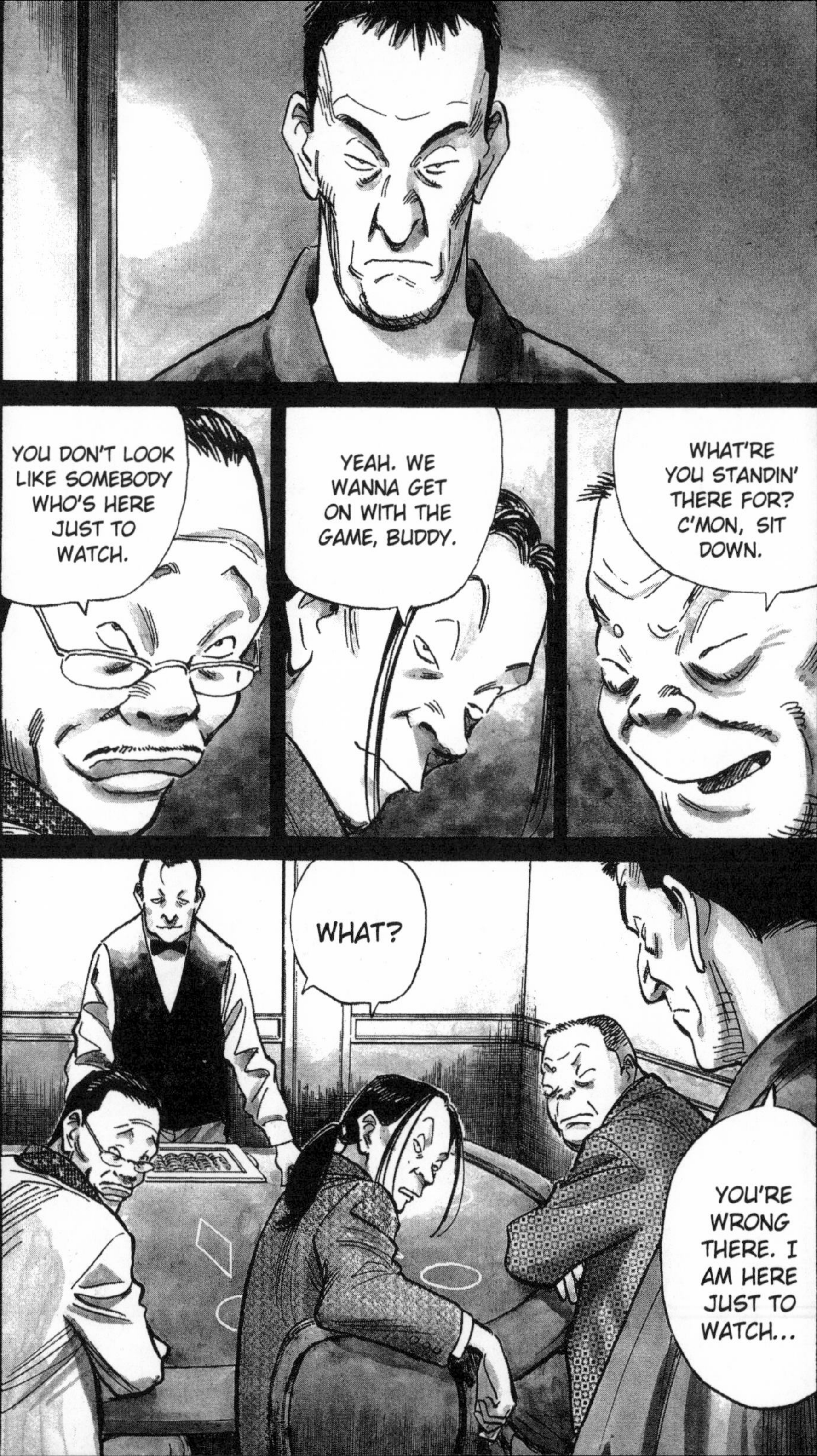
WHAT'RE YOU STANDIN' THERE FOR? C'MON, SIT DOWN.
YEAH. WE WANNA GET ON WITH THE GAME, BUDDY.
YOU DON'T LOOK LIKE SOMEBODY WHO'S HERE JUST TO WATCH.
WHAT?
YOU'RE WRONG THERE. I AM HERE JUST TO WATCH...

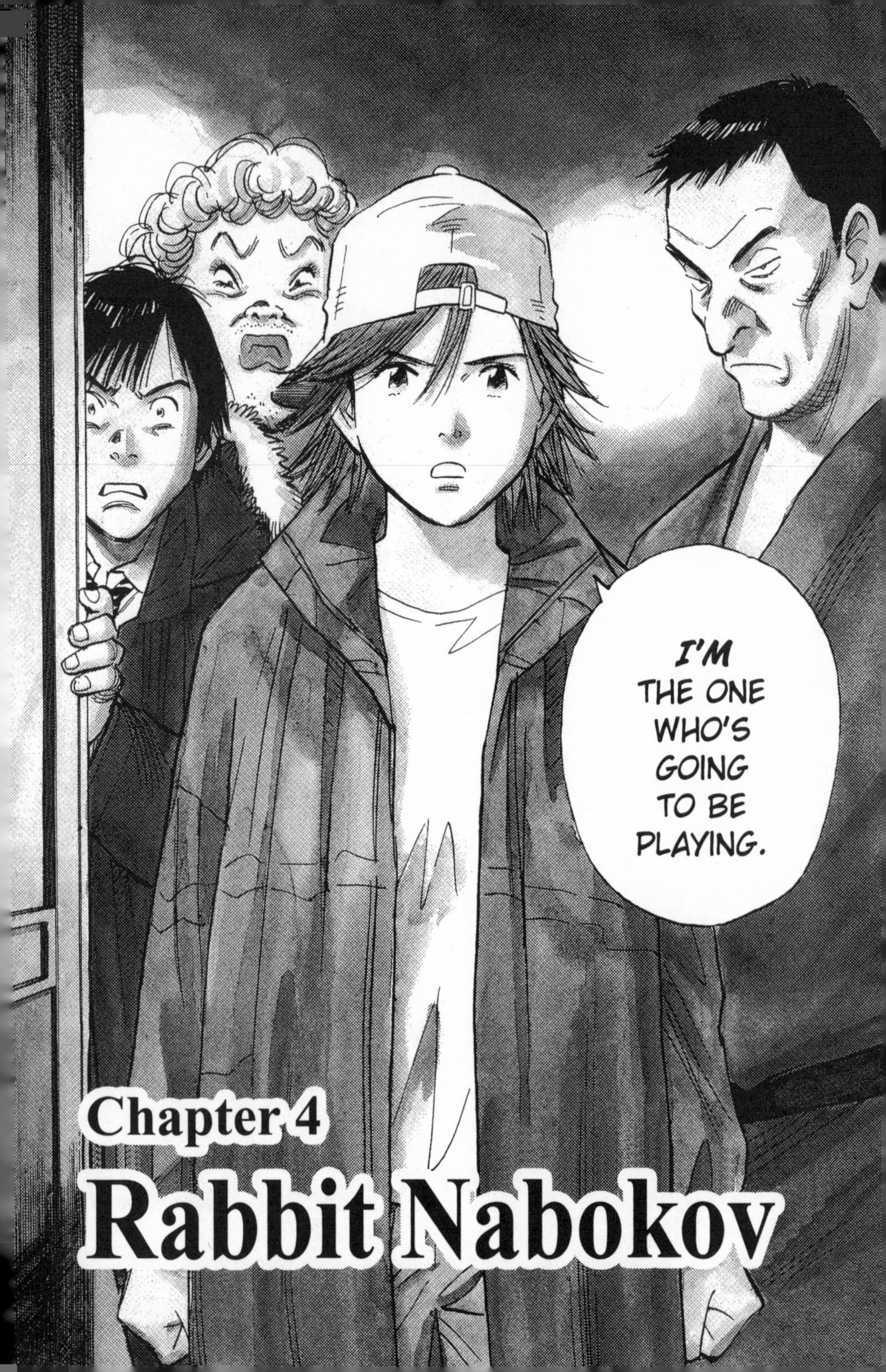
I'M THE ONE WHO'S GOING TO BE PLAYING.

Chapter 4
Rabbit Nabokov

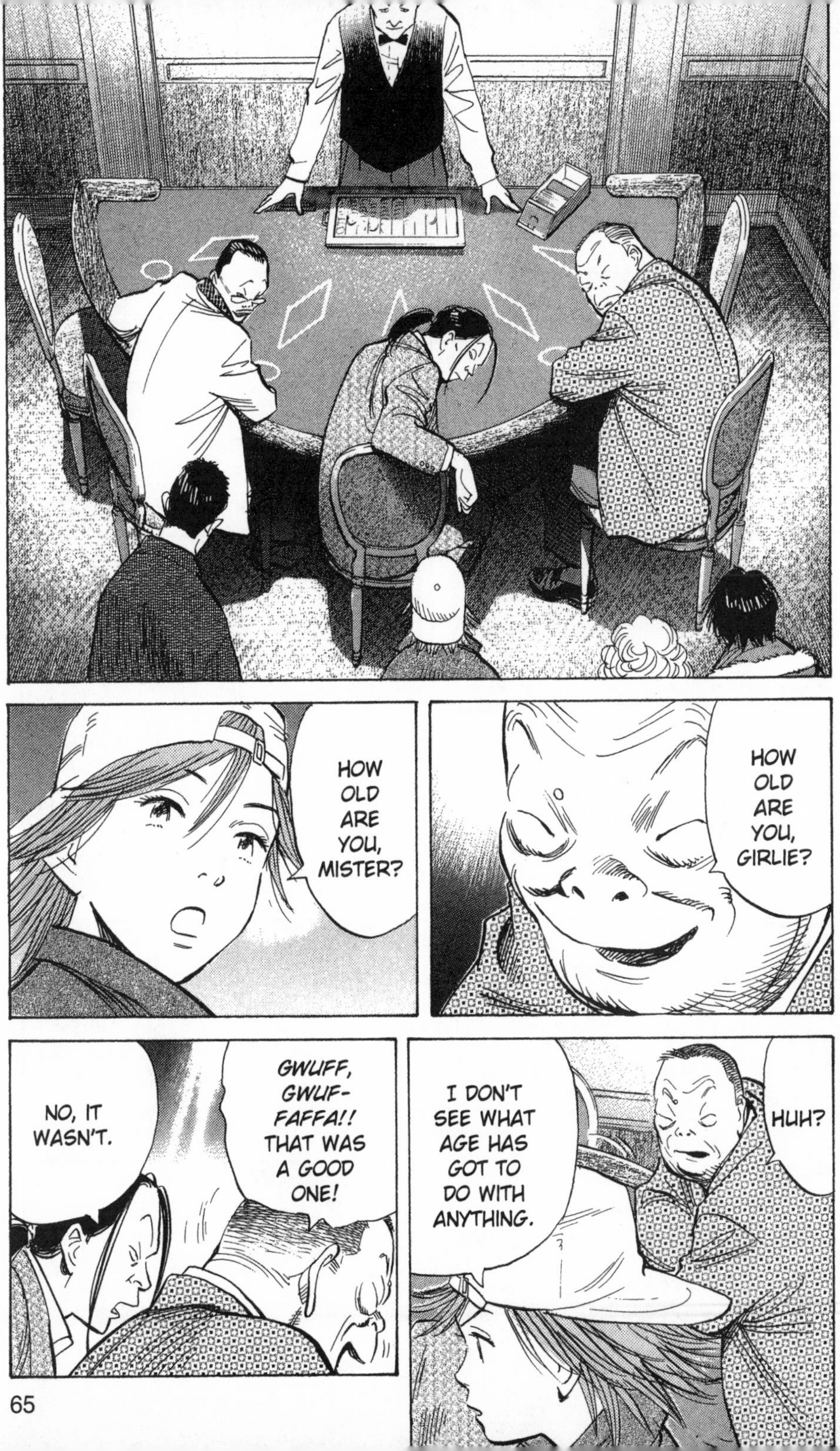
HOW OLD ARE YOU, GIRLIE?
HOW OLD ARE YOU, MISTER?
HUH?
I DON'T SEE WHAT AGE HAS GOT TO DO WITH ANYTHING.
GWUFF, GWUF-FAFFA!! THAT WAS A GOOD ONE!
NO, IT WASN'T.

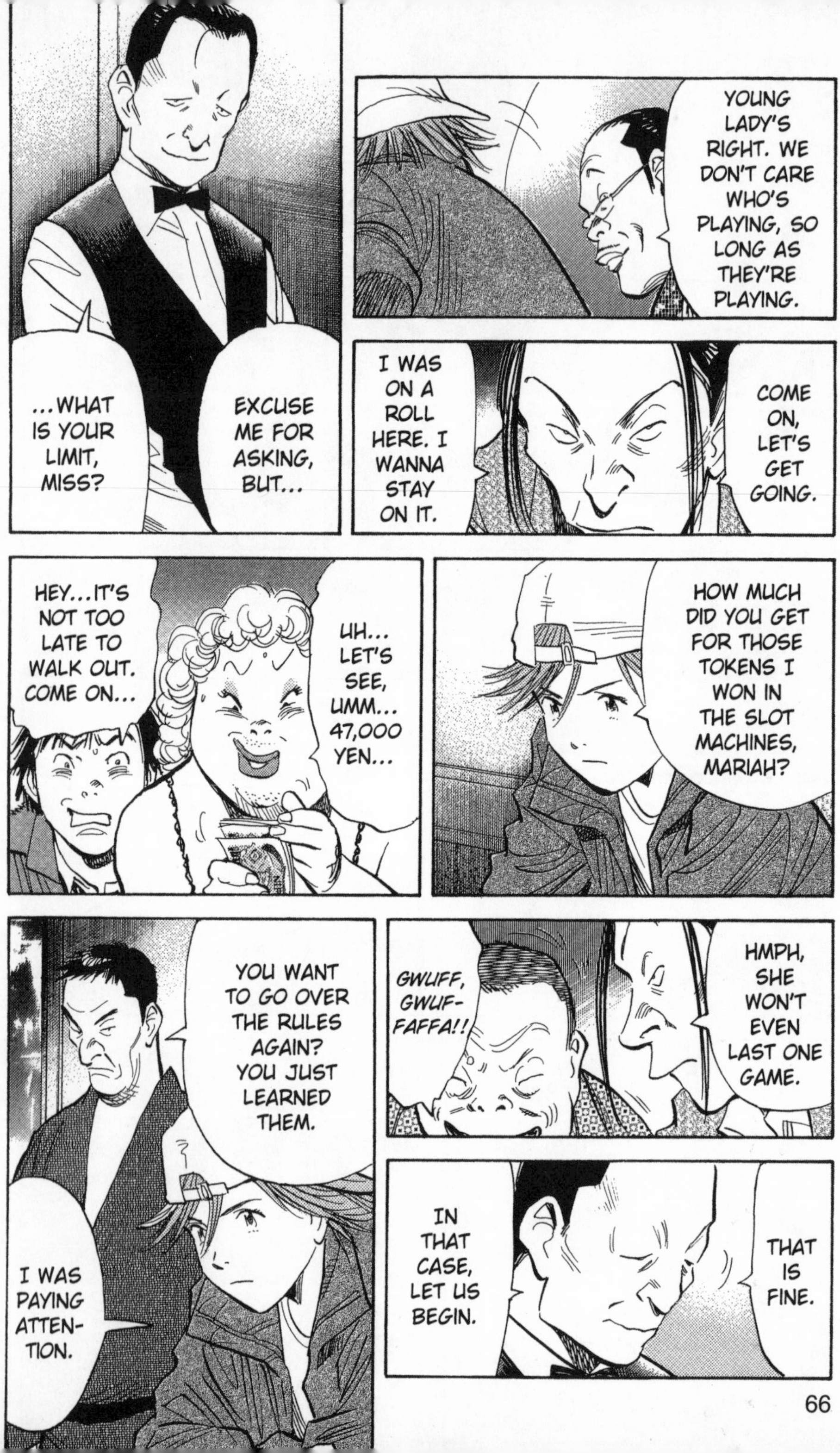
YOUNG LADY'S RIGHT. WE DON'T CARE WHO'S PLAYING, SO LONG AS THEY'RE PLAYING.
COME ON, LET'S GET GOING.
I WAS ON A ROLL HERE. I WANNA STAY ON IT.
EXCUSE ME FOR ASKING, BUT...
...WHAT IS YOUR LIMIT, MISS?
HOW MUCH DID YOU GET FOR THOSE TOKENS I WON IN THE SLOT MACHINES, MARIAH?
UH... LET'S SEE, UMM... 47,000 YEN...
HEY... IT'S NOT TOO LATE TO WALK OUT. COME ON...
HMPH, SHE WON'T EVEN LAST ONE GAME.
GWUFF, GWUF-FAFFA!!
THAT IS FINE.
IN THAT CASE, LET US BEGIN.
YOU WANT TO GO OVER THE RULES AGAIN? YOU JUST LEARNED THEM.
I WAS PAYING ATTEN-TION.

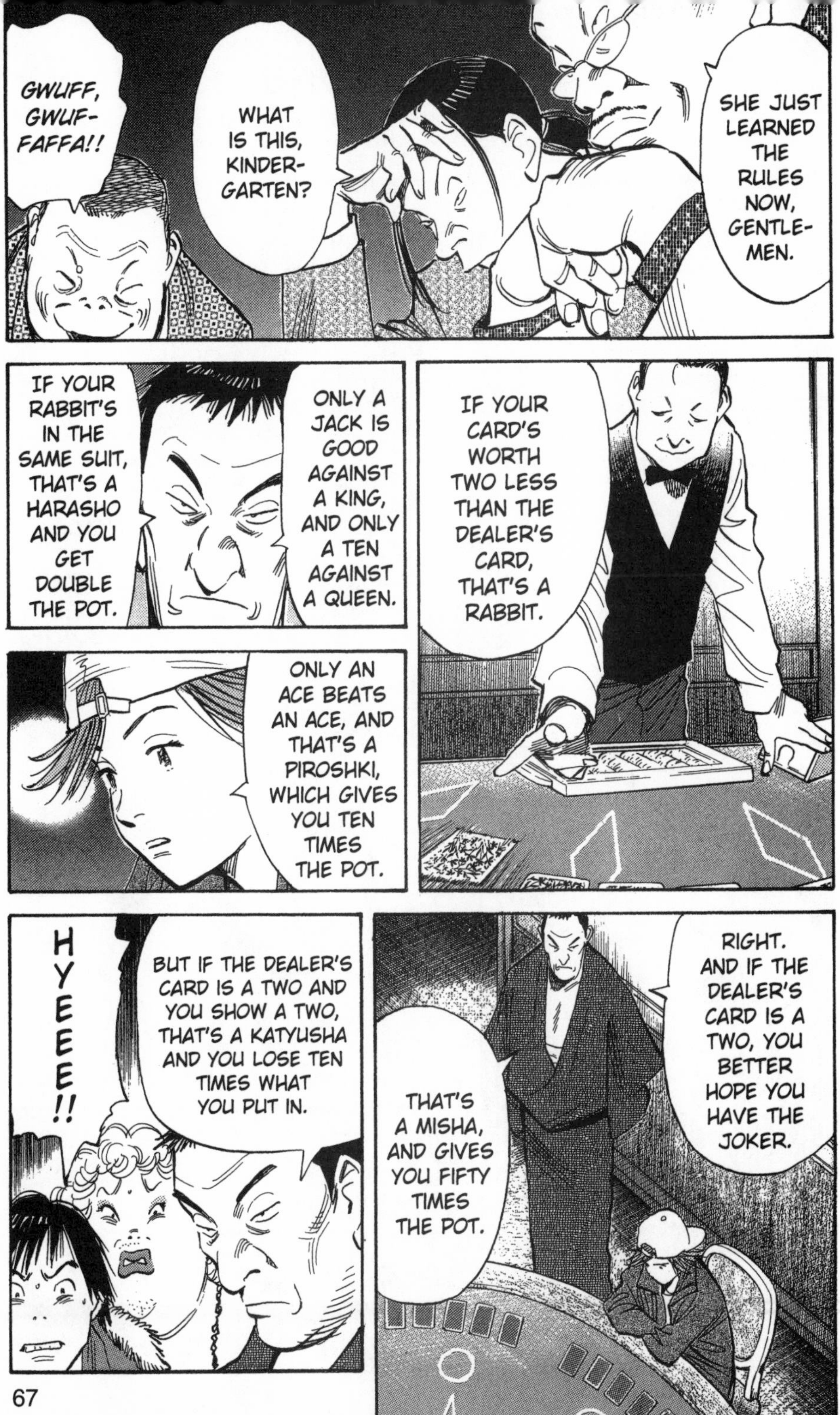
SHE JUST LEARNED THE RULES NOW, GENTLEMEN.
WHAT IS THIS, KINDERGARTEN?
GWUFF, GWUFFAFFA!!
IF YOUR CARD'S WORTH TWO LESS THAN THE DEALER'S CARD, THAT'S A RABBIT.
ONLY A JACK IS GOOD AGAINST A KING, AND ONLY A TEN AGAINST A QUEEN.
IF YOUR RABBIT'S IN THE SAME SUIT, THAT'S A HARASHO AND YOU GET DOUBLE THE POT.
ONLY AN ACE BEATS AN ACE, AND THAT'S A PIROSHKI, WHICH GIVES YOU TEN TIMES THE POT.
RIGHT. AND IF THE DEALER'S CARD IS A TWO, YOU BETTER HOPE YOU HAVE THE JOKER.
THAT'S A MISHA, AND GIVES YOU FIFTY TIMES THE POT.
BUT IF THE DEALER'S CARD IS A TWO AND YOU SHOW A TWO, THAT'S A KATYUSHA AND YOU LOSE TEN TIMES WHAT YOU PUT IN.
HYEEEE!!

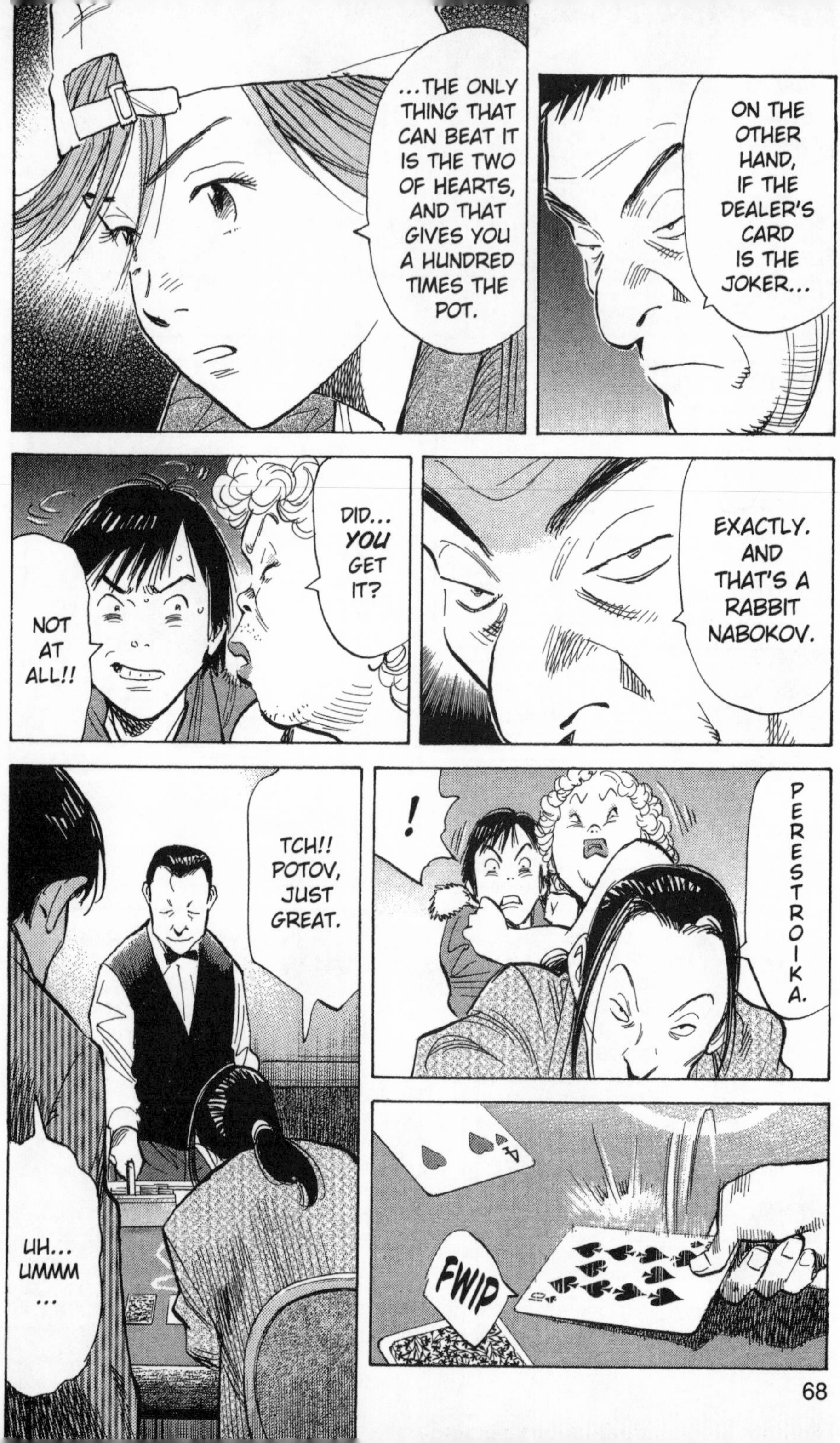
ON THE OTHER HAND, IF THE DEALER'S CARD IS THE JOKER...
...THE ONLY THING THAT CAN BEAT IT IS THE TWO OF HEARTS, AND THAT GIVES YOU A HUNDRED TIMES THE POT.
EXACTLY. AND THAT'S A RABBIT NABOKOV.
DID... *YOU* GET IT?
NOT AT ALL!!
PERESTROIKA.
!
FWIP
TCH!! POTOV, JUST GREAT.
UH... UMMM ...

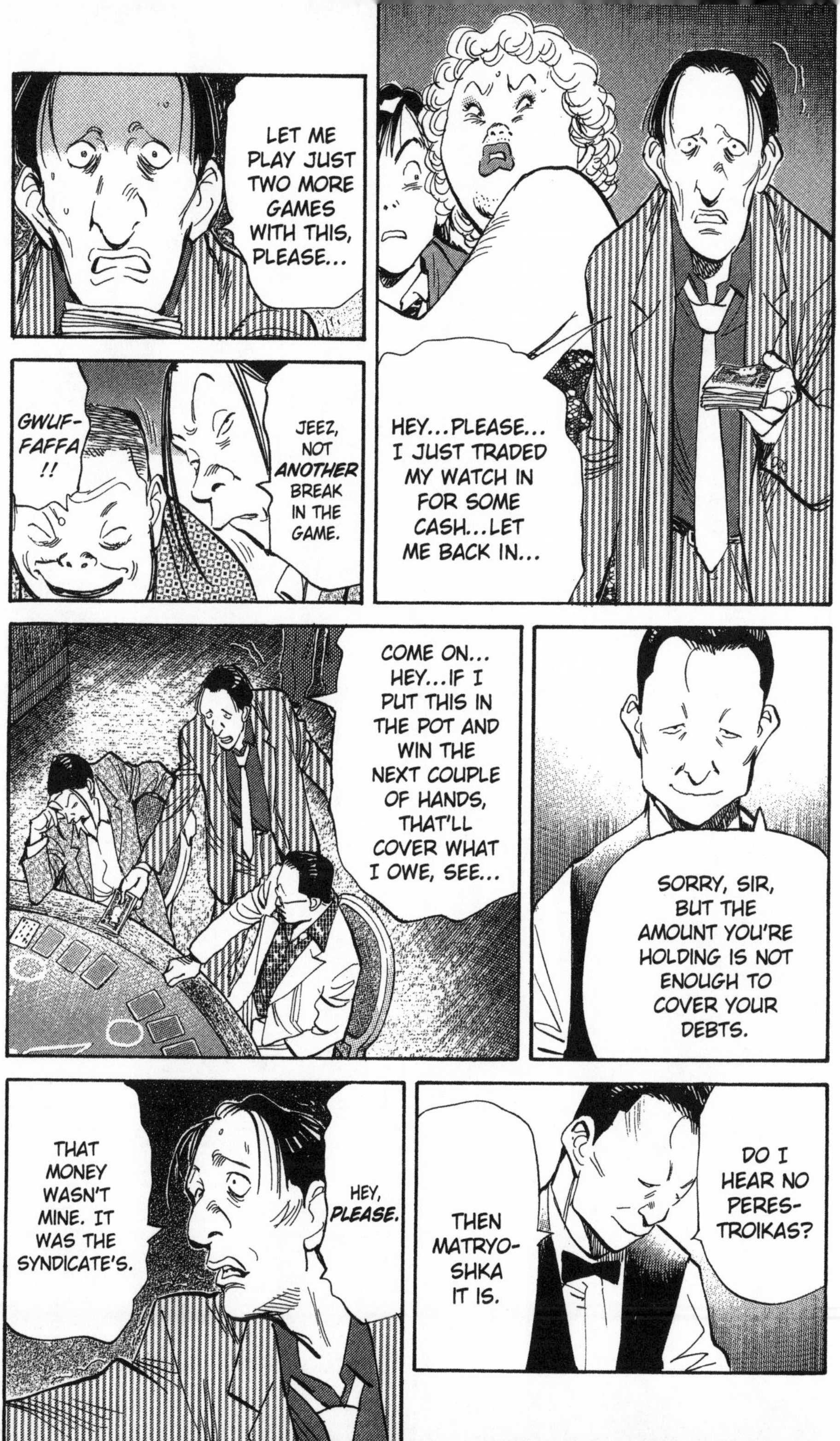
HEY...PLEASE... I JUST TRADED MY WATCH IN FOR SOME CASH...LET ME BACK IN...
LET ME PLAY JUST TWO MORE GAMES WITH THIS, PLEASE...
JEEZ, NOT ANOTHER BREAK IN THE GAME.
GWUF-FAFFA!!
SORRY, SIR, BUT THE AMOUNT YOU'RE HOLDING IS NOT ENOUGH TO COVER YOUR DEBTS.
COME ON... HEY...IF I PUT THIS IN THE POT AND WIN THE NEXT COUPLE OF HANDS, THAT'LL COVER WHAT I OWE, SEE...
DO I HEAR NO PERES-TROIKAS?
THEN MATRYO-SHKA IT IS.
HEY, PLEASE.
THAT MONEY WASN'T MINE. IT WAS THE SYNDICATE'S.

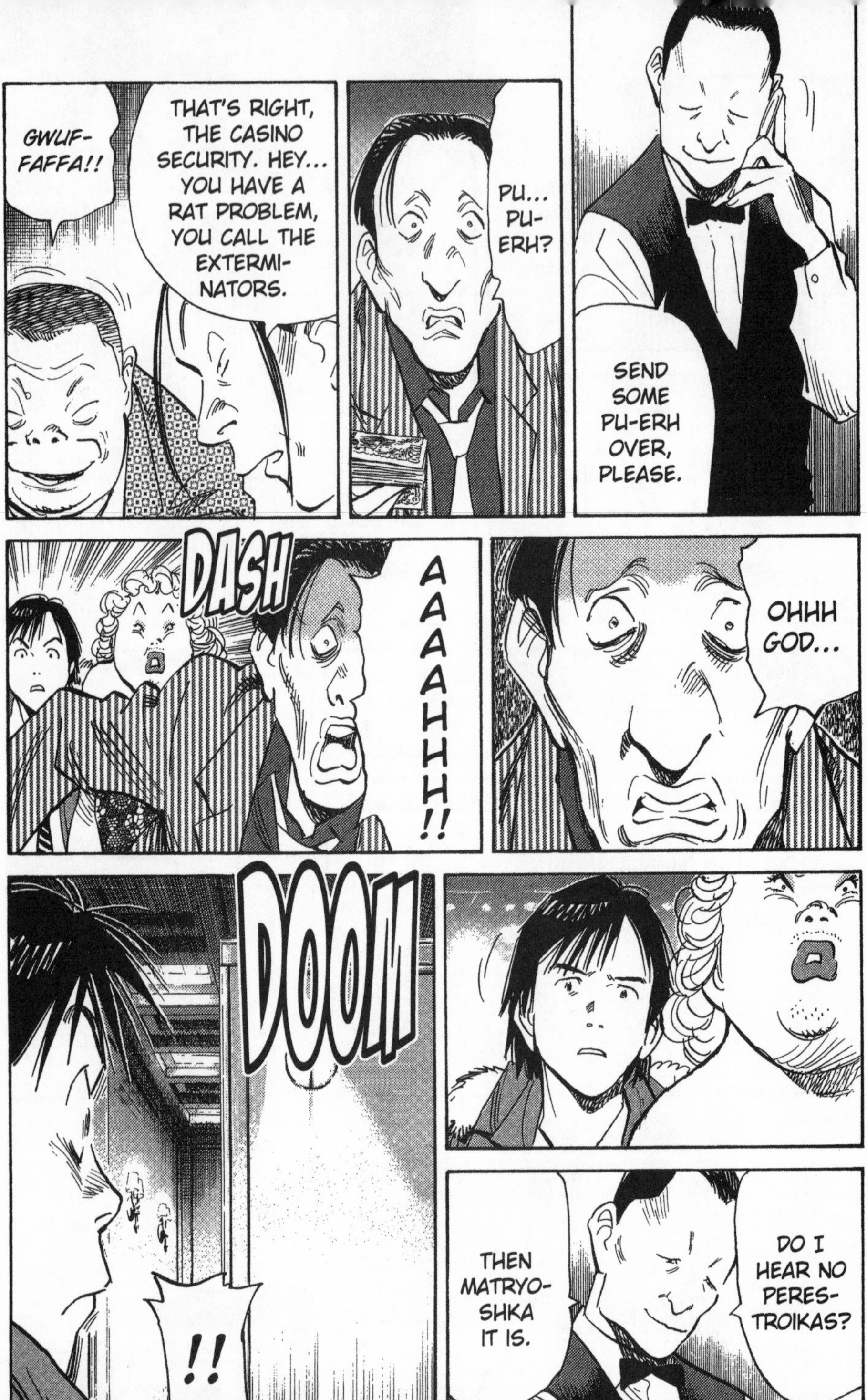
SEND SOME PU-ERH OVER, PLEASE.
PU... PU-ERH?
THAT'S RIGHT, THE CASINO SECURITY. HEY... YOU HAVE A RAT PROBLEM, YOU CALL THE EXTERMINATORS.
GWUF-FAFFA!!
OHHH GOD...
AAAAAHHH!!
DASH
DO I HEAR NO PERESTROIKAS?
THEN MATRYOSHKA IT IS.
DOOM
!!

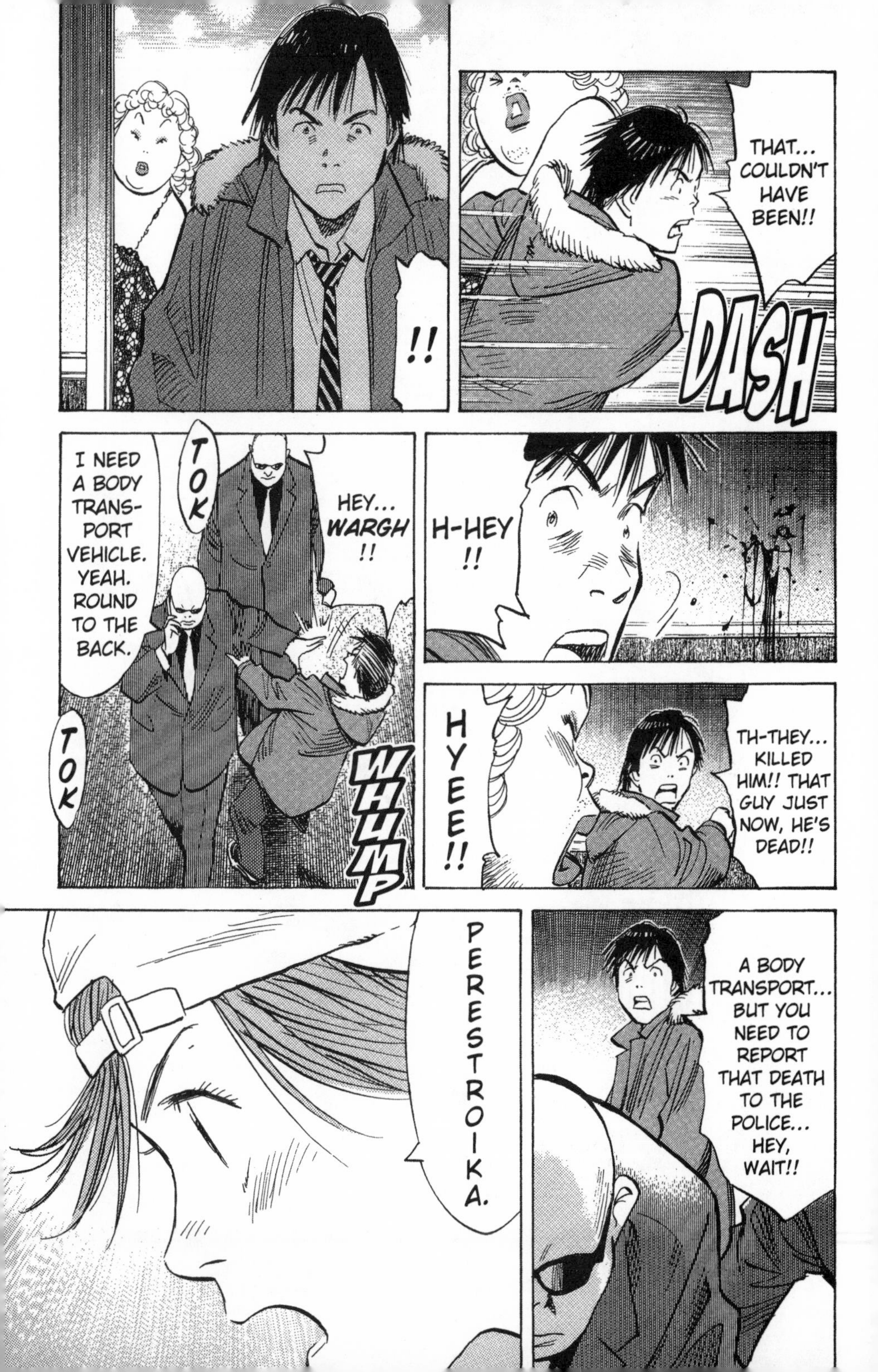
THAT... COULDN'T HAVE BEEN!!
DASH
!!
H-HEY !!
TH-THEY... KILLED HIM!! THAT GUY JUST NOW, HE'S DEAD!!
HYEE!!
HEY... WARGH !!
TOK
I NEED A BODY TRANS-PORT VEHICLE. YEAH. ROUND TO THE BACK.
TOK
WHUMP
A BODY TRANSPORT... BUT YOU NEED TO REPORT THAT DEATH TO THE POLICE... HEY, WAIT!!
PERESTROIKA.

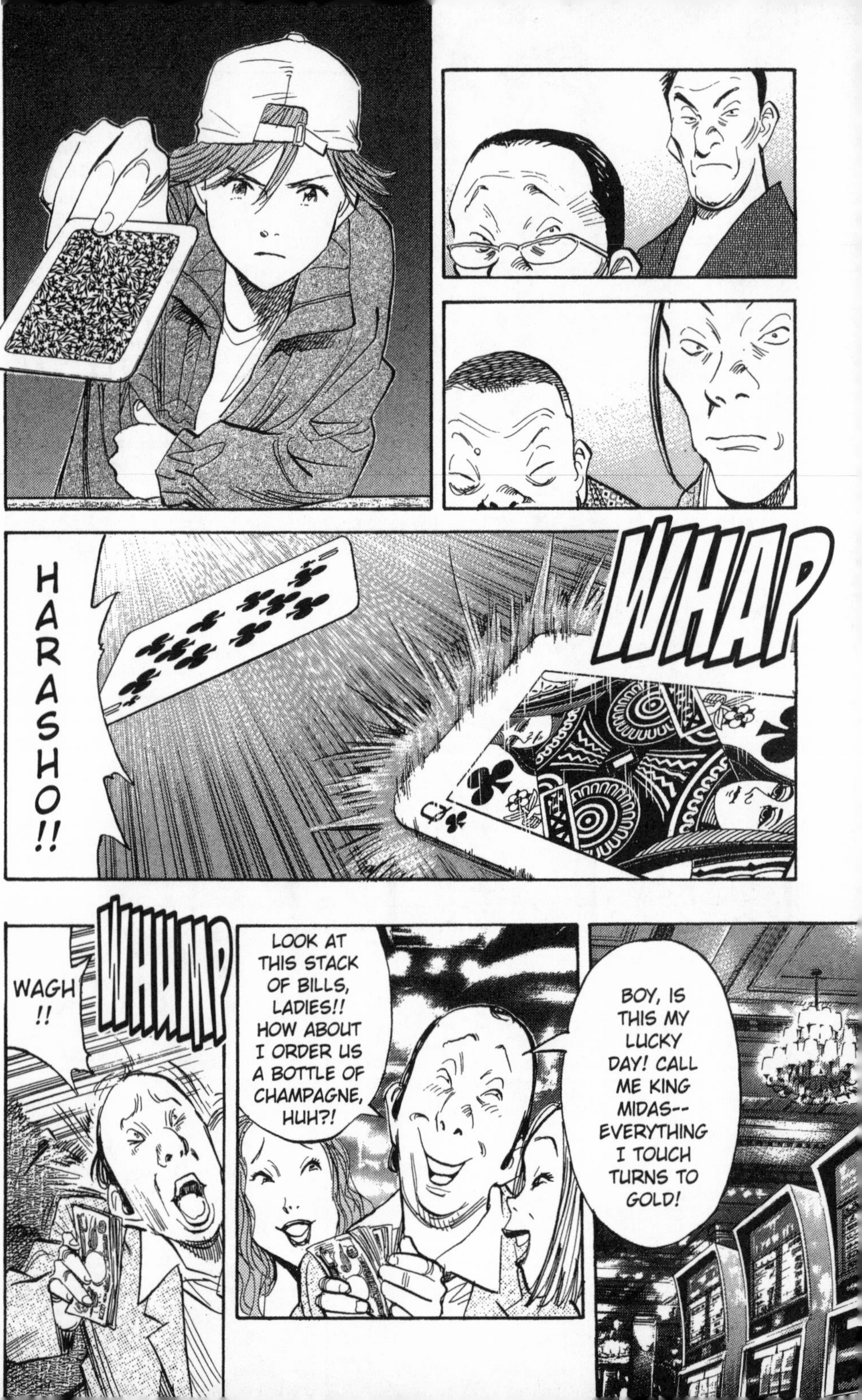
WHAP
HARASHO!!
BOY, IS THIS MY LUCKY DAY! CALL ME KING MIDAS-- EVERYTHING I TOUCH TURNS TO GOLD!
LOOK AT THIS STACK OF BILLS, LADIES!! HOW ABOUT I ORDER US A BOTTLE OF CHAMPAGNE, HUH?!
WHUMP
WAGH !!

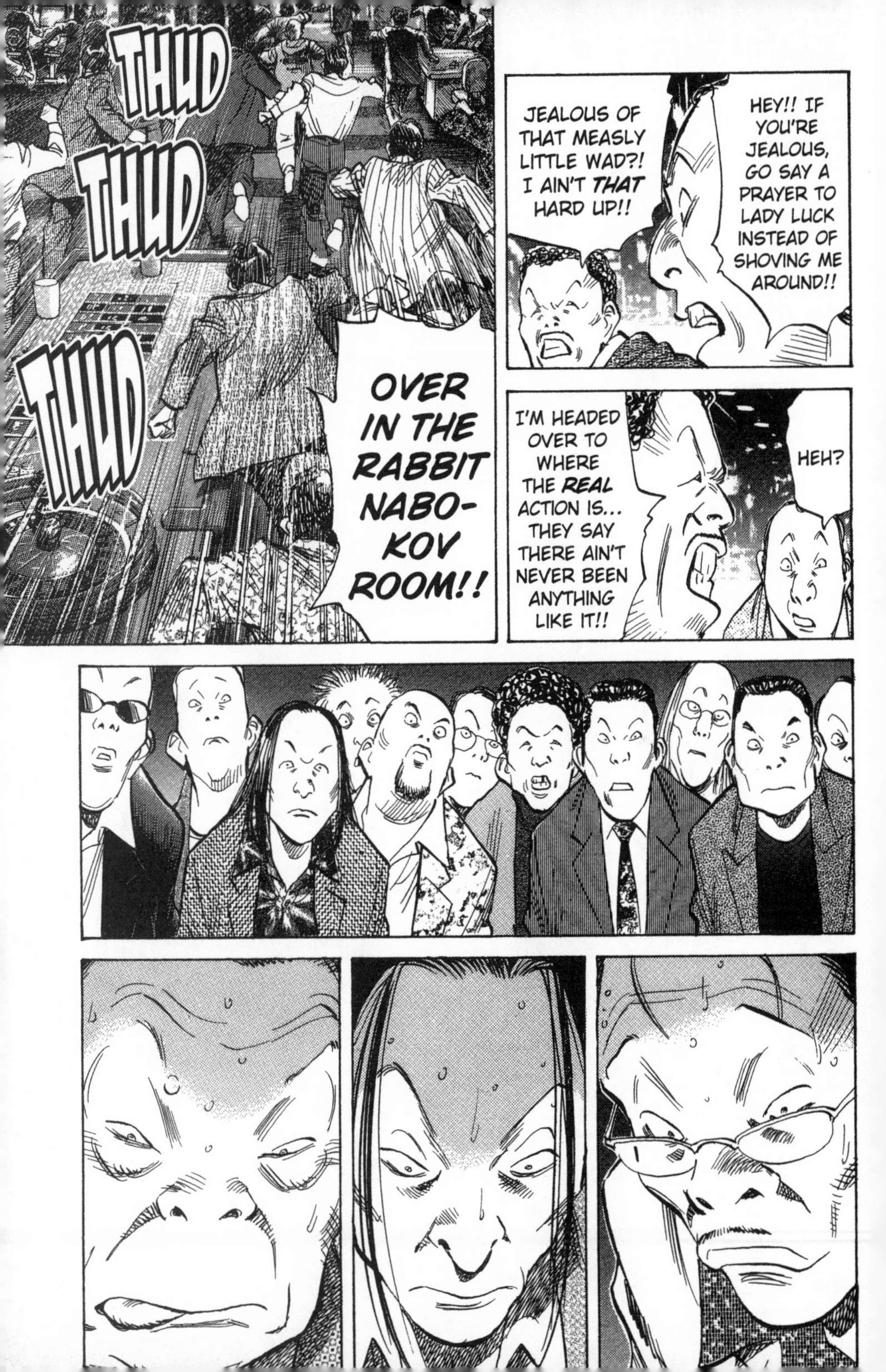
HEY!! IF YOU'RE JEALOUS, GO SAY A PRAYER TO LADY LUCK INSTEAD OF SHOVING ME AROUND!!
JEALOUS OF THAT MEASLY LITTLE WAD?! I AIN'T *THAT* HARD UP!!
I'M HEADED OVER TO WHERE THE *REAL* ACTION IS... THEY SAY THERE AIN'T NEVER BEEN ANYTHING LIKE IT!!
HEH?
OVER IN THE RABBIT NABOKOV ROOM!!
THUD
THUD
THUD

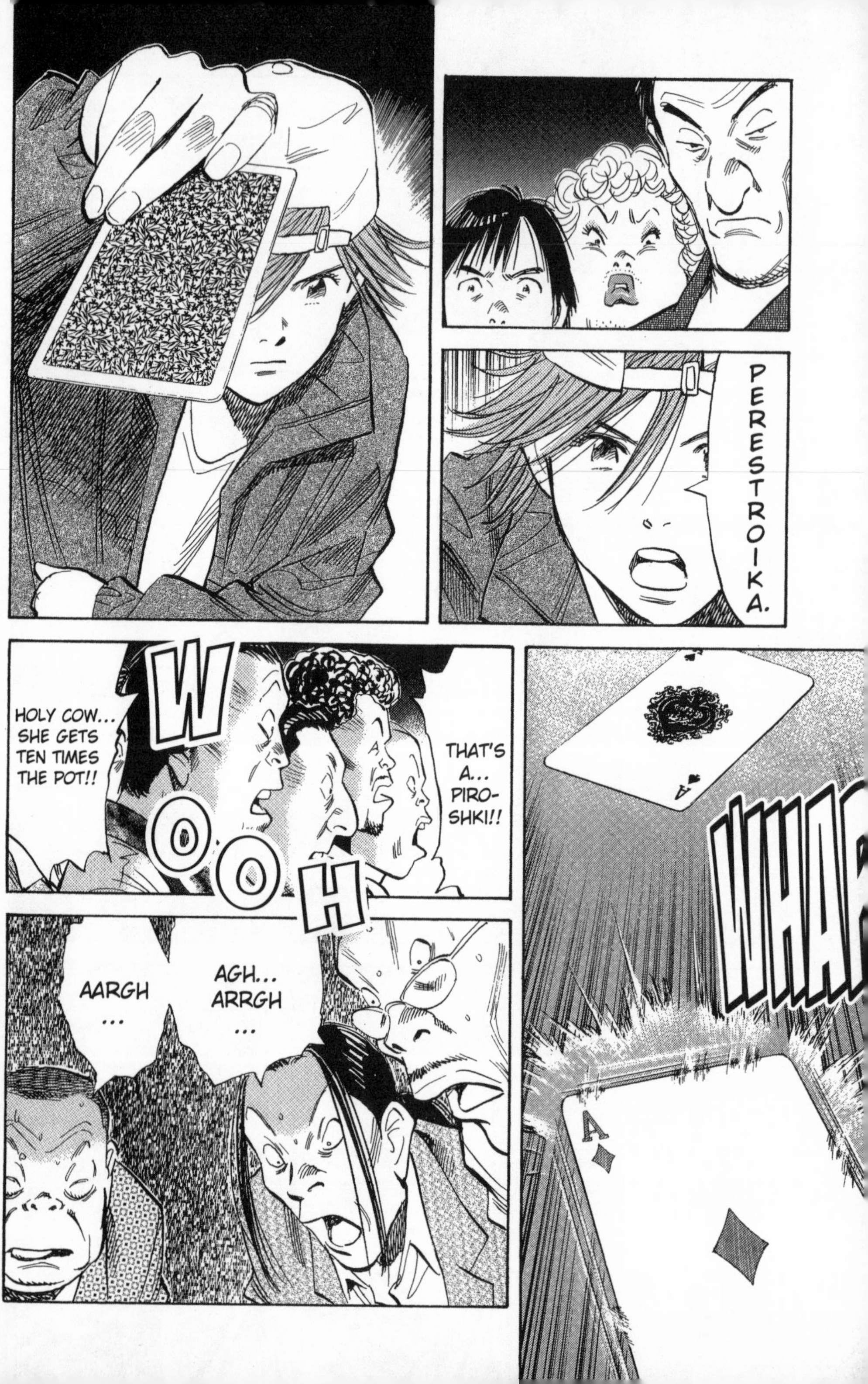
PERESTROIKA.
WHA
THAT'S A... PIROSHKI!!
WOOH
HOLY COW... SHE GETS TEN TIMES THE POT!!
AGH... ARRGH...
AARGH...

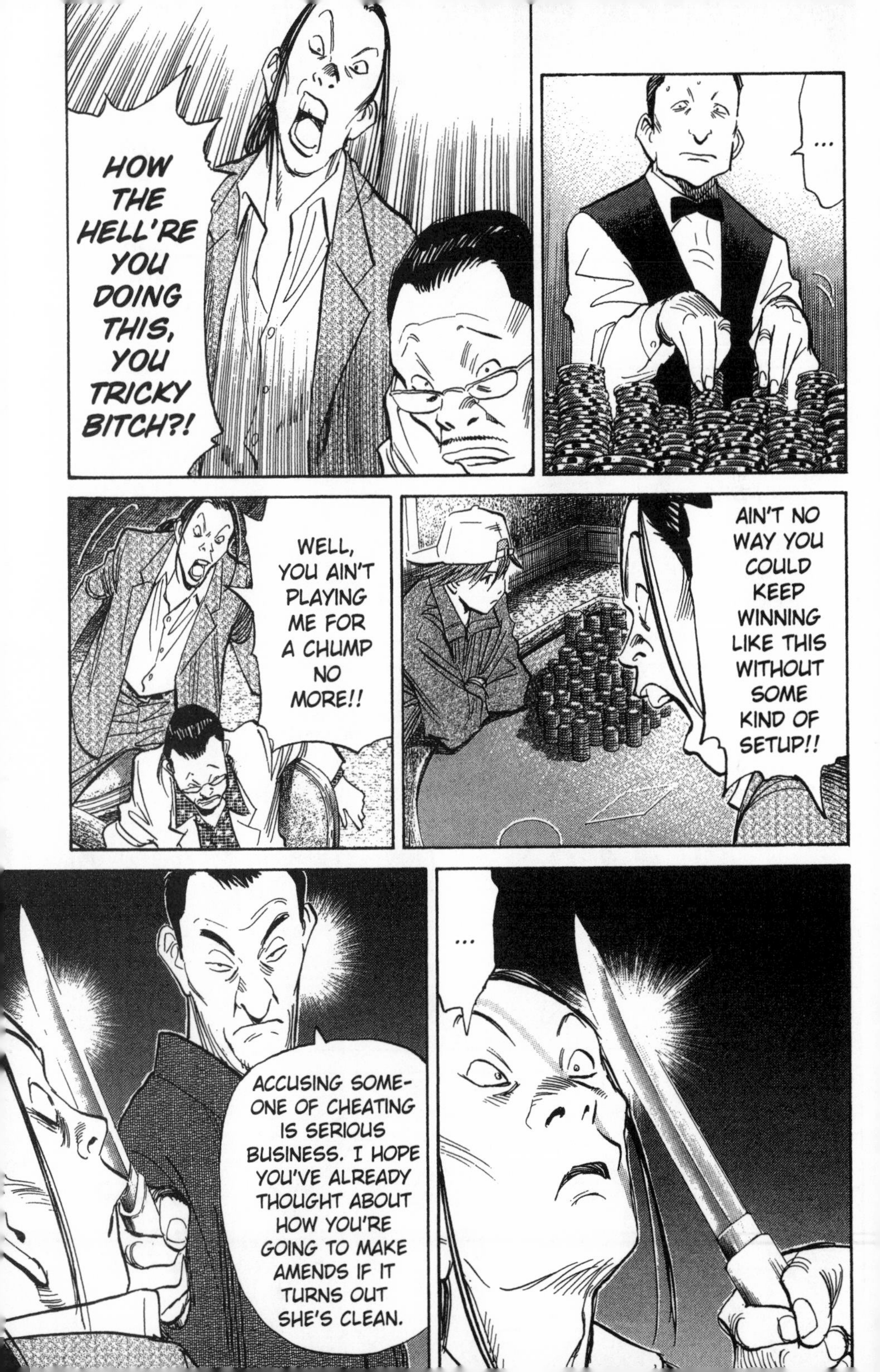
...
HOW THE HELL'RE YOU DOING THIS, YOU TRICKY BITCH?!
AIN'T NO WAY YOU COULD KEEP WINNING LIKE THIS WITHOUT SOME KIND OF SETUP!!
WELL, YOU AIN'T PLAYING ME FOR A CHUMP NO MORE!!
...
ACCUSING SOME-ONE OF CHEATING IS SERIOUS BUSINESS. I HOPE YOU'VE ALREADY THOUGHT ABOUT HOW YOU'RE GOING TO MAKE AMENDS IF IT TURNS OUT SHE'S CLEAN.

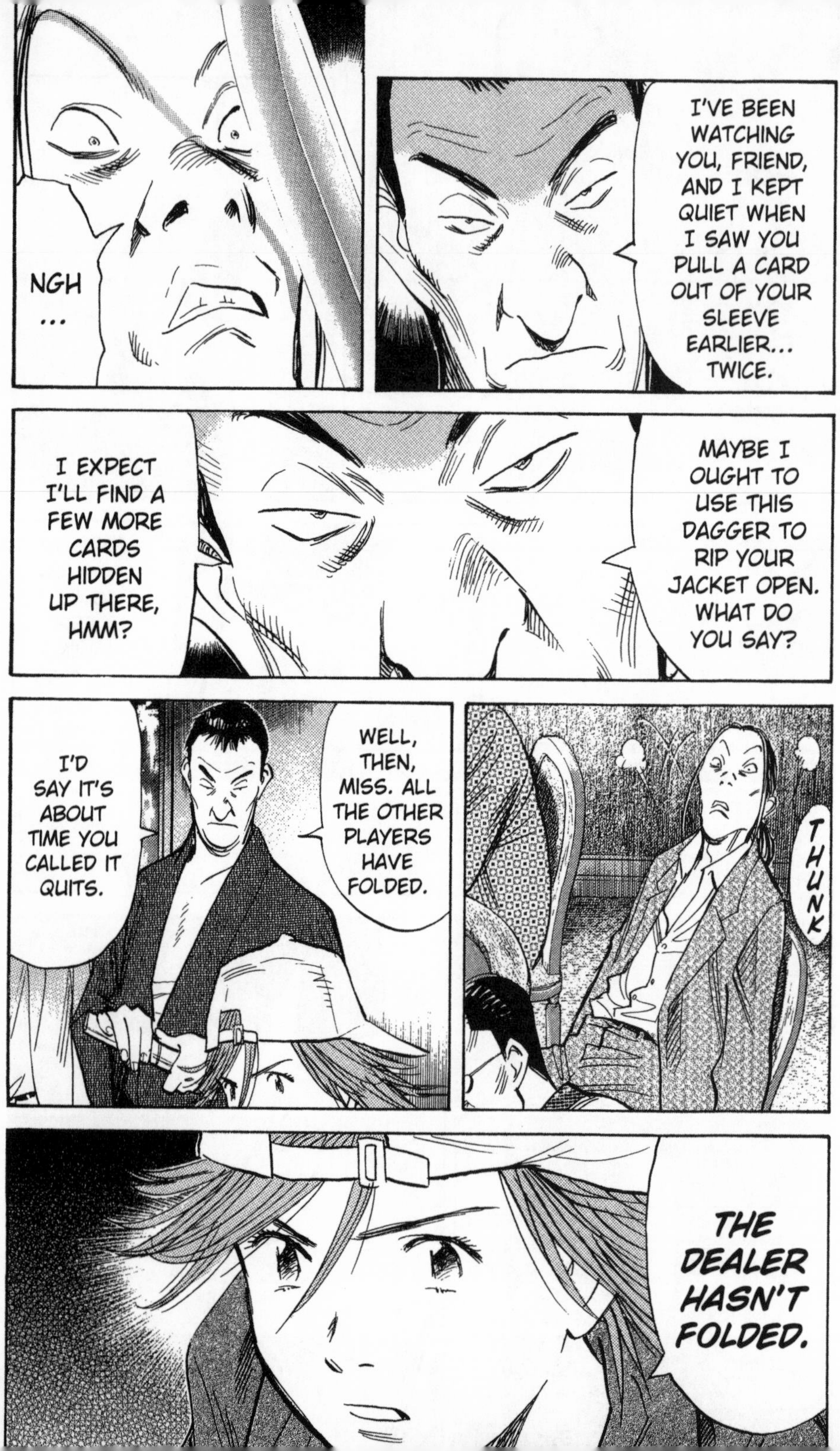
I'VE BEEN WATCHING YOU, FRIEND, AND I KEPT QUIET WHEN I SAW YOU PULL A CARD OUT OF YOUR SLEEVE EARLIER... TWICE.
NGH ...
MAYBE I OUGHT TO USE THIS DAGGER TO RIP YOUR JACKET OPEN. WHAT DO YOU SAY?
I EXPECT I'LL FIND A FEW MORE CARDS HIDDEN UP THERE, HMM?
THUNK
WELL, THEN, MISS. ALL THE OTHER PLAYERS HAVE FOLDED.
I'D SAY IT'S ABOUT TIME YOU CALLED IT QUITS.
THE DEALER HASN'T FOLDED.

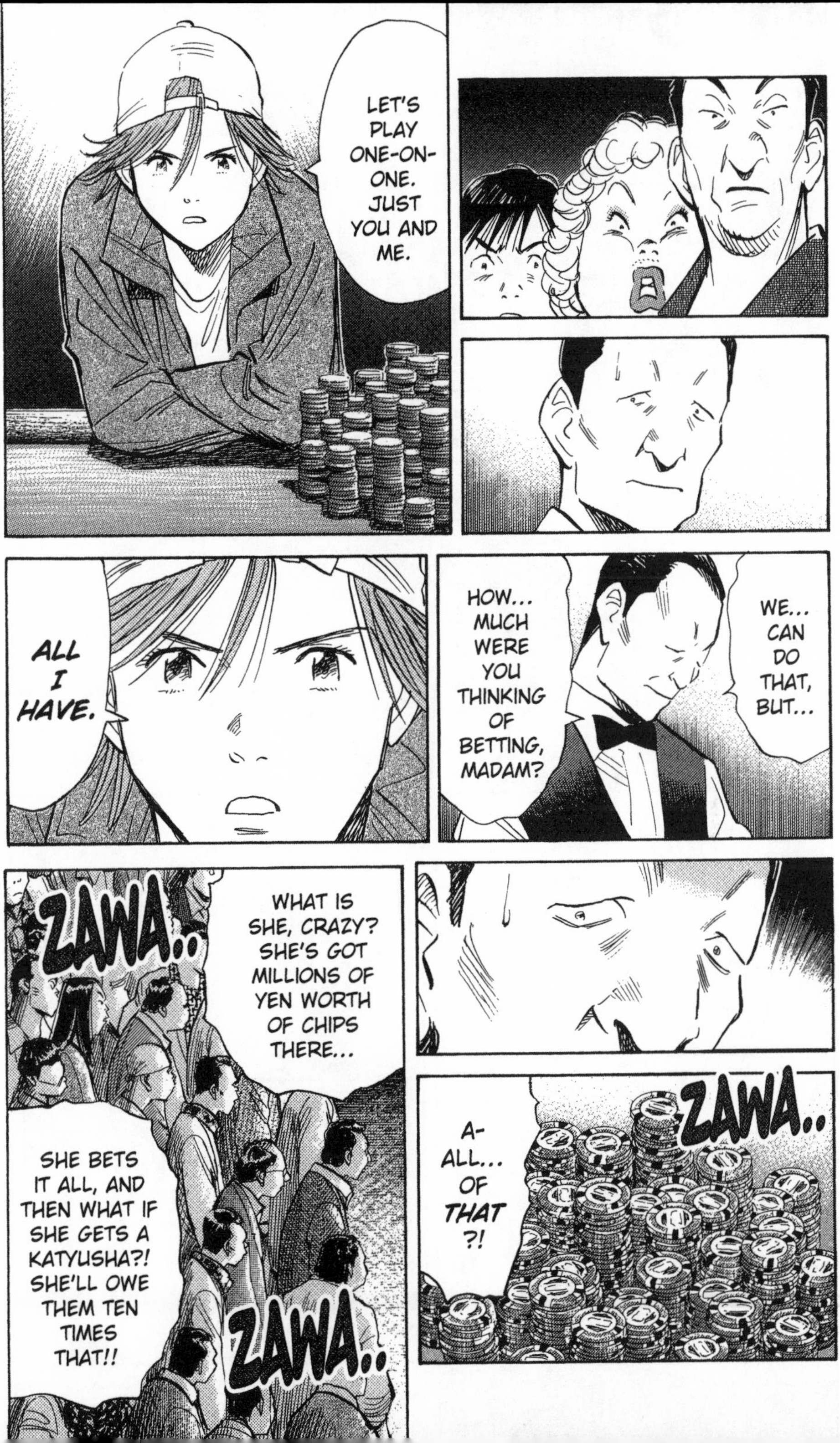
LET'S PLAY ONE-ON-ONE. JUST YOU AND ME.
WE... CAN DO THAT, BUT...
HOW... MUCH WERE YOU THINKING OF BETTING, MADAM?
ALL I HAVE.
ZAWA..
A- ALL... OF THAT?!
ZAWA..
WHAT IS SHE, CRAZY? SHE'S GOT MILLIONS OF YEN WORTH OF CHIPS THERE...
SHE BETS IT ALL, AND THEN WHAT IF SHE GETS A KATYUSHA?! SHE'LL OWE THEM TEN TIMES THAT!!
ZAWA..

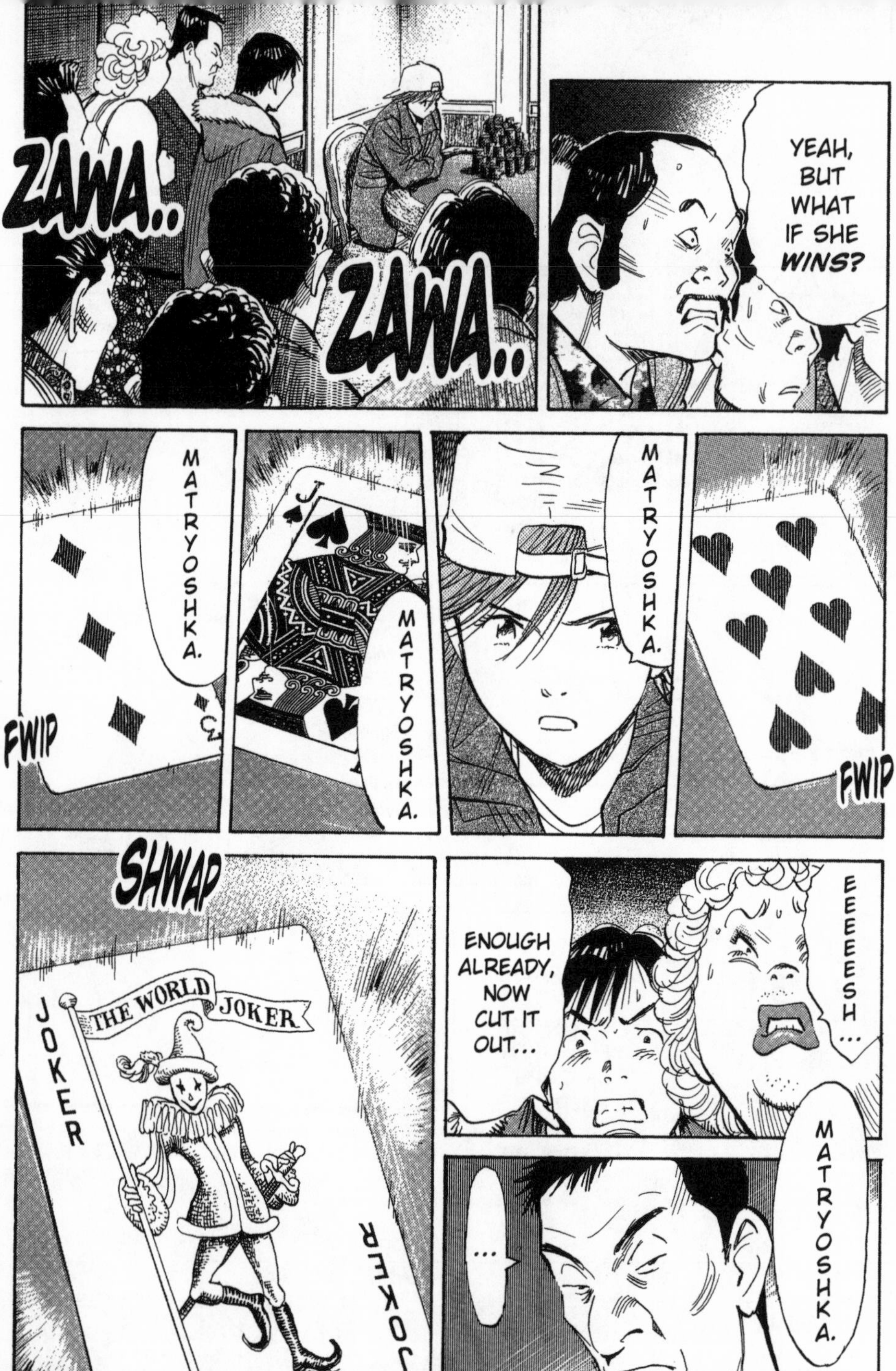

YEAH, BUT WHAT IF SHE WINS?
ZAWA..
ZAWA..
FWIP
MATRYOSHKA.
MATRYOSHKA.
MATRYOSHKA.
FWIP
EEEEEESH...
ENOUGH ALREADY, NOW CUT IT OUT...
MATRYOSHKA.
...
SHWAP
THE WORLD
JOKER
JOKER
JOKER

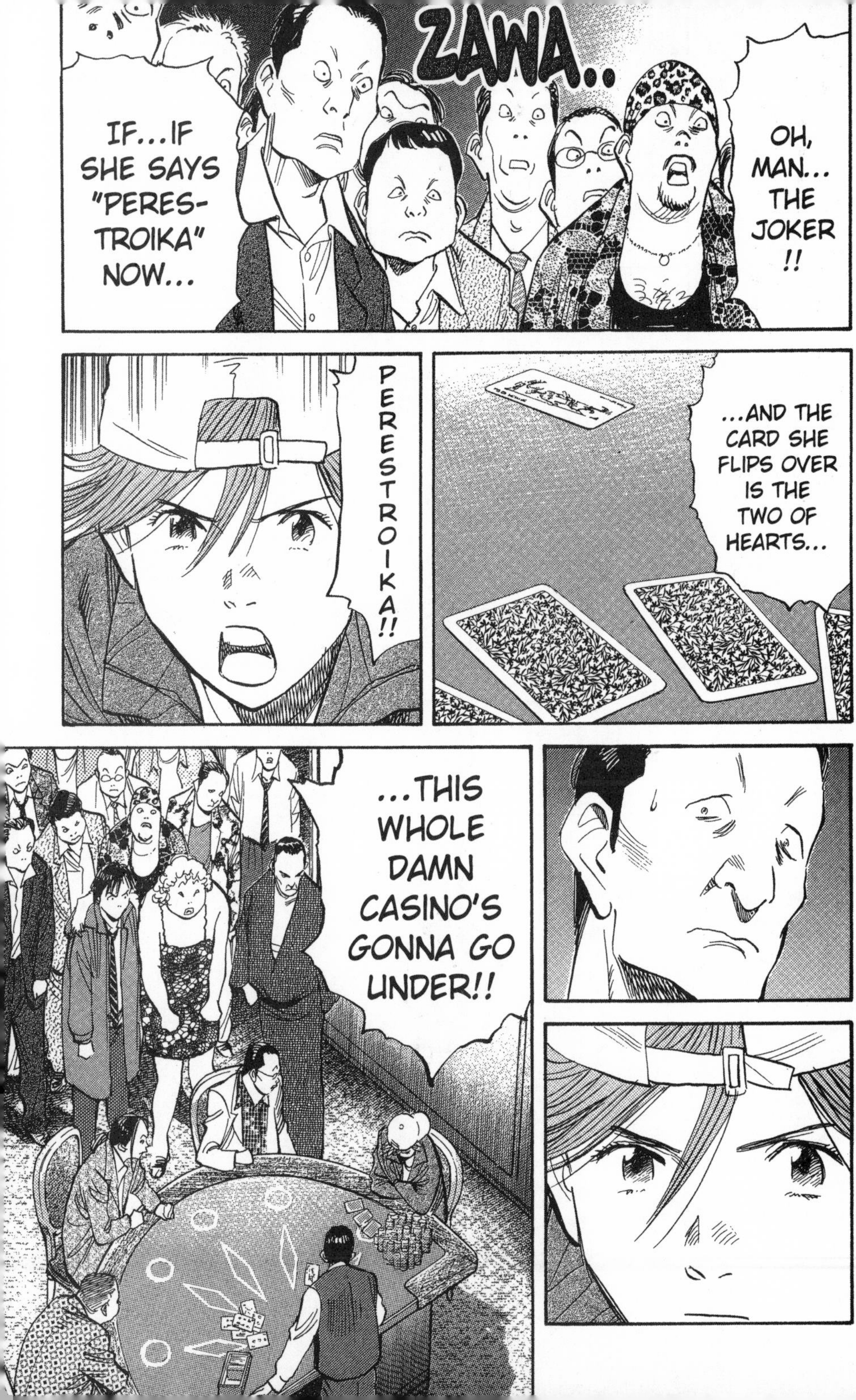
ZAWA..
OH, MAN... THE JOKER!!
IF...IF SHE SAYS "PERES-TROIKA" NOW...
...AND THE CARD SHE FLIPS OVER IS THE TWO OF HEARTS...
PERESTROIKA!!
...THIS WHOLE DAMN CASINO'S GONNA GO UNDER!!

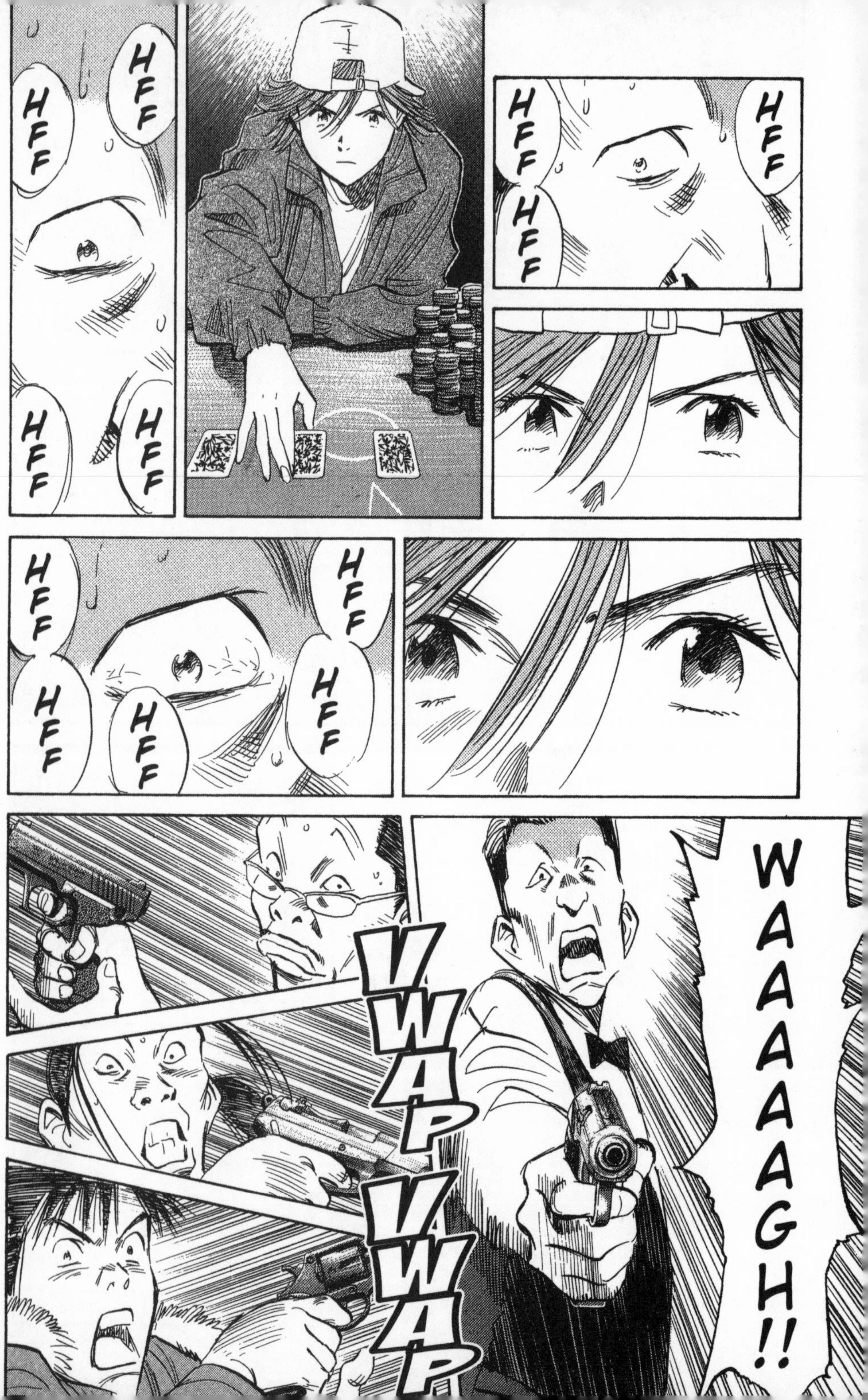
HFF
HFF HFF
HFF
HFF
HFF
HFF
HFF
HFF
HFF
HFF
HFF
HFF
WAAAAAAGH!!
VWAP
VWAP

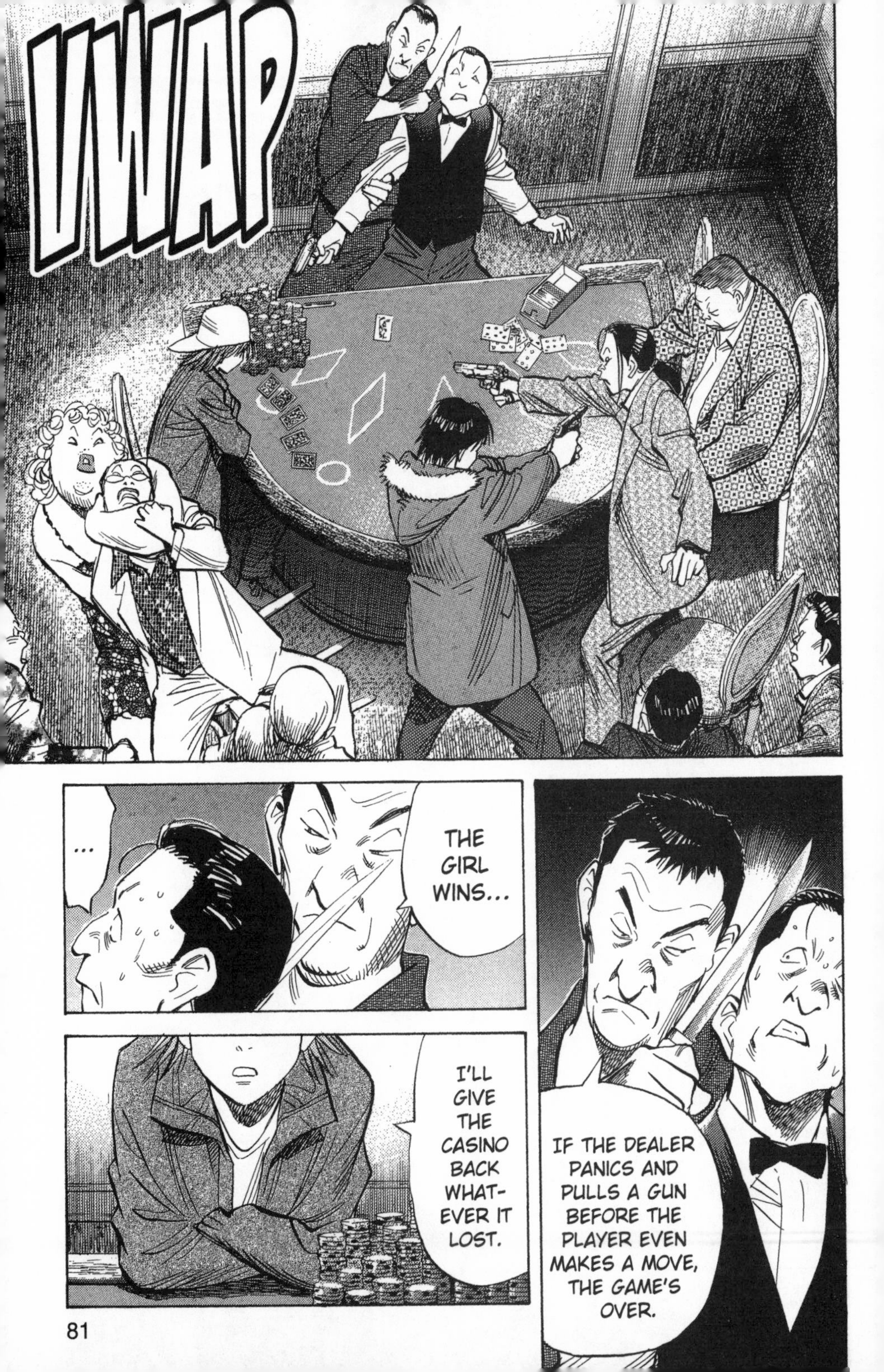
VWAP
IF THE DEALER PANICS AND PULLS A GUN BEFORE THE PLAYER EVEN MAKES A MOVE, THE GAME'S OVER.
THE GIRL WINS...
...
I'LL GIVE THE CASINO BACK WHAT-EVER IT LOST.

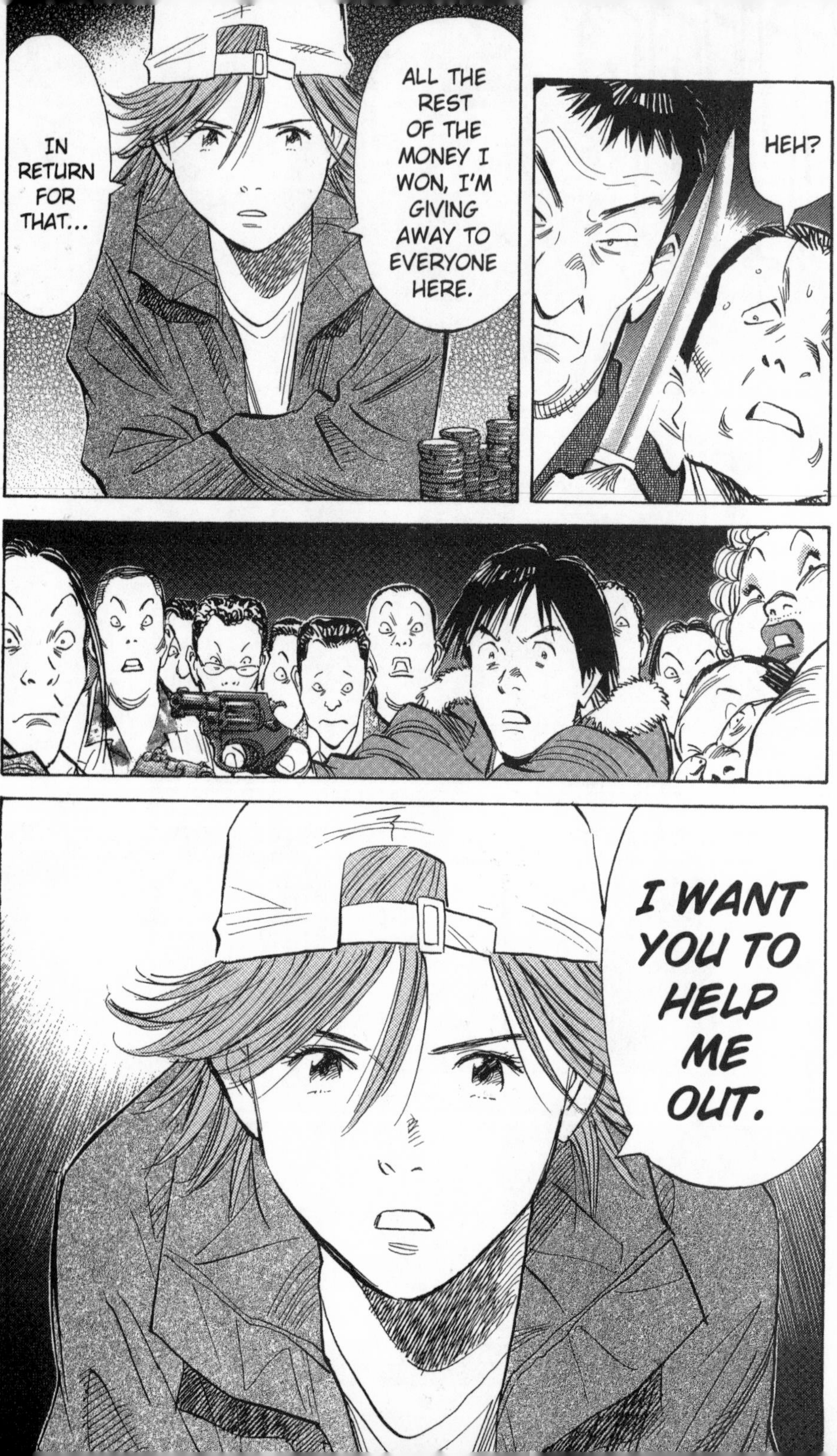
HEH?
ALL THE REST OF THE MONEY I WON, I'M GIVING AWAY TO EVERYONE HERE.
IN RETURN FOR THAT...
I WANT YOU TO HELP ME OUT.

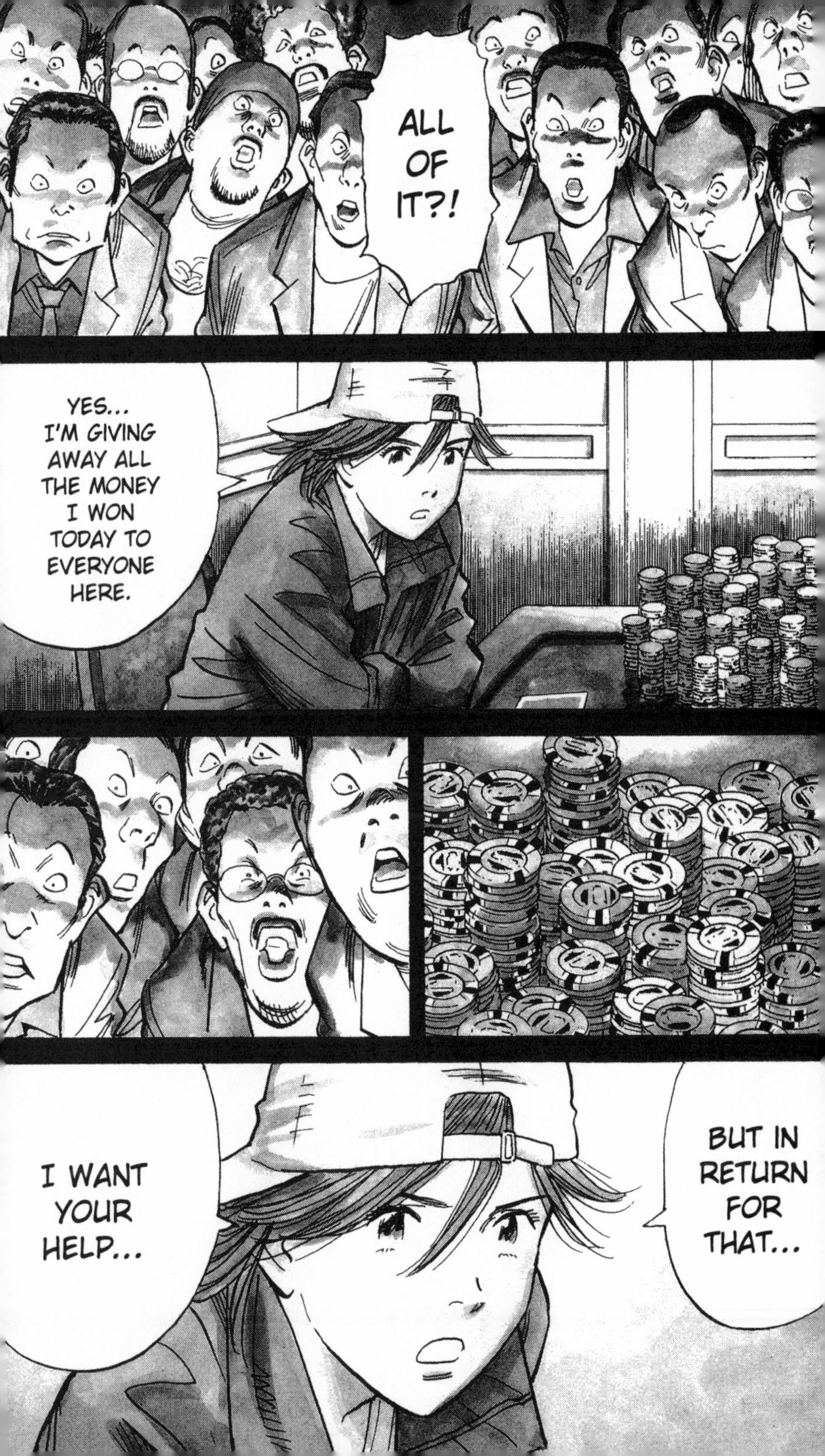
ALL OF IT?!
YES... I'M GIVING AWAY ALL THE MONEY I WON TODAY TO EVERYONE HERE.
BUT IN RETURN FOR THAT...
I WANT YOUR HELP...

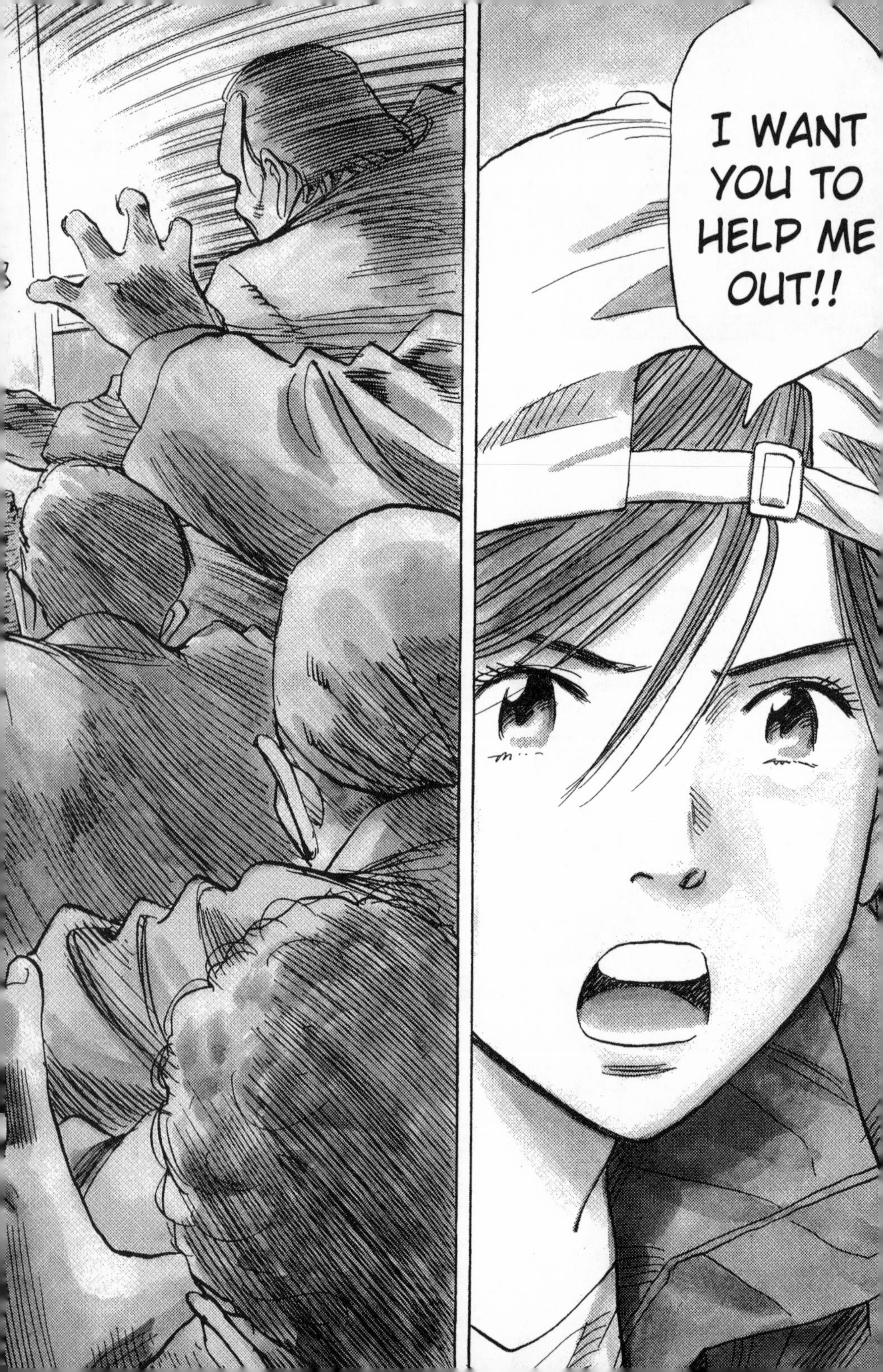
I WANT YOU TO HELP ME OUT!!

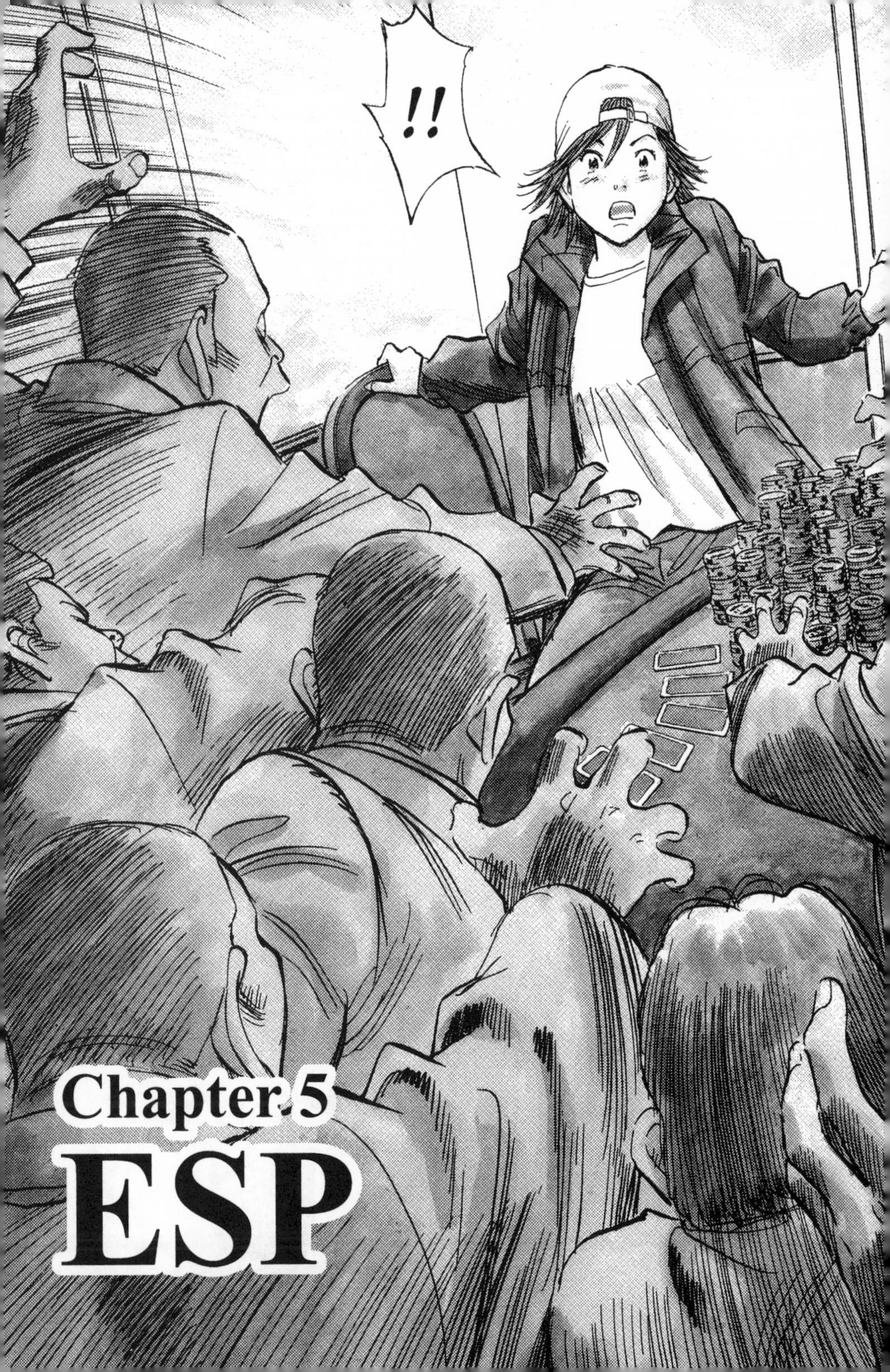
!!
Chapter 5
ESP

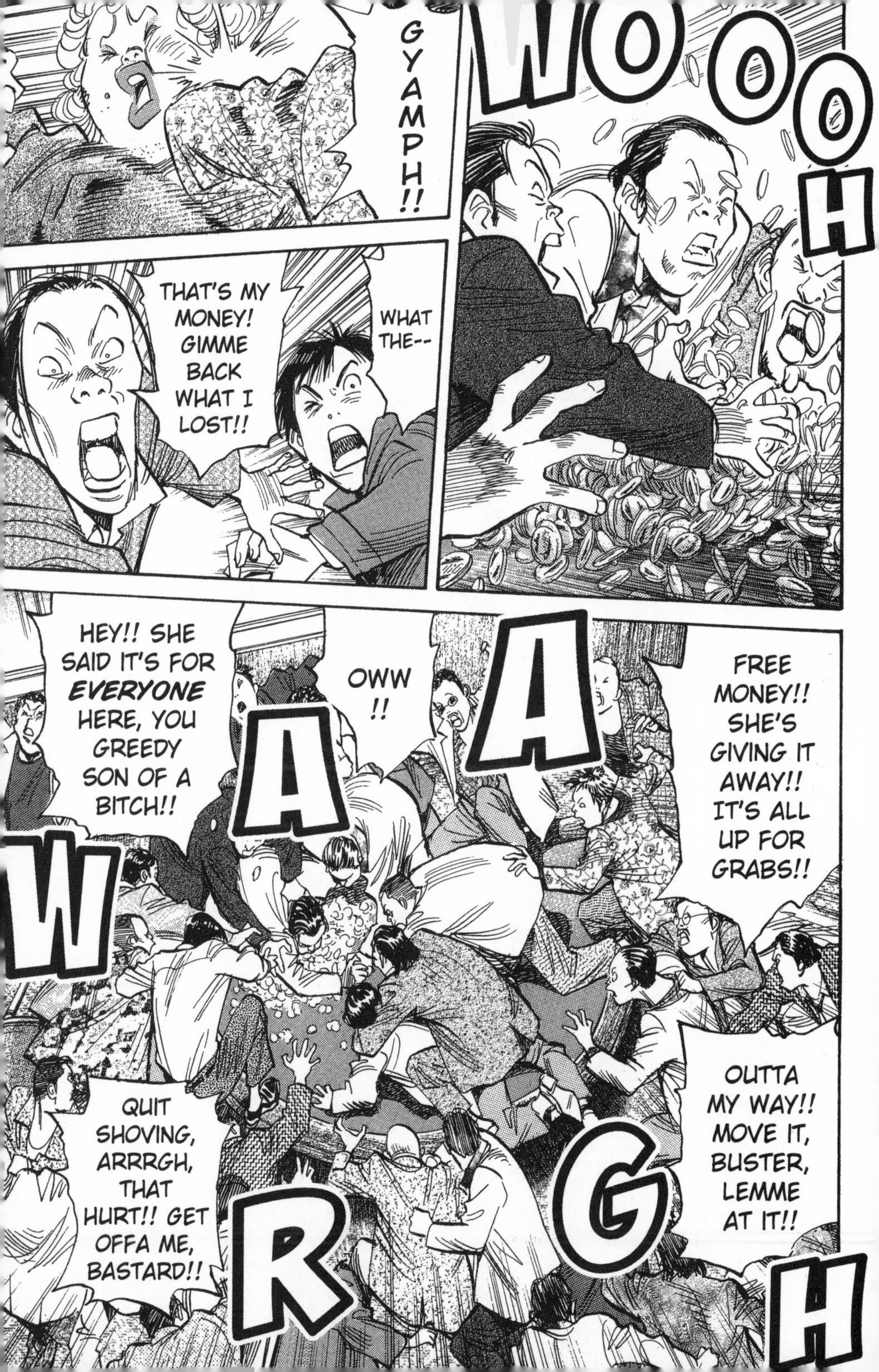
WOOOOH
GYAMPH!!
WHAT THE--
THAT'S MY MONEY! GIMME BACK WHAT I LOST!!
FREE MONEY!! SHE'S GIVING IT AWAY!! IT'S ALL UP FOR GRABS!!
OWW !!
HEY!! SHE SAID IT'S FOR EVERYONE HERE, YOU GREEDY SON OF A BITCH!!
WAAGRH
OUTTA MY WAY!! MOVE IT, BUSTER, LEMME AT IT!!
QUIT SHOVING, ARRRGH, THAT HURT!! GET OFFA ME, BASTARD!!

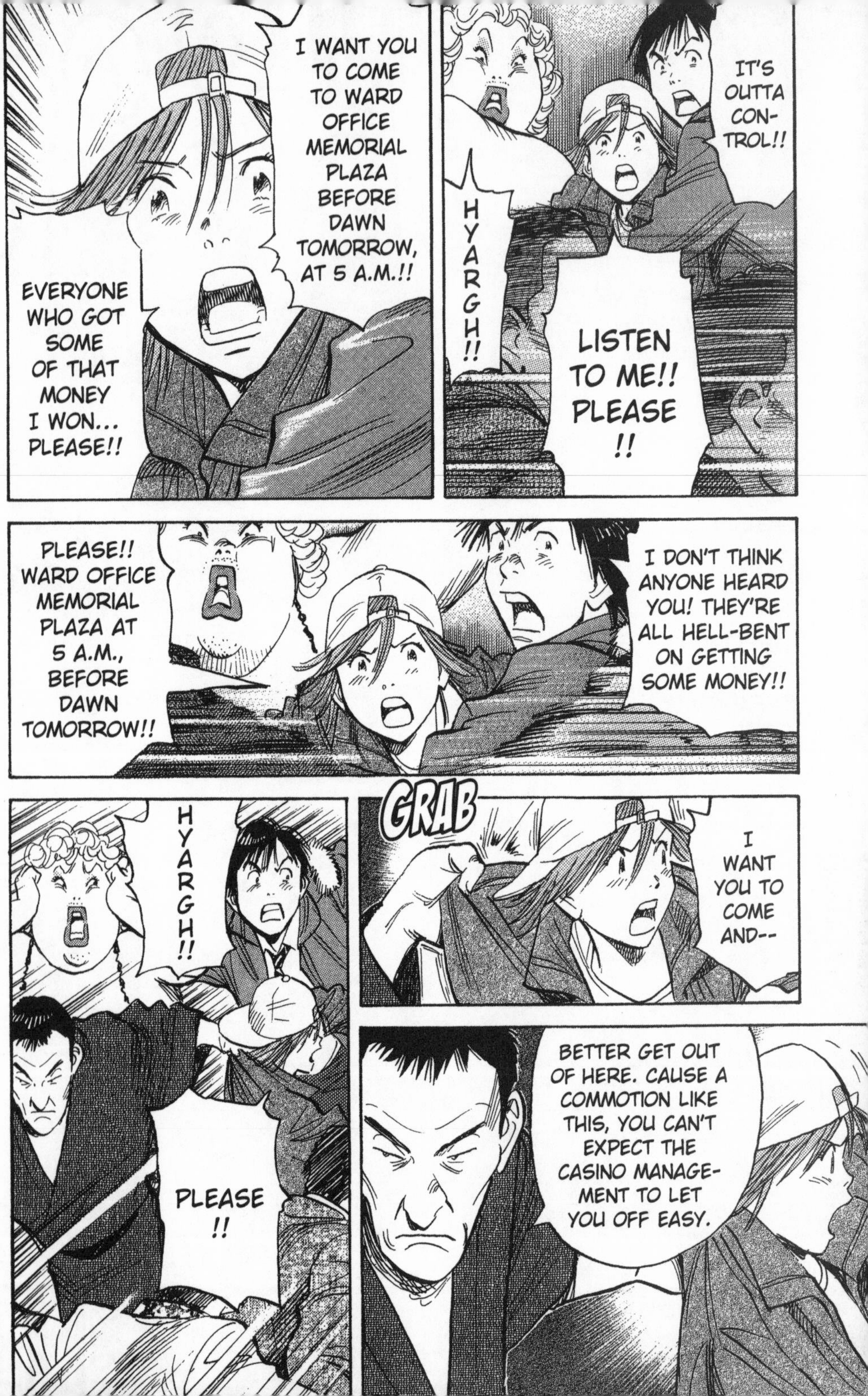
IT'S OUTTA CON-TROL!!
HYARGH!!
LISTEN TO ME!! PLEASE !!
I WANT YOU TO COME TO WARD OFFICE MEMORIAL PLAZA BEFORE DAWN TOMORROW, AT 5 A.M.!!
EVERYONE WHO GOT SOME OF THAT MONEY I WON... PLEASE!!
I DON'T THINK ANYONE HEARD YOU! THEY'RE ALL HELL-BENT ON GETTING SOME MONEY!!
PLEASE!! WARD OFFICE MEMORIAL PLAZA AT 5 A.M., BEFORE DAWN TOMORROW!!
GRAB
I WANT YOU TO COME AND--
BETTER GET OUT OF HERE. CAUSE A COMMOTION LIKE THIS, YOU CAN'T EXPECT THE CASINO MANAGE-MENT TO LET YOU OFF EASY.
HYARGH!!
PLEASE !!

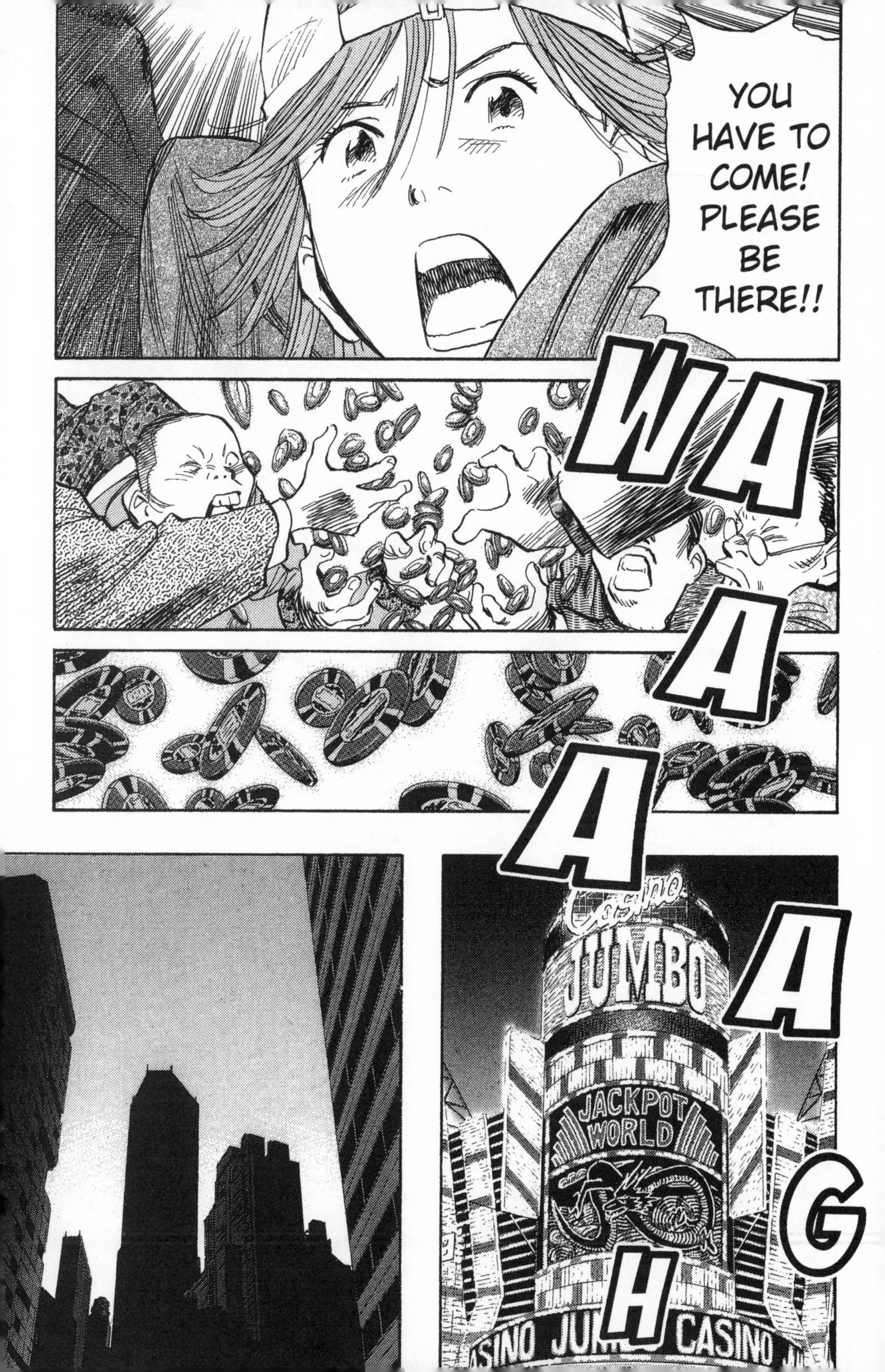
YOU HAVE TO COME! PLEASE BE THERE!!
WAAAAA
Casino
JUMBO
JACKPOT WORLD
GH
CASINO JUMBO CASINO

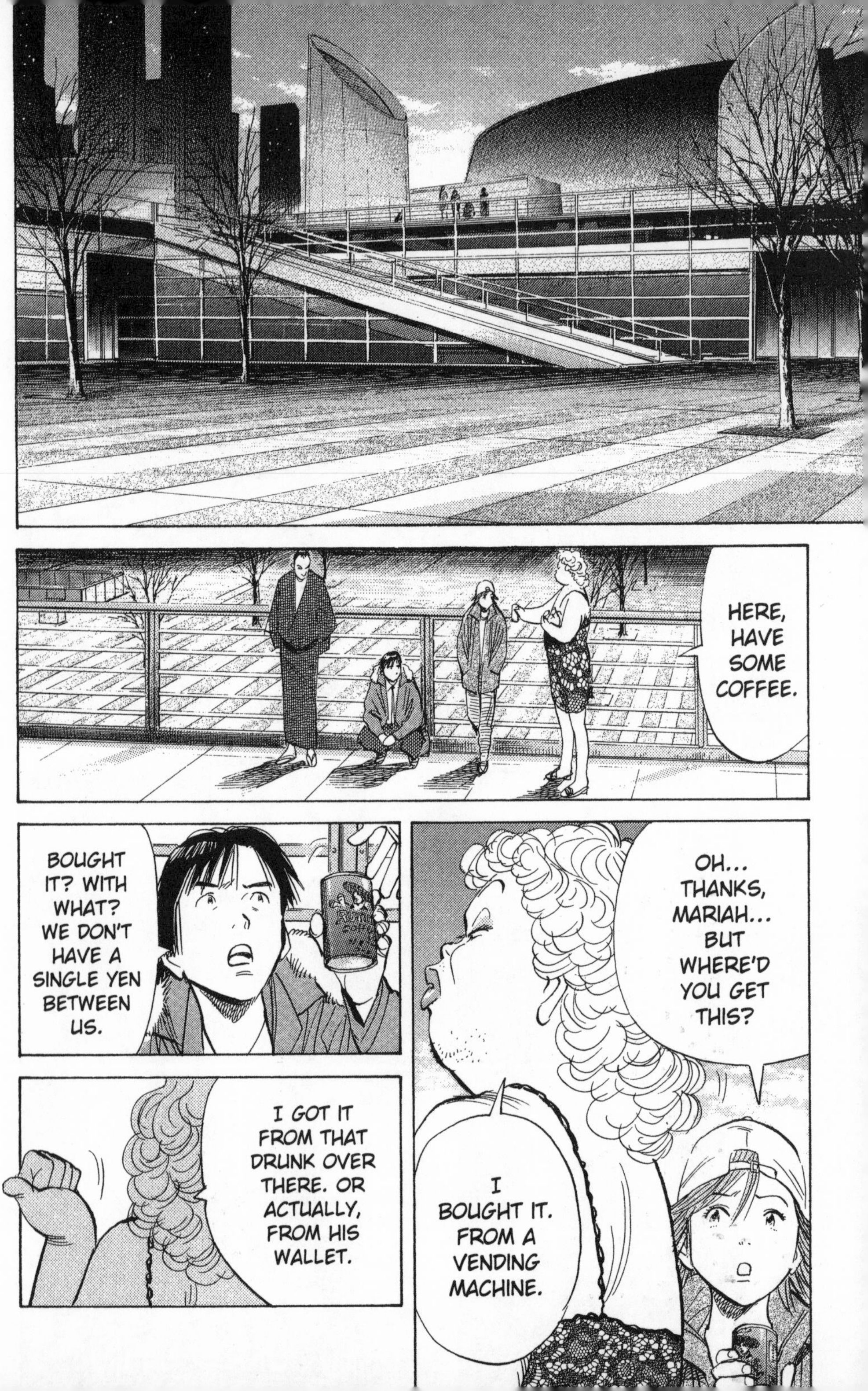
HERE, HAVE SOME COFFEE.
OH... THANKS, MARIAH... BUT WHERE'D YOU GET THIS?
I BOUGHT IT. FROM A VENDING MACHINE.
BOUGHT IT? WITH WHAT? WE DON'T HAVE A SINGLE YEN BETWEEN US.
I GOT IT FROM THAT DRUNK OVER THERE. OR ACTUALLY, FROM HIS WALLET.

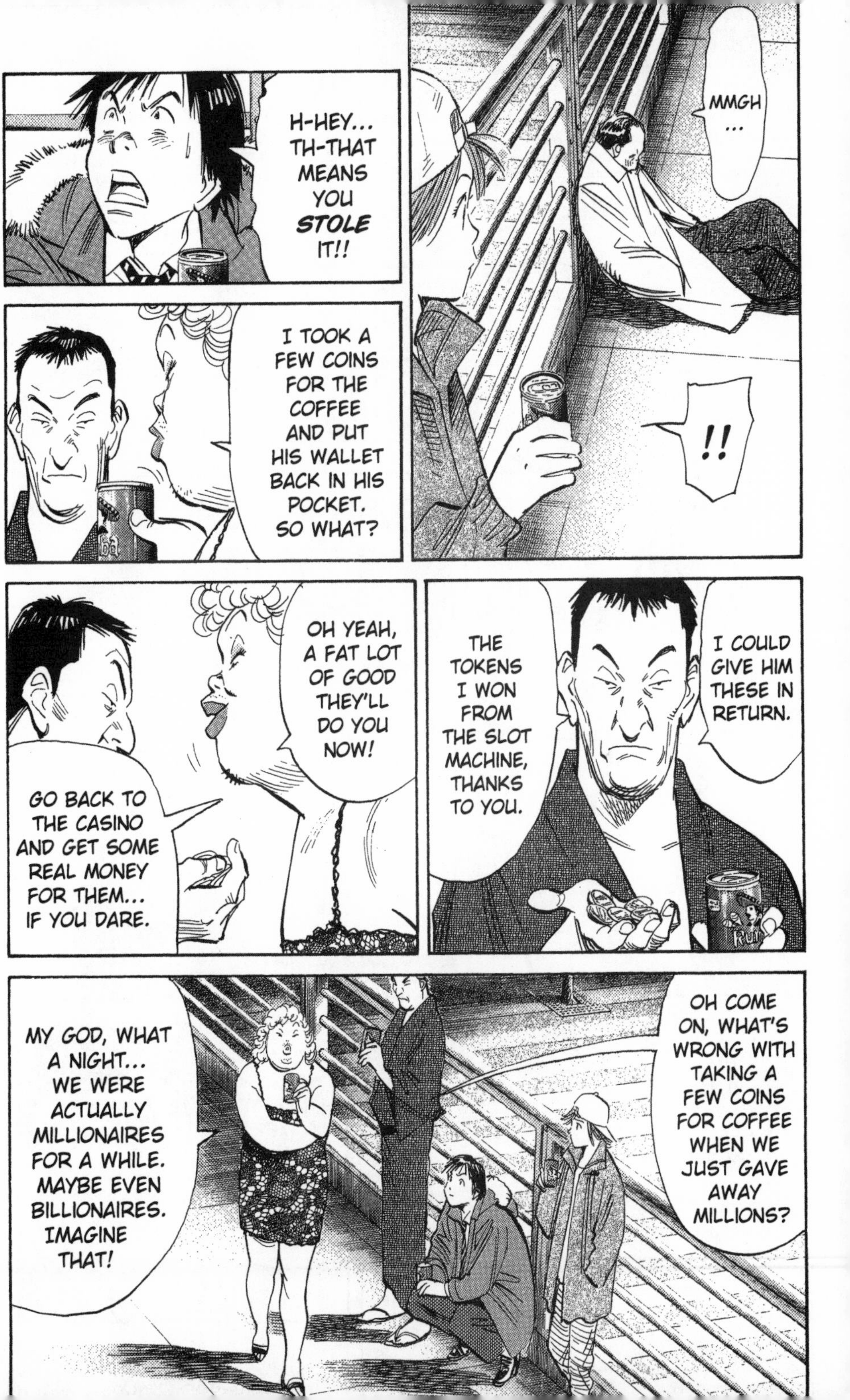
MMGH ...
!!
H-HEY... TH-THAT MEANS YOU **STOLE** IT!!
I TOOK A FEW COINS FOR THE COFFEE AND PUT HIS WALLET BACK IN HIS POCKET. SO WHAT?
I COULD GIVE HIM THESE IN RETURN.
THE TOKENS I WON FROM THE SLOT MACHINE, THANKS TO YOU.
OH YEAH, A FAT LOT OF GOOD THEY'LL DO YOU NOW!
GO BACK TO THE CASINO AND GET SOME REAL MONEY FOR THEM... IF YOU DARE.
OH COME ON, WHAT'S WRONG WITH TAKING A FEW COINS FOR COFFEE WHEN WE JUST GAVE AWAY MILLIONS?
MY GOD, WHAT A NIGHT... WE WERE ACTUALLY MILLIONAIRES FOR A WHILE. MAYBE EVEN BILLIONAIRES. IMAGINE THAT!

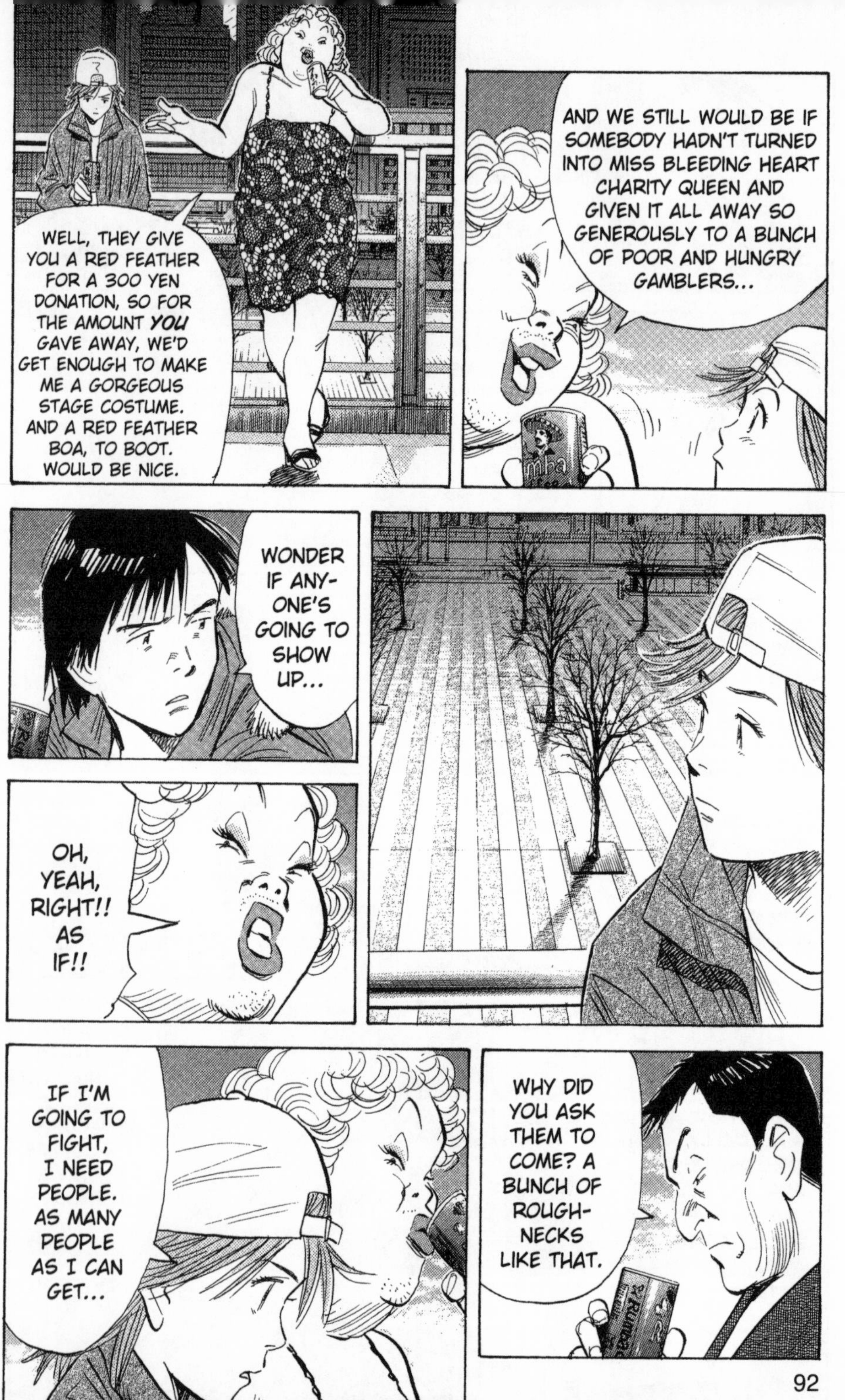
AND WE STILL WOULD BE IF SOMEBODY HADN'T TURNED INTO MISS BLEEDING HEART CHARITY QUEEN AND GIVEN IT ALL AWAY SO GENEROUSLY TO A BUNCH OF POOR AND HUNGRY GAMBLERS...
WELL, THEY GIVE YOU A RED FEATHER FOR A 300 YEN DONATION, SO FOR THE AMOUNT *YOU* GAVE AWAY, WE'D GET ENOUGH TO MAKE ME A GORGEOUS STAGE COSTUME. AND A RED FEATHER BOA, TO BOOT. WOULD BE NICE.
WONDER IF ANY-ONE'S GOING TO SHOW UP...
OH, YEAH, RIGHT!! AS IF!!
WHY DID YOU ASK THEM TO COME? A BUNCH OF ROUGH-NECKS LIKE THAT.
IF I'M GOING TO FIGHT, I NEED PEOPLE. AS MANY PEOPLE AS I CAN GET...

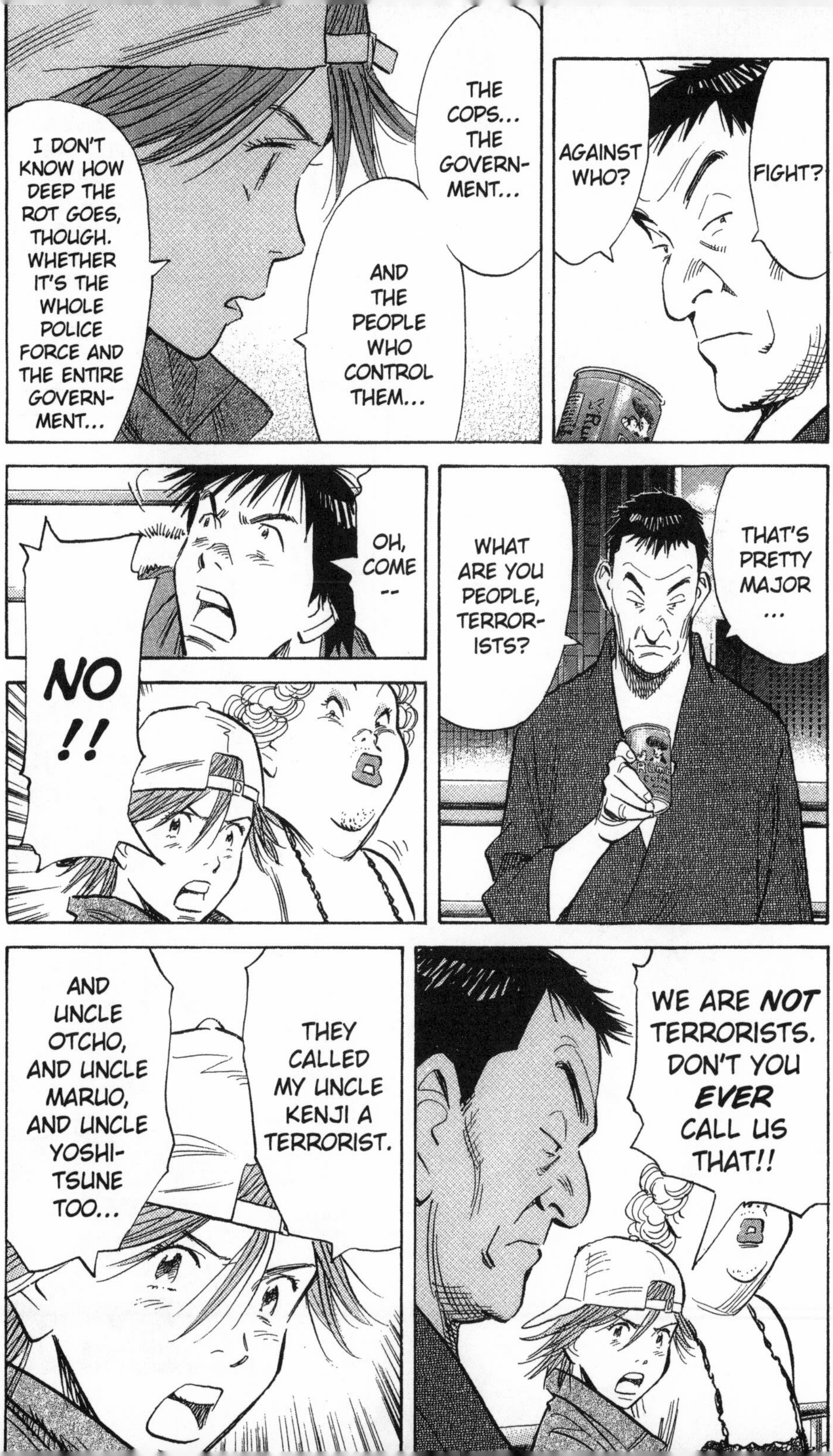
FIGHT?
AGAINST WHO?
THE COPS... THE GOVERNMENT...
AND THE PEOPLE WHO CONTROL THEM...
I DON'T KNOW HOW DEEP THE ROT GOES, THOUGH. WHETHER IT'S THE WHOLE POLICE FORCE AND THE ENTIRE GOVERNMENT...
THAT'S PRETTY MAJOR ...
WHAT ARE YOU PEOPLE, TERRORISTS?
OH, COME --
NO!!
WE ARE NOT TERRORISTS. DON'T YOU EVER CALL US THAT!!
THEY CALLED MY UNCLE KENJI A TERRORIST.
AND UNCLE OTCHO, AND UNCLE MARUO, AND UNCLE YOSHITSUNE TOO...

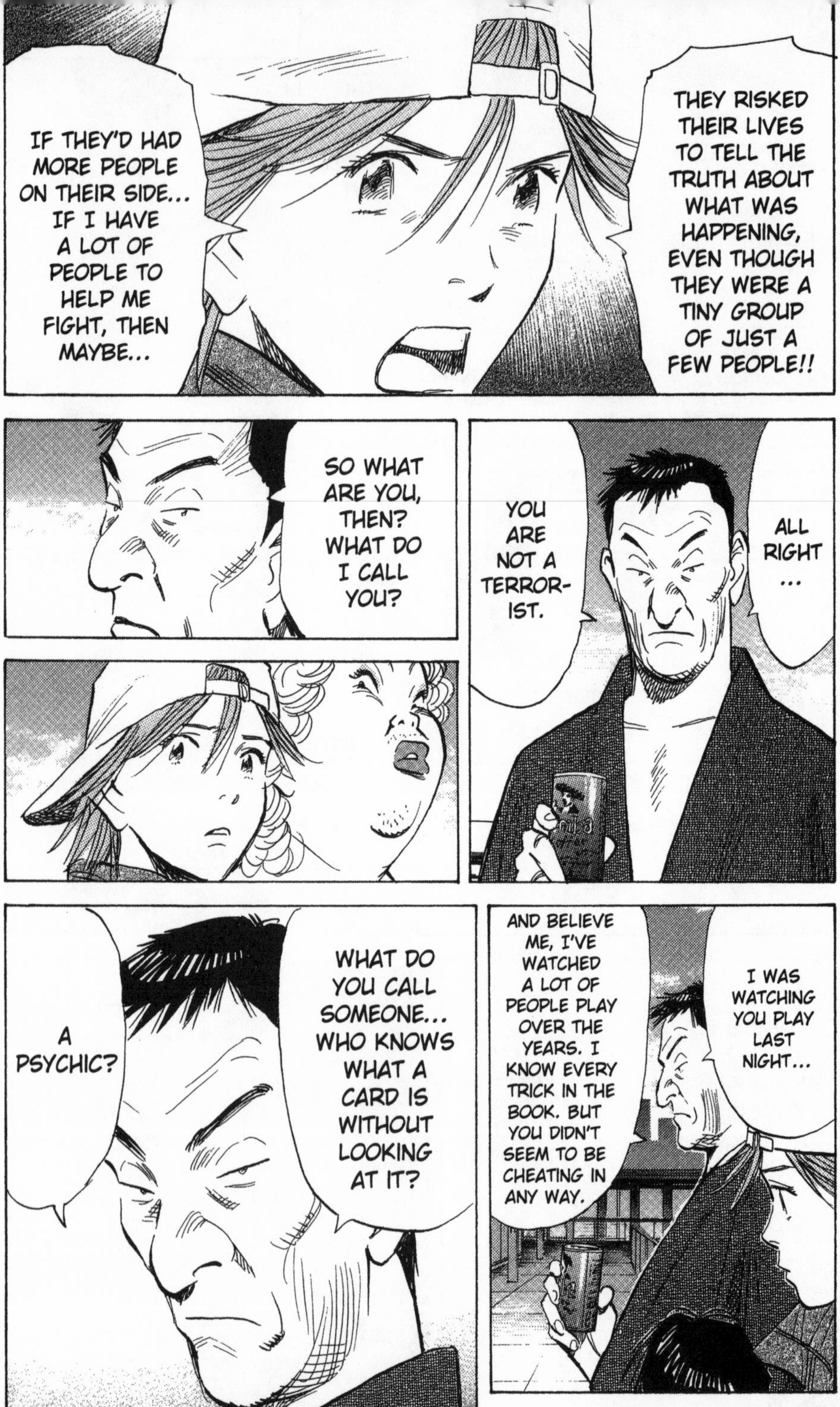
THEY RISKED THEIR LIVES TO TELL THE TRUTH ABOUT WHAT WAS HAPPENING, EVEN THOUGH THEY WERE A TINY GROUP OF JUST A FEW PEOPLE!!
IF THEY'D HAD MORE PEOPLE ON THEIR SIDE... IF I HAVE A LOT OF PEOPLE TO HELP ME FIGHT, THEN MAYBE...
ALL RIGHT...
YOU ARE NOT A TERROR-IST.
SO WHAT ARE YOU, THEN? WHAT DO I CALL YOU?
I WAS WATCHING YOU PLAY LAST NIGHT...
AND BELIEVE ME, I'VE WATCHED A LOT OF PEOPLE PLAY OVER THE YEARS. I KNOW EVERY TRICK IN THE BOOK. BUT YOU DIDN'T SEEM TO BE CHEATING IN ANY WAY.
WHAT DO YOU CALL SOMEONE... WHO KNOWS WHAT A CARD IS WITHOUT LOOKING AT IT?
A PSYCHIC?

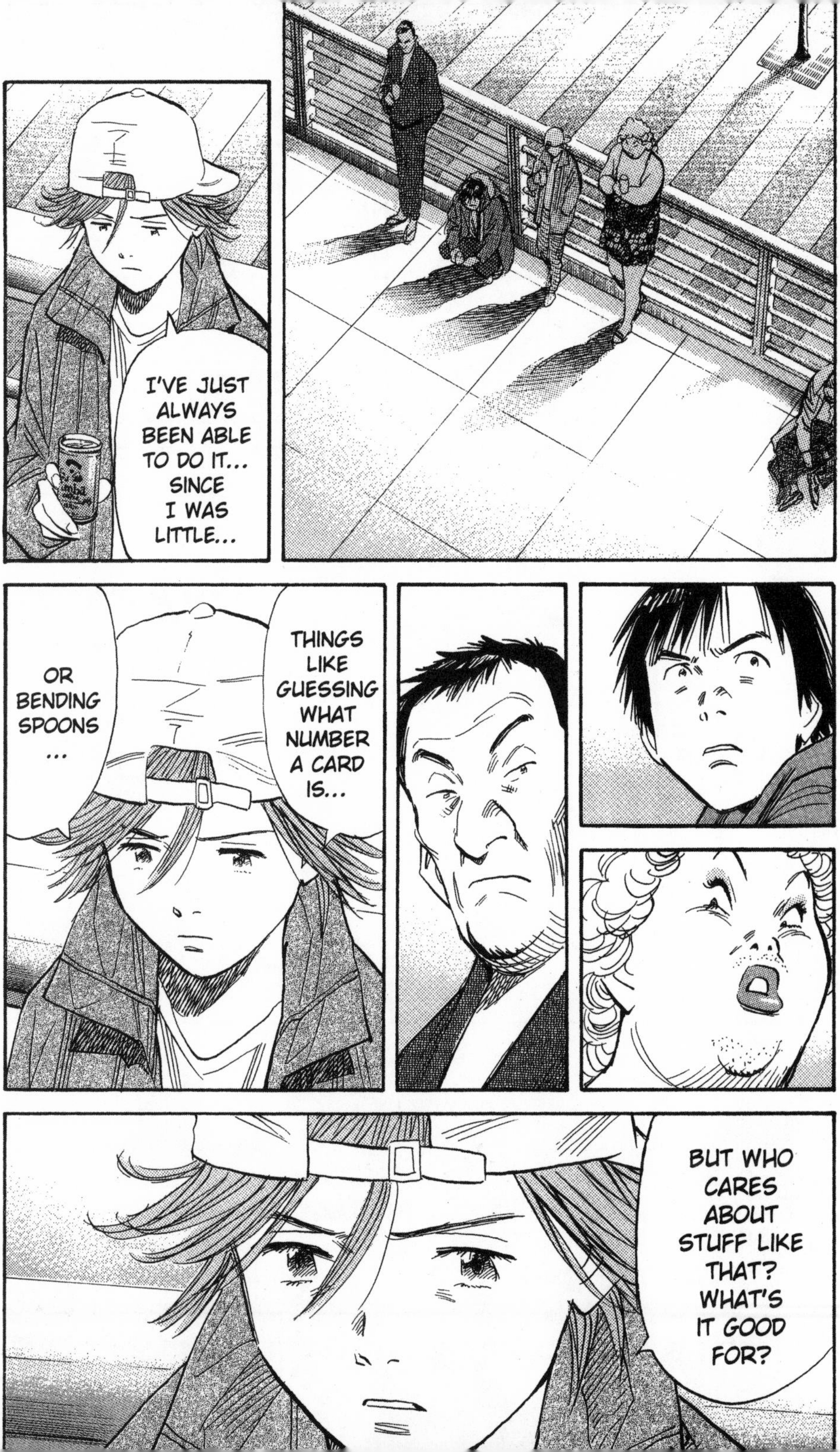
I'VE JUST ALWAYS BEEN ABLE TO DO IT... SINCE I WAS LITTLE...
THINGS LIKE GUESSING WHAT NUMBER A CARD IS...
OR BENDING SPOONS...
BUT WHO CARES ABOUT STUFF LIKE THAT? WHAT'S IT GOOD FOR?

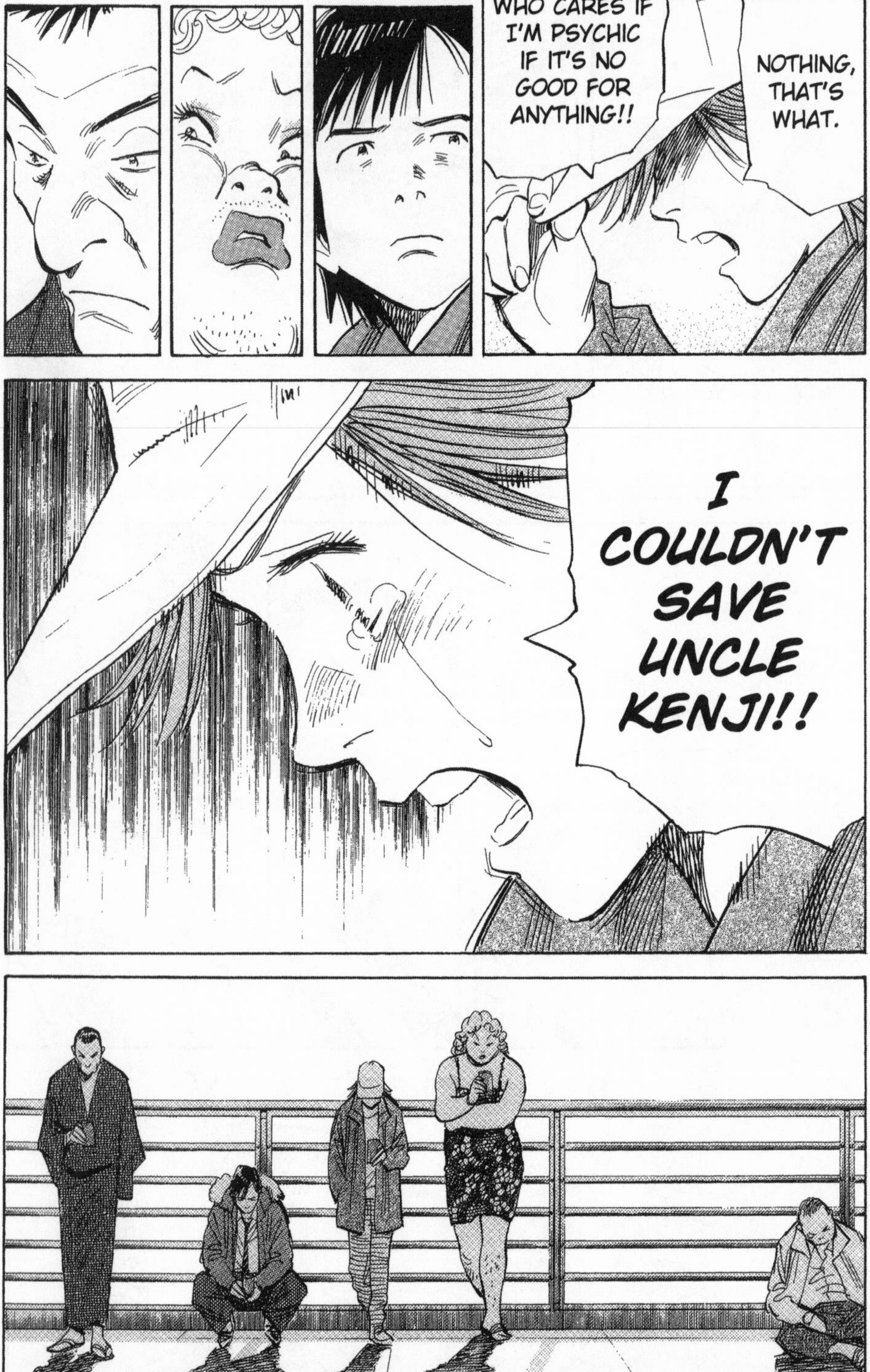
NOTHING, THAT'S WHAT.
WHO CARES IF I'M PSYCHIC IF IT'S NO GOOD FOR ANYTHING!!
I COULDN'T SAVE UNCLE KENJI!!

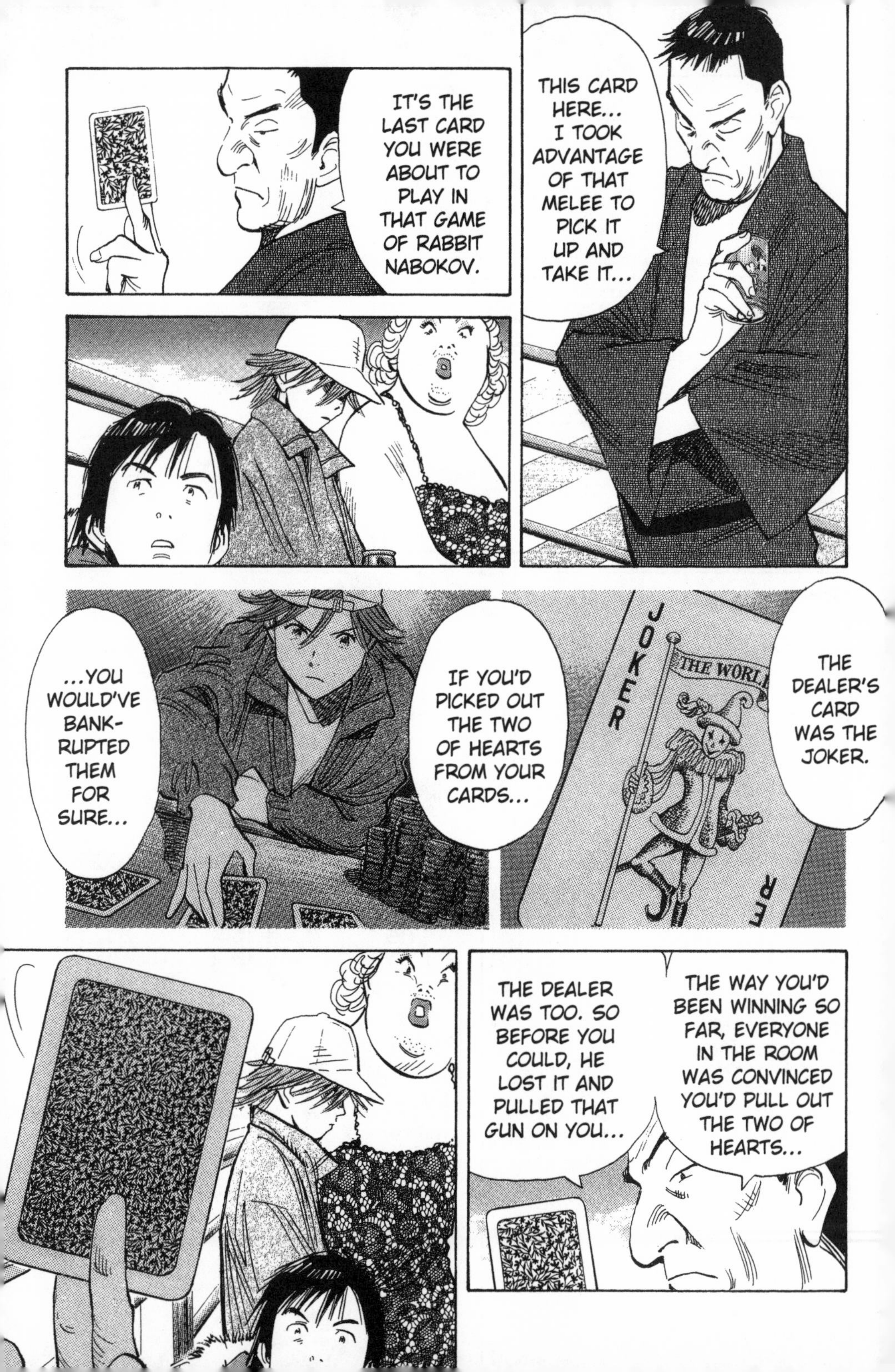

THIS CARD HERE... I TOOK ADVANTAGE OF THAT MELEE TO PICK IT UP AND TAKE IT...
IT'S THE LAST CARD YOU WERE ABOUT TO PLAY IN THAT GAME OF RABBIT NABOKOV.
THE DEALER'S CARD WAS THE JOKER.
JOKER
IF YOU'D PICKED OUT THE TWO OF HEARTS FROM YOUR CARDS...
...YOU WOULD'VE BANK-RUPTED THEM FOR SURE...
THE WAY YOU'D BEEN WINNING SO FAR, EVERYONE IN THE ROOM WAS CONVINCED YOU'D PULL OUT THE TWO OF HEARTS...
THE DEALER WAS TOO. SO BEFORE YOU COULD, HE LOST IT AND PULLED THAT GUN ON YOU...

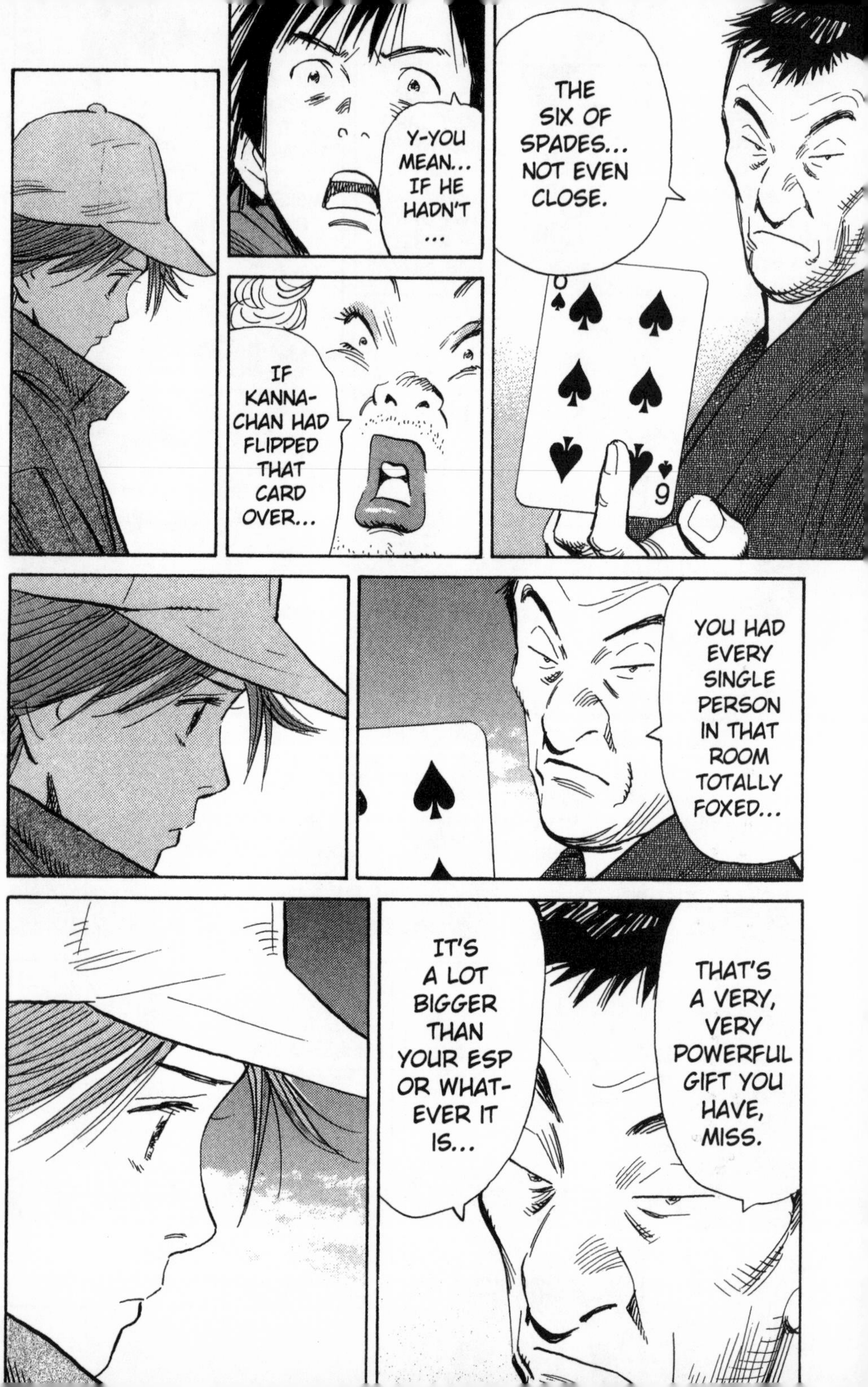
THE SIX OF SPADES... NOT EVEN CLOSE.
Y-YOU MEAN... IF HE HADN'T ...
IF KANNA-CHAN HAD FLIPPED THAT CARD OVER...
YOU HAD EVERY SINGLE PERSON IN THAT ROOM TOTALLY FOXED...
THAT'S A VERY, VERY POWERFUL GIFT YOU HAVE, MISS.
IT'S A LOT BIGGER THAN YOUR ESP OR WHAT-EVER IT IS...

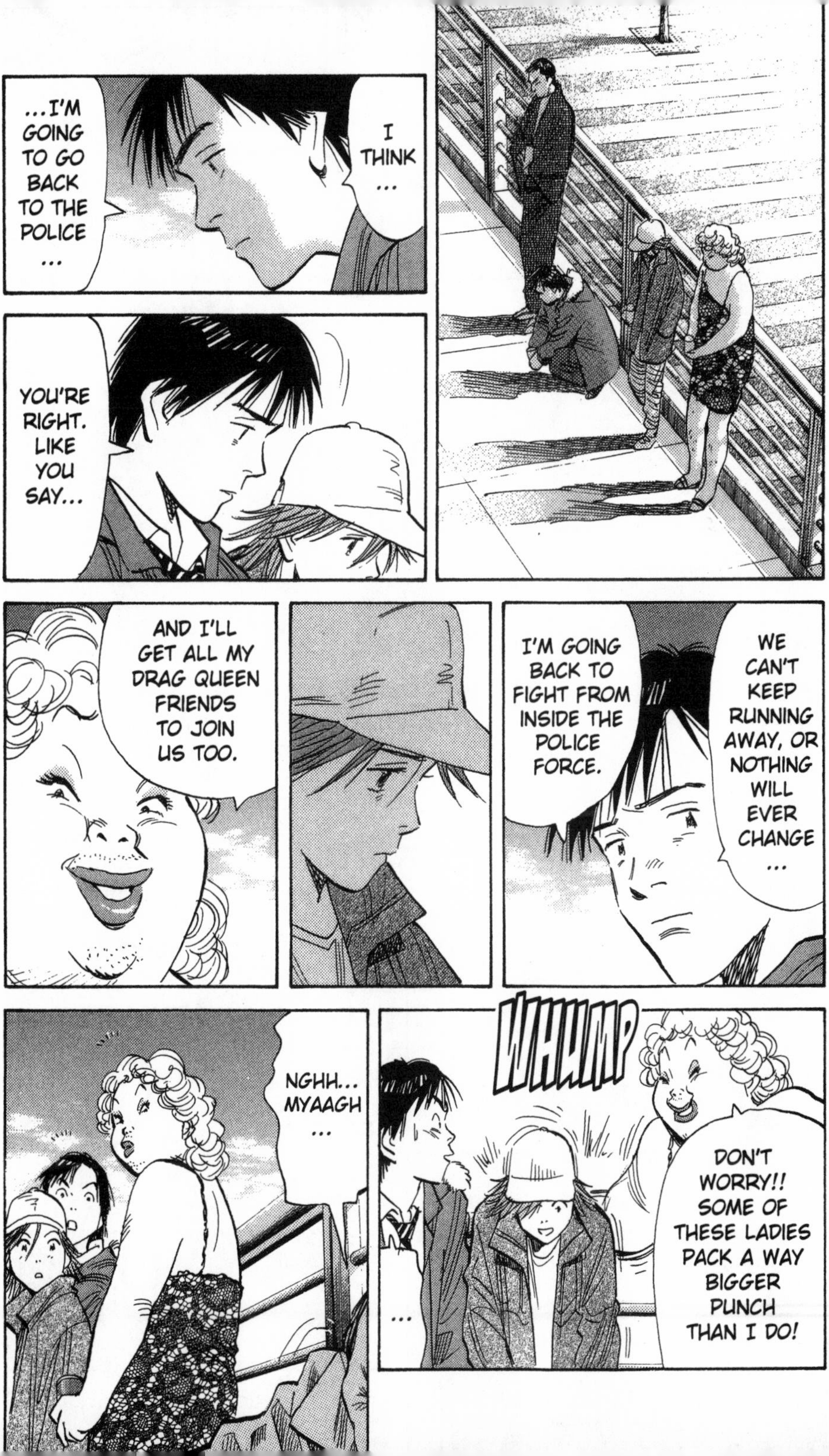
I THINK ...
...I'M GOING TO GO BACK TO THE POLICE ...
YOU'RE RIGHT. LIKE YOU SAY...
WE CAN'T KEEP RUNNING AWAY, OR NOTHING WILL EVER CHANGE ...
I'M GOING BACK TO FIGHT FROM INSIDE THE POLICE FORCE.
AND I'LL GET ALL MY DRAG QUEEN FRIENDS TO JOIN US TOO.
WHUMP
DON'T WORRY!! SOME OF THESE LADIES PACK A WAY BIGGER PUNCH THAN I DO!
...
NGHH... MYAAGH ...

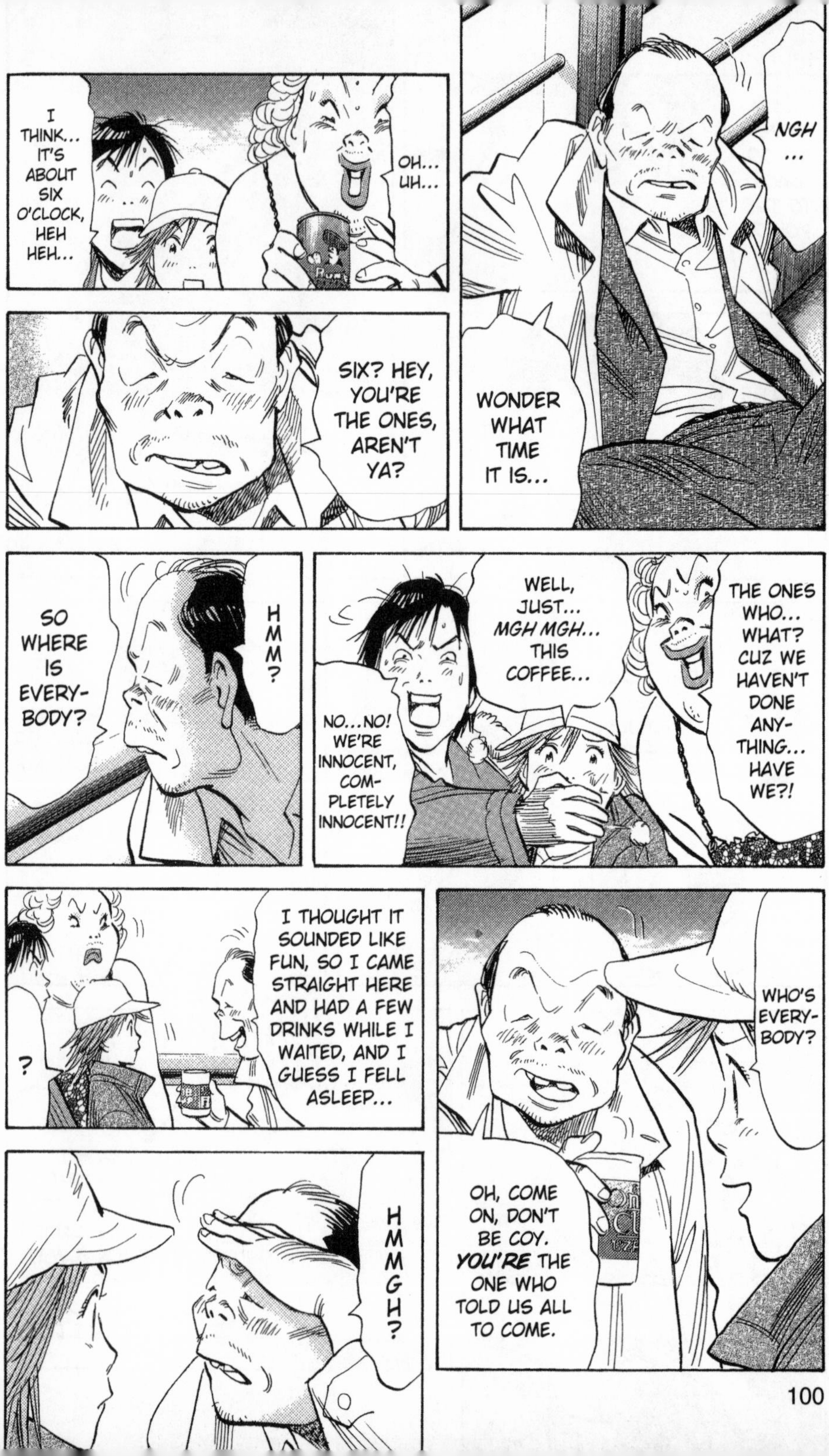
NGH...
WONDER WHAT TIME IT IS...
OH... UH...
I THINK... IT'S ABOUT SIX O'CLOCK, HEH HEH...
SIX? HEY, YOU'RE THE ONES, AREN'T YA?
THE ONES WHO... WHAT? CUZ WE HAVEN'T DONE ANY-THING... HAVE WE?!
WELL, JUST... *MGH MGH...* THIS COFFEE...
NO...NO! WE'RE INNOCENT, COM-PLETELY INNOCENT!!
HMM?
SO WHERE IS EVERY-BODY?
WHO'S EVERY-BODY?
OH, COME ON, DON'T BE COY. ***YOU'RE*** THE ONE WHO TOLD US ALL TO COME.
I THOUGHT IT SOUNDED LIKE FUN, SO I CAME STRAIGHT HERE AND HAD A FEW DRINKS WHILE I WAITED, AND I GUESS I FELL ASLEEP...
?
HMMGH?

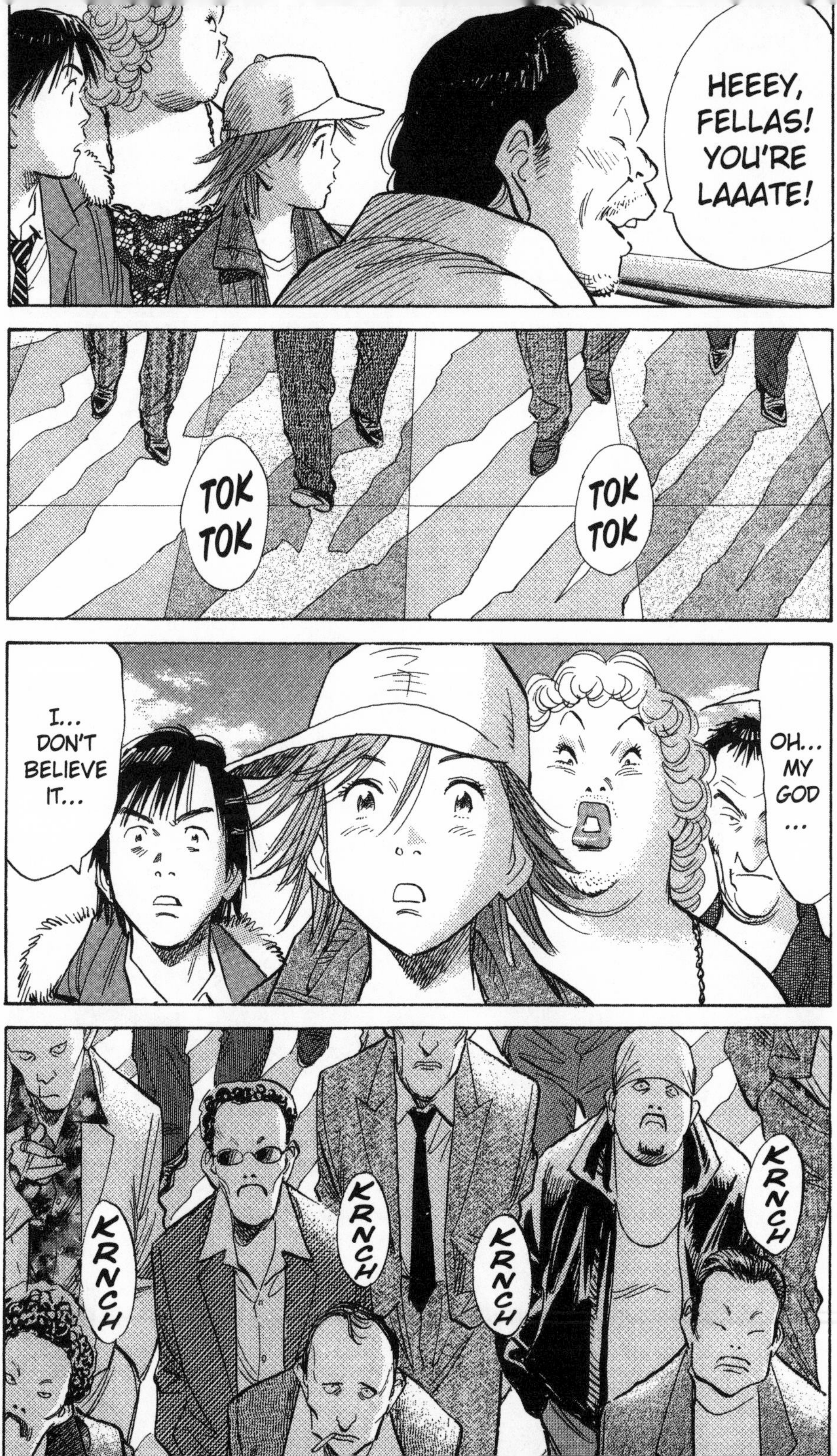
HEEEY, FELLAS! YOU'RE LAAATE!
TOK TOK
TOK TOK
OH... MY GOD ...
I... DON'T BELIEVE IT...
KRNCH
KRNCH
KRNCH
KRNCH

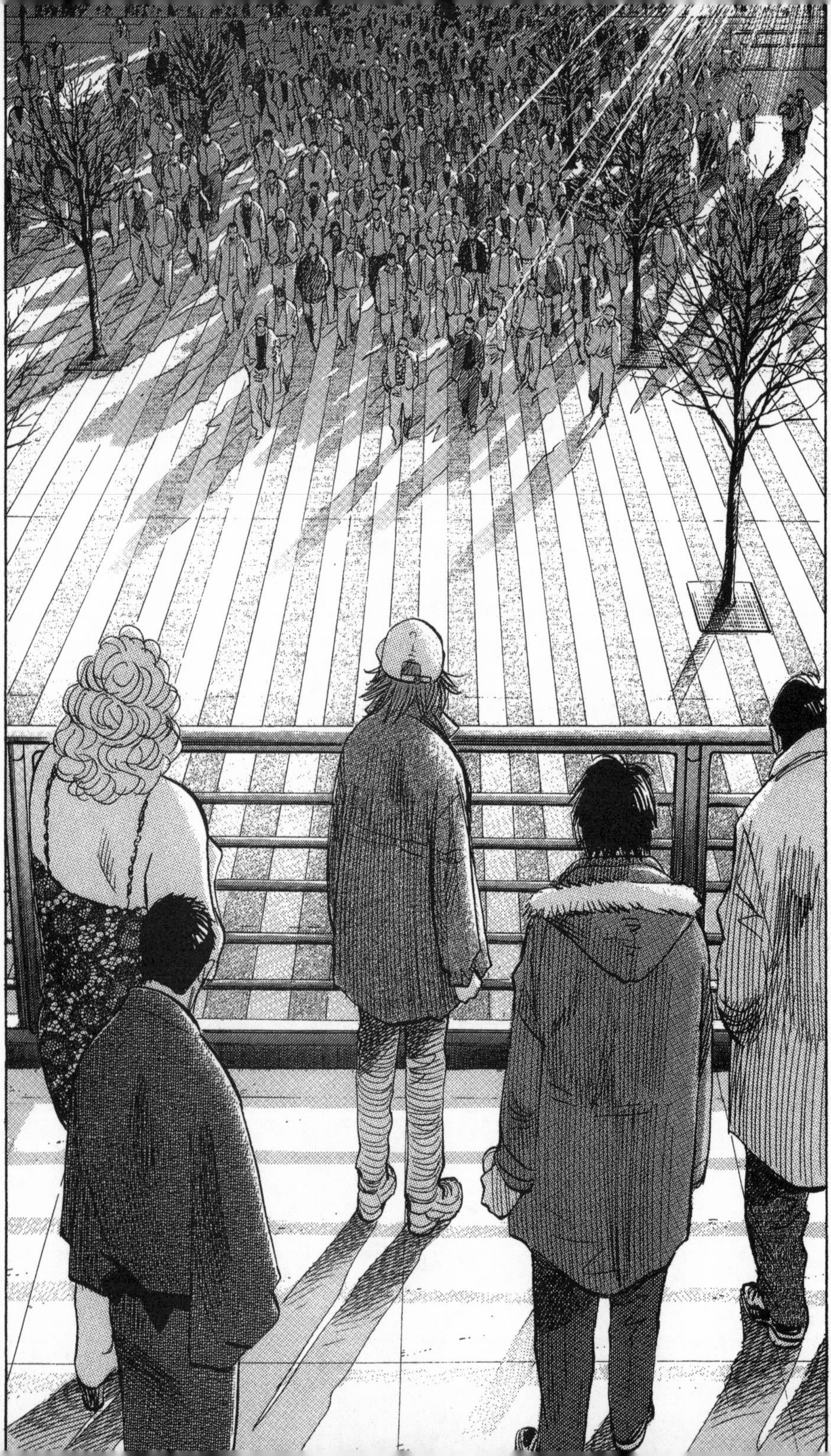

Chapter 6 Confession

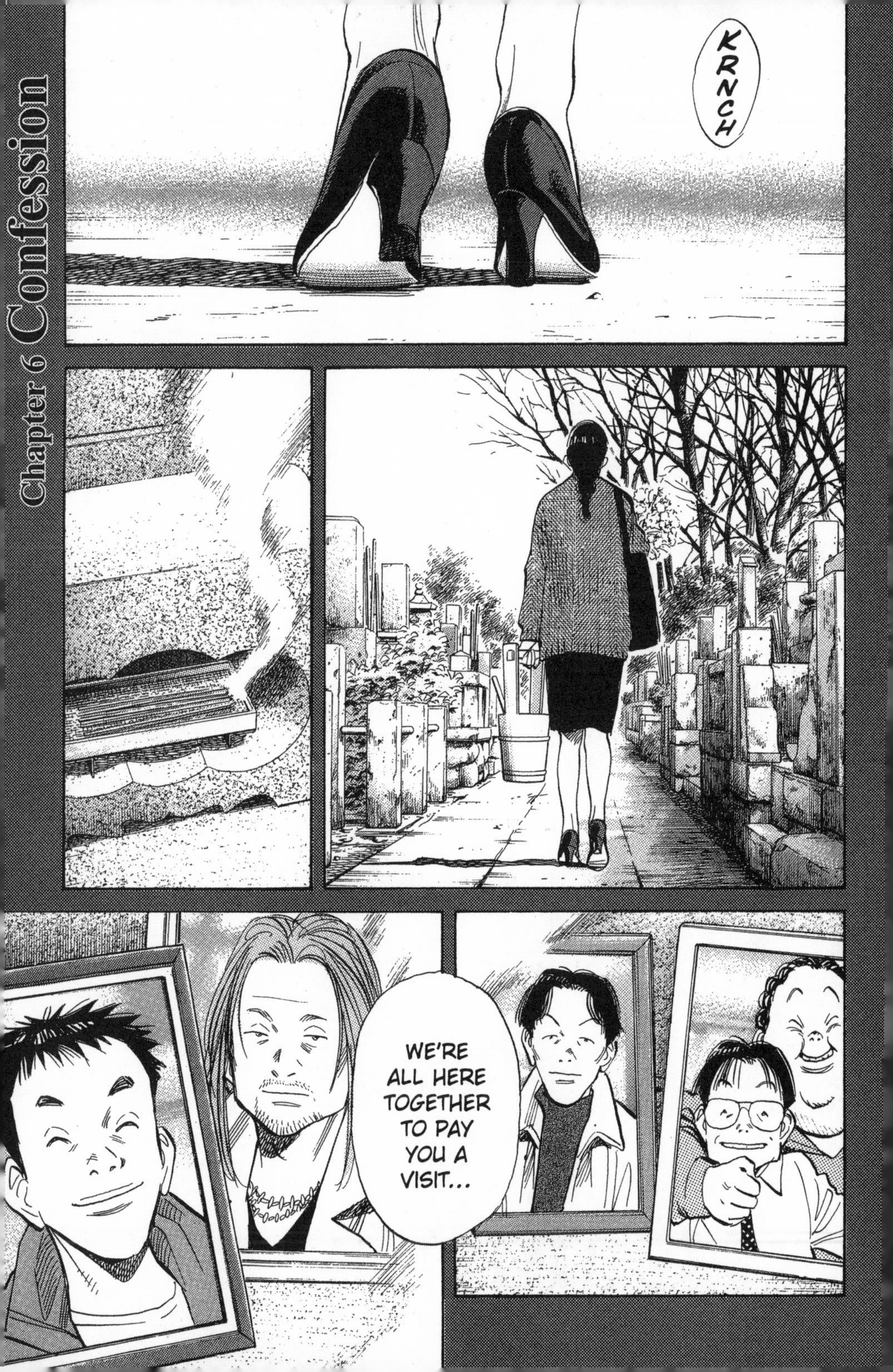
KRNCH
WE'RE ALL HERE TOGETHER TO PAY YOU A VISIT...

...MON-CHAN.

*Grave of Shimon Masaaki

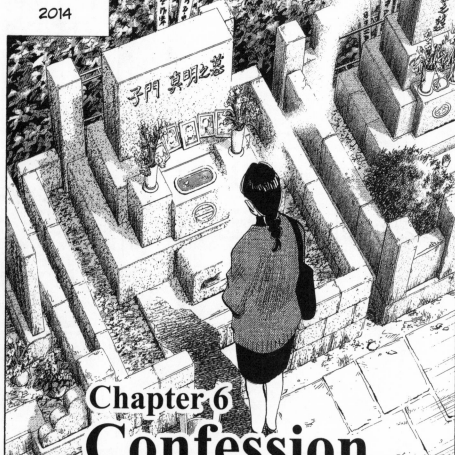

2014

Chapter 6
Confession

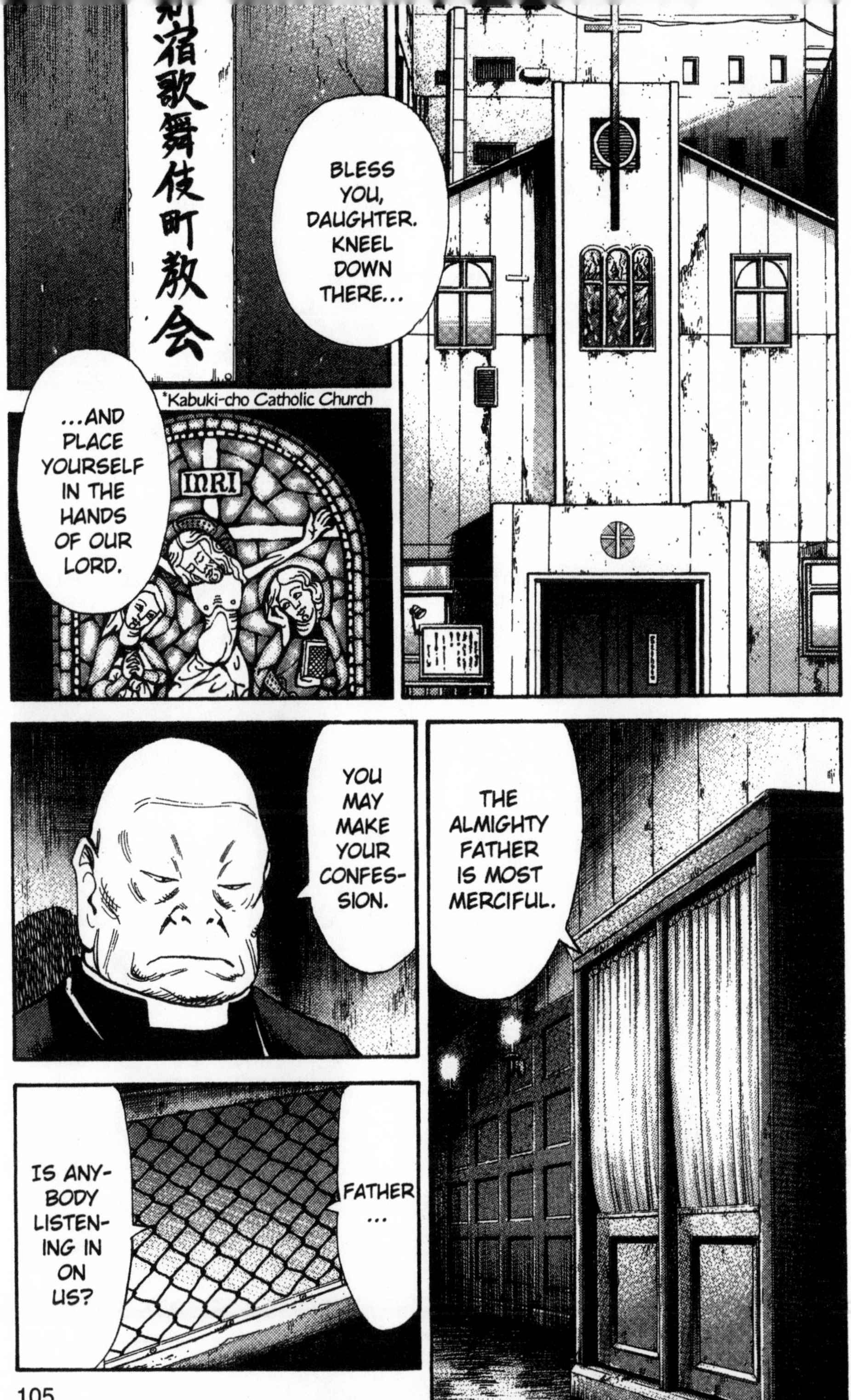
BLESS YOU, DAUGHTER. KNEEL DOWN THERE...
宿歌舞伎町教会
*Kabuki-cho Catholic Church
INRI
...AND PLACE YOURSELF IN THE HANDS OF OUR LORD.
THE ALMIGHTY FATHER IS MOST MERCIFUL.
YOU MAY MAKE YOUR CONFES-SION.
FATHER...
IS ANY-BODY LISTEN-ING IN ON US?

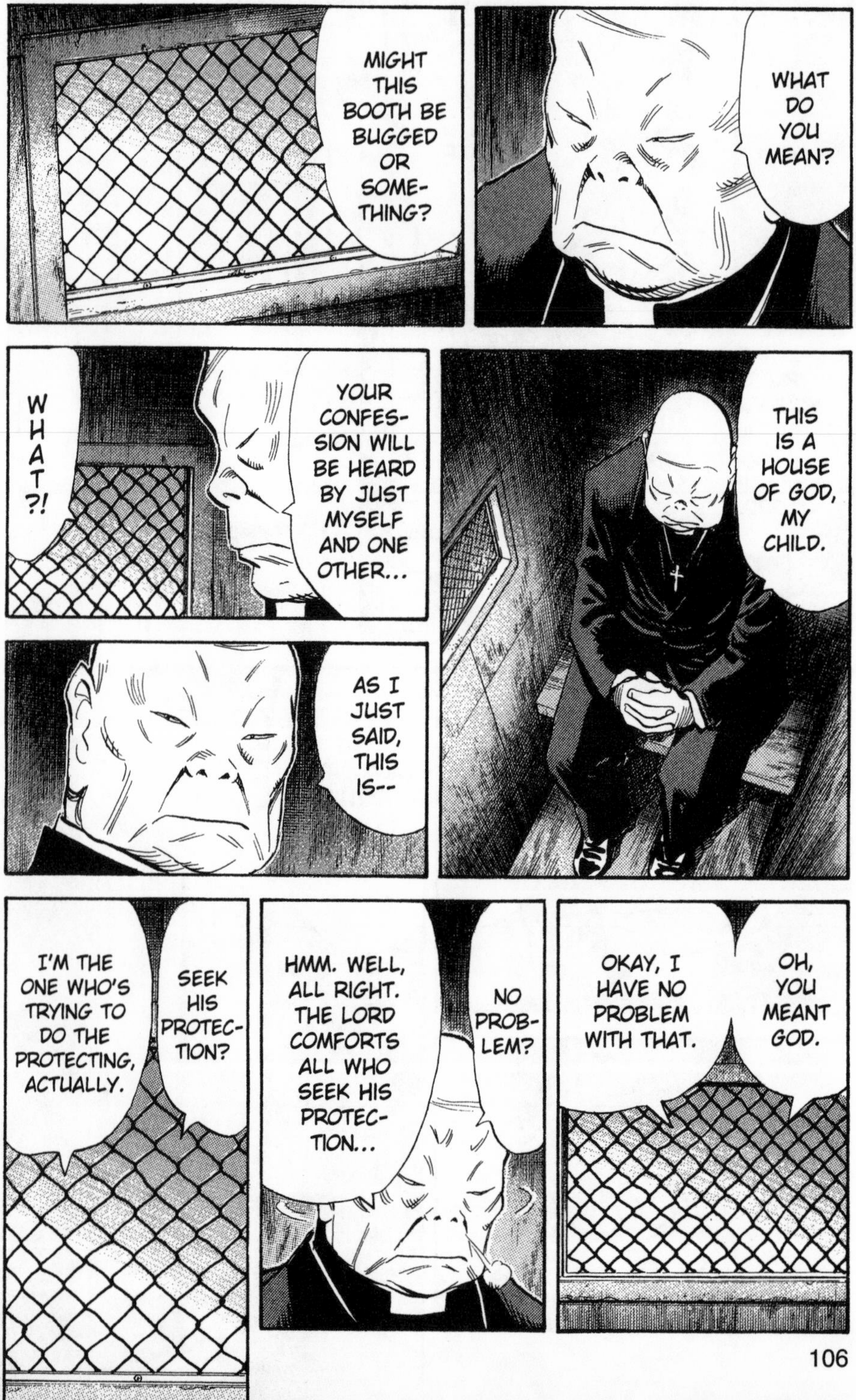
WHAT DO YOU MEAN?
MIGHT THIS BOOTH BE BUGGED OR SOMETHING?
THIS IS A HOUSE OF GOD, MY CHILD.
YOUR CONFESSION WILL BE HEARD BY JUST MYSELF AND ONE OTHER...
WHAT?!
AS I JUST SAID, THIS IS--
OH, YOU MEANT GOD.
OKAY, I HAVE NO PROBLEM WITH THAT.
NO PROBLEM?
HMM. WELL, ALL RIGHT. THE LORD COMFORTS ALL WHO SEEK HIS PROTECTION...
SEEK HIS PROTECTION?
I'M THE ONE WHO'S TRYING TO DO THE PROTECTING, ACTUALLY.

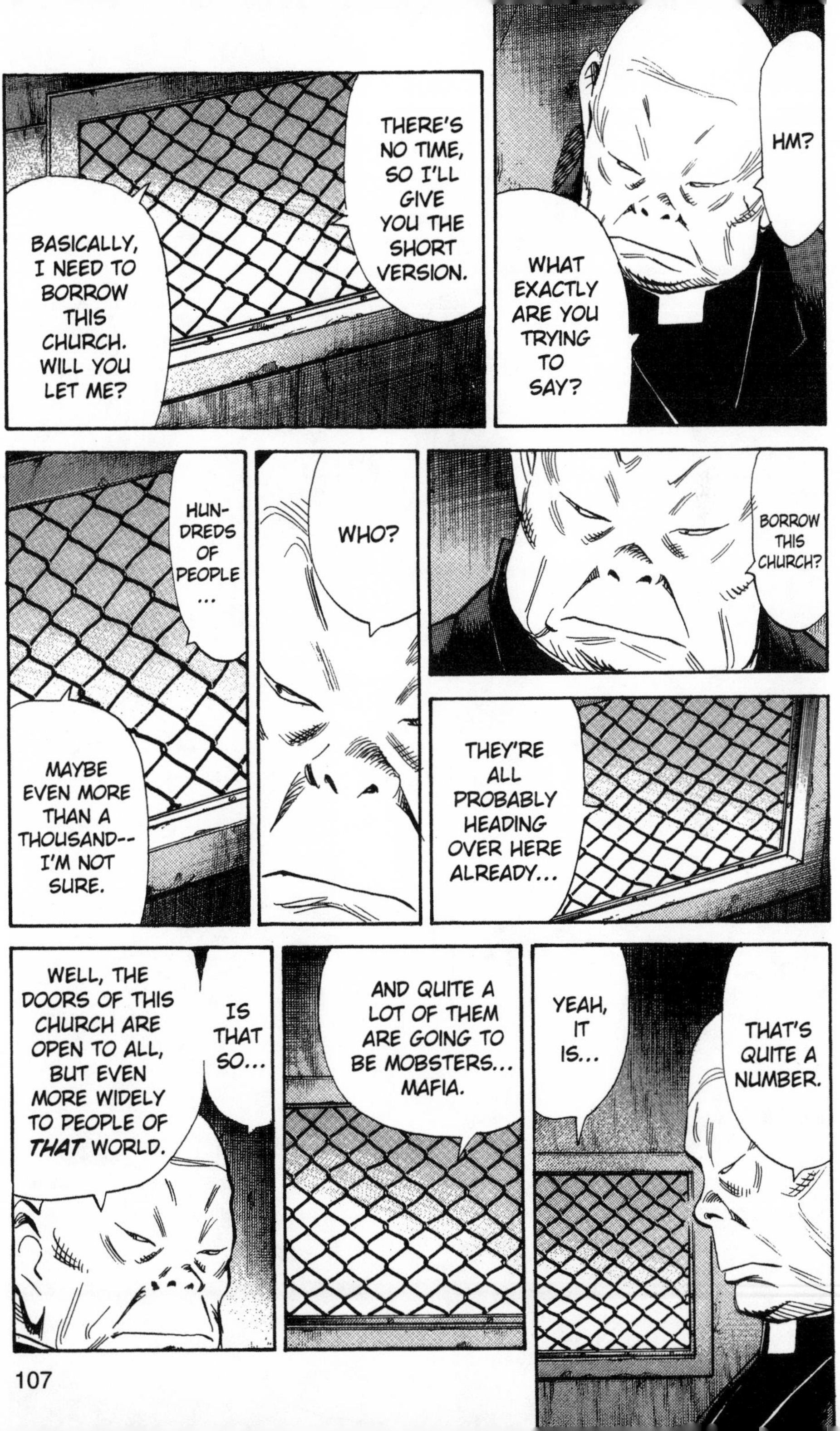
HM?
WHAT EXACTLY ARE YOU TRYING TO SAY?
THERE'S NO TIME, SO I'LL GIVE YOU THE SHORT VERSION.
BASICALLY, I NEED TO BORROW THIS CHURCH. WILL YOU LET ME?
BORROW THIS CHURCH?
THEY'RE ALL PROBABLY HEADING OVER HERE ALREADY...
WHO?
HUN-DREDS OF PEOPLE ...
MAYBE EVEN MORE THAN A THOUSAND-- I'M NOT SURE.
THAT'S QUITE A NUMBER.
YEAH, IT IS...
AND QUITE A LOT OF THEM ARE GOING TO BE MOBSTERS... MAFIA.
IS THAT SO...
WELL, THE DOORS OF THIS CHURCH ARE OPEN TO ALL, BUT EVEN MORE WIDELY TO PEOPLE OF *THAT* WORLD.

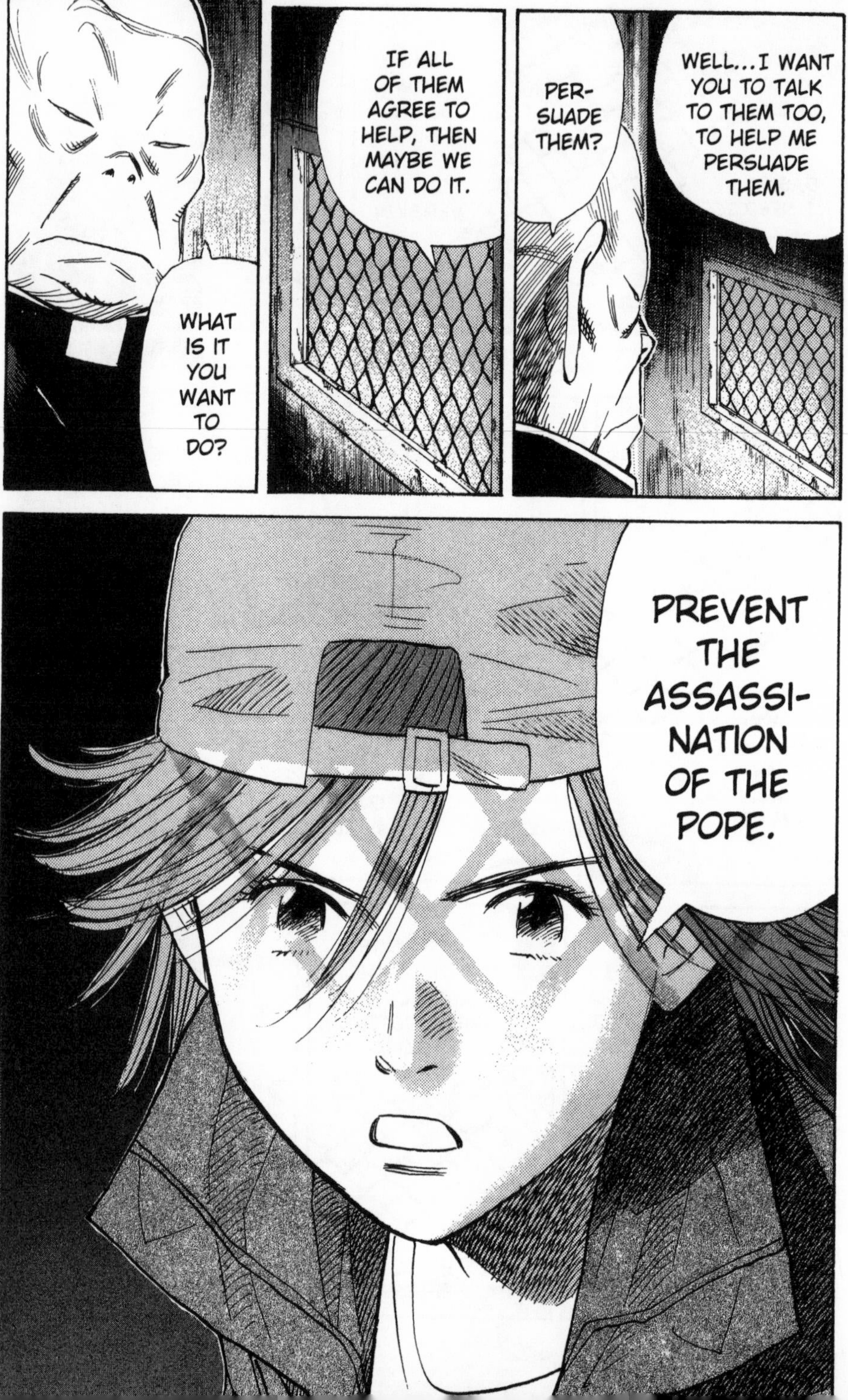
WELL...I WANT YOU TO TALK TO THEM TOO, TO HELP ME PERSUADE THEM.
PER-SUADE THEM?
IF ALL OF THEM AGREE TO HELP, THEN MAYBE WE CAN DO IT.
WHAT IS IT YOU WANT TO DO?
PREVENT THE ASSASSI-NATION OF THE POPE.

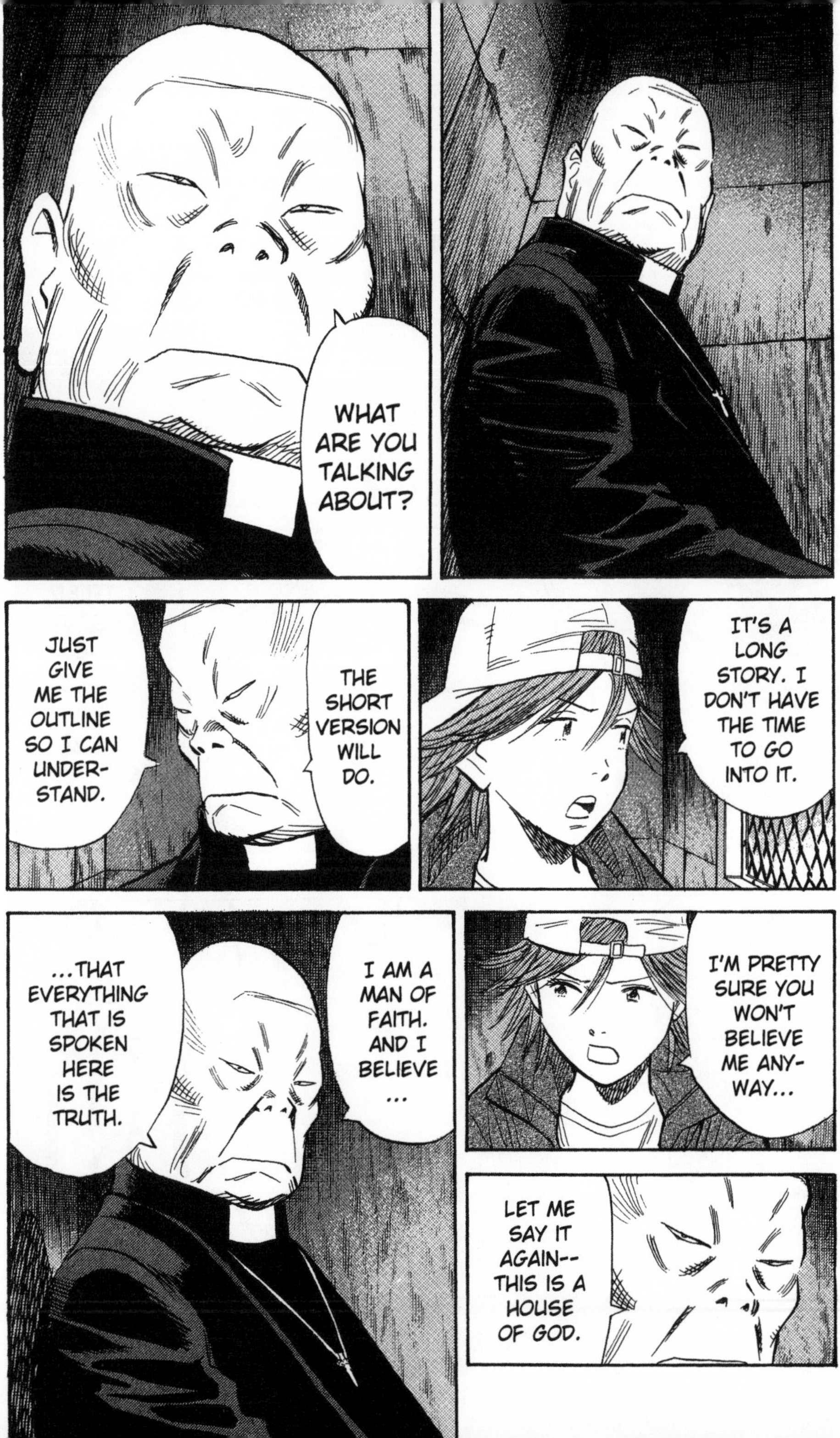
WHAT ARE YOU TALKING ABOUT?
IT'S A LONG STORY. I DON'T HAVE THE TIME TO GO INTO IT.
THE SHORT VERSION WILL DO.
JUST GIVE ME THE OUTLINE SO I CAN UNDER-STAND.
I'M PRETTY SURE YOU WON'T BELIEVE ME ANY-WAY...
LET ME SAY IT AGAIN-- THIS IS A HOUSE OF GOD.
I AM A MAN OF FAITH. AND I BELIEVE ...
...THAT EVERYTHING THAT IS SPOKEN HERE IS THE TRUTH.

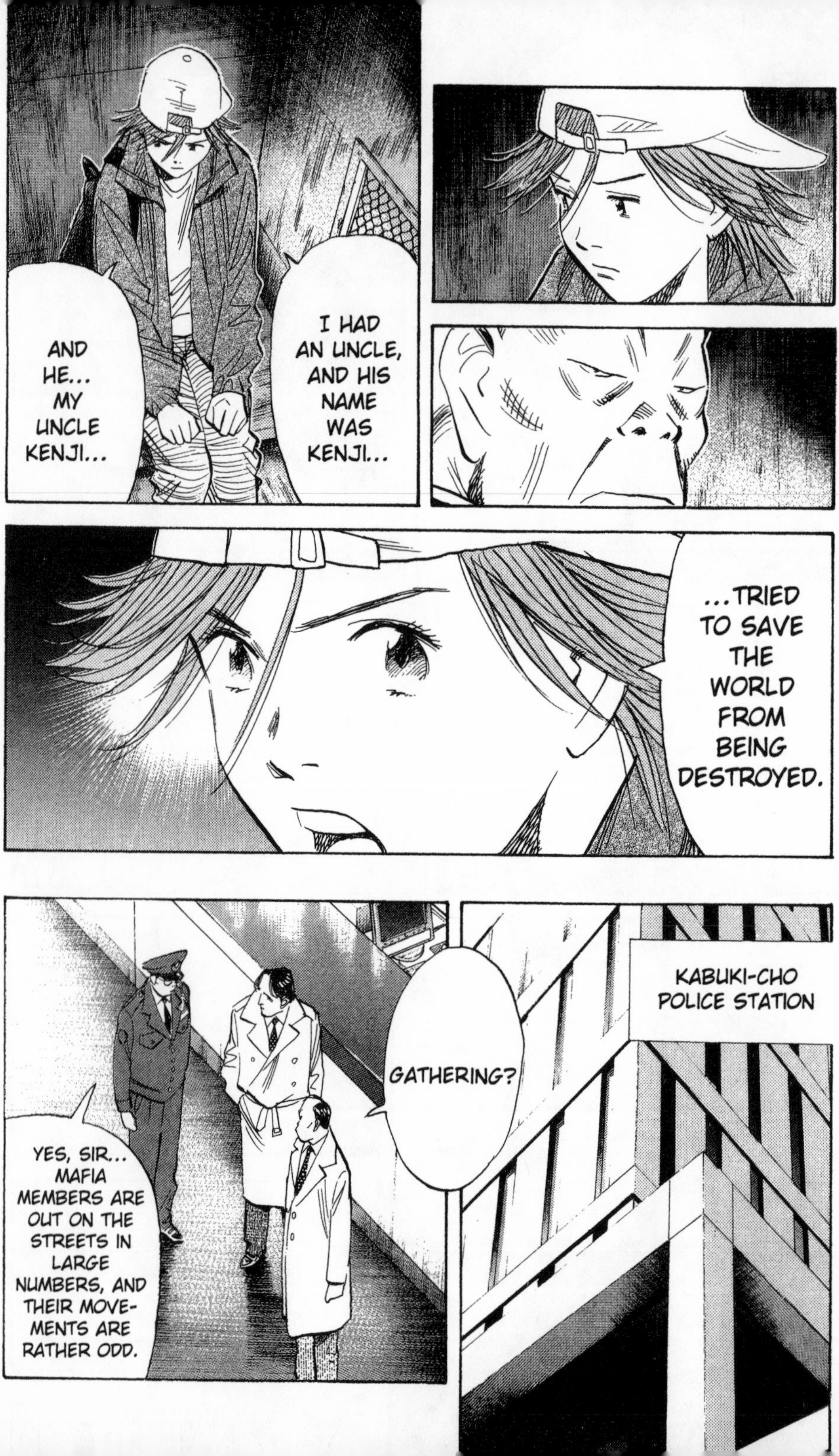
I HAD AN UNCLE, AND HIS NAME WAS KENJI...
AND HE... MY UNCLE KENJI...
...TRIED TO SAVE THE WORLD FROM BEING DESTROYED.
KABUKI-CHO POLICE STATION
GATHERING?
YES, SIR... MAFIA MEMBERS ARE OUT ON THE STREETS IN LARGE NUMBERS, AND THEIR MOVE-MENTS ARE RATHER ODD.

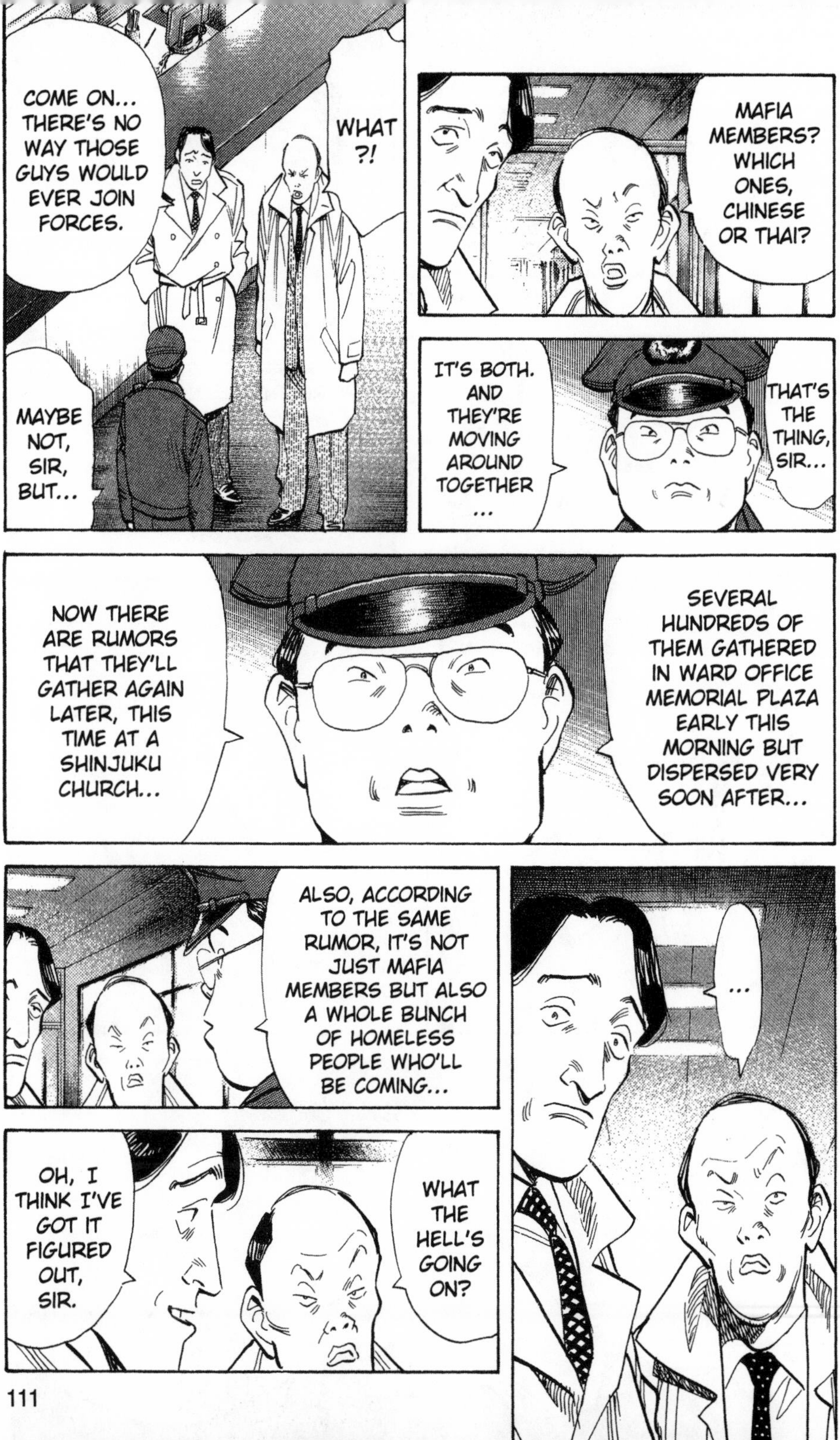
MAFIA MEMBERS? WHICH ONES, CHINESE OR THAI?
THAT'S THE THING, SIR...
IT'S BOTH. AND THEY'RE MOVING AROUND TOGETHER ...
WHAT ?!
COME ON... THERE'S NO WAY THOSE GUYS WOULD EVER JOIN FORCES.
MAYBE NOT, SIR, BUT...
SEVERAL HUNDREDS OF THEM GATHERED IN WARD OFFICE MEMORIAL PLAZA EARLY THIS MORNING BUT DISPERSED VERY SOON AFTER...
NOW THERE ARE RUMORS THAT THEY'LL GATHER AGAIN LATER, THIS TIME AT A SHINJUKU CHURCH...
...
ALSO, ACCORDING TO THE SAME RUMOR, IT'S NOT JUST MAFIA MEMBERS BUT ALSO A WHOLE BUNCH OF HOMELESS PEOPLE WHO'LL BE COMING...
WHAT THE HELL'S GOING ON?
OH, I THINK I'VE GOT IT FIGURED OUT, SIR.

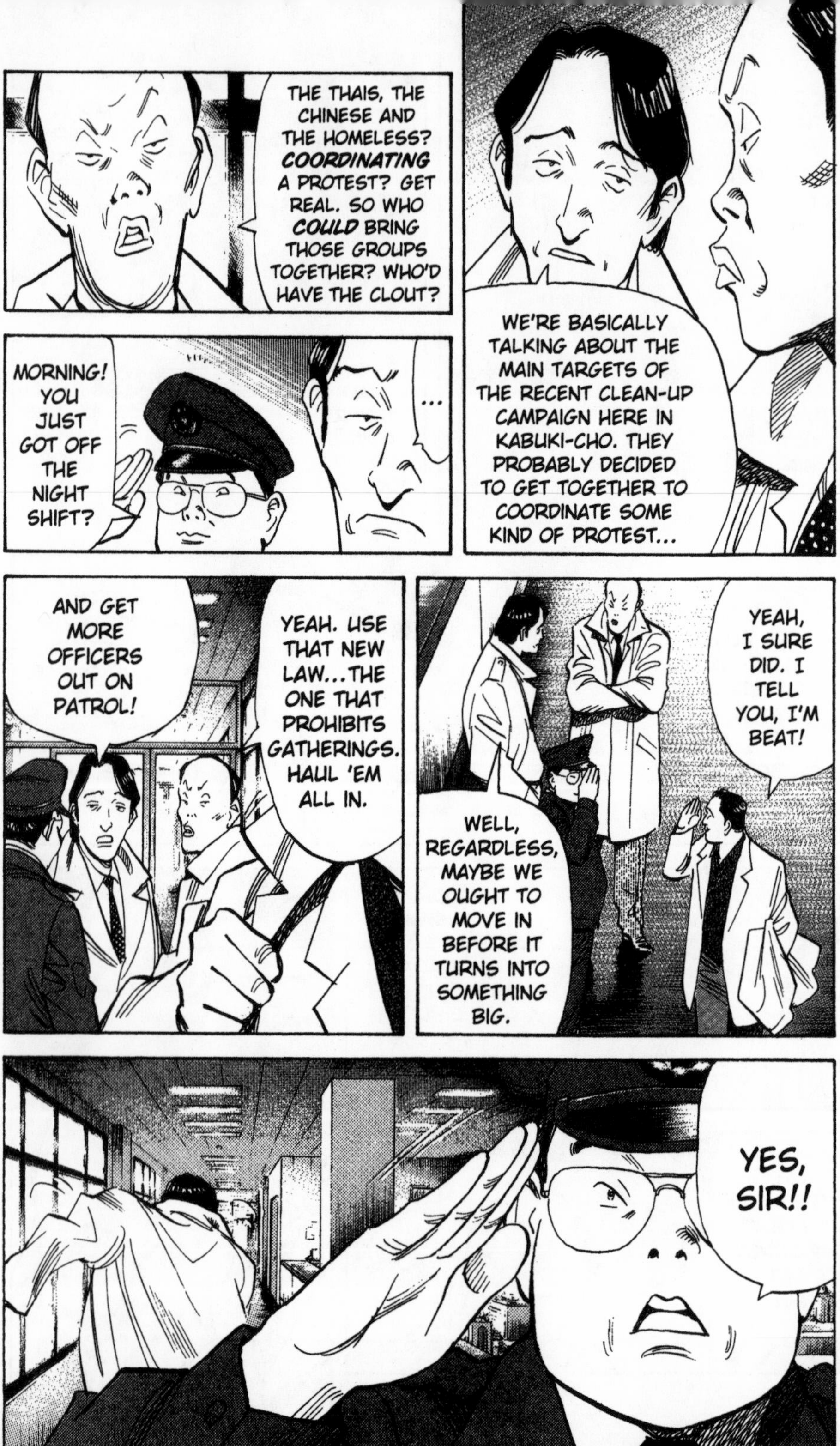
WE'RE BASICALLY TALKING ABOUT THE MAIN TARGETS OF THE RECENT CLEAN-UP CAMPAIGN HERE IN KABUKI-CHO. THEY PROBABLY DECIDED TO GET TOGETHER TO COORDINATE SOME KIND OF PROTEST...
THE THAIS, THE CHINESE AND THE HOMELESS? COORDINATING A PROTEST? GET REAL. SO WHO COULD BRING THOSE GROUPS TOGETHER? WHO'D HAVE THE CLOUT?
...
MORNING! YOU JUST GOT OFF THE NIGHT SHIFT?
YEAH, I SURE DID. I TELL YOU, I'M BEAT!
WELL, REGARDLESS, MAYBE WE OUGHT TO MOVE IN BEFORE IT TURNS INTO SOMETHING BIG.
YEAH. USE THAT NEW LAW...THE ONE THAT PROHIBITS GATHERINGS. HAUL 'EM ALL IN.
AND GET MORE OFFICERS OUT ON PATROL!
YES, SIR!!

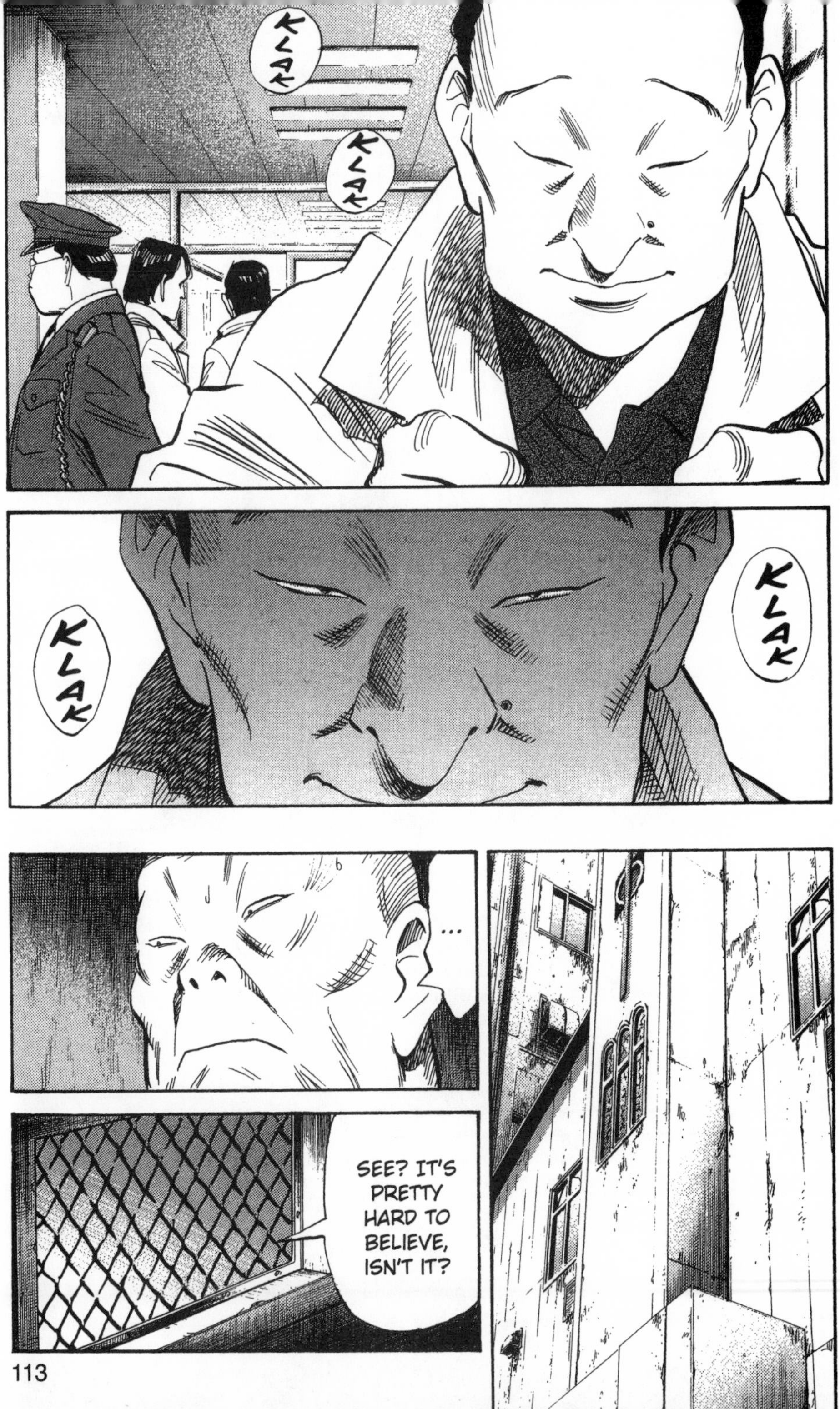
KLAK
KLAK
KLAK
KLAK
...
SEE? IT'S PRETTY HARD TO BELIEVE, ISN'T IT?

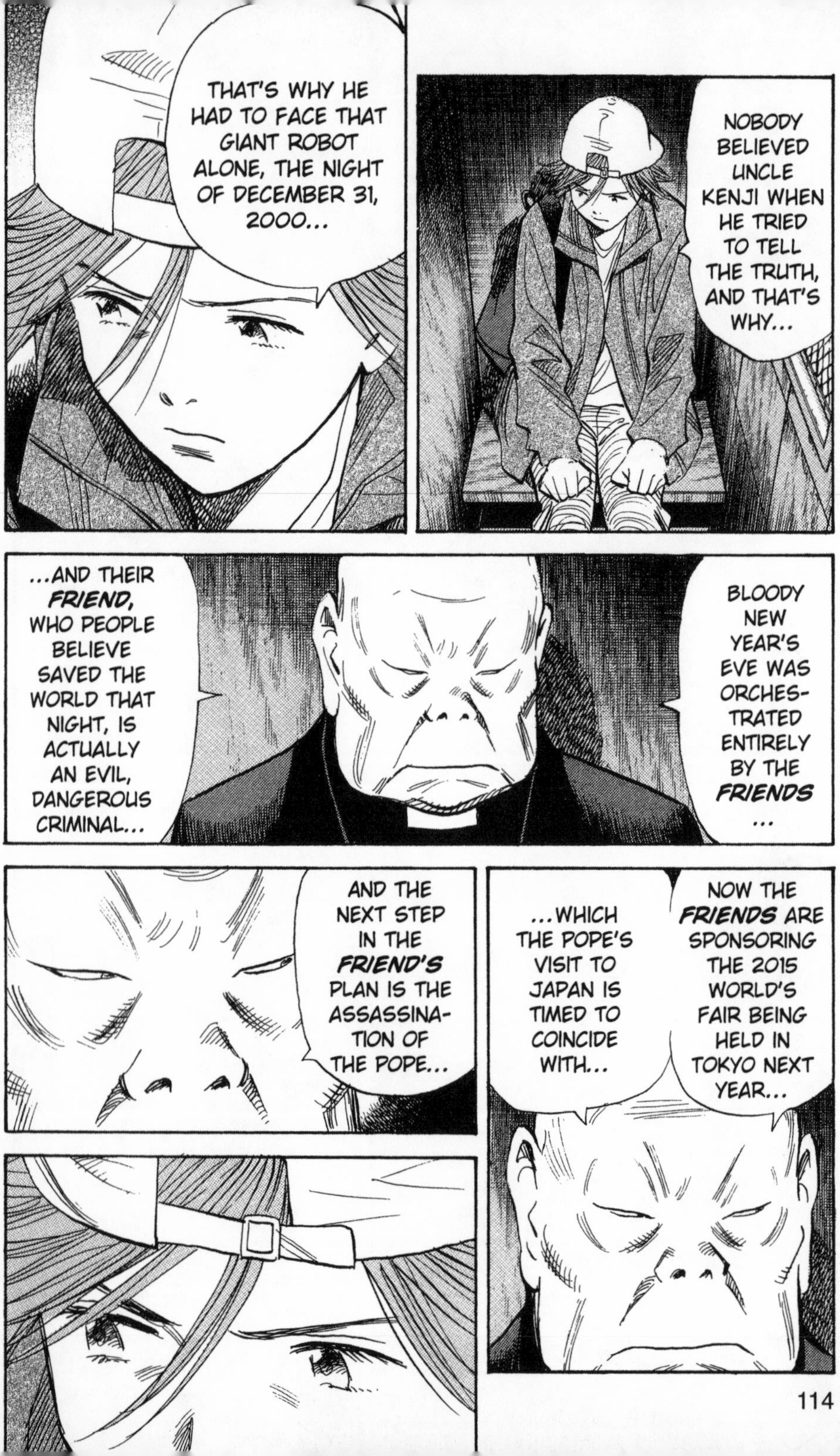

NOBODY BELIEVED UNCLE KENJI WHEN HE TRIED TO TELL THE TRUTH, AND THAT'S WHY...
THAT'S WHY HE HAD TO FACE THAT GIANT ROBOT ALONE, THE NIGHT OF DECEMBER 31, 2000...
BLOODY NEW YEAR'S EVE WAS ORCHES-TRATED ENTIRELY BY THE *FRIENDS* ...
...AND THEIR *FRIEND,* WHO PEOPLE BELIEVE SAVED THE WORLD THAT NIGHT, IS ACTUALLY AN EVIL, DANGEROUS CRIMINAL...
NOW THE *FRIENDS* ARE SPONSORING THE 2015 WORLD'S FAIR BEING HELD IN TOKYO NEXT YEAR...
...WHICH THE POPE'S VISIT TO JAPAN IS TIMED TO COINCIDE WITH...
AND THE NEXT STEP IN THE *FRIEND'S* PLAN IS THE ASSASSINA-TION OF THE POPE...

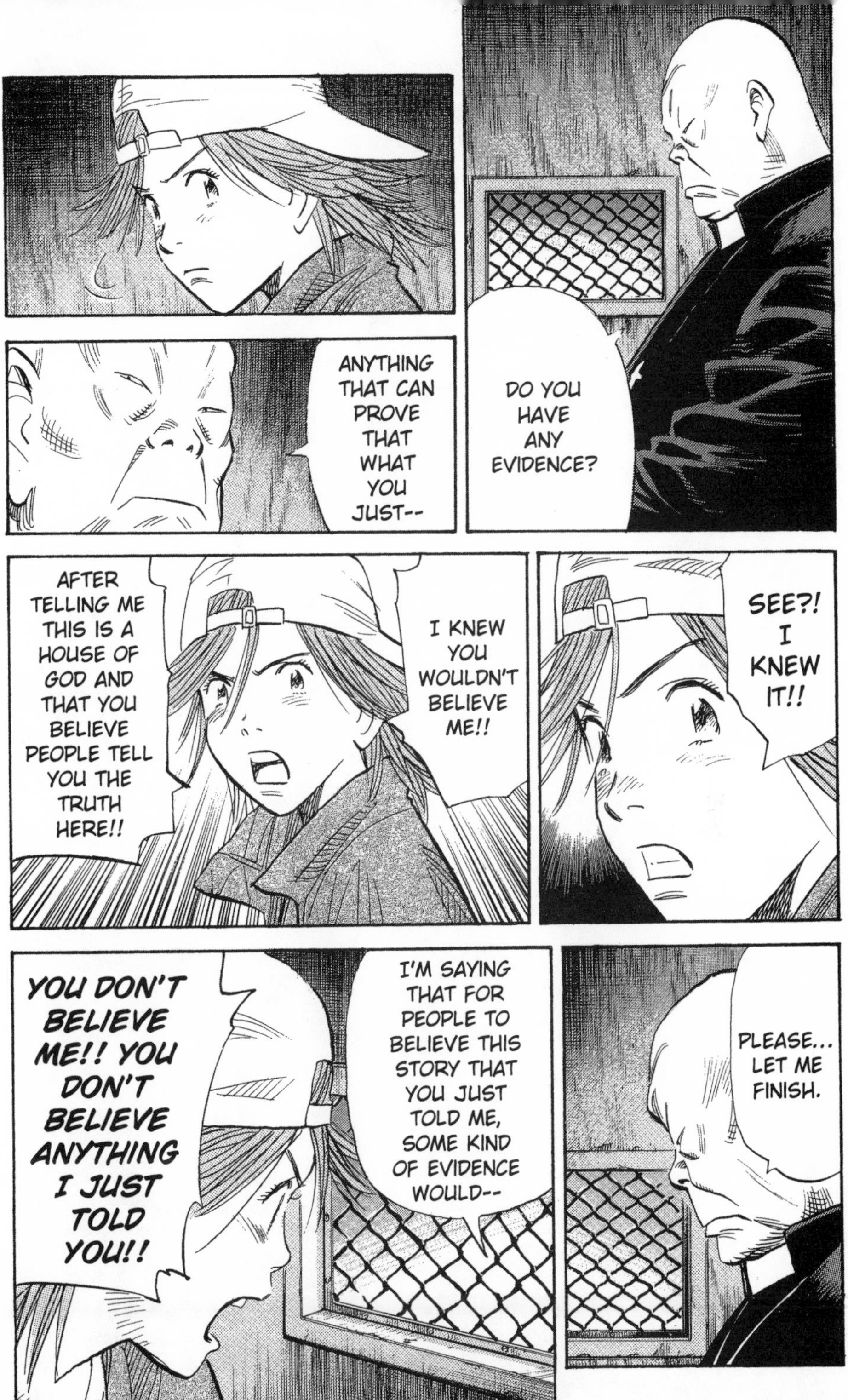
DO YOU HAVE ANY EVIDENCE?
ANYTHING THAT CAN PROVE THAT WHAT YOU JUST--
SEE?! I KNEW IT!!
I KNEW YOU WOULDN'T BELIEVE ME!!
AFTER TELLING ME THIS IS A HOUSE OF GOD AND THAT YOU BELIEVE PEOPLE TELL YOU THE TRUTH HERE!!
PLEASE... LET ME FINISH.
I'M SAYING THAT FOR PEOPLE TO BELIEVE THIS STORY THAT YOU JUST TOLD ME, SOME KIND OF EVIDENCE WOULD--
YOU DON'T BELIEVE ME!! YOU DON'T BELIEVE ANYTHING I JUST TOLD YOU!!

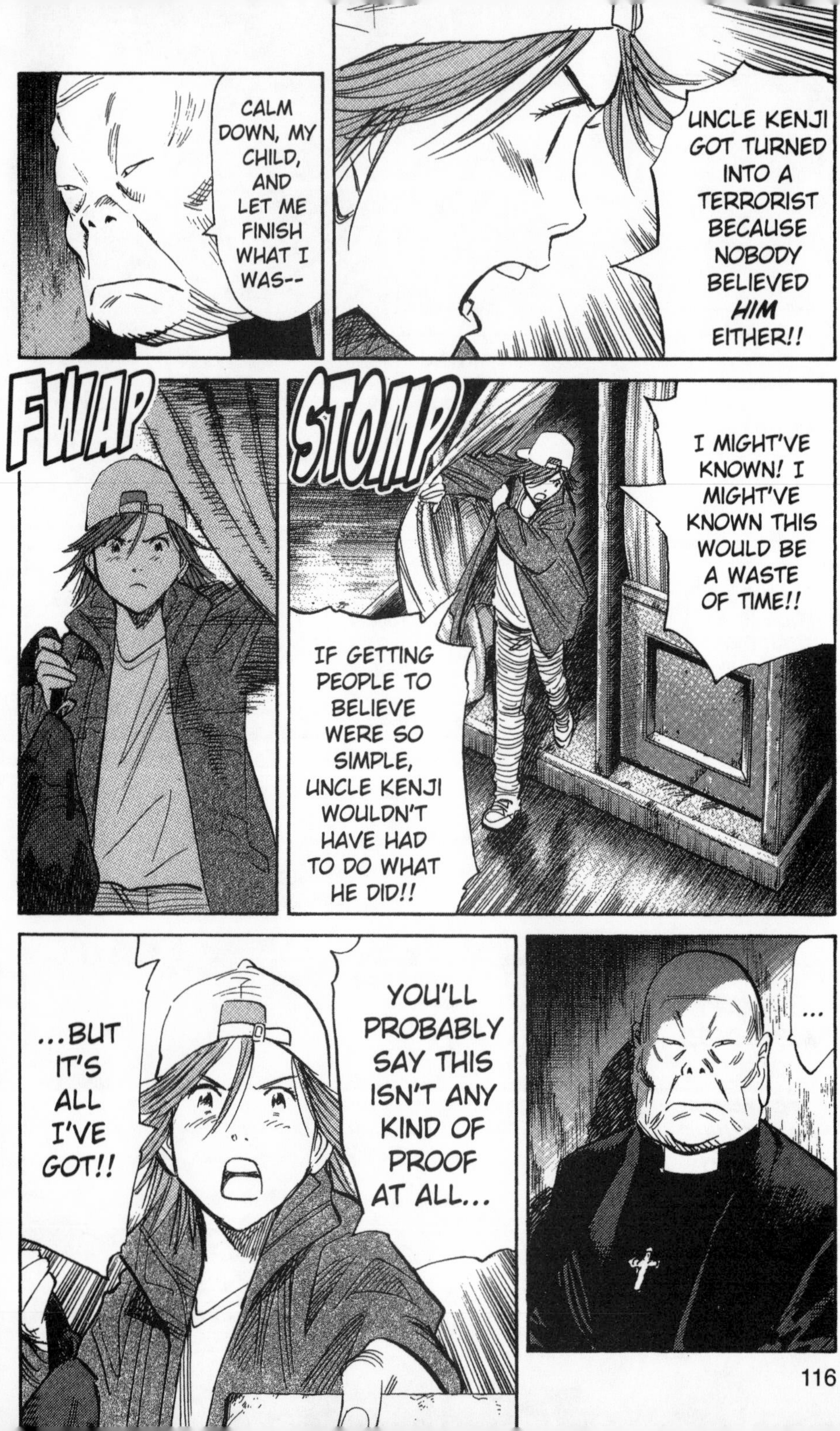
UNCLE KENJI GOT TURNED INTO A TERRORIST BECAUSE NOBODY BELIEVED *HIM* EITHER!!
CALM DOWN, MY CHILD, AND LET ME FINISH WHAT I WAS--
STOMP
I MIGHT'VE KNOWN! I MIGHT'VE KNOWN THIS WOULD BE A WASTE OF TIME!!
IF GETTING PEOPLE TO BELIEVE WERE SO SIMPLE, UNCLE KENJI WOULDN'T HAVE HAD TO DO WHAT HE DID!!
FWAP
...
YOU'LL PROBABLY SAY THIS ISN'T ANY KIND OF PROOF AT ALL...
...BUT IT'S ALL I'VE GOT!!

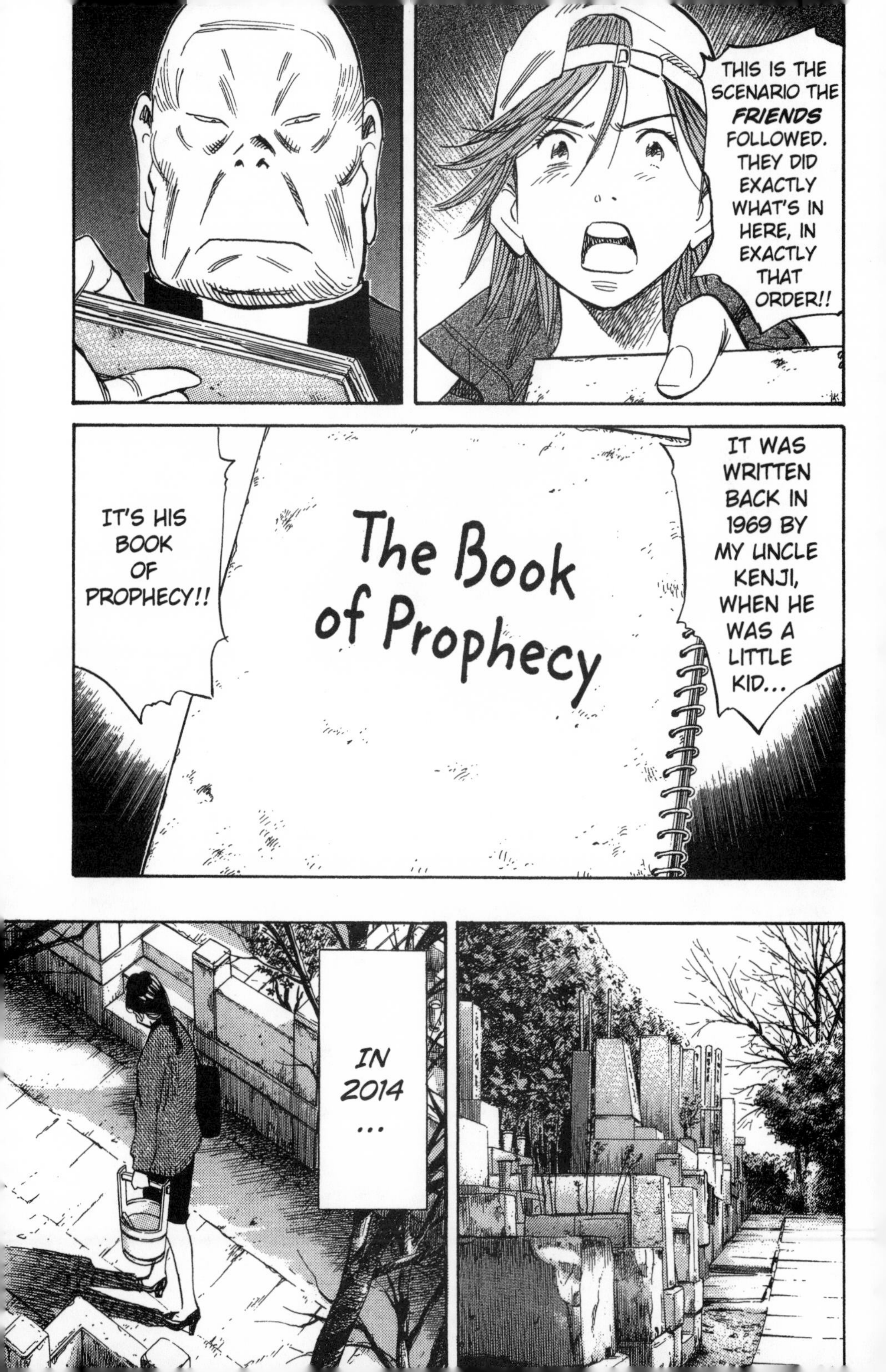
THIS IS THE SCENARIO THE FRIENDS FOLLOWED. THEY DID EXACTLY WHAT'S IN HERE, IN EXACTLY THAT ORDER!!
IT WAS WRITTEN BACK IN 1969 BY MY UNCLE KENJI, WHEN HE WAS A LITTLE KID...
The Book of Prophecy
IT'S HIS BOOK OF PROPHECY!!
IN 2014 ...

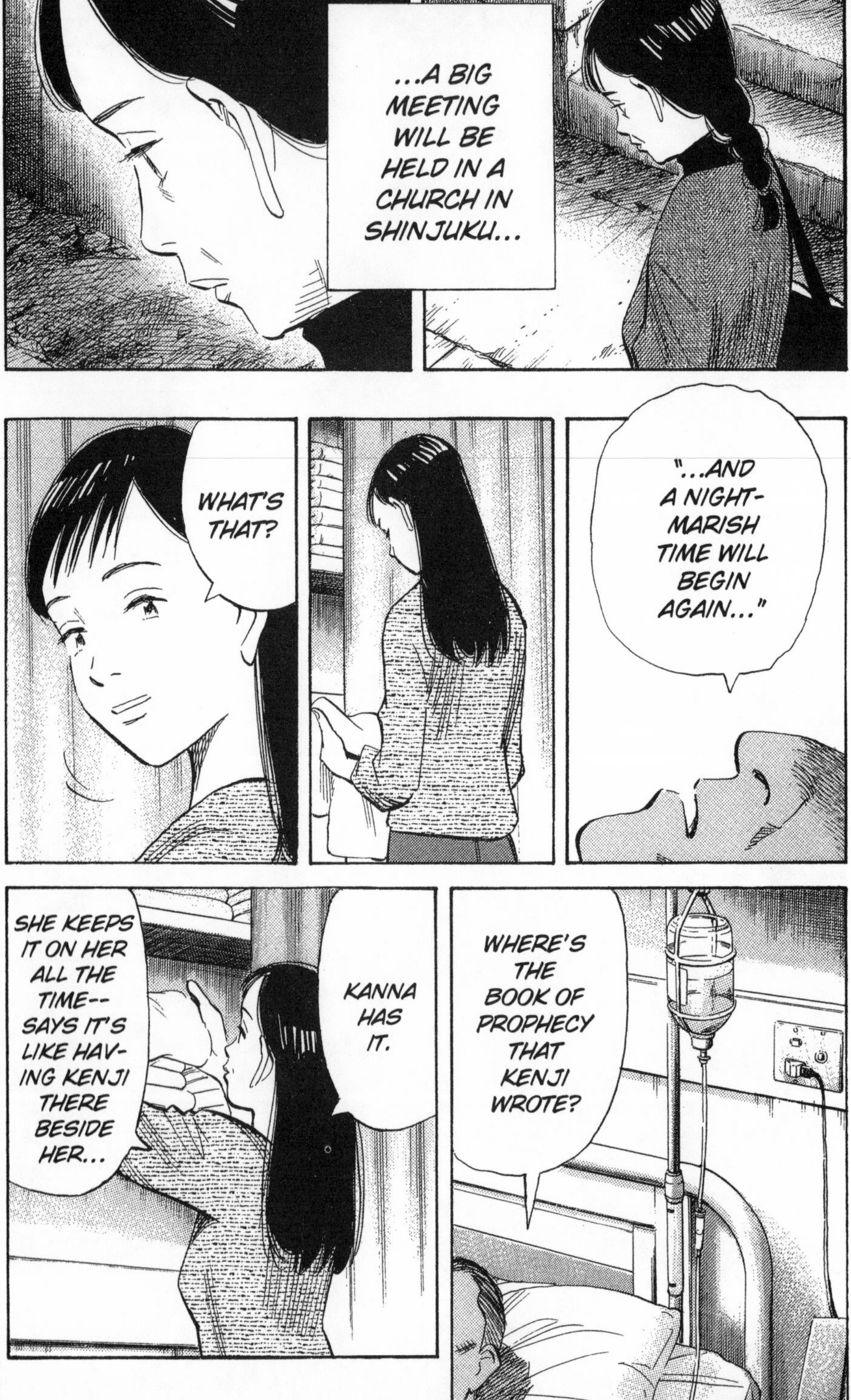
...A BIG MEETING WILL BE HELD IN A CHURCH IN SHINJUKU...
"...AND A NIGHT-MARISH TIME WILL BEGIN AGAIN..."
WHAT'S THAT?
WHERE'S THE BOOK OF PROPHECY THAT KENJI WROTE?
KANNA HAS IT.
SHE KEEPS IT ON HER ALL THE TIME-- SAYS IT'S LIKE HAV-ING KENJI THERE BESIDE HER...

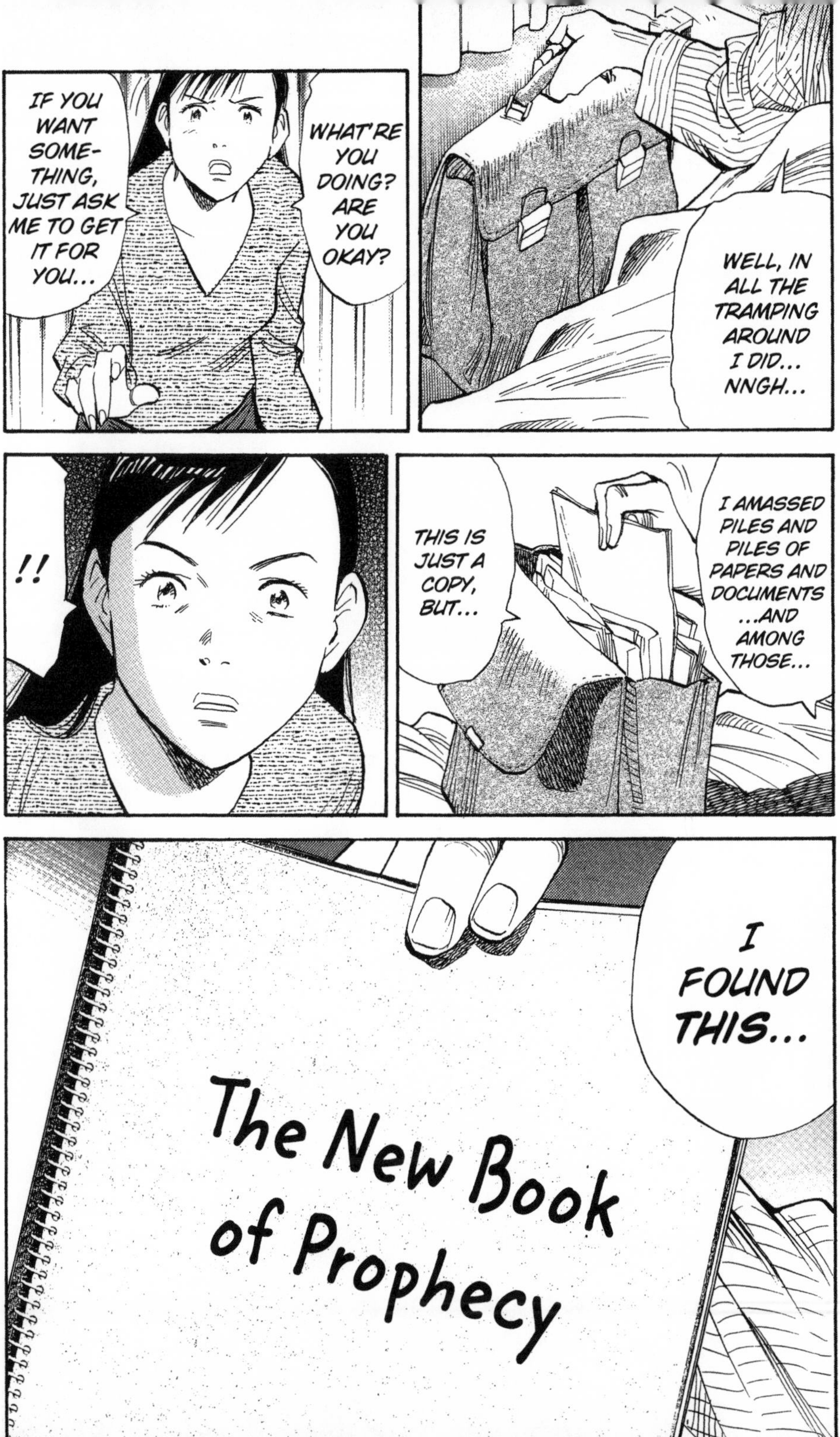
WELL, IN ALL THE TRAMPING AROUND I DID... NNGH...
WHAT'RE YOU DOING? ARE YOU OKAY?
IF YOU WANT SOME-THING, JUST ASK ME TO GET IT FOR YOU...
I AMASSED PILES AND PILES OF PAPERS AND DOCUMENTS ...AND AMONG THOSE...
THIS IS JUST A COPY, BUT...
!!
I FOUND **THIS...**
The New Book of Prophecy

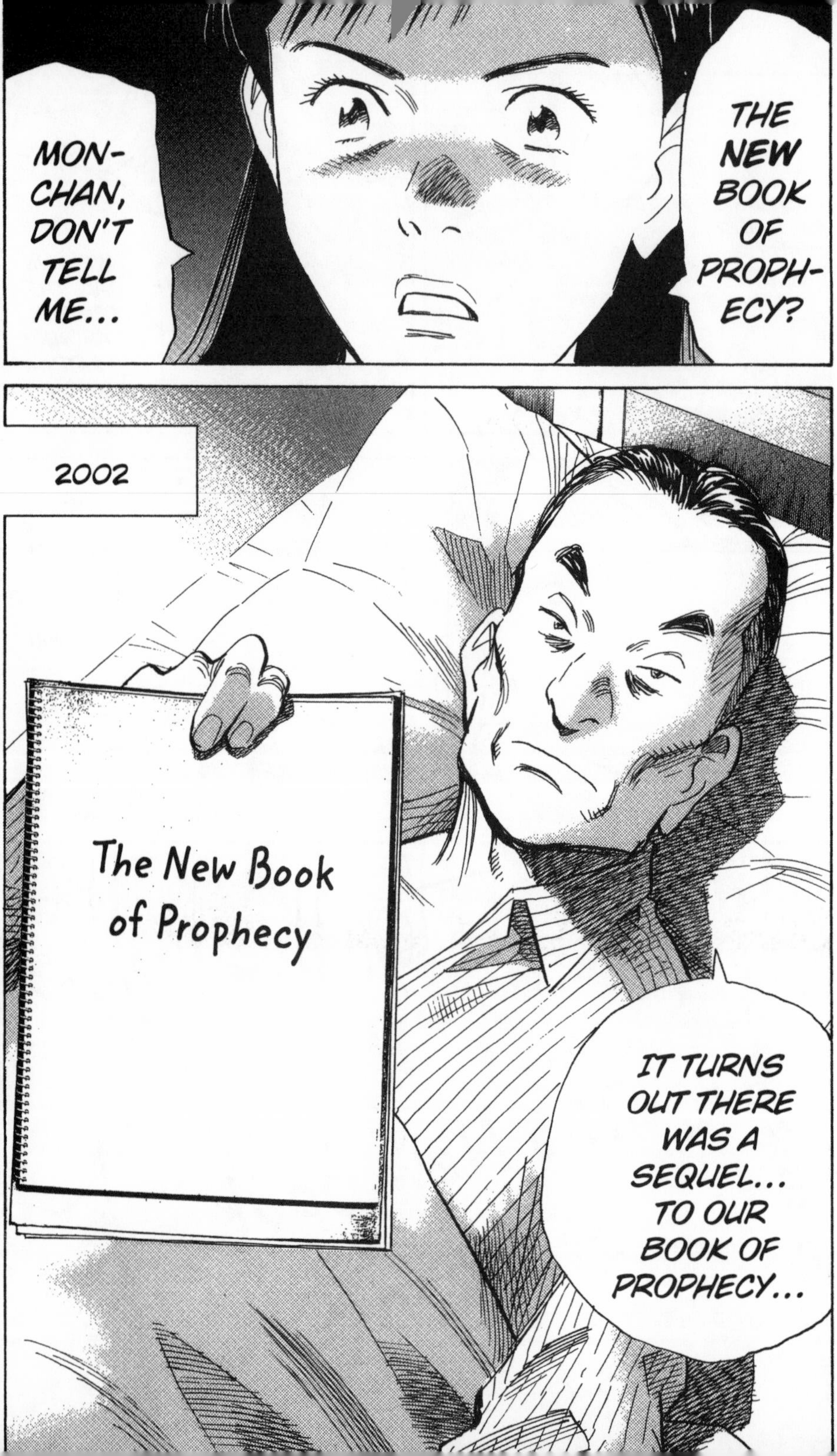

THE NEW BOOK OF PROPH-ECY?
MON-CHAN, DON'T TELL ME...
2002
The New Book of Prophecy
IT TURNS OUT THERE WAS A SEQUEL... TO OUR BOOK OF PROPHECY...

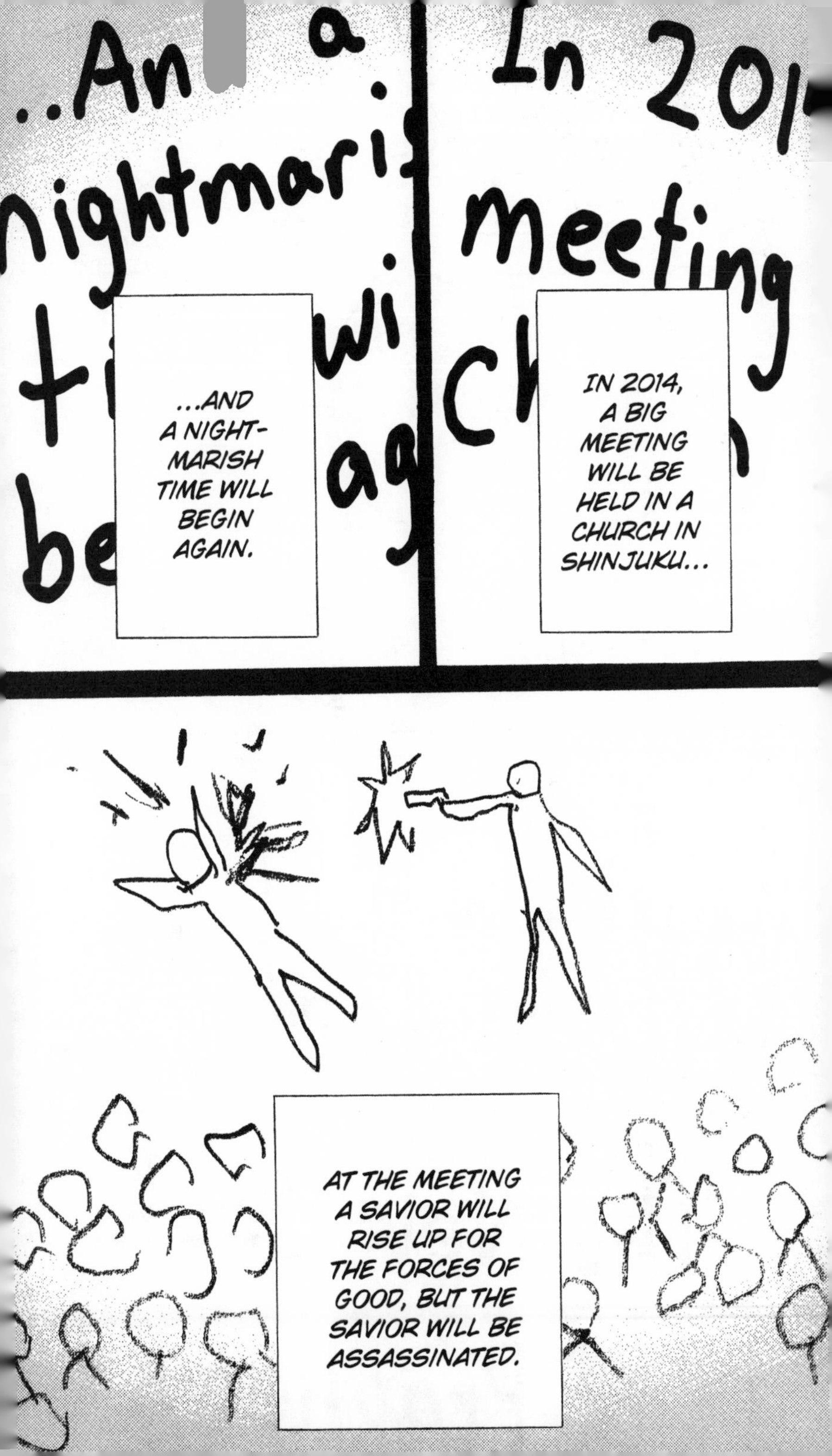
IN 2014, A BIG MEETING WILL BE HELD IN A CHURCH IN SHINJUKU...
...AND A NIGHT-MARISH TIME WILL BEGIN AGAIN.
AT THE MEETING A SAVIOR WILL RISE UP FOR THE FORCES OF GOOD, BUT THE SAVIOR WILL BE ASSASSINATED.

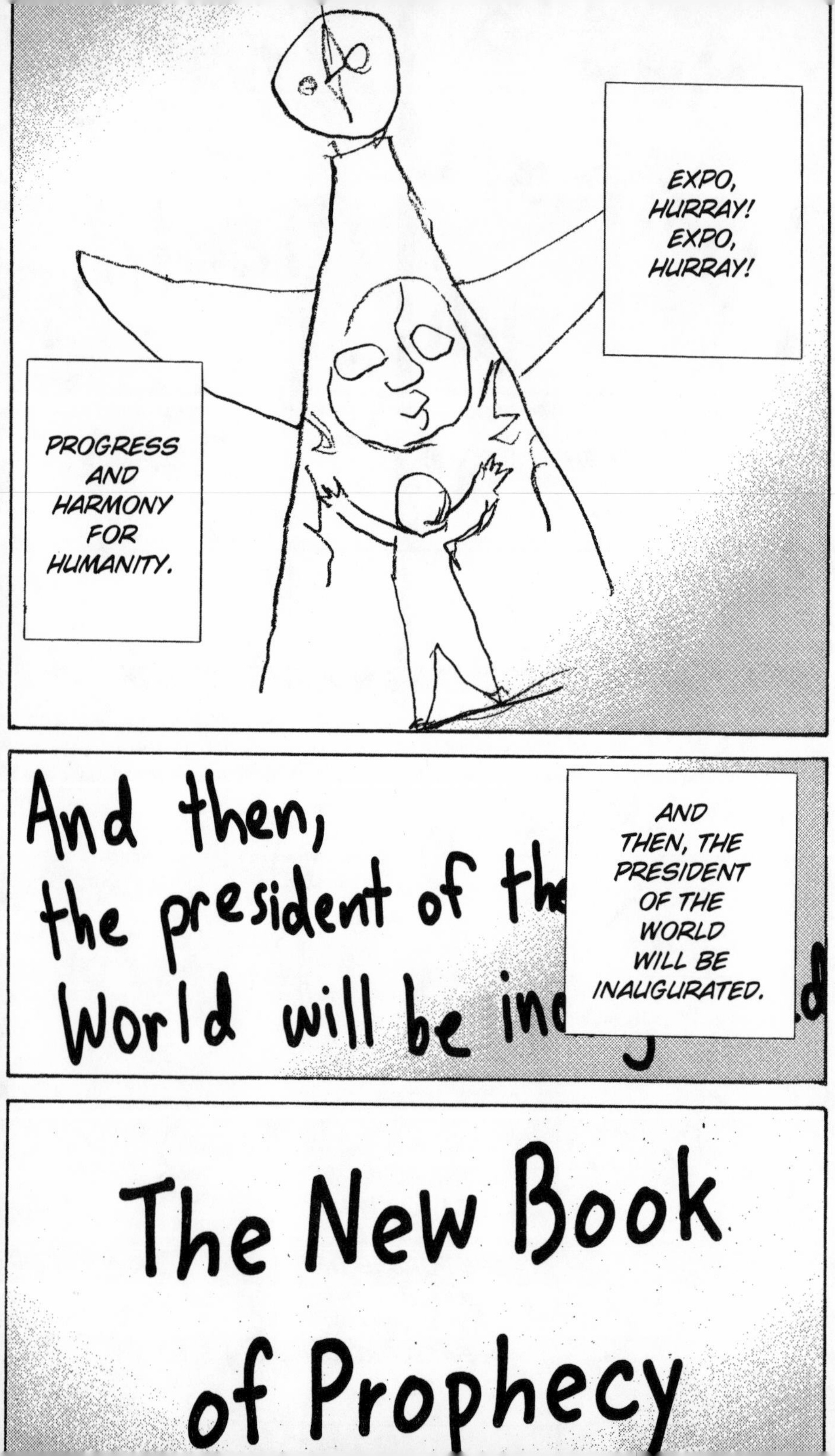

EXPO, HURRAY! EXPO, HURRAY!
PROGRESS AND HARMONY FOR HUMANITY.
AND THEN, THE PRESIDENT OF THE WORLD WILL BE INAUGURATED.
And then,
the president of th
World will be in
The New Book of Prophecy

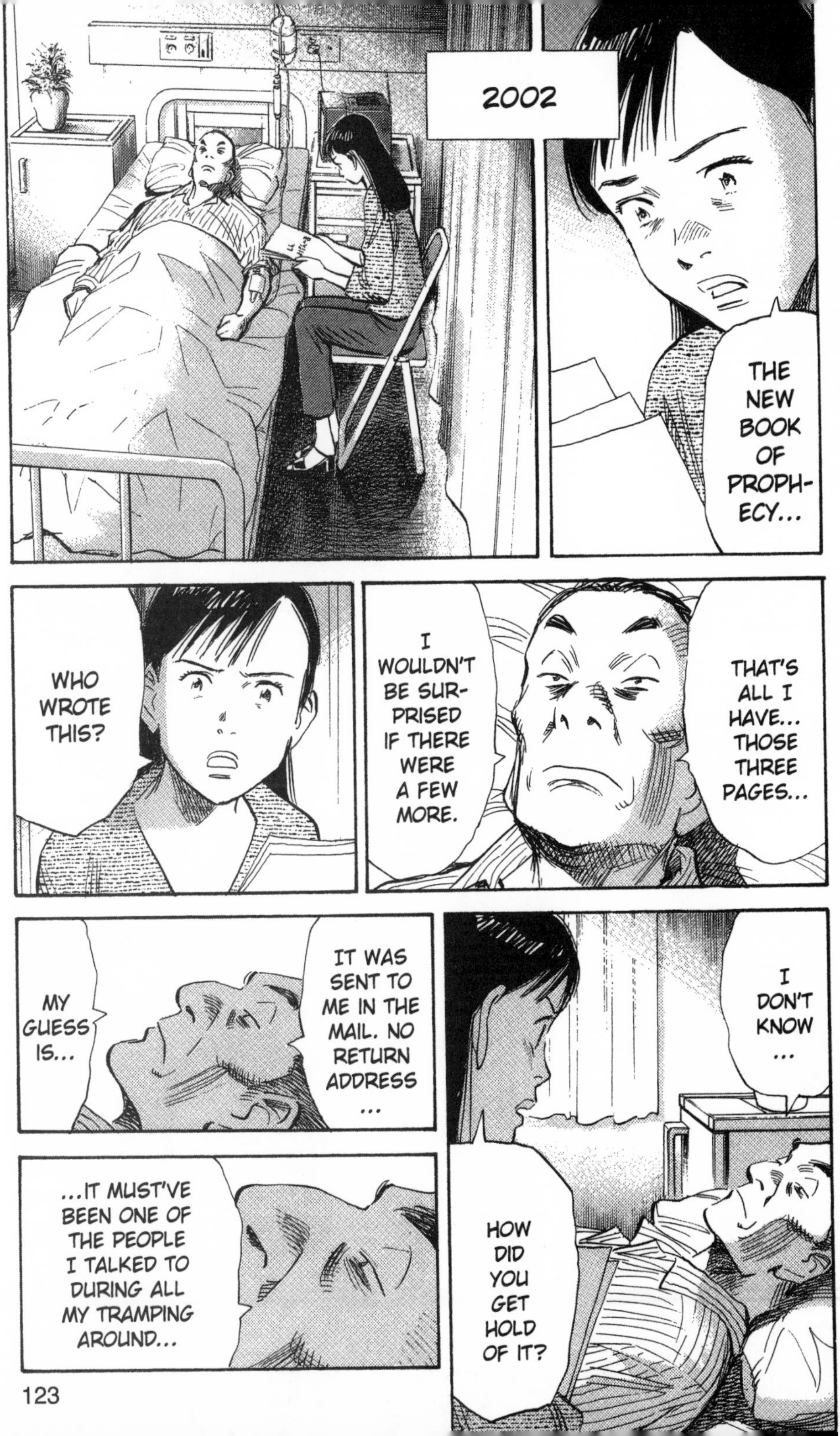
2002
THE NEW BOOK OF PROPHECY...
THAT'S ALL I HAVE... THOSE THREE PAGES...
I WOULDN'T BE SURPRISED IF THERE WERE A FEW MORE.
WHO WROTE THIS?
I DON'T KNOW ...
HOW DID YOU GET HOLD OF IT?
IT WAS SENT TO ME IN THE MAIL. NO RETURN ADDRESS ...
MY GUESS IS...
...IT MUST'VE BEEN ONE OF THE PEOPLE I TALKED TO DURING ALL MY TRAMPING AROUND...

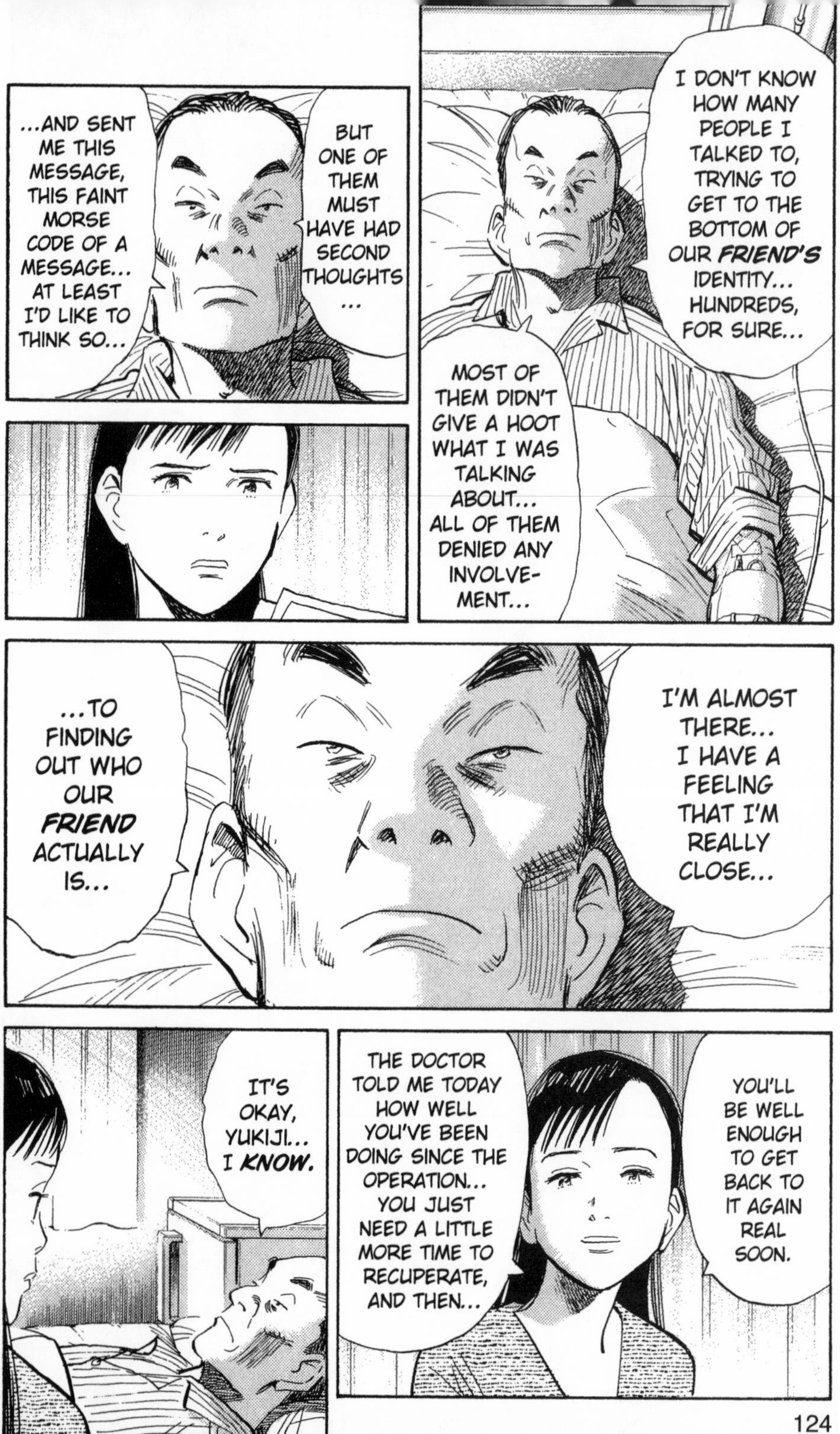
I DON'T KNOW HOW MANY PEOPLE I TALKED TO, TRYING TO GET TO THE BOTTOM OF OUR ***FRIEND'S*** IDENTITY... HUNDREDS, FOR SURE...
MOST OF THEM DIDN'T GIVE A HOOT WHAT I WAS TALKING ABOUT... ALL OF THEM DENIED ANY INVOLVE-MENT...
BUT ONE OF THEM MUST HAVE HAD SECOND THOUGHTS...
...AND SENT ME THIS MESSAGE, THIS FAINT MORSE CODE OF A MESSAGE... AT LEAST I'D LIKE TO THINK SO...
I'M ALMOST THERE... I HAVE A FEELING THAT I'M REALLY CLOSE...
...TO FINDING OUT WHO OUR ***FRIEND*** ACTUALLY IS...
YOU'LL BE WELL ENOUGH TO GET BACK TO IT AGAIN REAL SOON.
THE DOCTOR TOLD ME TODAY HOW WELL YOU'VE BEEN DOING SINCE THE OPERATION... YOU JUST NEED A LITTLE MORE TIME TO RECUPERATE, AND THEN...
IT'S OKAY, YUKIJI... I ***KNOW.***

...

IT'S MY OWN BODY, AFTER ALL...

I CAN TELL I DON'T HAVE MUCH TIME LEFT...

I'M GOING TO KEEP FIGHTING TO THE BITTER END...

BUT...

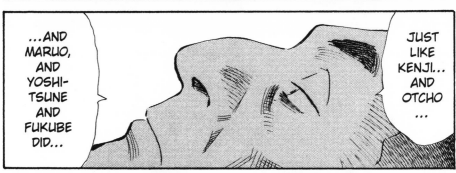

JUST LIKE KENJI... AND OTCHO...

...AND MARUO, AND YOSHI-TSUNE AND FUKUBE DID...

I'M GOING TO FIGHT...

...TO SAVE THE WORLD...

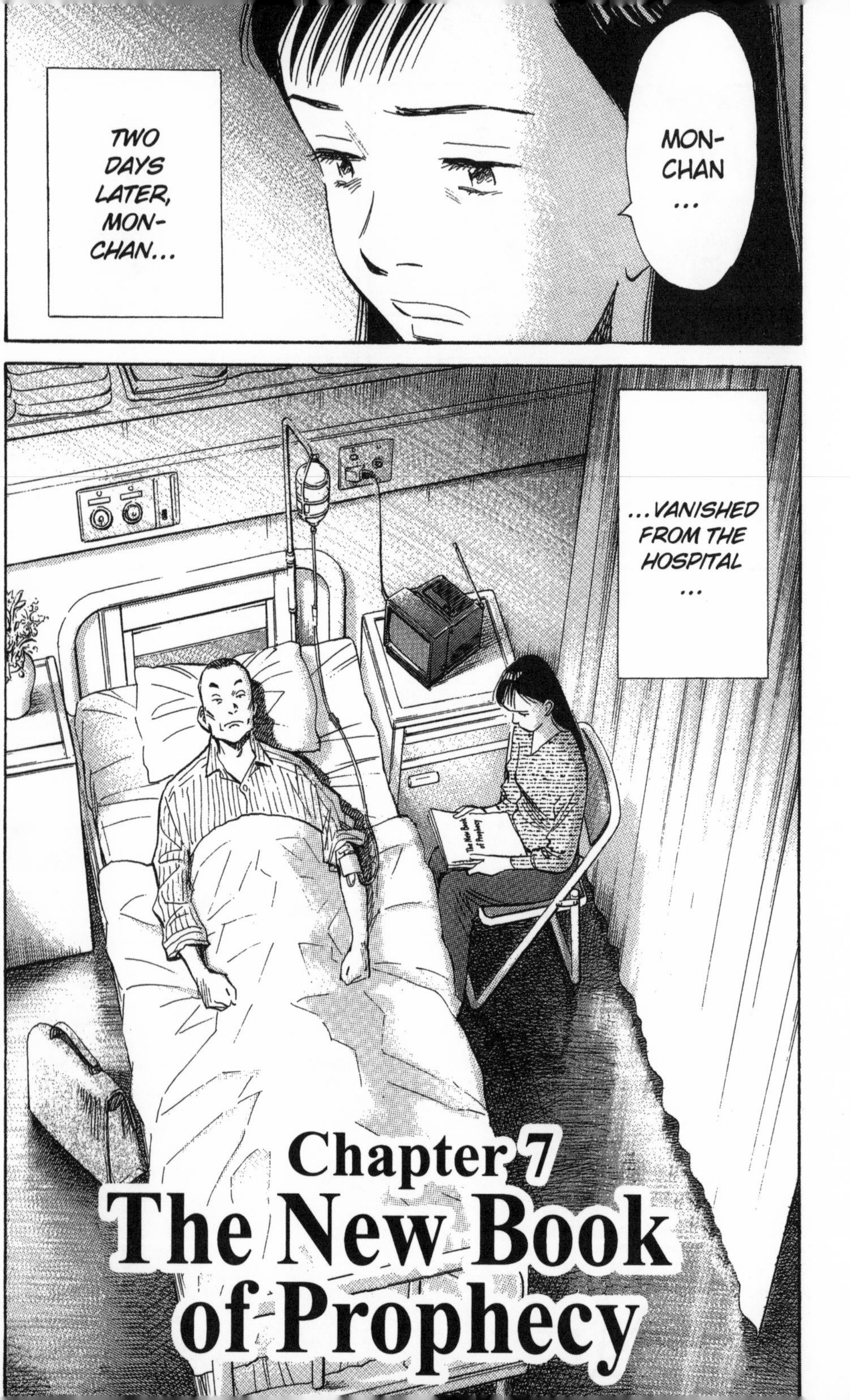
MON-CHAN...
TWO DAYS LATER, MON-CHAN...
...VANISHED FROM THE HOSPITAL...
Chapter 7
The New Book of Prophecy

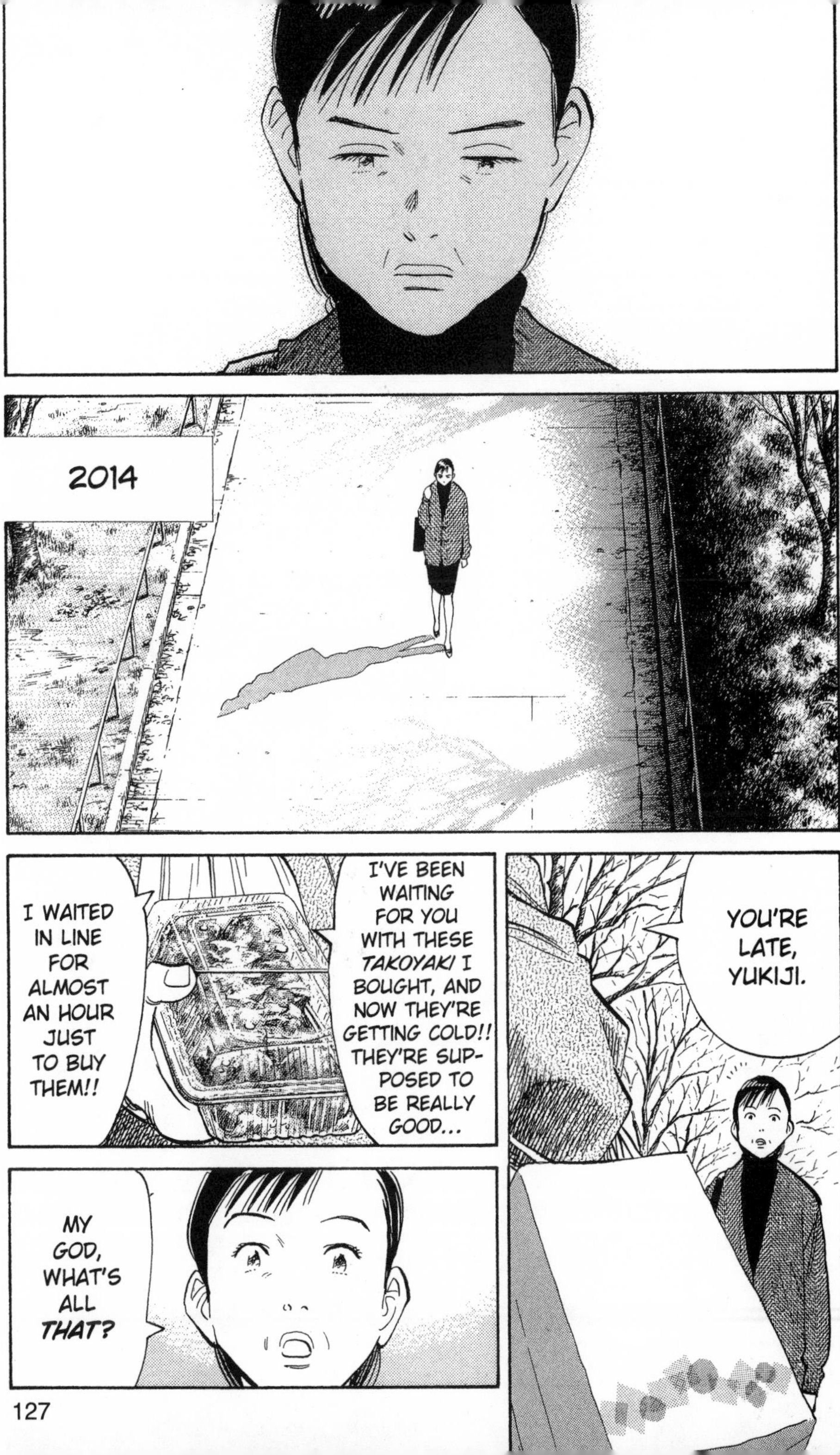
2014
YOU'RE LATE, YUKIJI.
I'VE BEEN WAITING FOR YOU WITH THESE *TAKOYAKI* I BOUGHT, AND NOW THEY'RE GETTING COLD!! THEY'RE SUP-POSED TO BE REALLY GOOD...
I WAITED IN LINE FOR ALMOST AN HOUR JUST TO BUY THEM!!
MY GOD, WHAT'S ALL ***THAT***?

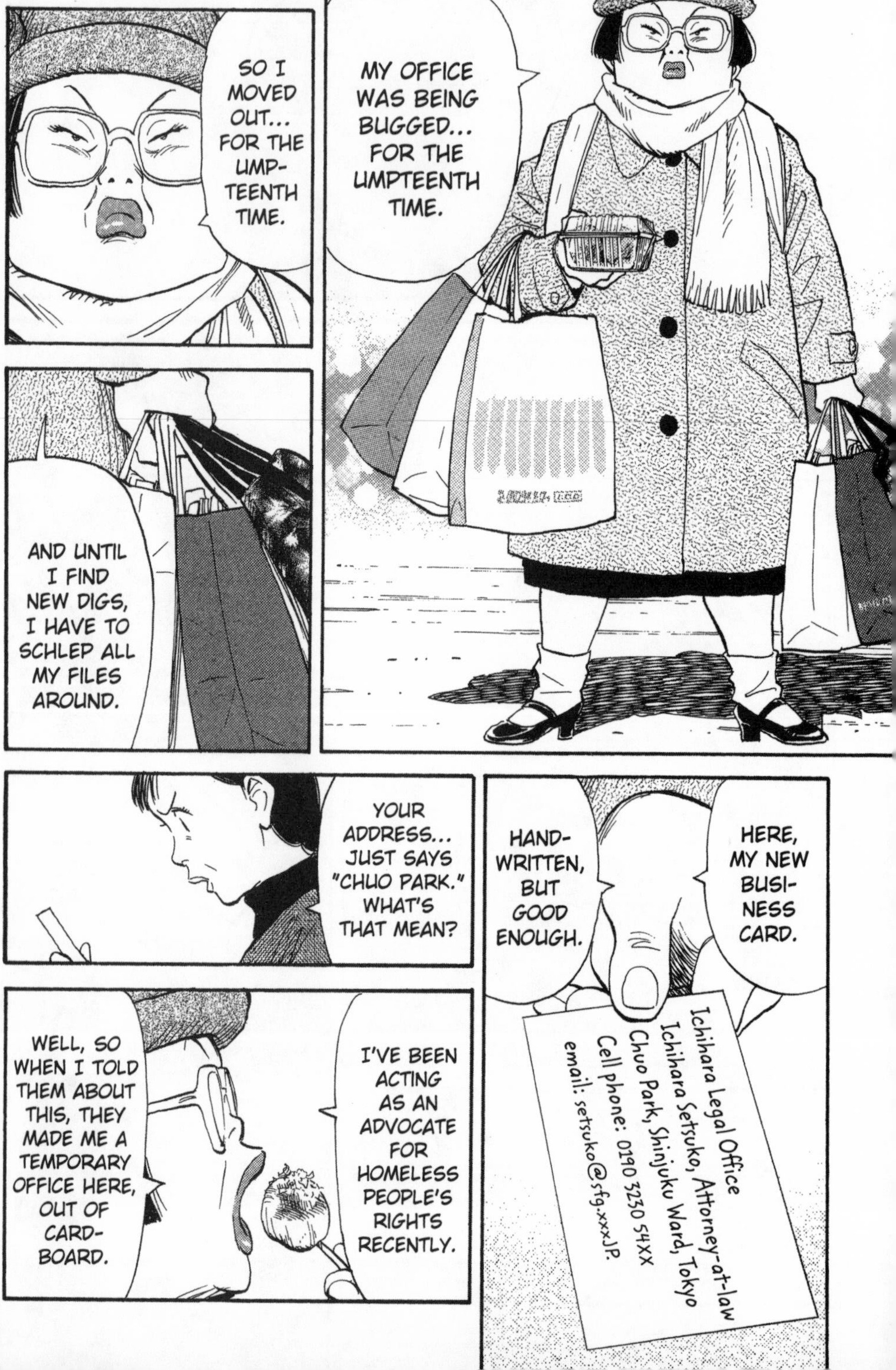
MY OFFICE WAS BEING BUGGED... FOR THE UMPTEENTH TIME.
SO I MOVED OUT... FOR THE UMP-TEENTH TIME.
AND UNTIL I FIND NEW DIGS, I HAVE TO SCHLEP ALL MY FILES AROUND.
HERE, MY NEW BUSI-NESS CARD.
HAND-WRITTEN, BUT GOOD ENOUGH.
Ichihara Legal Office
Ichihara Setsuko, Attorney-at-law
Chuo Park, Shinjuku Ward, Tokyo
Cell phone: 0190 3230 54XX
email: setsuko@sfg.xxxJP.
YOUR ADDRESS... JUST SAYS "CHUO PARK." WHAT'S THAT MEAN?
I'VE BEEN ACTING AS AN ADVOCATE FOR HOMELESS PEOPLE'S RIGHTS RECENTLY.
WELL, SO WHEN I TOLD THEM ABOUT THIS, THEY MADE ME A TEMPORARY OFFICE HERE, OUT OF CARD-BOARD.

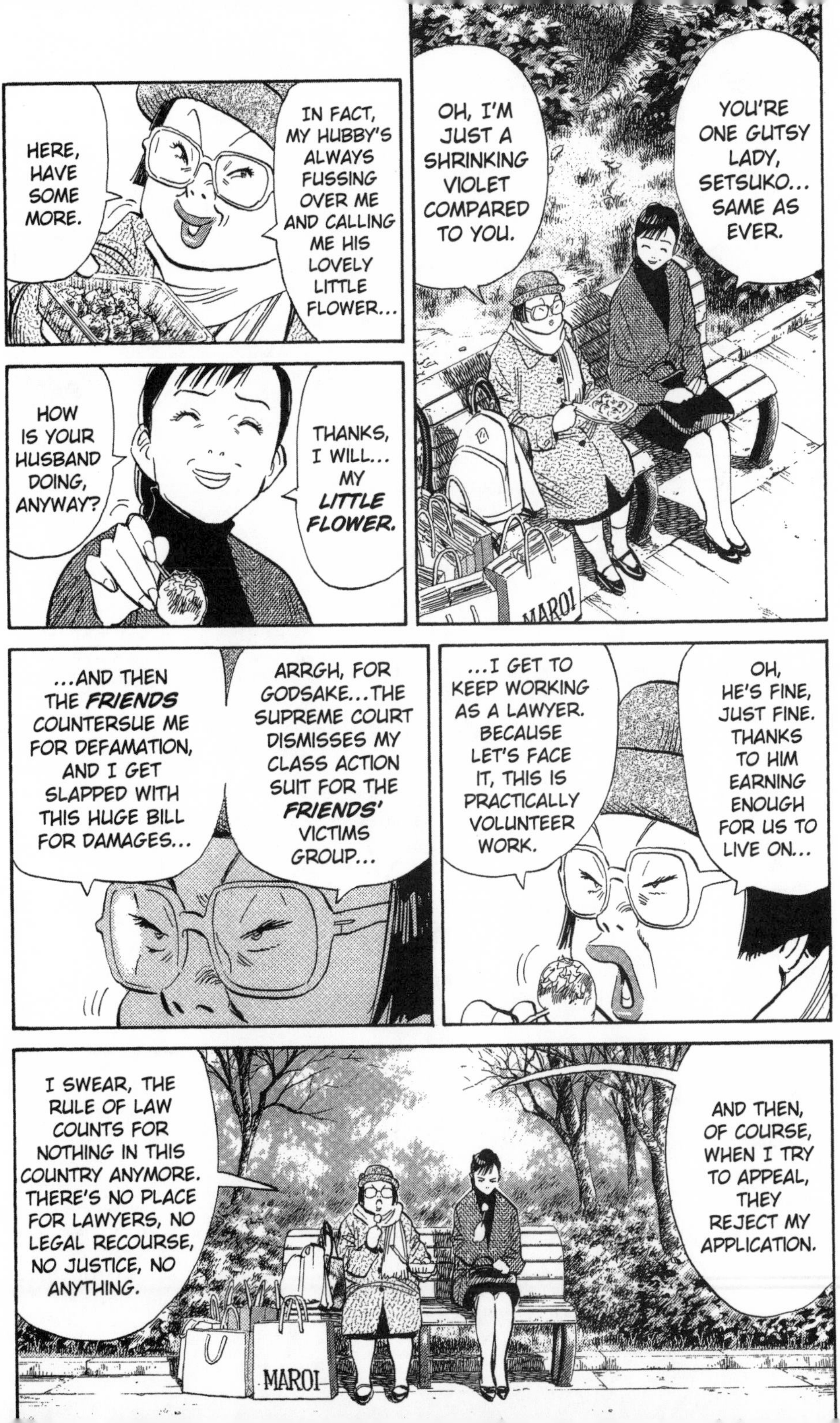

YOU'RE ONE GUTSY LADY, SETSUKO... SAME AS EVER.
OH, I'M JUST A SHRINKING VIOLET COMPARED TO YOU.
IN FACT, MY HUBBY'S ALWAYS FUSSING OVER ME AND CALLING ME HIS LOVELY LITTLE FLOWER...
HERE, HAVE SOME MORE.
THANKS, I WILL... MY *LITTLE FLOWER.*
HOW IS YOUR HUSBAND DOING, ANYWAY?
MAROI
OH, HE'S FINE, JUST FINE. THANKS TO HIM EARNING ENOUGH FOR US TO LIVE ON...
...I GET TO KEEP WORKING AS A LAWYER. BECAUSE LET'S FACE IT, THIS IS PRACTICALLY VOLUNTEER WORK.
ARRGH, FOR GODSAKE...THE SUPREME COURT DISMISSES MY CLASS ACTION SUIT FOR THE *FRIENDS'* VICTIMS GROUP...
...AND THEN THE *FRIENDS* COUNTERSUE ME FOR DEFAMATION, AND I GET SLAPPED WITH THIS HUGE BILL FOR DAMAGES...
AND THEN, OF COURSE, WHEN I TRY TO APPEAL, THEY REJECT MY APPLICATION.
I SWEAR, THE RULE OF LAW COUNTS FOR NOTHING IN THIS COUNTRY ANYMORE. THERE'S NO PLACE FOR LAWYERS, NO LEGAL RECOURSE, NO JUSTICE, NO ANYTHING.
MAROI

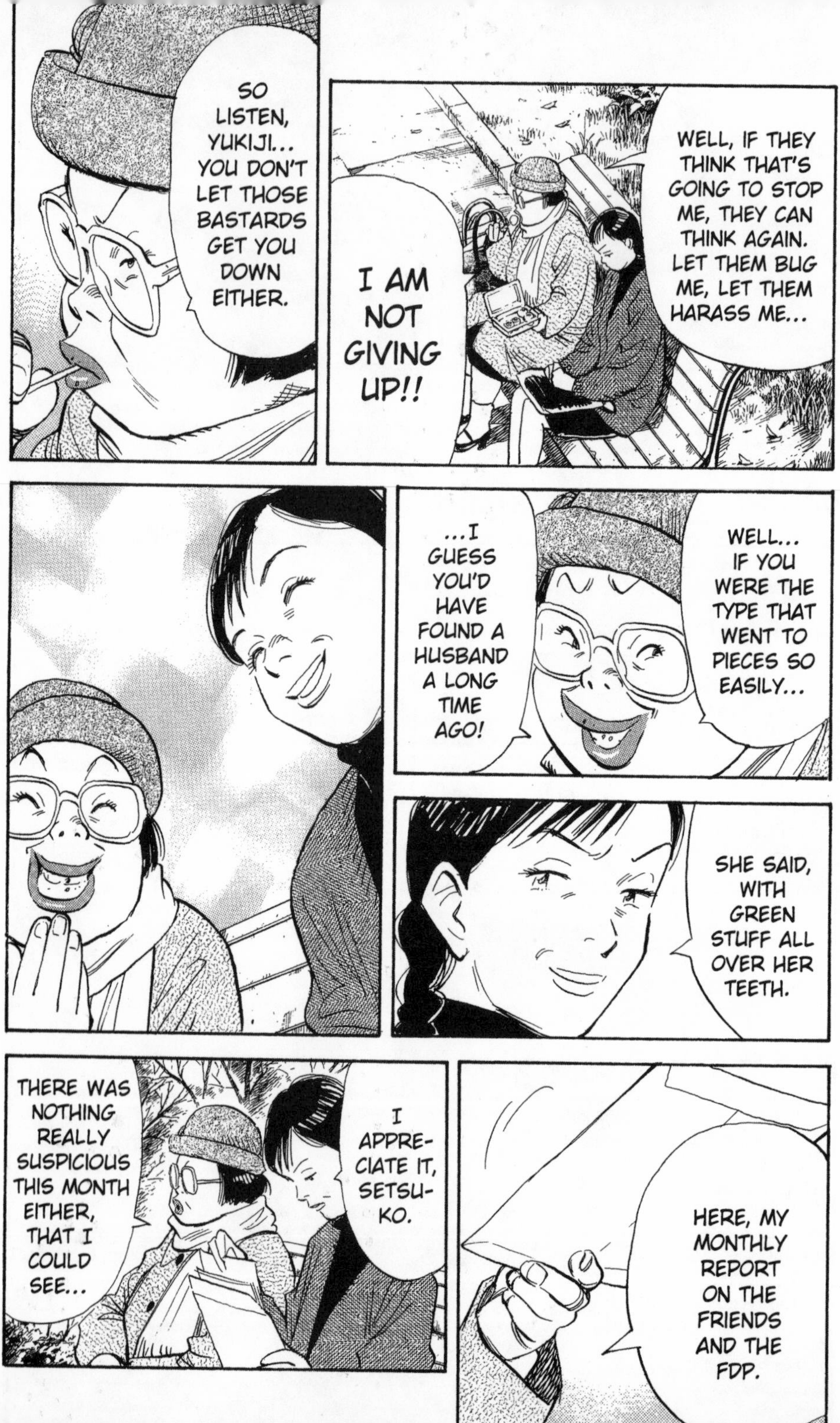
WELL, IF THEY THINK THAT'S GOING TO STOP ME, THEY CAN THINK AGAIN. LET THEM BUG ME, LET THEM HARASS ME...
I AM NOT GIVING UP!!
SO LISTEN, YUKIJI... YOU DON'T LET THOSE BASTARDS GET YOU DOWN EITHER.
WELL... IF YOU WERE THE TYPE THAT WENT TO PIECES SO EASILY...
...I GUESS YOU'D HAVE FOUND A HUSBAND A LONG TIME AGO!
SHE SAID, WITH GREEN STUFF ALL OVER HER TEETH.
HERE, MY MONTHLY REPORT ON THE FRIENDS AND THE FDP.
I APPRECIATE IT, SETSUKO.
THERE WAS NOTHING REALLY SUSPICIOUS THIS MONTH EITHER, THAT I COULD SEE...

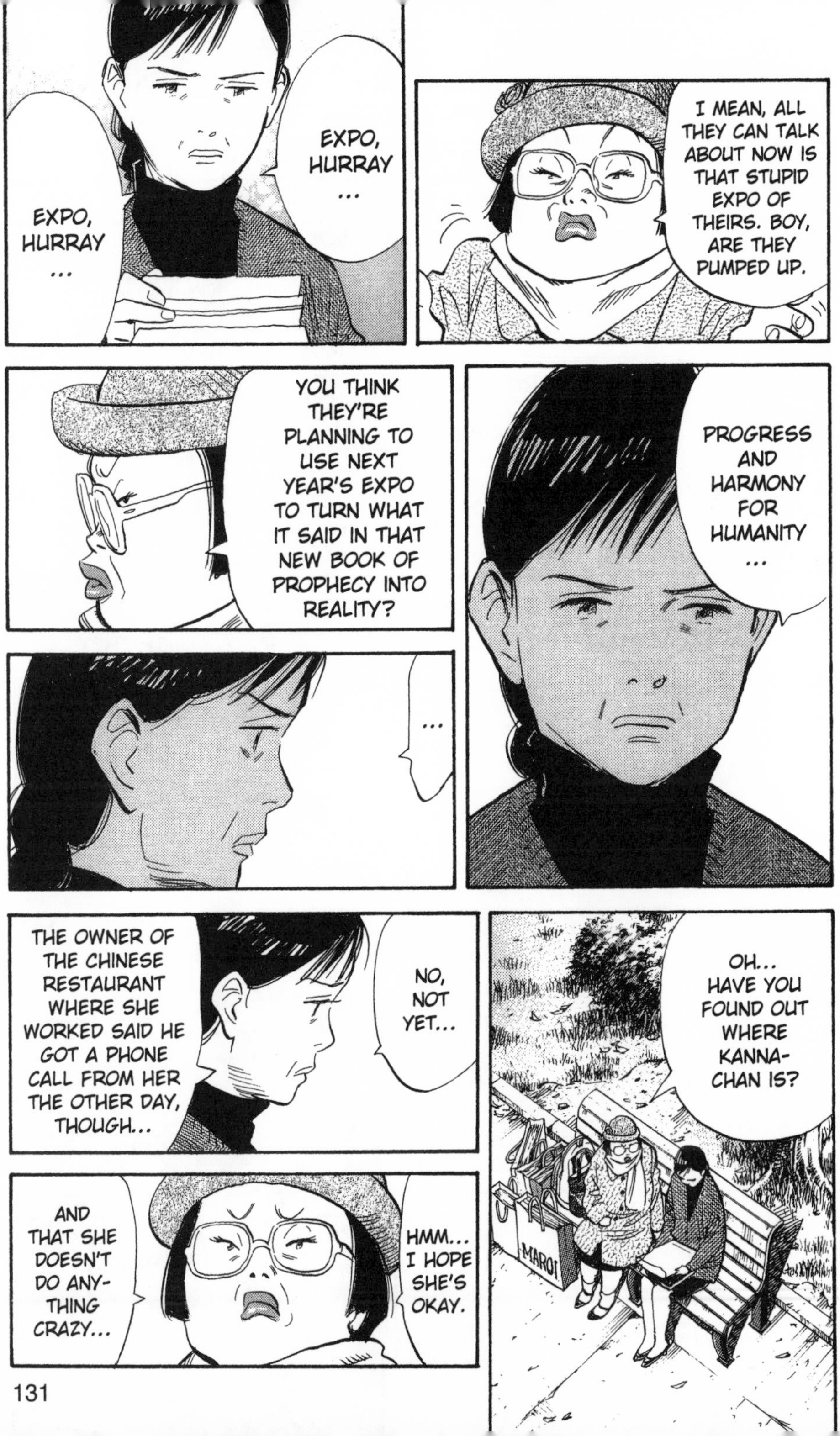
I MEAN, ALL THEY CAN TALK ABOUT NOW IS THAT STUPID EXPO OF THEIRS. BOY, ARE THEY PUMPED UP.
EXPO, HURRAY ...
EXPO, HURRAY ...
PROGRESS AND HARMONY FOR HUMANITY ...
YOU THINK THEY'RE PLANNING TO USE NEXT YEAR'S EXPO TO TURN WHAT IT SAID IN THAT NEW BOOK OF PROPHECY INTO REALITY?
...
OH... HAVE YOU FOUND OUT WHERE KANNA-CHAN IS?
NO, NOT YET...
THE OWNER OF THE CHINESE RESTAURANT WHERE SHE WORKED SAID HE GOT A PHONE CALL FROM HER THE OTHER DAY, THOUGH...
HMM... I HOPE SHE'S OKAY.
AND THAT SHE DOESN'T DO ANY-THING CRAZY...
MARUI

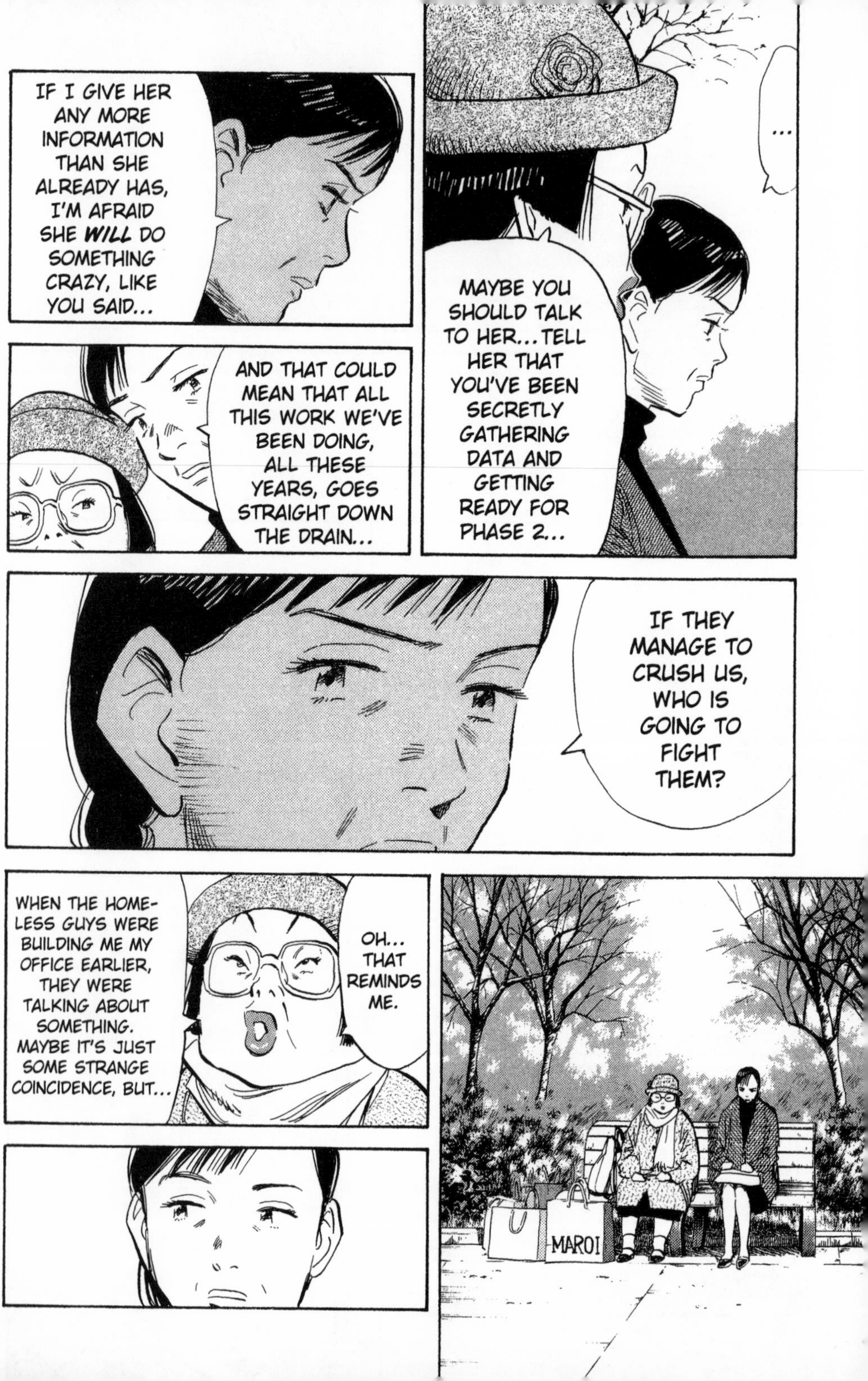
...
MAYBE YOU SHOULD TALK TO HER... TELL HER THAT YOU'VE BEEN SECRETLY GATHERING DATA AND GETTING READY FOR PHASE 2...
IF I GIVE HER ANY MORE INFORMATION THAN SHE ALREADY HAS, I'M AFRAID SHE ***WILL*** DO SOMETHING CRAZY, LIKE YOU SAID...
AND THAT COULD MEAN THAT ALL THIS WORK WE'VE BEEN DOING, ALL THESE YEARS, GOES STRAIGHT DOWN THE DRAIN...
IF THEY MANAGE TO CRUSH US, WHO IS GOING TO FIGHT THEM?
MAROI
OH... THAT REMINDS ME.
WHEN THE HOME-LESS GUYS WERE BUILDING ME MY OFFICE EARLIER, THEY WERE TALKING ABOUT SOMETHING. MAYBE IT'S JUST SOME STRANGE COINCIDENCE, BUT...

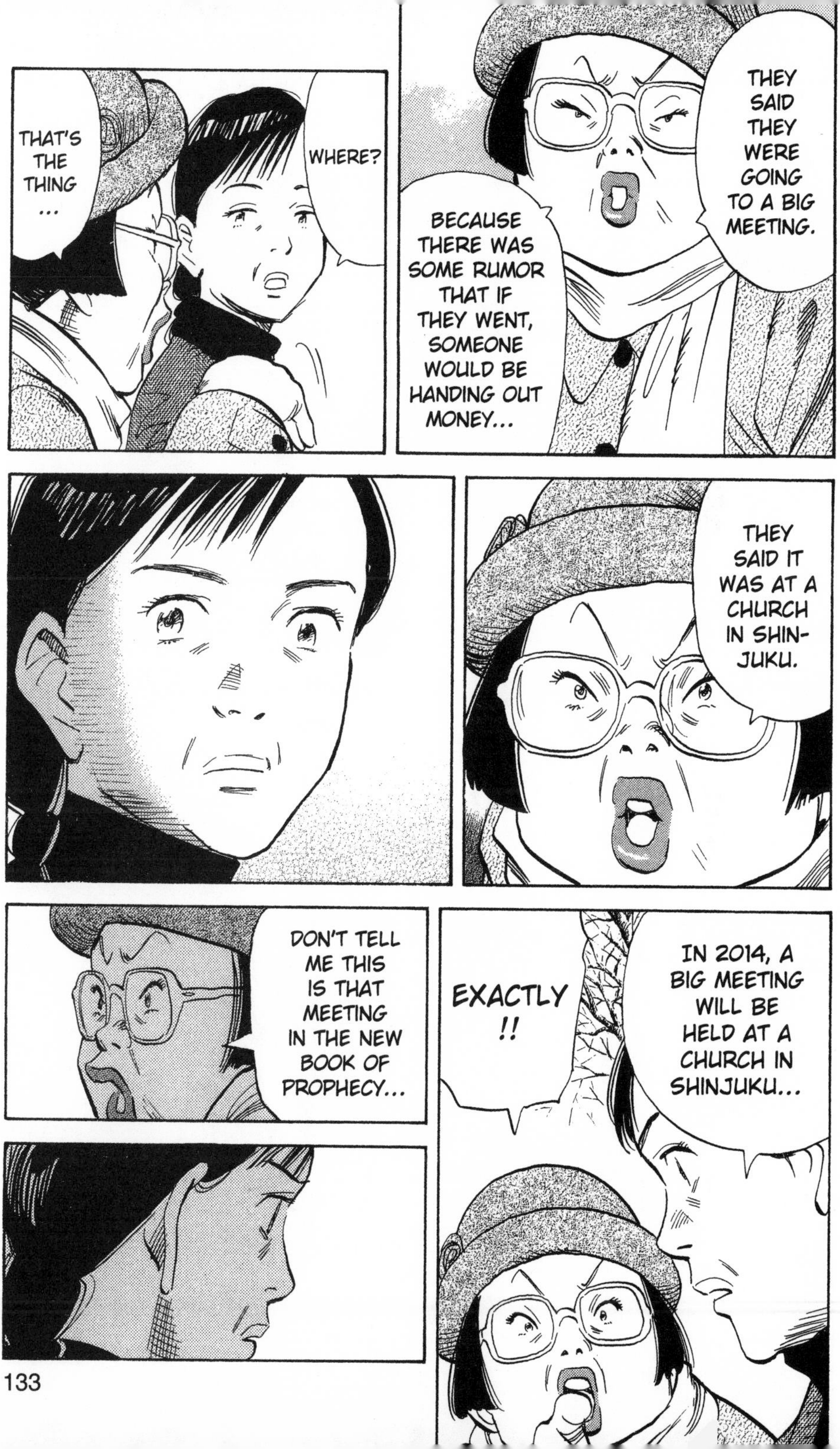
THEY SAID THEY WERE GOING TO A BIG MEETING.
BECAUSE THERE WAS SOME RUMOR THAT IF THEY WENT, SOMEONE WOULD BE HANDING OUT MONEY...
WHERE?
THAT'S THE THING ...
THEY SAID IT WAS AT A CHURCH IN SHIN-JUKU.
IN 2014, A BIG MEETING WILL BE HELD AT A CHURCH IN SHINJUKU...
EXACTLY !!
DON'T TELL ME THIS IS THAT MEETING IN THE NEW BOOK OF PROPHECY...

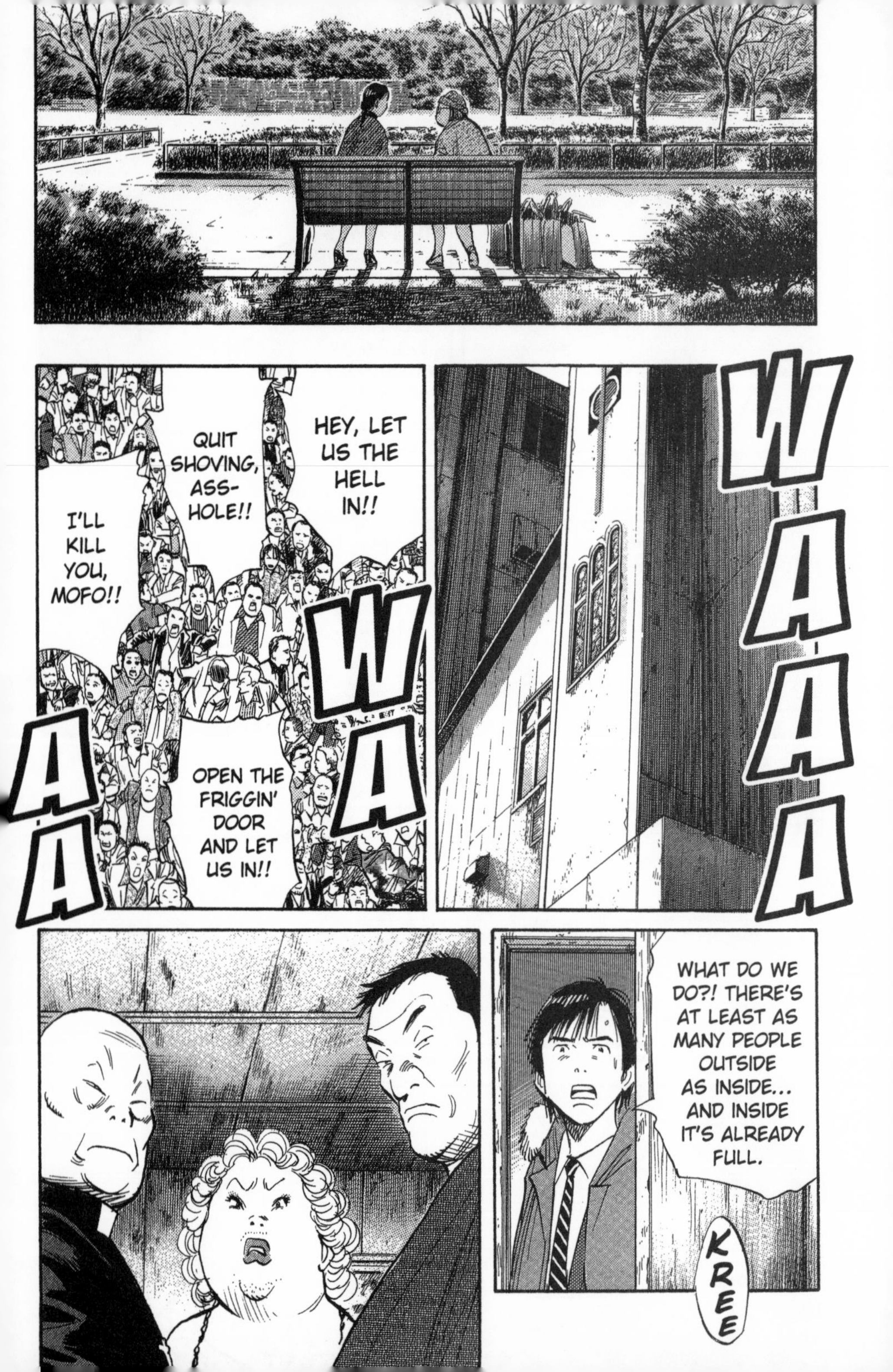
WAAAA
HEY, LET US THE HELL IN!!
QUIT SHOVING, ASS-HOLE!!
I'LL KILL YOU, MOFO!!
WA
OPEN THE FRIGGIN' DOOR AND LET US IN!!
AA
WHAT DO WE DO?! THERE'S AT LEAST AS MANY PEOPLE OUTSIDE AS INSIDE... AND INSIDE IT'S ALREADY FULL.
KREE

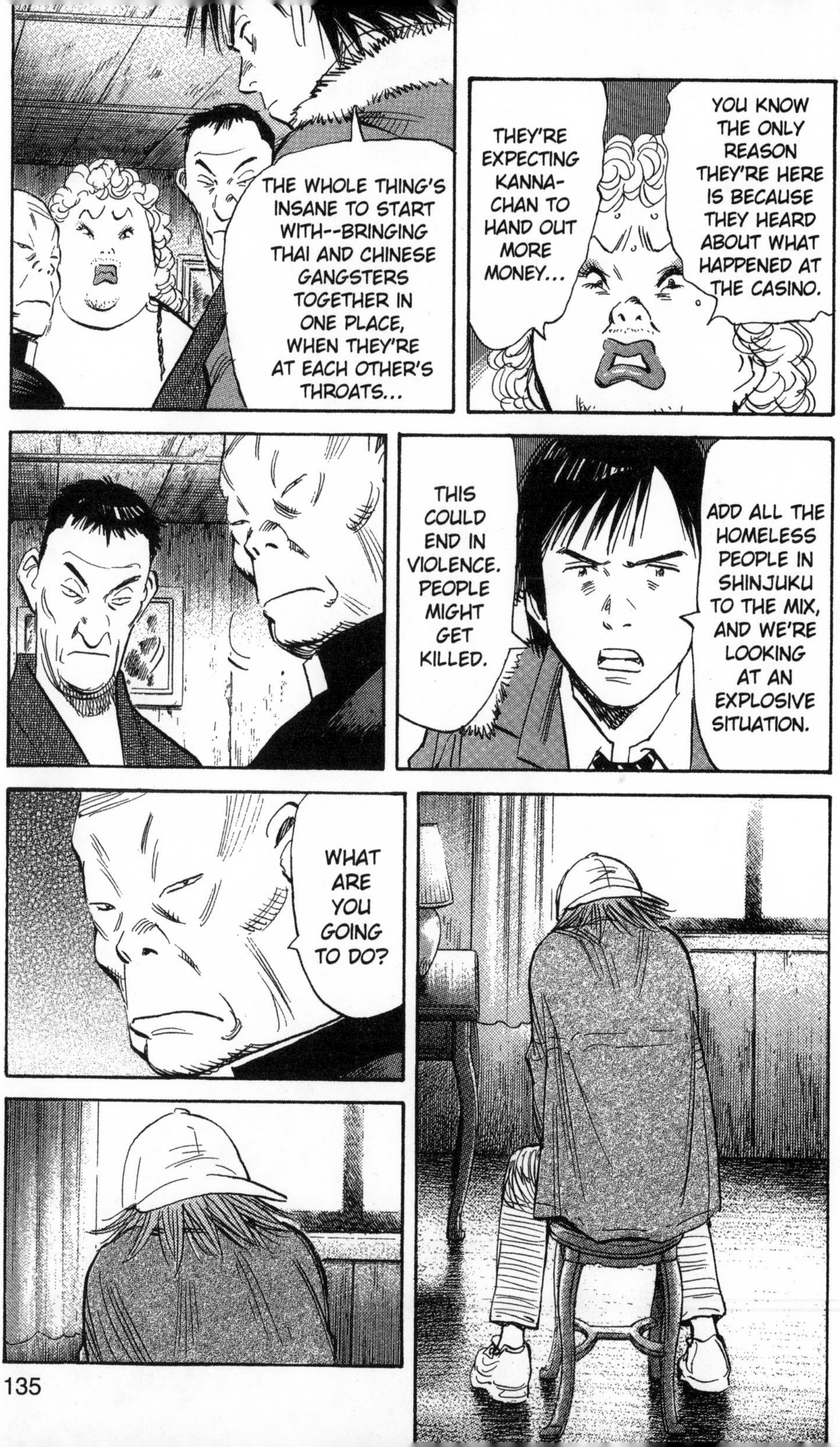
YOU KNOW THE ONLY REASON THEY'RE HERE IS BECAUSE THEY HEARD ABOUT WHAT HAPPENED AT THE CASINO.
THEY'RE EXPECTING KANNA-CHAN TO HAND OUT MORE MONEY...
THE WHOLE THING'S INSANE TO START WITH--BRINGING THAI AND CHINESE GANGSTERS TOGETHER IN ONE PLACE, WHEN THEY'RE AT EACH OTHER'S THROATS...
ADD ALL THE HOMELESS PEOPLE IN SHINJUKU TO THE MIX, AND WE'RE LOOKING AT AN EXPLOSIVE SITUATION.
THIS COULD END IN VIOLENCE. PEOPLE MIGHT GET KILLED.
WHAT ARE YOU GOING TO DO?

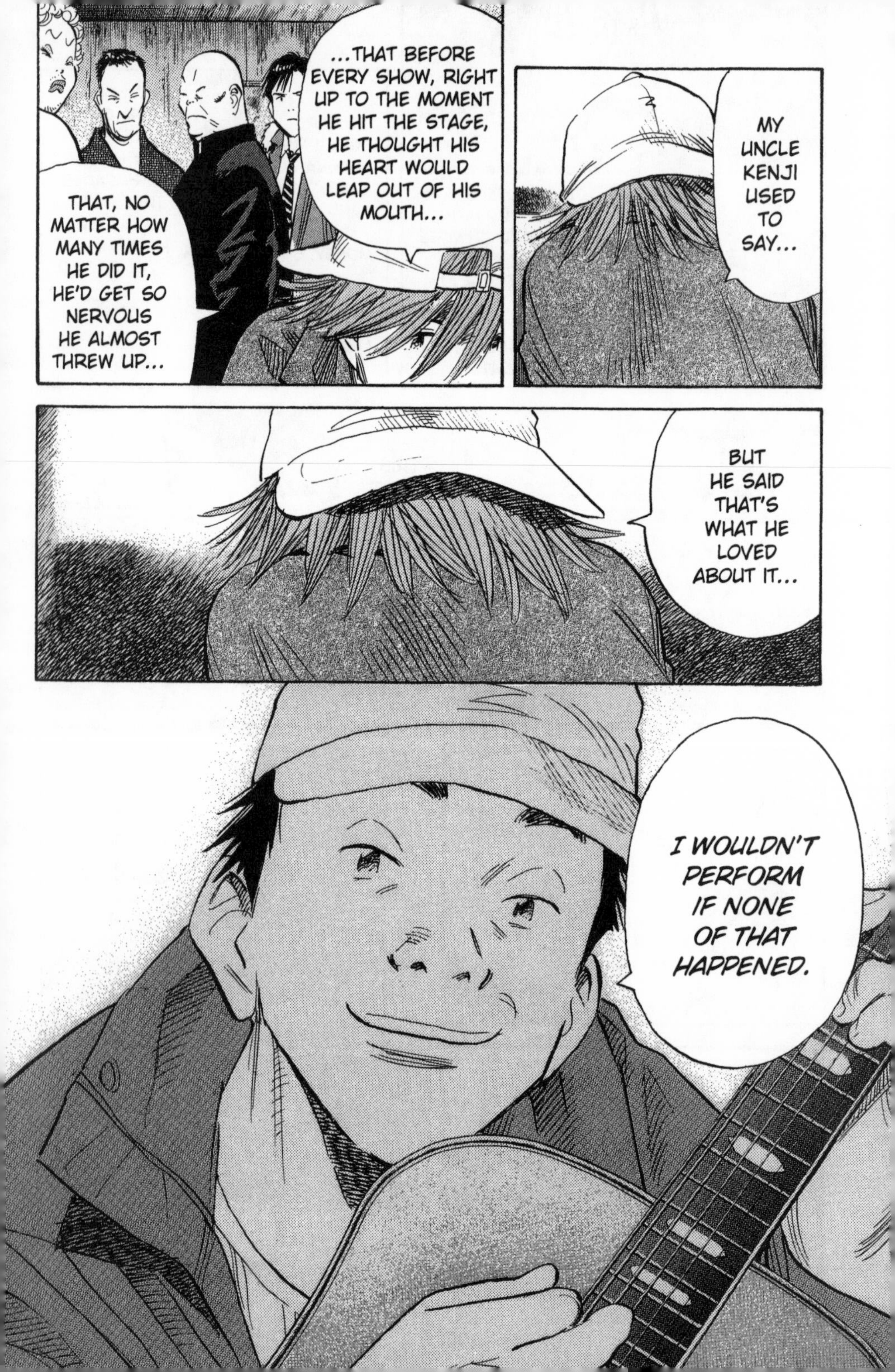
MY UNCLE KENJI USED TO SAY...
...THAT BEFORE EVERY SHOW, RIGHT UP TO THE MOMENT HE HIT THE STAGE, HE THOUGHT HIS HEART WOULD LEAP OUT OF HIS MOUTH...
THAT, NO MATTER HOW MANY TIMES HE DID IT, HE'D GET SO NERVOUS HE ALMOST THREW UP...
BUT HE SAID THAT'S WHAT HE LOVED ABOUT IT...
I WOULDN'T PERFORM IF NONE OF THAT HAPPENED.

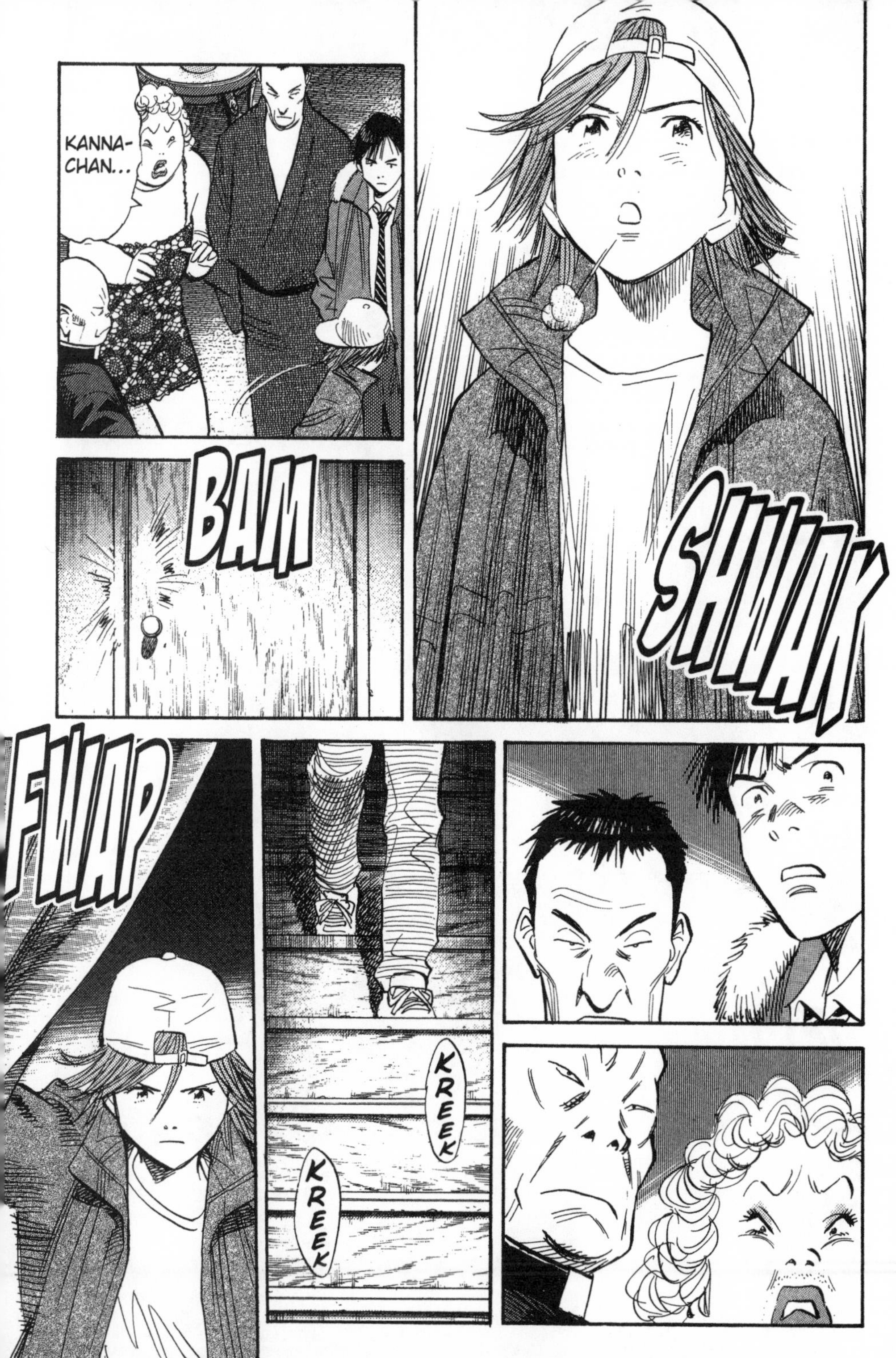
SHWAK
KANNA-CHAN...
BAM
KREEK
KREEK
FWAP

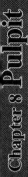

Chapter 8 Pulpit

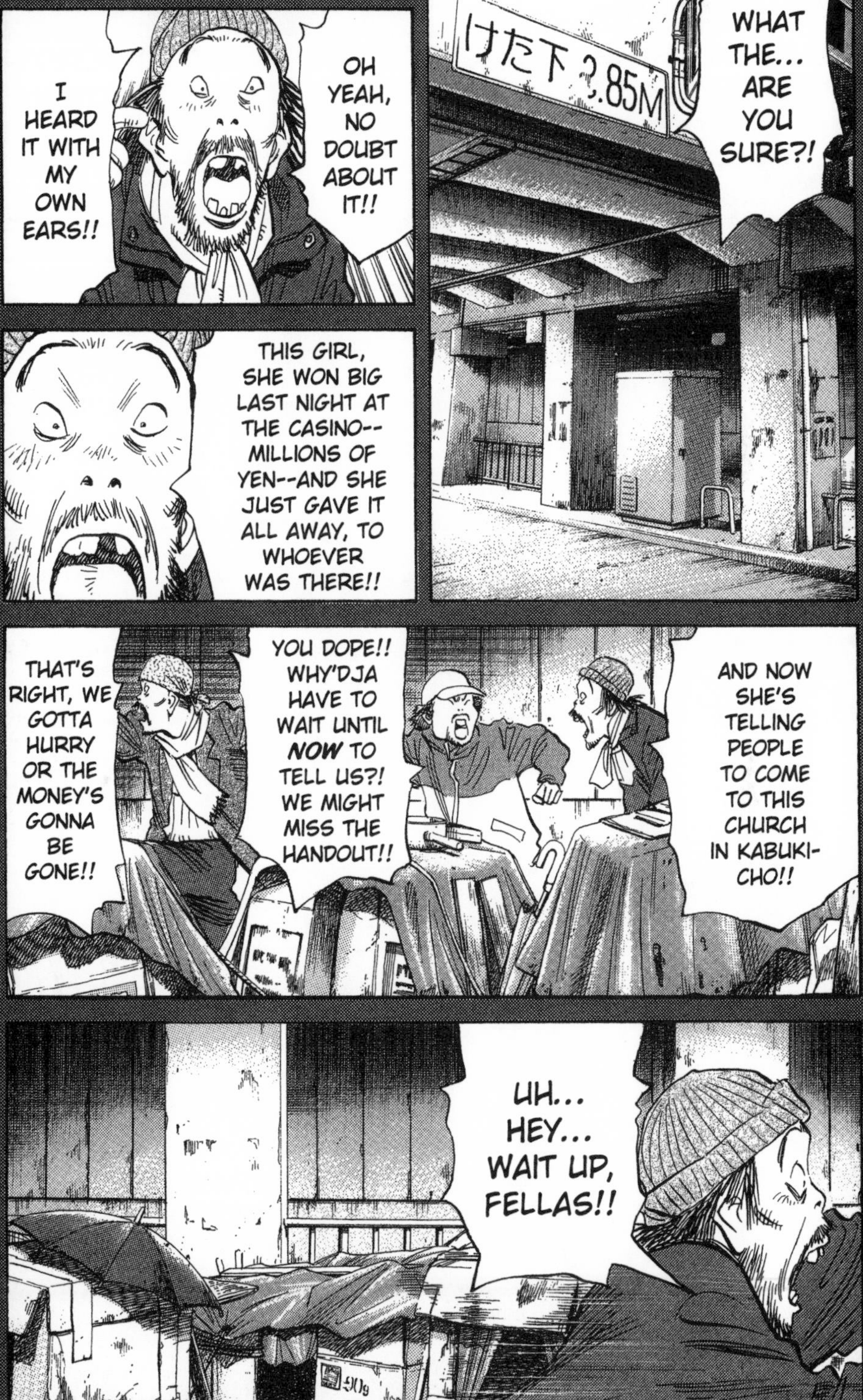
けた下 3.85M
WHAT THE... ARE YOU SURE?!
OH YEAH, NO DOUBT ABOUT IT!!
I HEARD IT WITH MY OWN EARS!!
THIS GIRL, SHE WON BIG LAST NIGHT AT THE CASINO--MILLIONS OF YEN--AND SHE JUST GAVE IT ALL AWAY, TO WHOEVER WAS THERE!!
AND NOW SHE'S TELLING PEOPLE TO COME TO THIS CHURCH IN KABUKI-CHO!!
YOU DOPE!! WHY'DJA HAVE TO WAIT UNTIL ***NOW*** TO TELL US?! WE MIGHT MISS THE HANDOUT!!
THAT'S RIGHT, WE GOTTA HURRY OR THE MONEY'S GONNA BE GONE!!
UH... HEY... WAIT UP, FELLAS!!

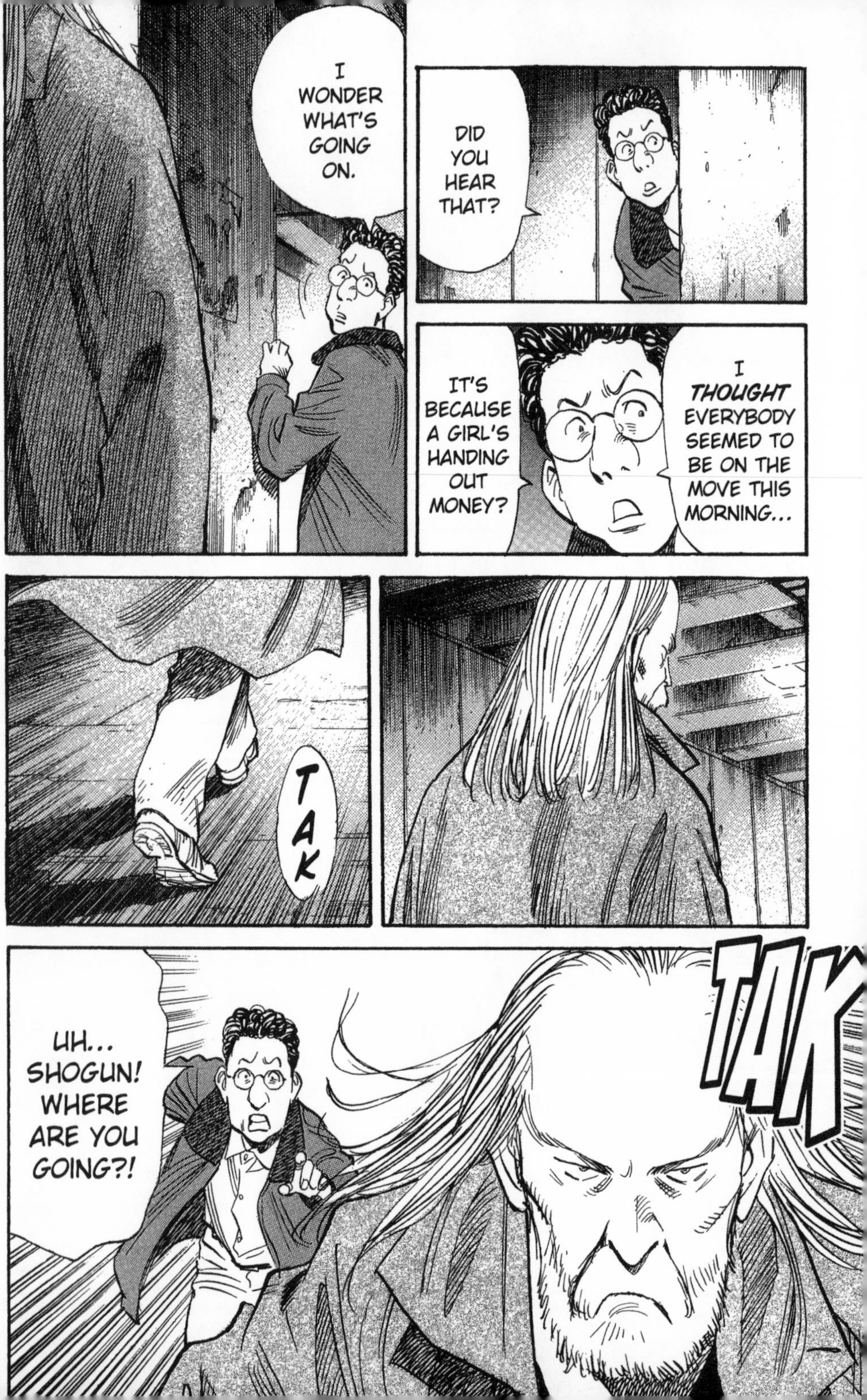
DID YOU HEAR THAT?
I *THOUGHT* EVERYBODY SEEMED TO BE ON THE MOVE THIS MORNING...
IT'S BECAUSE A GIRL'S HANDING OUT MONEY?
I WONDER WHAT'S GOING ON.
TAK
TAK
UH... SHOGUN! WHERE ARE YOU GOING?!

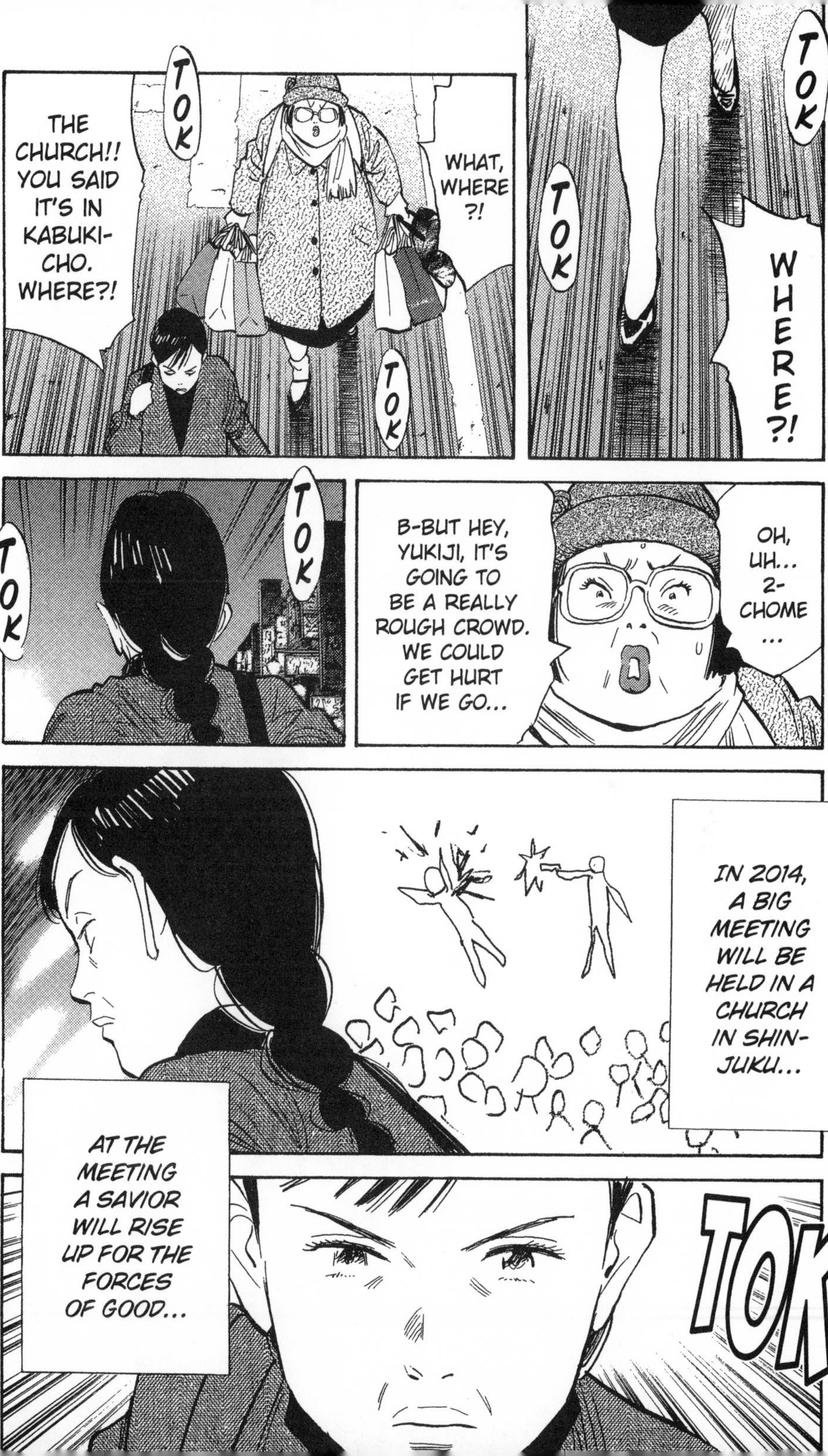
TOK
TOK
WHERE?!
WHAT, WHERE?!
TOK
THE CHURCH!! YOU SAID IT'S IN KABUKI-CHO. WHERE?!
TOK
OH, UH... 2-CHOME...
B-BUT HEY, YUKIJI, IT'S GOING TO BE A REALLY ROUGH CROWD. WE COULD GET HURT IF WE GO...
TOK
TOK
IN 2014, A BIG MEETING WILL BE HELD IN A CHURCH IN SHIN-JUKU...
AT THE MEETING A SAVIOR WILL RISE UP FOR THE FORCES OF GOOD...
TOK

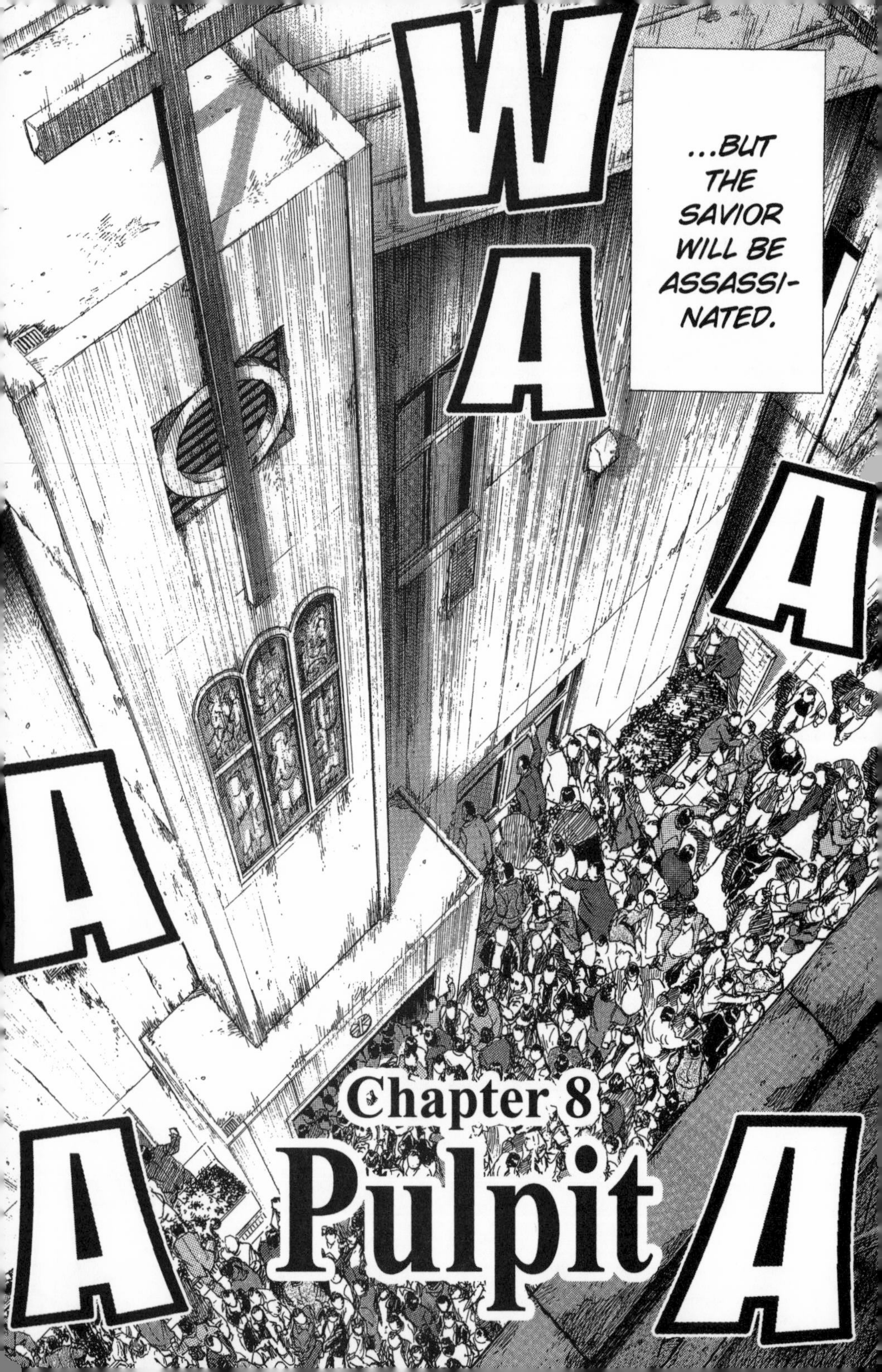
...BUT THE SAVIOR WILL BE ASSASSINATED.
WAAAAA
Chapter 8
Pulpit

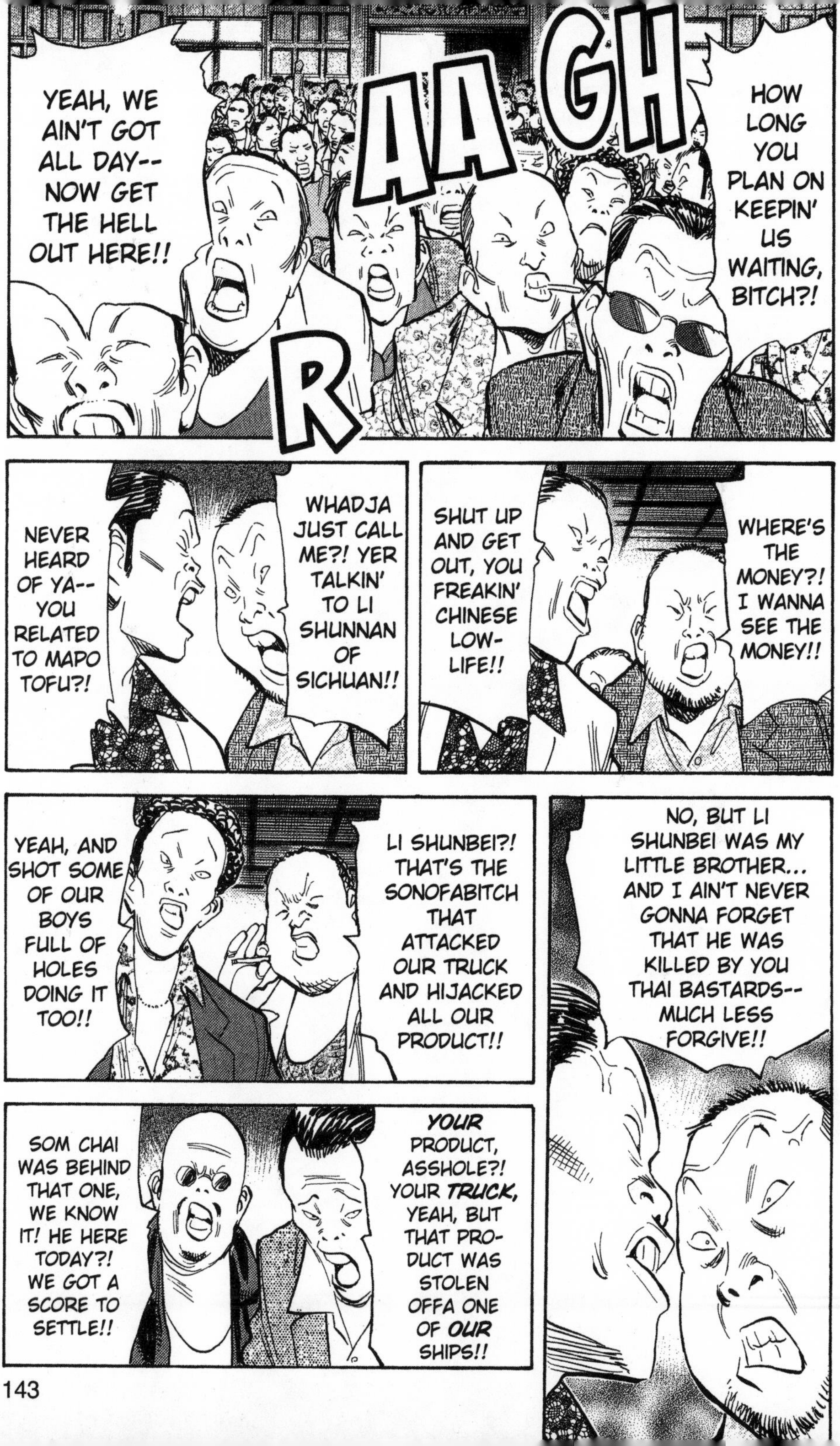

HOW LONG YOU PLAN ON KEEPIN' US WAITING, BITCH?!
AAGH
R
YEAH, WE AIN'T GOT ALL DAY-- NOW GET THE HELL OUT HERE!!
WHERE'S THE MONEY?! I WANNA SEE THE MONEY!!
SHUT UP AND GET OUT, YOU FREAKIN' CHINESE LOW-LIFE!!
WHADJA JUST CALL ME?! YER TALKIN' TO LI SHUNNAN OF SICHUAN!!
NEVER HEARD OF YA-- YOU RELATED TO MAPO TOFU?!
NO, BUT LI SHUNBEI WAS MY LITTLE BROTHER... AND I AIN'T NEVER GONNA FORGET THAT HE WAS KILLED BY YOU THAI BASTARDS-- MUCH LESS FORGIVE!!
LI SHUNBEI?! THAT'S THE SONOFABITCH THAT ATTACKED OUR TRUCK AND HIJACKED ALL OUR PRODUCT!!
YEAH, AND SHOT SOME OF OUR BOYS FULL OF HOLES DOING IT TOO!!
YOUR PRODUCT, ASSHOLE?! YOUR *TRUCK*, YEAH, BUT THAT PRO-DUCT WAS STOLEN OFFA ONE OF *OUR* SHIPS!!
SOM CHAI WAS BEHIND THAT ONE, WE KNOW IT! HE HERE TODAY?! WE GOT A SCORE TO SETTLE!!

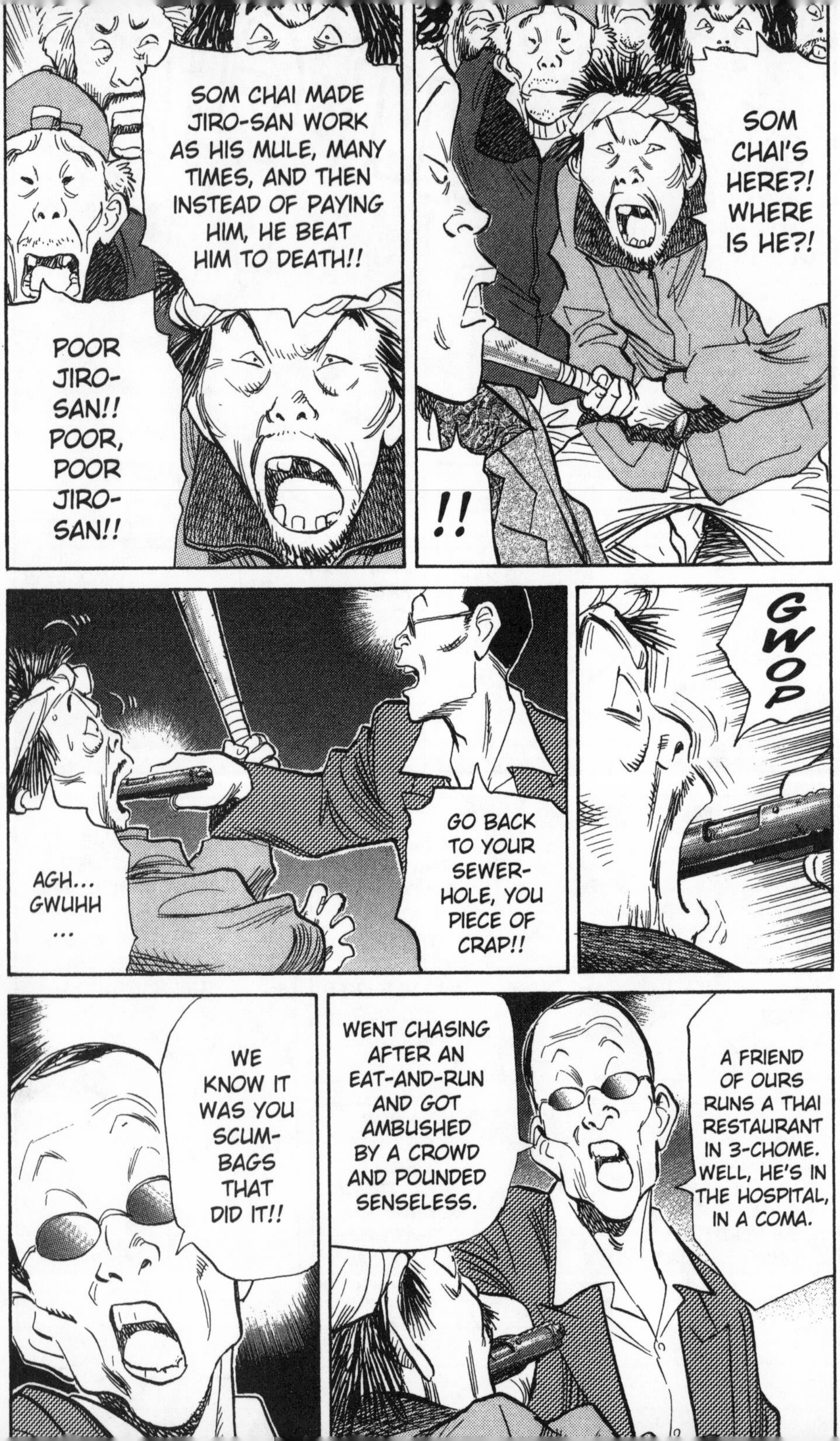
SOM CHAI'S HERE?! WHERE IS HE?!
!!
SOM CHAI MADE JIRO-SAN WORK AS HIS MULE, MANY TIMES, AND THEN INSTEAD OF PAYING HIM, HE BEAT HIM TO DEATH!!
POOR JIRO-SAN!! POOR, POOR JIRO-SAN!!
GWOP
GO BACK TO YOUR SEWER-HOLE, YOU PIECE OF CRAP!!
AGH... GWUHH ...
A FRIEND OF OURS RUNS A THAI RESTAURANT IN 3-CHOME. WELL, HE'S IN THE HOSPITAL, IN A COMA.
WENT CHASING AFTER AN EAT-AND-RUN AND GOT AMBUSHED BY A CROWD AND POUNDED SENSELESS.
WE KNOW IT WAS YOU SCUM-BAGS THAT DID IT!!

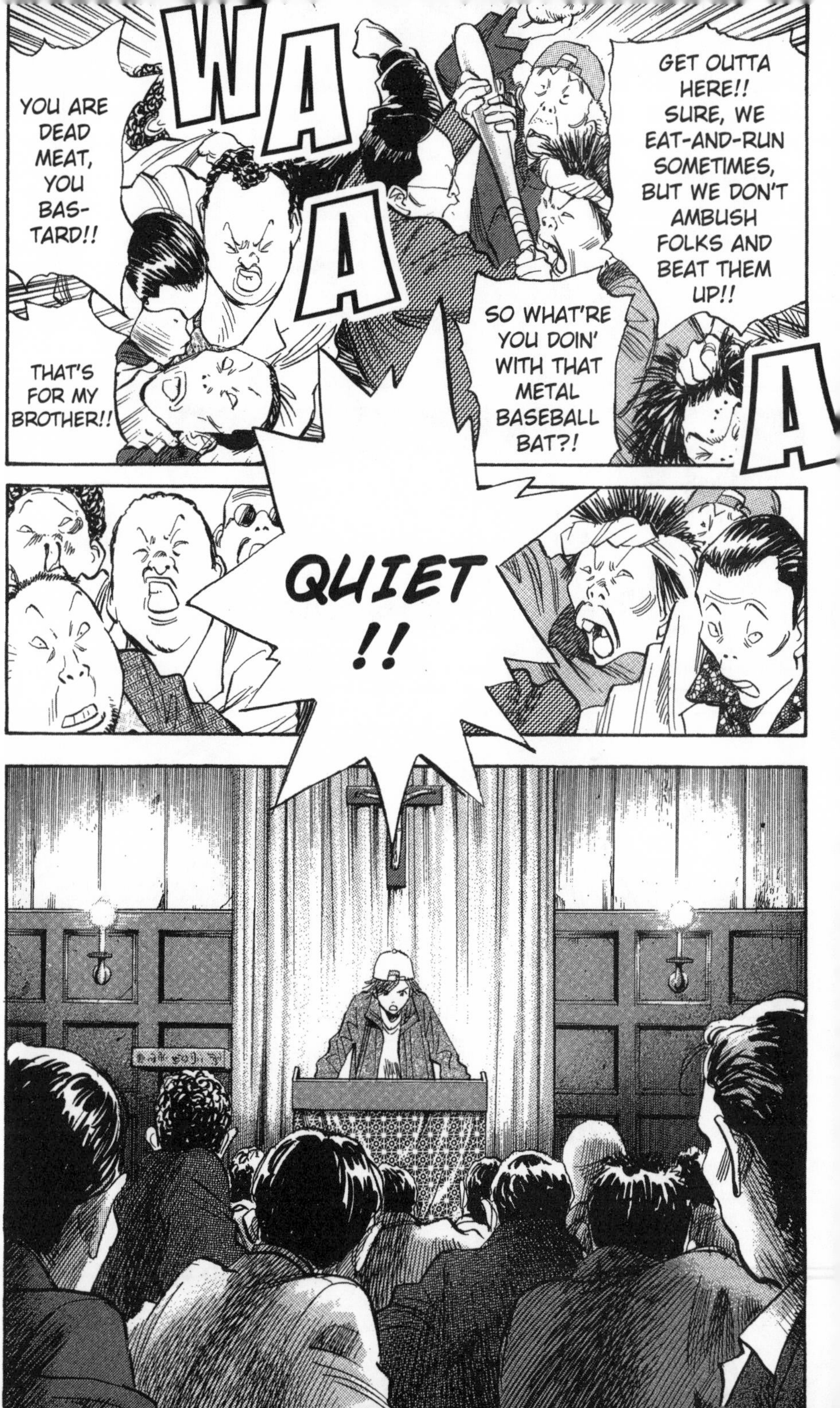
GET OUTTA HERE!! SURE, WE EAT-AND-RUN SOMETIMES, BUT WE DON'T AMBUSH FOLKS AND BEAT THEM UP!!
SO WHAT'RE YOU DOIN' WITH THAT METAL BASEBALL BAT?!
WA A A
YOU ARE DEAD MEAT, YOU BAS-TARD!!
THAT'S FOR MY BROTHER!!
QUIET !!

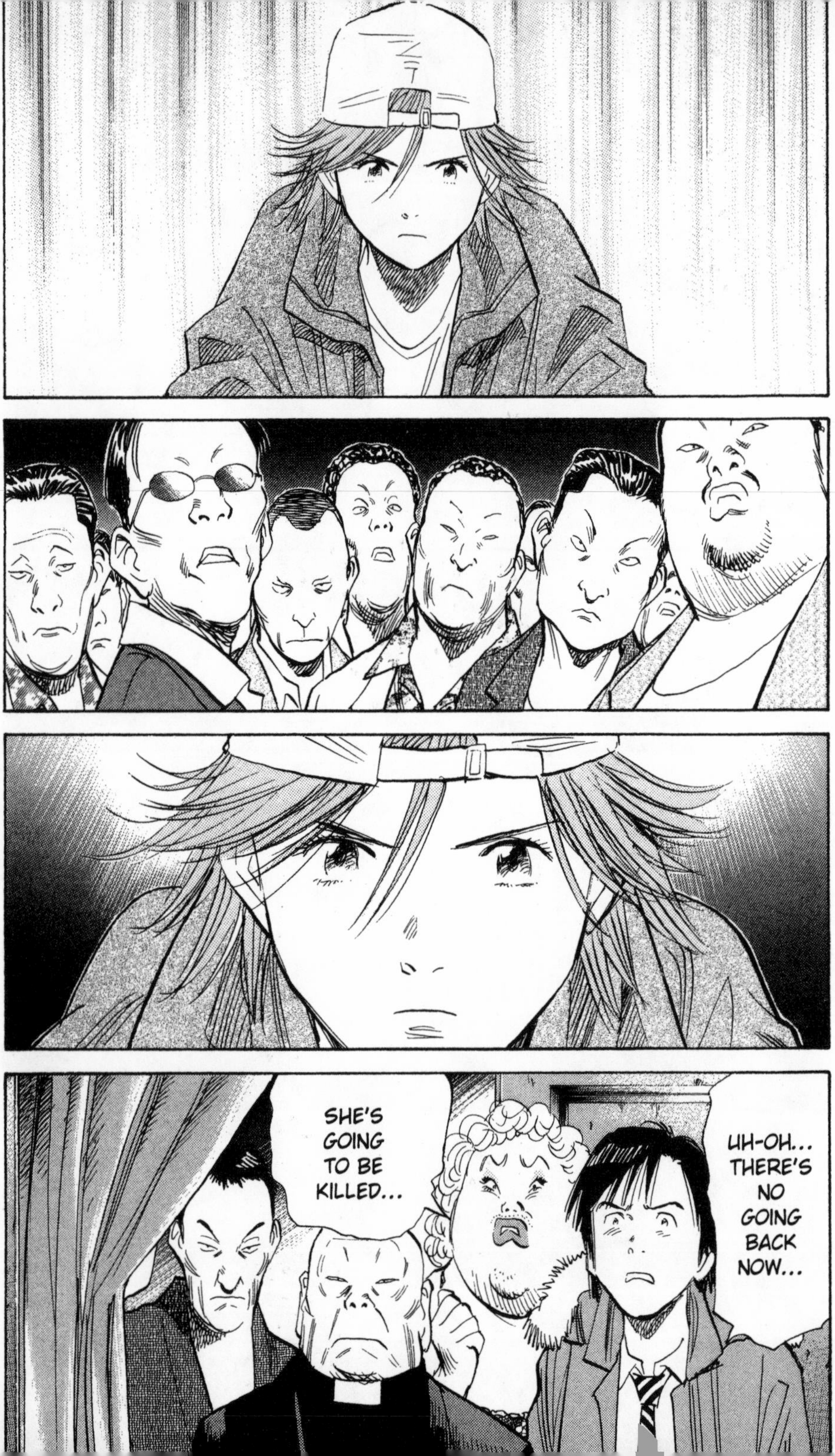
UH-OH... THERE'S NO GOING BACK NOW...
SHE'S GOING TO BE KILLED...

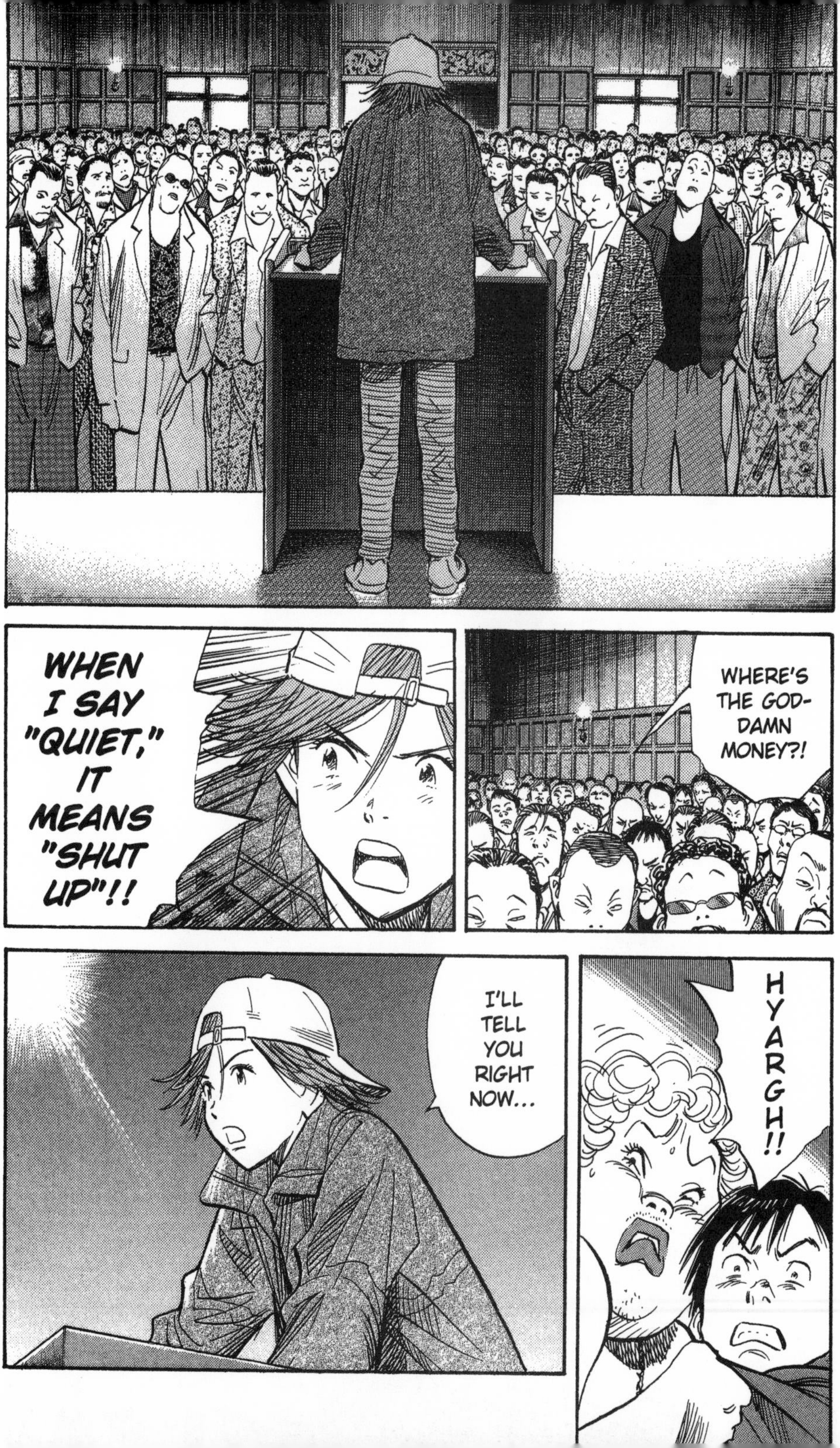
WHERE'S THE GOD-DAMN MONEY?!
WHEN I SAY "QUIET," IT MEANS "SHUT UP"!!
HYARGH!!
I'LL TELL YOU RIGHT NOW...

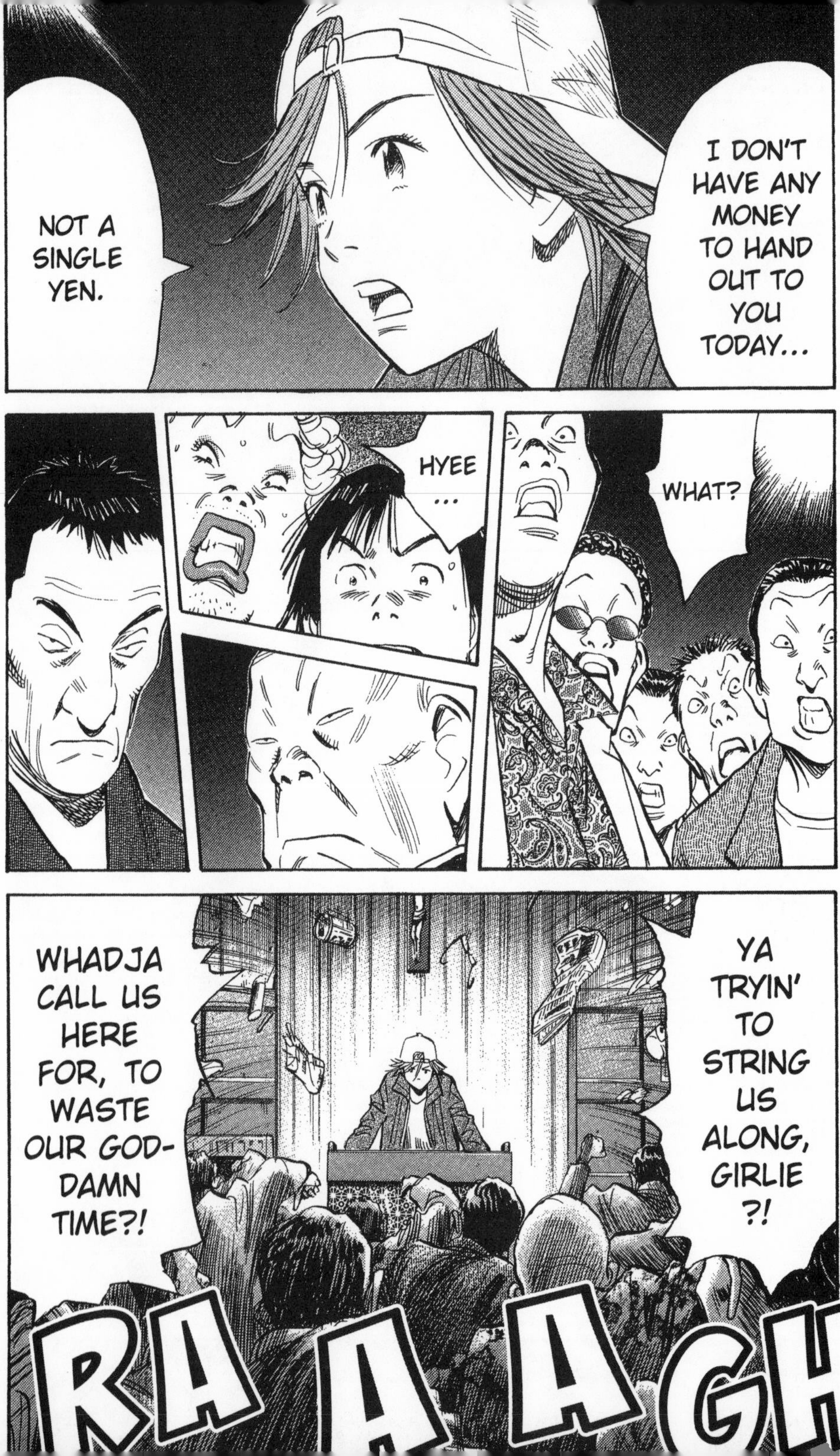
I DON'T HAVE ANY MONEY TO HAND OUT TO YOU TODAY...
NOT A SINGLE YEN.
WHAT?
HYEE ...
YA TRYIN' TO STRING US ALONG, GIRLIE ?!
WHADJA CALL US HERE FOR, TO WASTE OUR GOD-DAMN TIME?!
RAAAGH

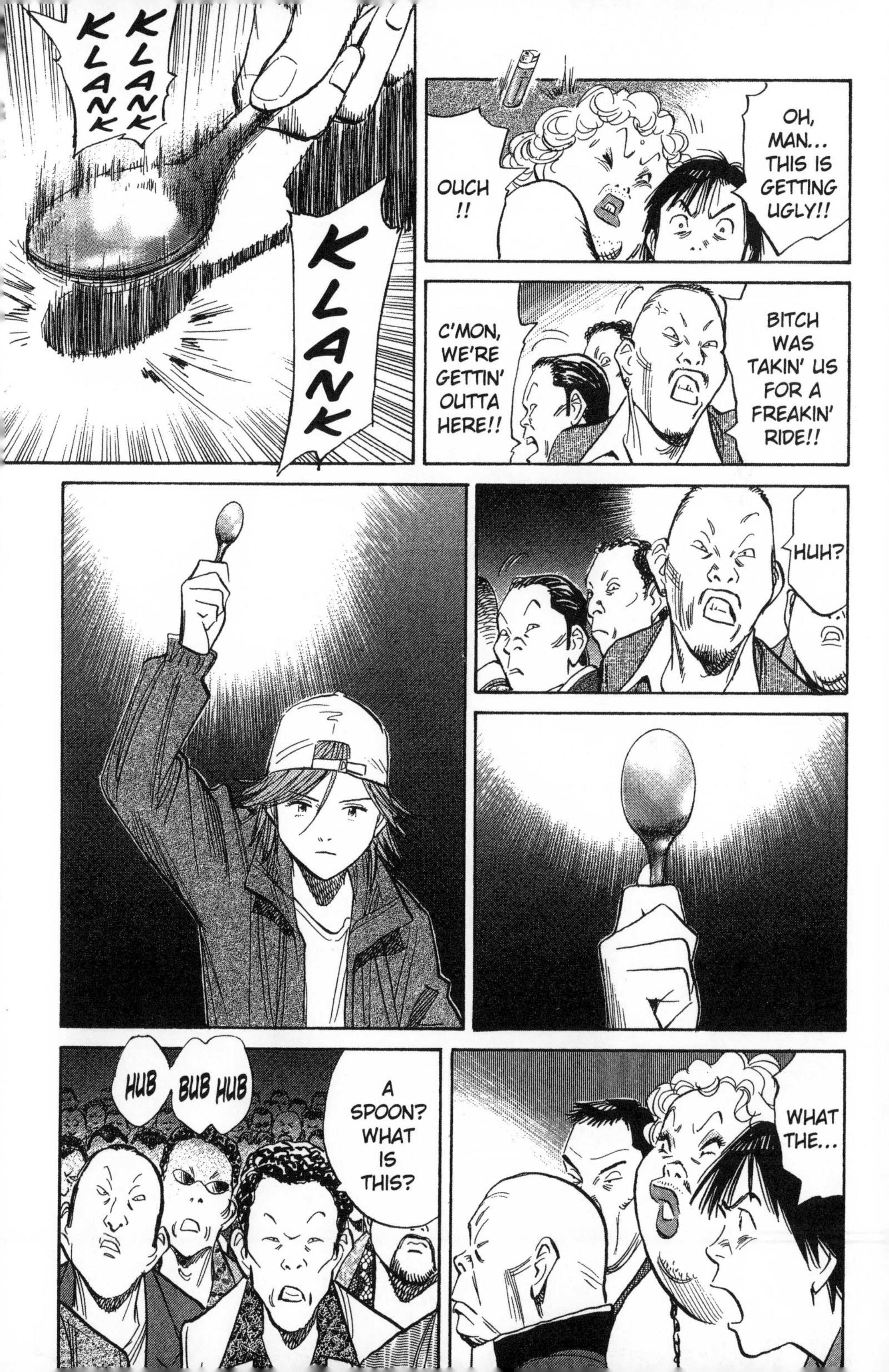

OH, MAN... THIS IS GETTING UGLY!!
OUCH !!
BITCH WAS TAKIN' US FOR A FREAKIN' RIDE!!
C'MON, WE'RE GETTIN' OUTTA HERE!!
KLANK KLANK
KLANK
HUH?
WHAT THE...
A SPOON? WHAT IS THIS?
HUB BUB HUB

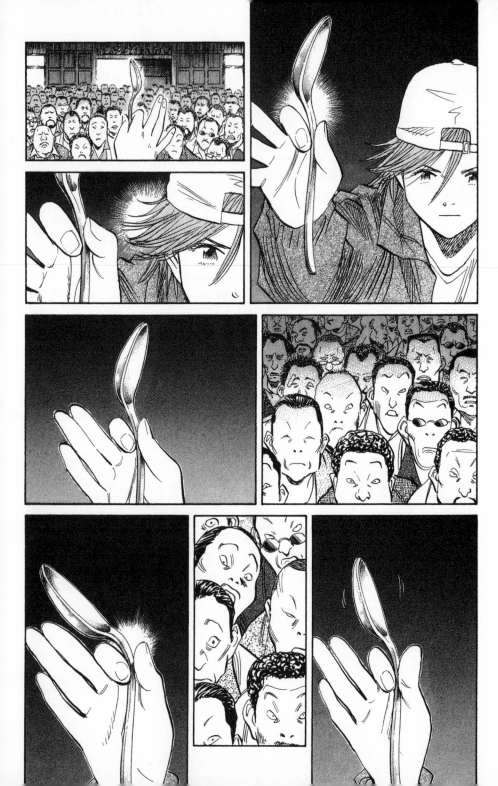

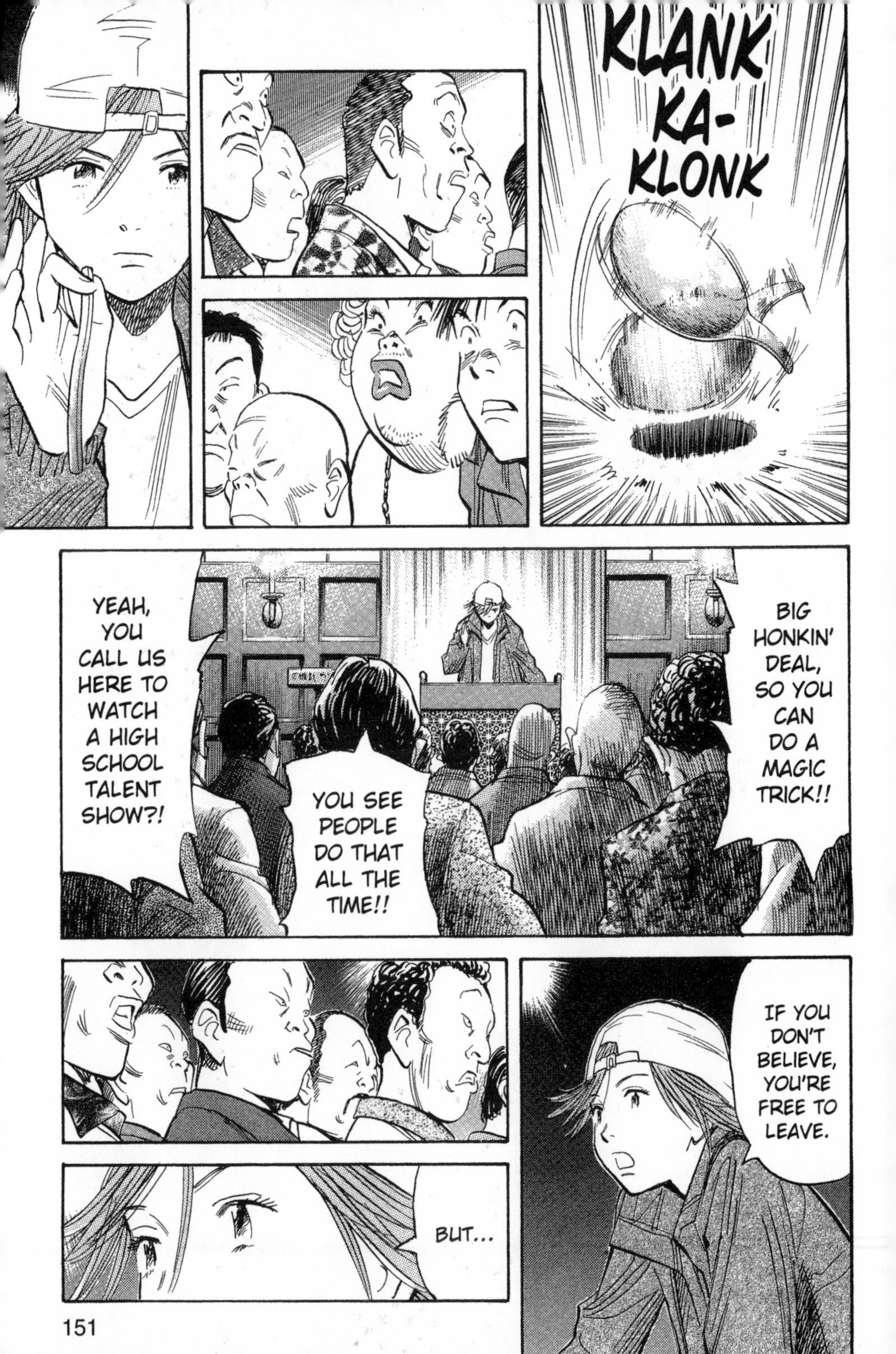
KLANK KA-KLONK
BIG HONKIN' DEAL, SO YOU CAN DO A MAGIC TRICK!!
YEAH, YOU CALL US HERE TO WATCH A HIGH SCHOOL TALENT SHOW?!
YOU SEE PEOPLE DO THAT ALL THE TIME!!
IF YOU DON'T BELIEVE, YOU'RE FREE TO LEAVE.
BUT...

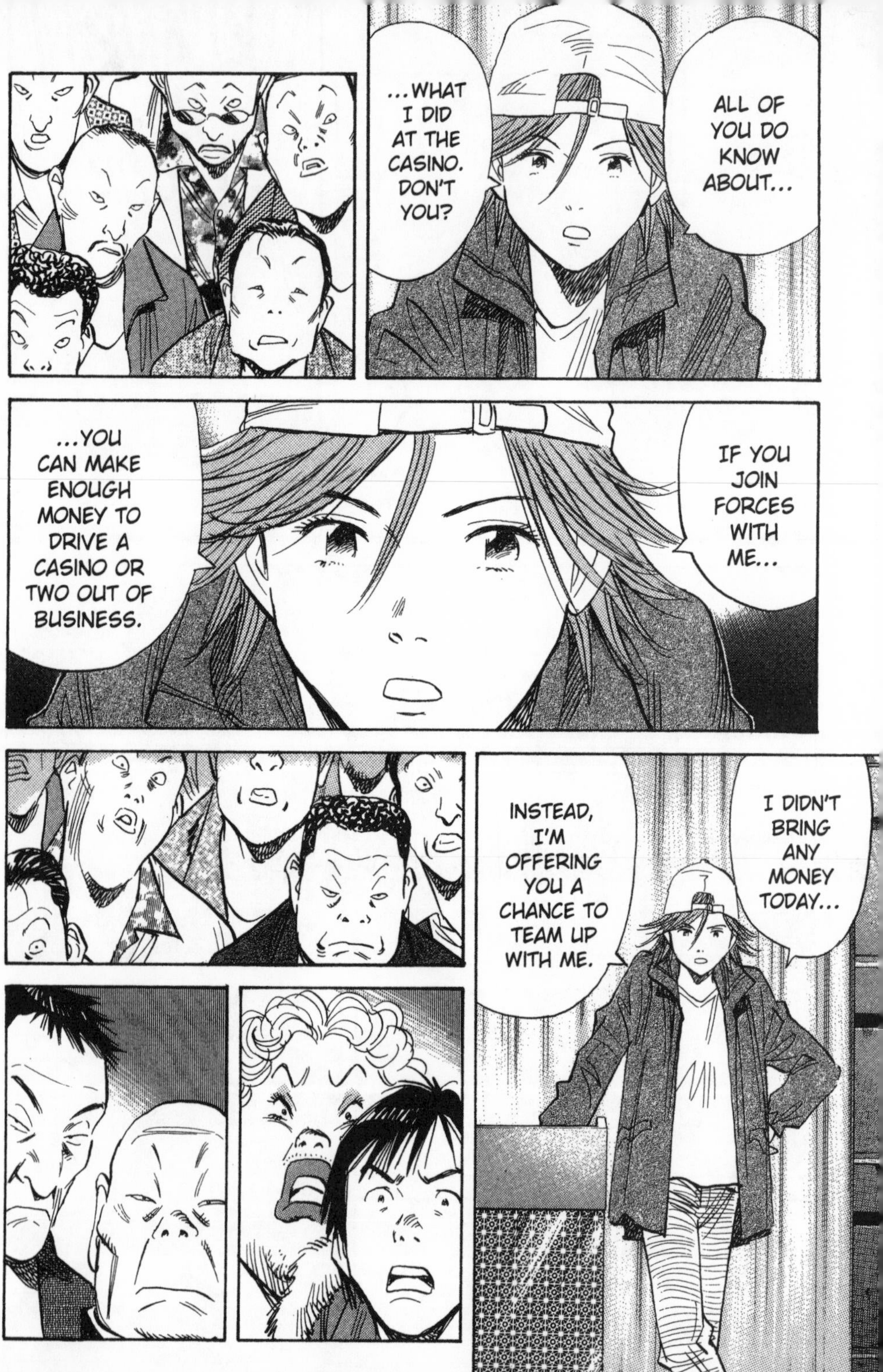
ALL OF YOU DO KNOW ABOUT...
...WHAT I DID AT THE CASINO. DON'T YOU?
IF YOU JOIN FORCES WITH ME...
...YOU CAN MAKE ENOUGH MONEY TO DRIVE A CASINO OR TWO OUT OF BUSINESS.
I DIDN'T BRING ANY MONEY TODAY...
INSTEAD, I'M OFFERING YOU A CHANCE TO TEAM UP WITH ME.

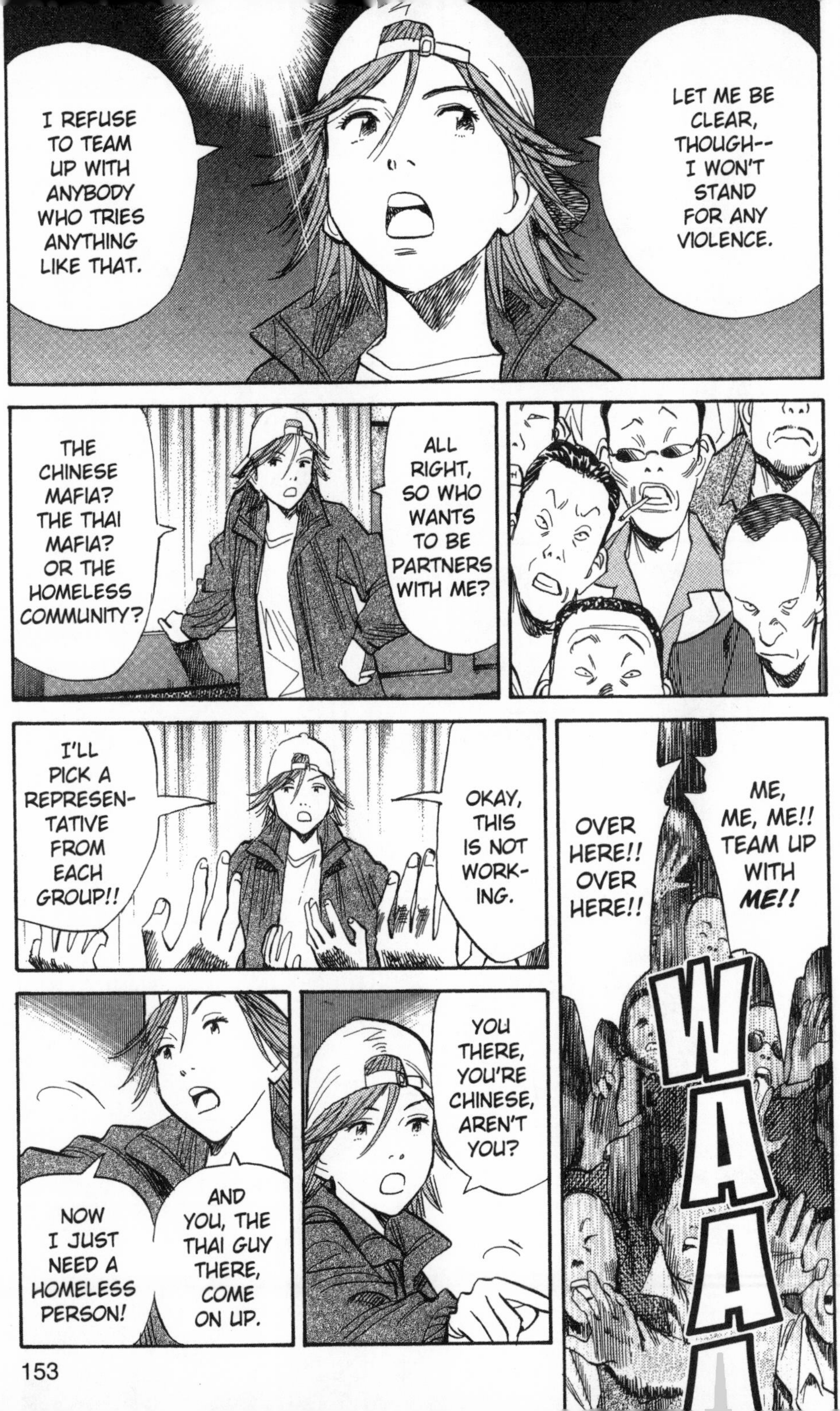
LET ME BE CLEAR, THOUGH-- I WON'T STAND FOR ANY VIOLENCE.
I REFUSE TO TEAM UP WITH ANYBODY WHO TRIES ANYTHING LIKE THAT.
ALL RIGHT, SO WHO WANTS TO BE PARTNERS WITH ME?
THE CHINESE MAFIA? THE THAI MAFIA? OR THE HOMELESS COMMUNITY?
ME, ME, ME!! TEAM UP WITH *ME!!*
OVER HERE!! OVER HERE!!
WAA
OKAY, THIS IS NOT WORK-ING.
I'LL PICK A REPRESEN-TATIVE FROM EACH GROUP!!
YOU THERE, YOU'RE CHINESE, AREN'T YOU?
AND YOU, THE THAI GUY THERE, COME ON UP.
NOW I JUST NEED A HOMELESS PERSON!

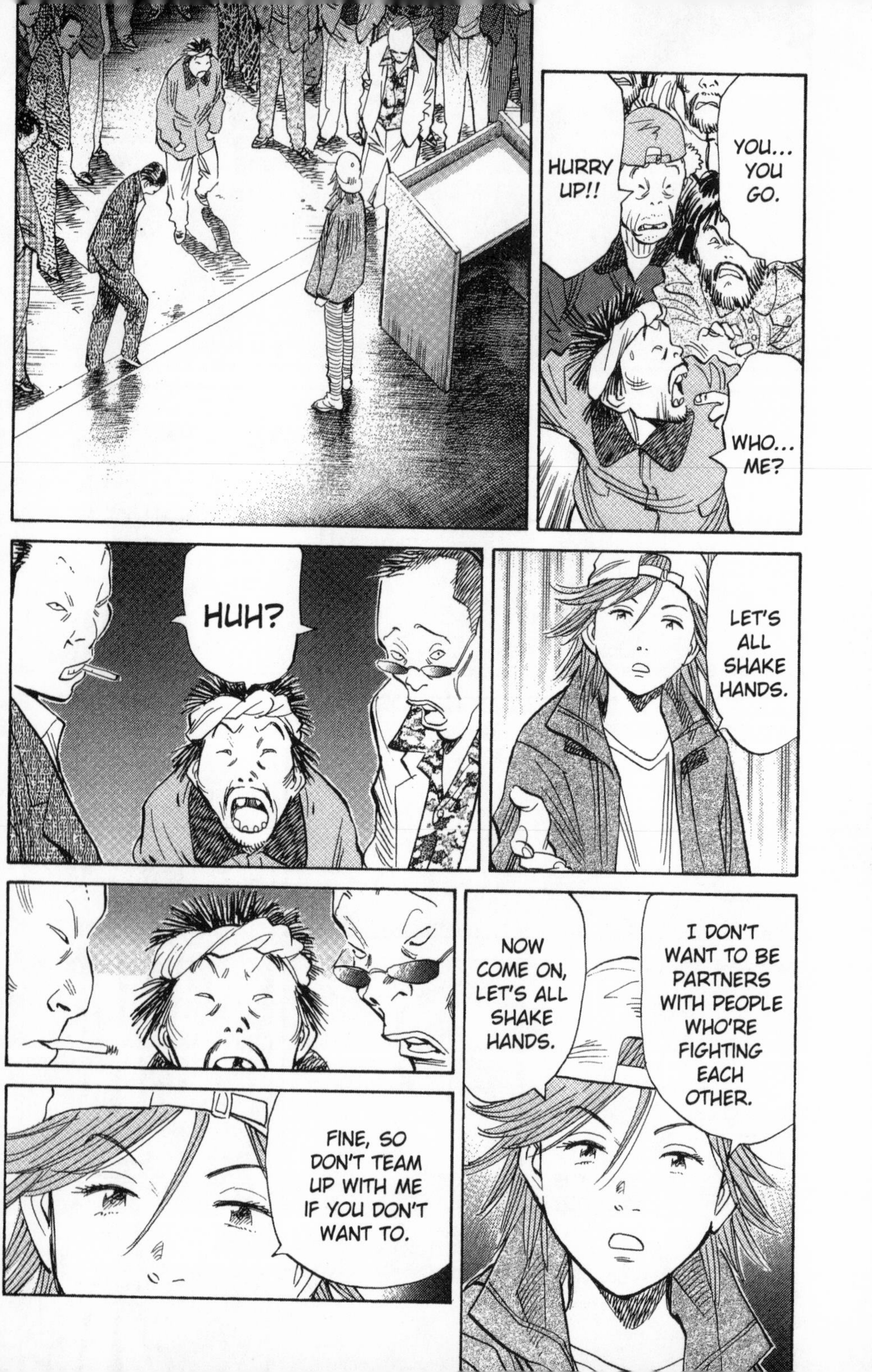
YOU... YOU GO.
HURRY UP!!
WHO... ME?
LET'S ALL SHAKE HANDS.
HUH?
I DON'T WANT TO BE PARTNERS WITH PEOPLE WHO'RE FIGHTING EACH OTHER.
NOW COME ON, LET'S ALL SHAKE HANDS.
FINE, SO DON'T TEAM UP WITH ME IF YOU DON'T WANT TO.

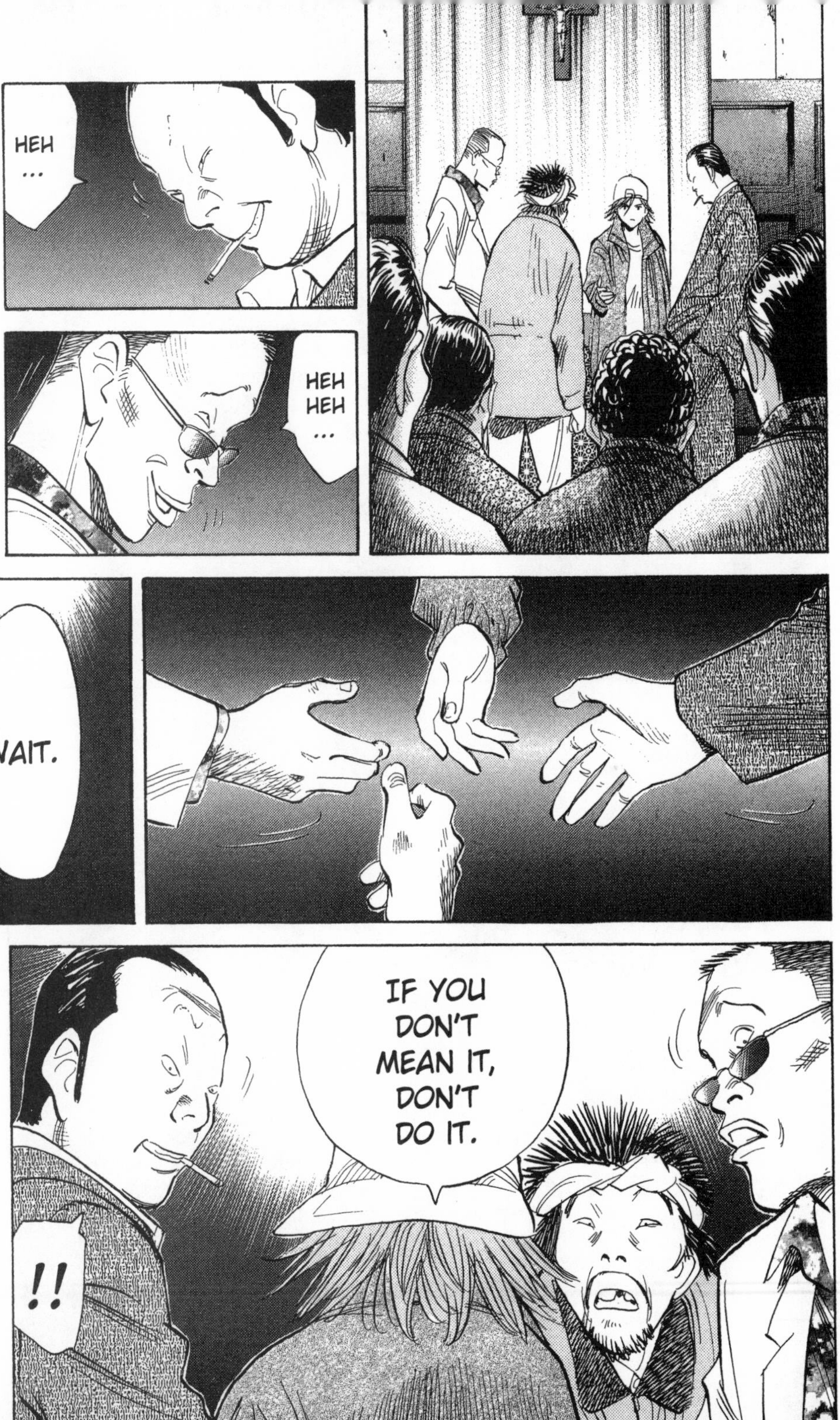
HEH ...
HEH HEH ...
WAIT.
IF YOU DON'T MEAN IT, DON'T DO IT.
!!

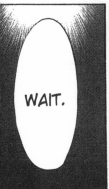

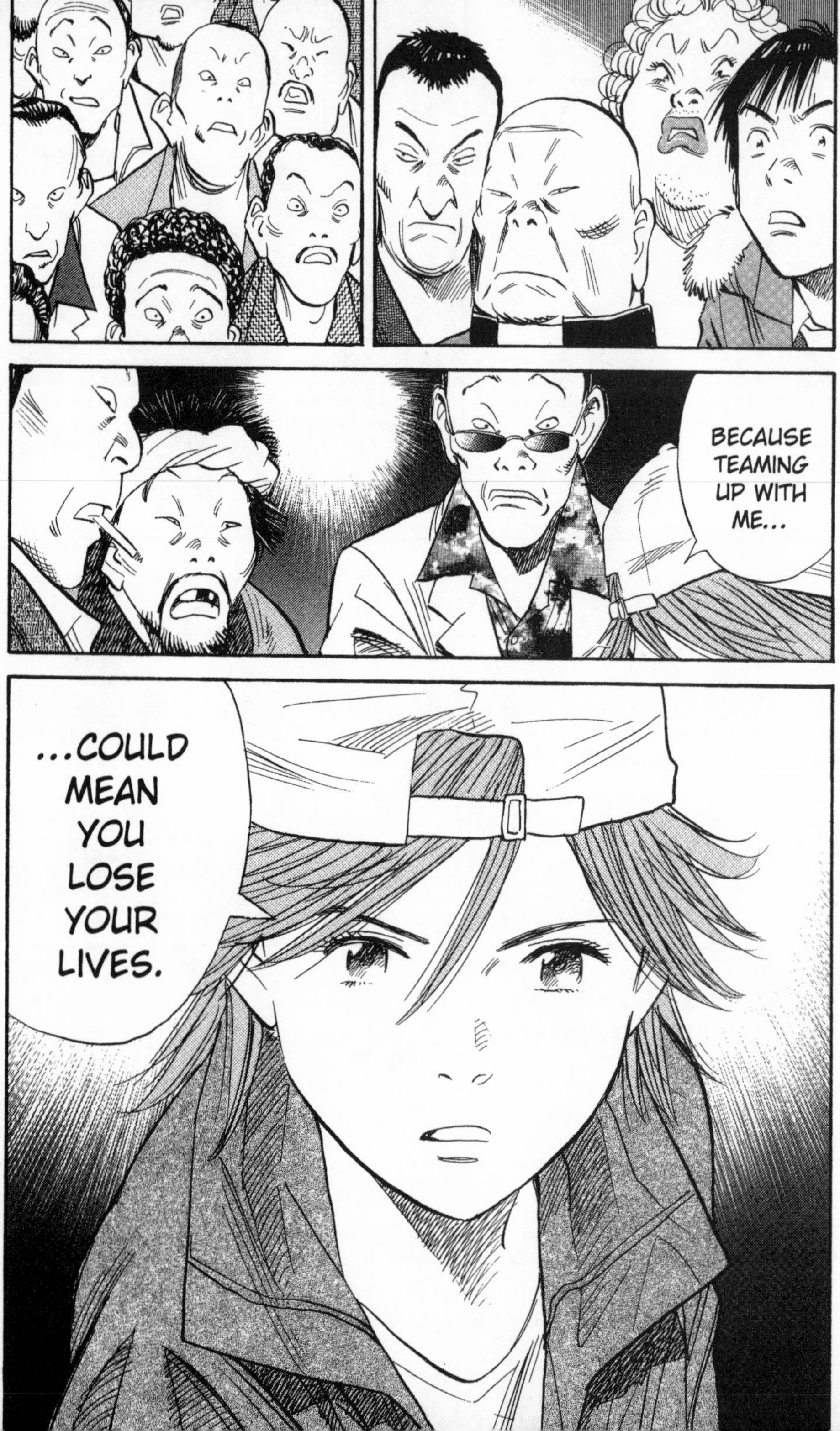
BECAUSE TEAMING UP WITH ME...
...COULD MEAN YOU LOSE YOUR LIVES.

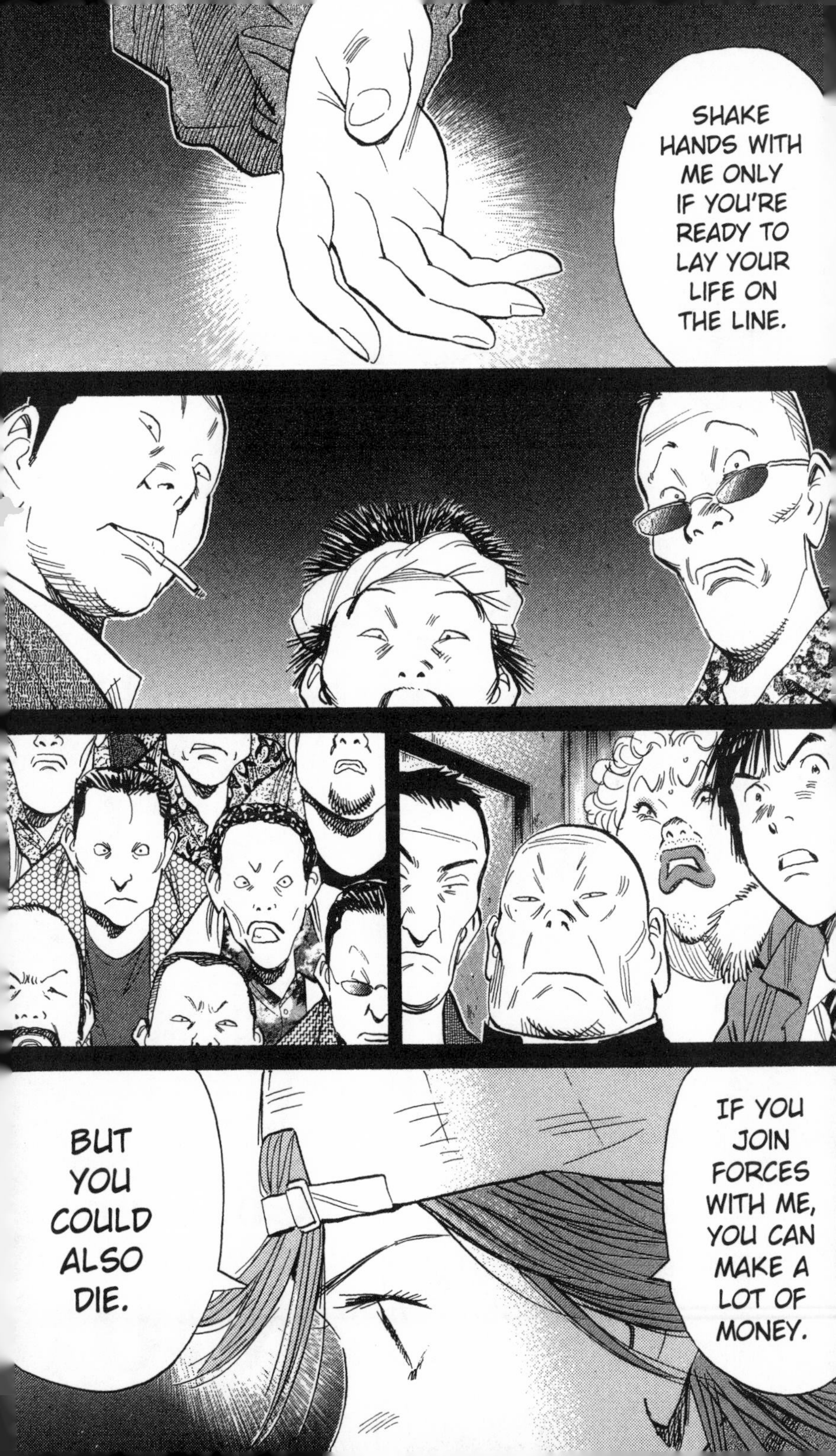
SHAKE HANDS WITH ME ONLY IF YOU'RE READY TO LAY YOUR LIFE ON THE LINE.
IF YOU JOIN FORCES WITH ME, YOU CAN MAKE A LOT OF MONEY.
BUT YOU COULD ALSO DIE.

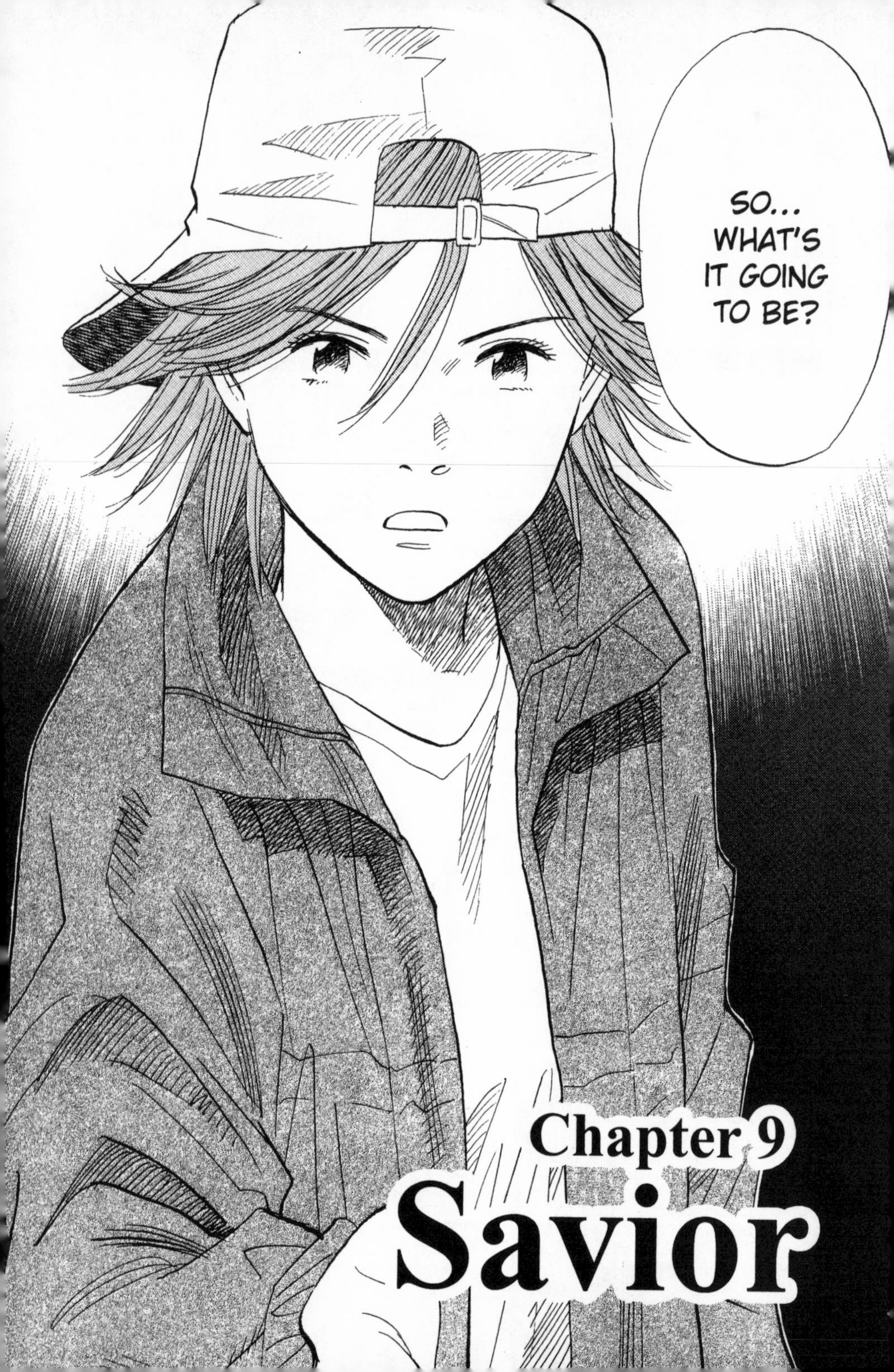
SO... WHAT'S IT GOING TO BE?
Chapter 9
Savior

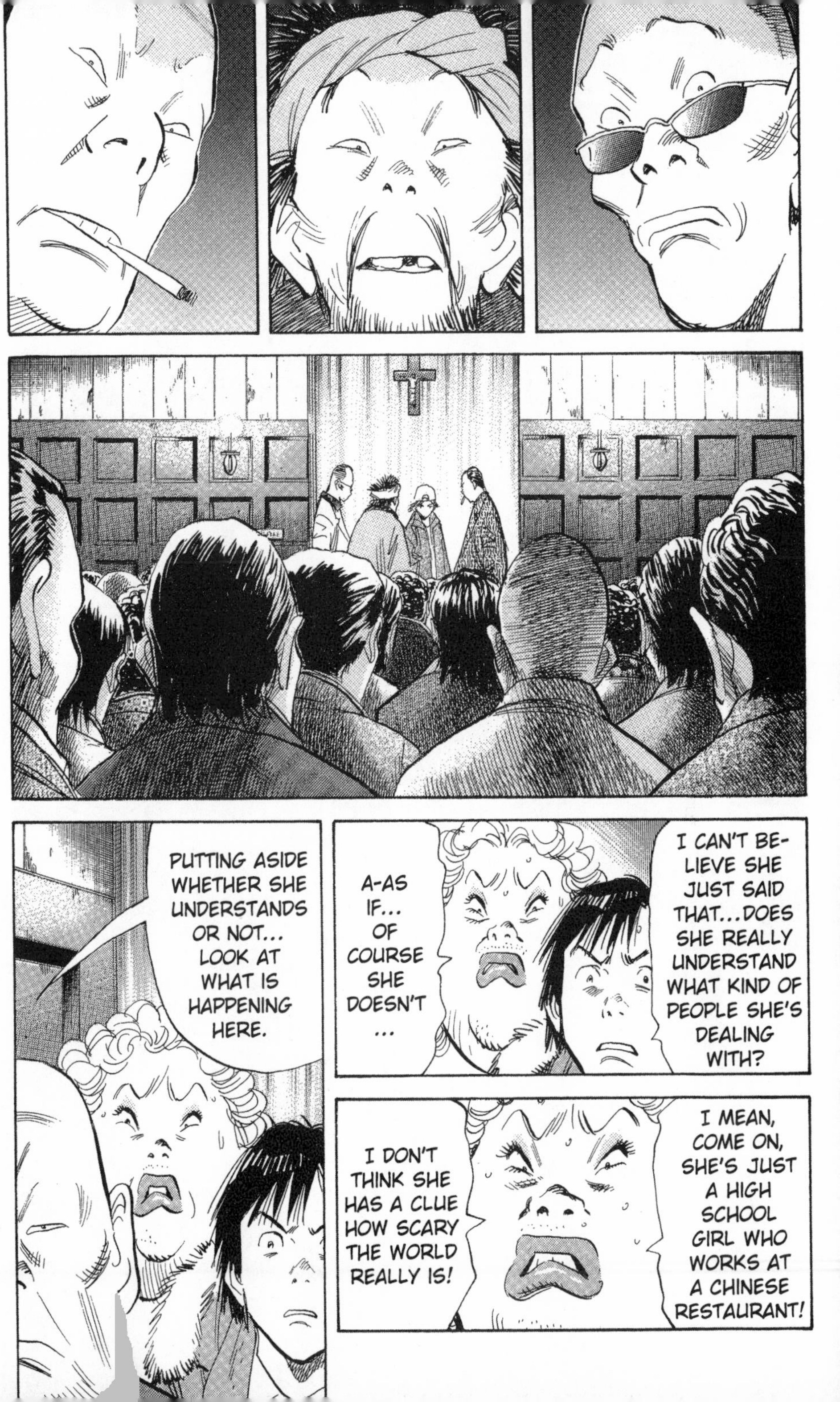
I CAN'T BE-LIEVE SHE JUST SAID THAT...DOES SHE REALLY UNDERSTAND WHAT KIND OF PEOPLE SHE'S DEALING WITH?
A-AS IF... OF COURSE SHE DOESN'T ...
I MEAN, COME ON, SHE'S JUST A HIGH SCHOOL GIRL WHO WORKS AT A CHINESE RESTAURANT!
I DON'T THINK SHE HAS A CLUE HOW SCARY THE WORLD REALLY IS!
PUTTING ASIDE WHETHER SHE UNDERSTANDS OR NOT... LOOK AT WHAT IS HAPPENING HERE.

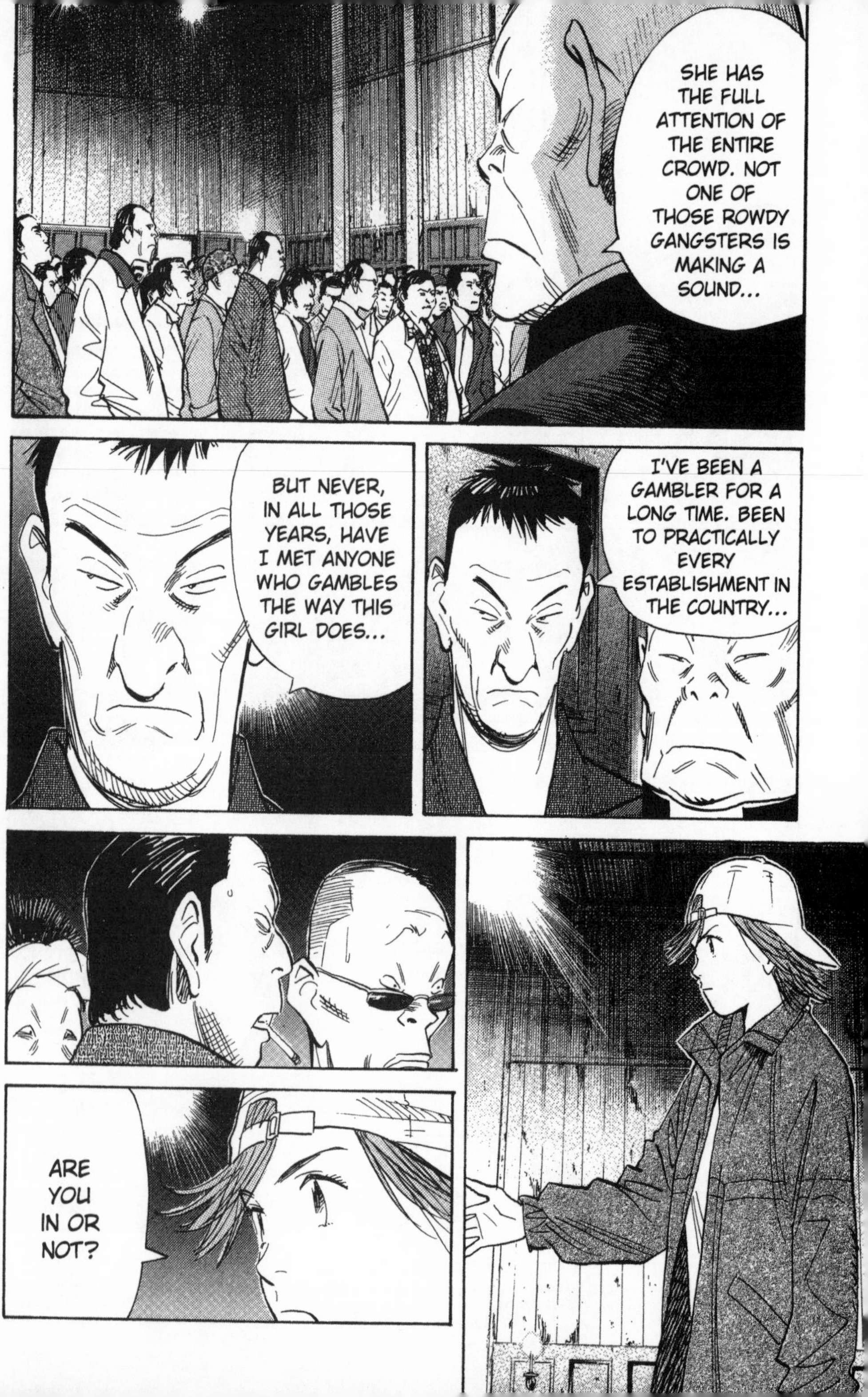
SHE HAS THE FULL ATTENTION OF THE ENTIRE CROWD. NOT ONE OF THOSE ROWDY GANGSTERS IS MAKING A SOUND...
I'VE BEEN A GAMBLER FOR A LONG TIME. BEEN TO PRACTICALLY EVERY ESTABLISHMENT IN THE COUNTRY...
BUT NEVER, IN ALL THOSE YEARS, HAVE I MET ANYONE WHO GAMBLES THE WAY THIS GIRL DOES...
ARE YOU IN OR NOT?

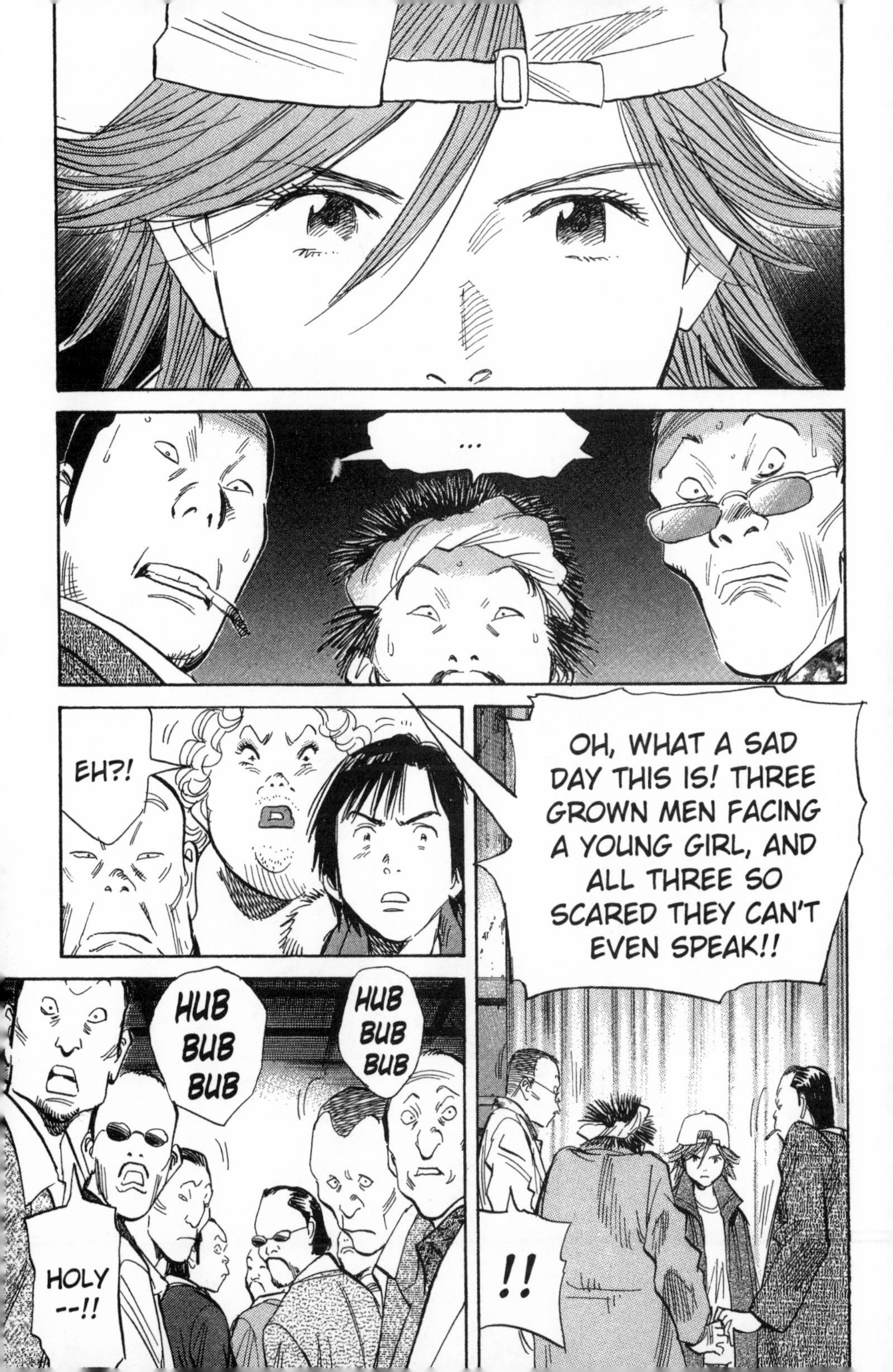
...
OH, WHAT A SAD DAY THIS IS! THREE GROWN MEN FACING A YOUNG GIRL, AND ALL THREE SO SCARED THEY CAN'T EVEN SPEAK!!
!!
EH?!
HUB BUB BUB
HUB BUB BUB
HOLY --!!

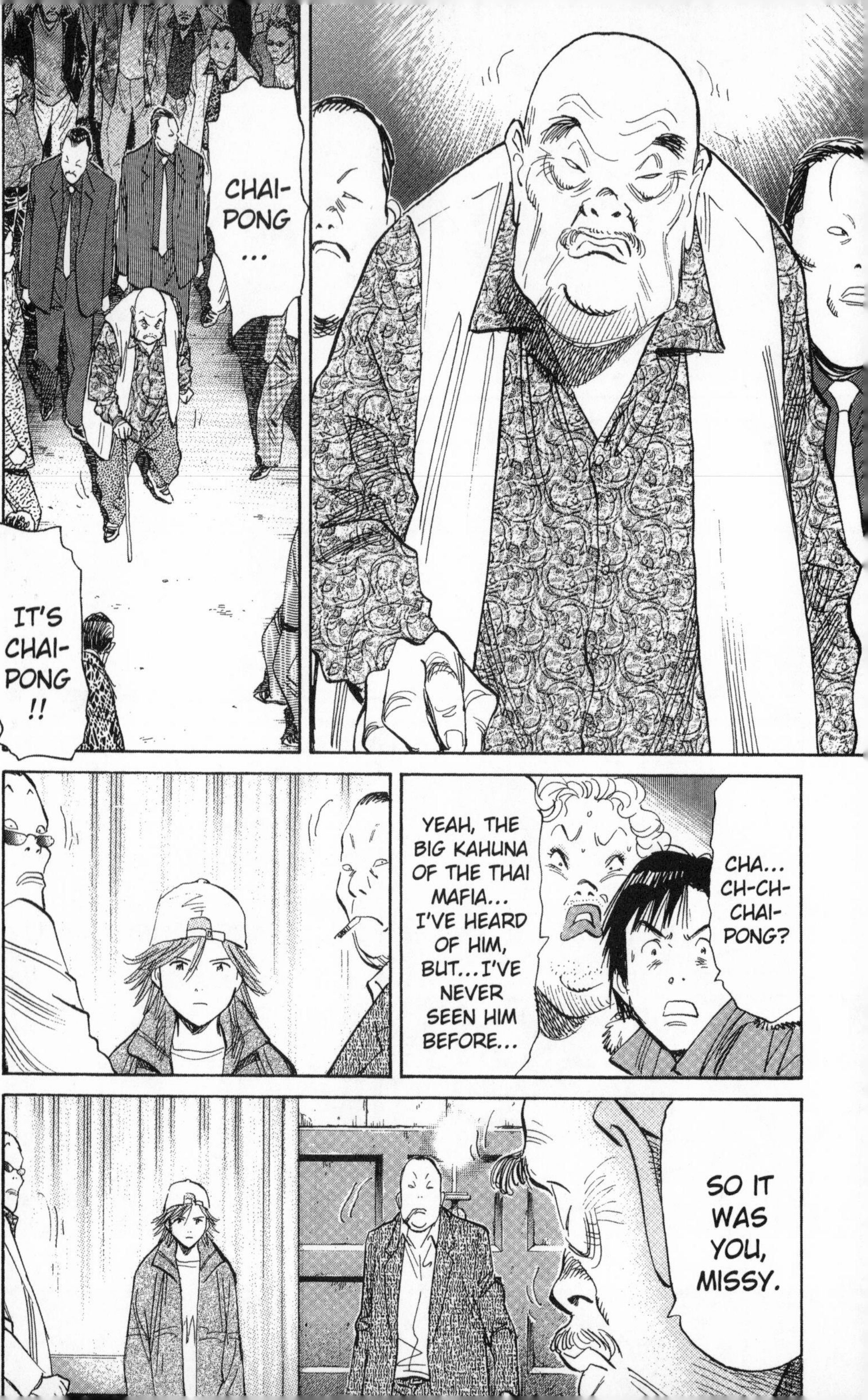
CHAI-PONG...
IT'S CHAI-PONG!!
CHA... CH-CH-CHAI-PONG?
YEAH, THE BIG KAHUNA OF THE THAI MAFIA... I'VE HEARD OF HIM, BUT...I'VE NEVER SEEN HIM BEFORE...
SO IT WAS YOU, MISSY.

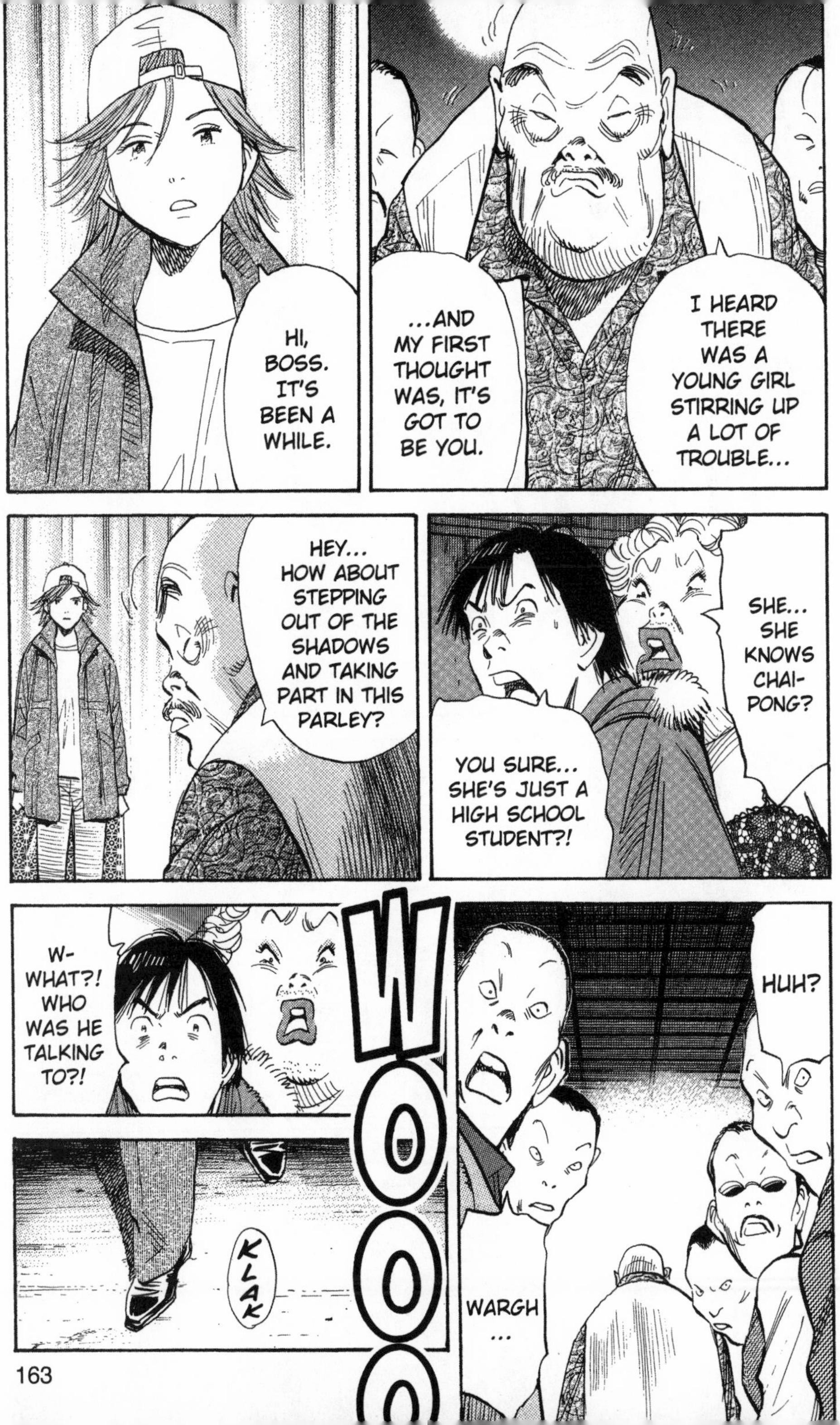
I HEARD THERE WAS A YOUNG GIRL STIRRING UP A LOT OF TROUBLE...
...AND MY FIRST THOUGHT WAS, IT'S GOT TO BE YOU.
HI, BOSS. IT'S BEEN A WHILE.
SHE... SHE KNOWS CHAI-PONG?
YOU SURE... SHE'S JUST A HIGH SCHOOL STUDENT?!
HEY... HOW ABOUT STEPPING OUT OF THE SHADOWS AND TAKING PART IN THIS PARLEY?
HUH?
WARGH...
WOOO
W-WHAT?! WHO WAS HE TALKING TO?!
KLAK

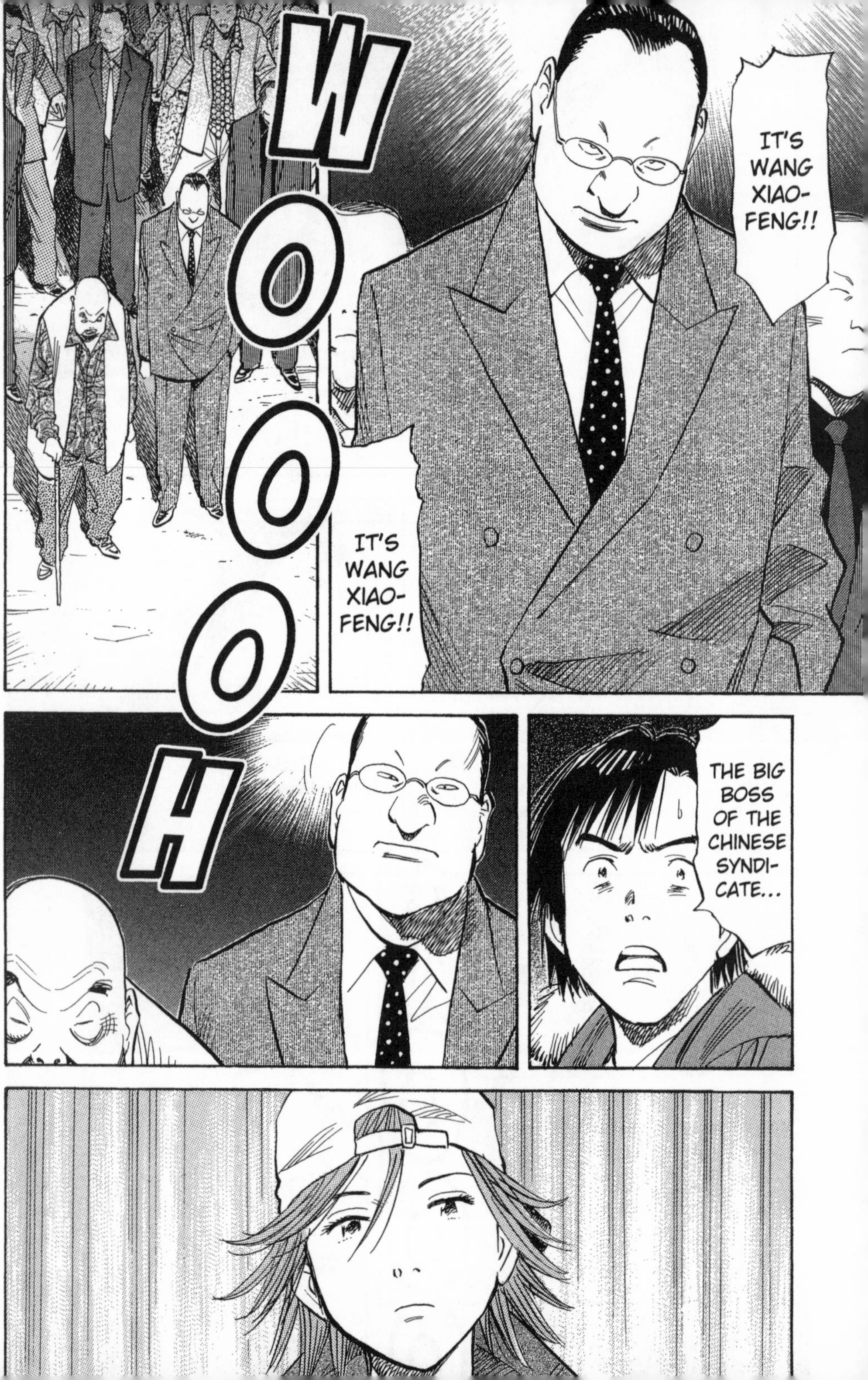
IT'S WANG XIAO-FENG!!
IT'S WANG XIAO-FENG!!
WOOOOH
THE BIG BOSS OF THE CHINESE SYNDICATE...

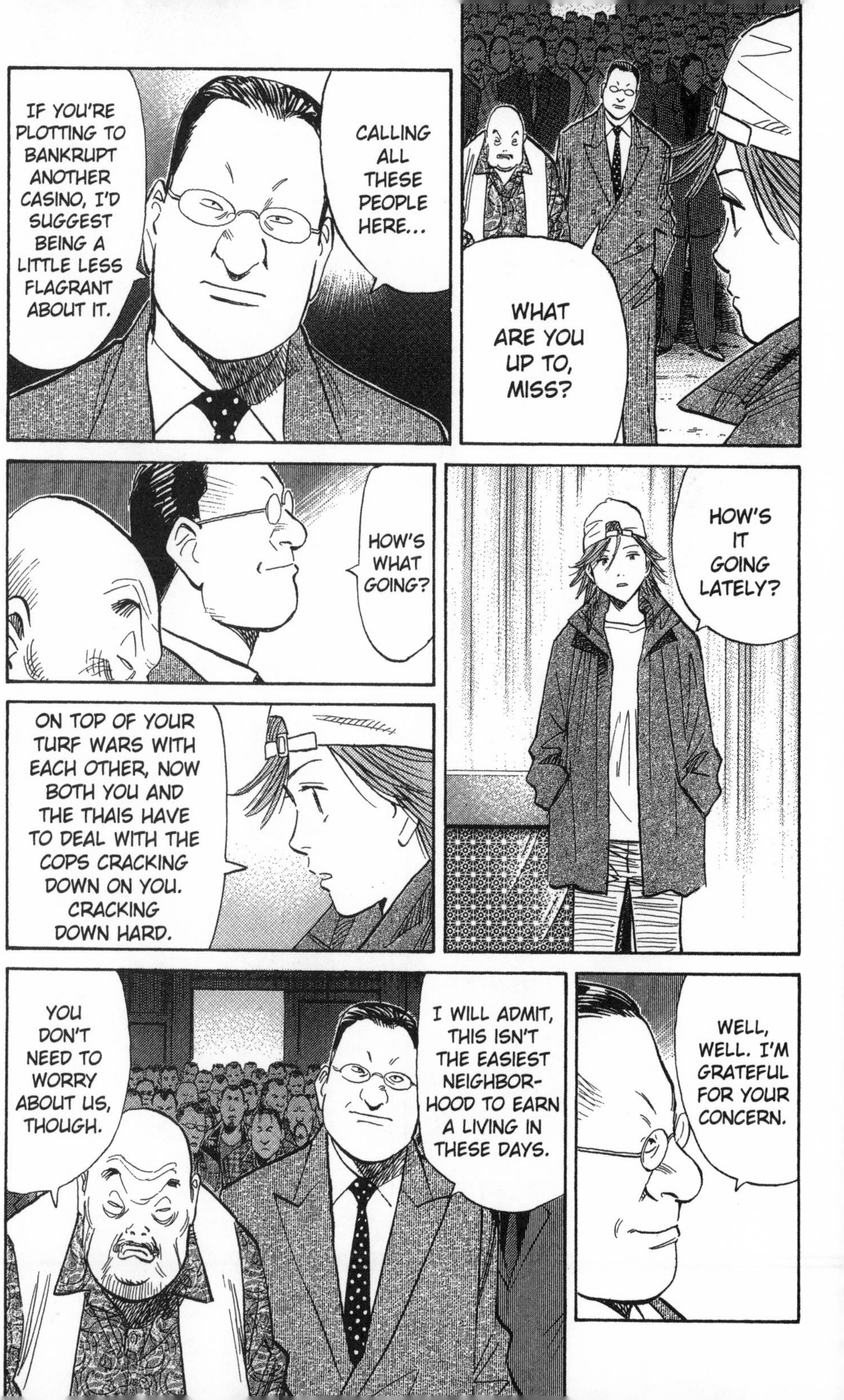
WHAT ARE YOU UP TO, MISS?
CALLING ALL THESE PEOPLE HERE...
IF YOU'RE PLOTTING TO BANKRUPT ANOTHER CASINO, I'D SUGGEST BEING A LITTLE LESS FLAGRANT ABOUT IT.
HOW'S IT GOING LATELY?
HOW'S WHAT GOING?
ON TOP OF YOUR TURF WARS WITH EACH OTHER, NOW BOTH YOU AND THE THAIS HAVE TO DEAL WITH THE COPS CRACKING DOWN ON YOU. CRACKING DOWN HARD.
WELL, WELL. I'M GRATEFUL FOR YOUR CONCERN.
I WILL ADMIT, THIS ISN'T THE EASIEST NEIGHBOR-HOOD TO EARN A LIVING IN THESE DAYS.
YOU DON'T NEED TO WORRY ABOUT US, THOUGH.

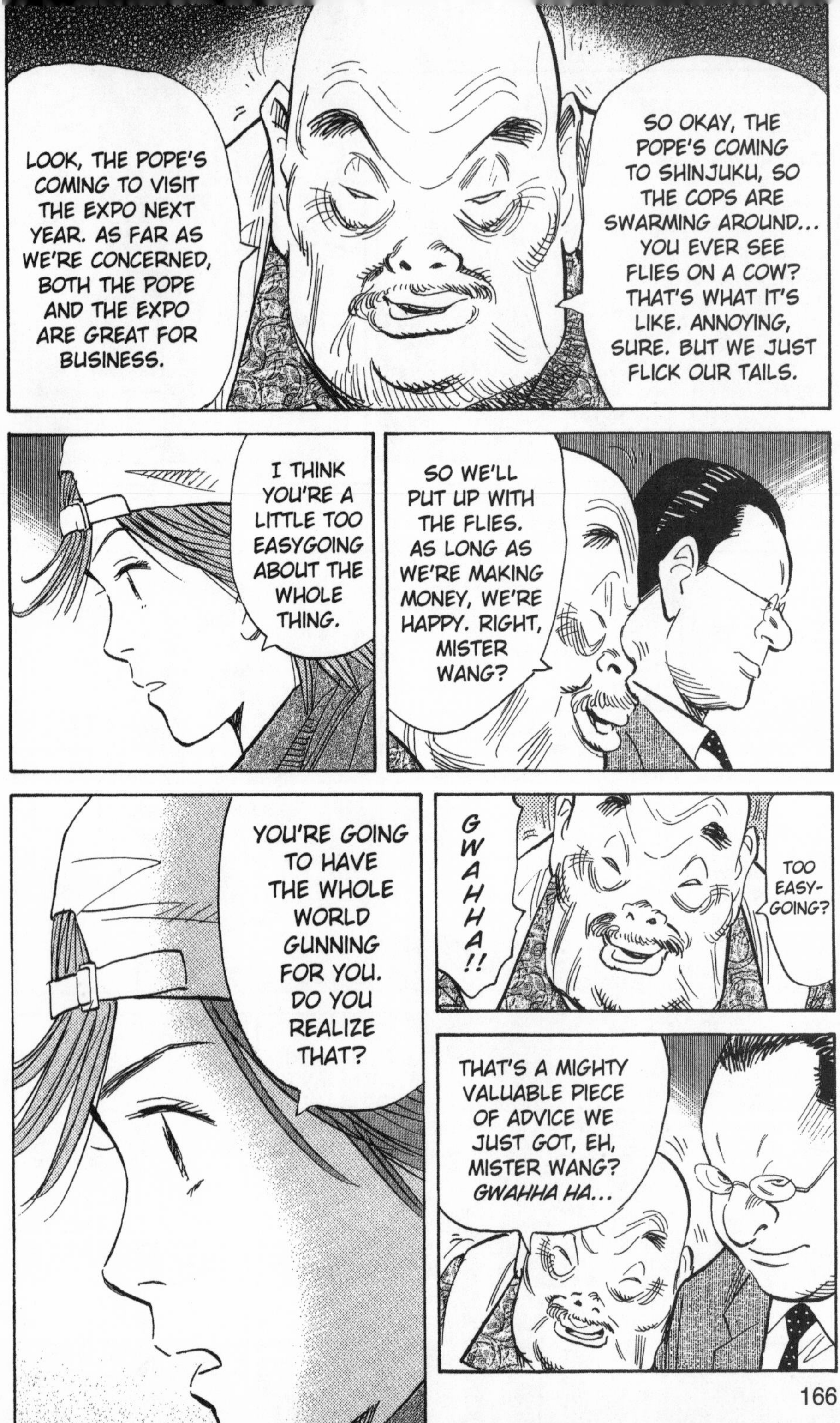
SO OKAY, THE POPE'S COMING TO SHINJUKU, SO THE COPS ARE SWARMING AROUND... YOU EVER SEE FLIES ON A COW? THAT'S WHAT IT'S LIKE. ANNOYING, SURE. BUT WE JUST FLICK OUR TAILS.
LOOK, THE POPE'S COMING TO VISIT THE EXPO NEXT YEAR. AS FAR AS WE'RE CONCERNED, BOTH THE POPE AND THE EXPO ARE GREAT FOR BUSINESS.
SO WE'LL PUT UP WITH THE FLIES. AS LONG AS WE'RE MAKING MONEY, WE'RE HAPPY. RIGHT, MISTER WANG?
I THINK YOU'RE A LITTLE TOO EASYGOING ABOUT THE WHOLE THING.
TOO EASY-GOING?
GWAHHA!!
THAT'S A MIGHTY VALUABLE PIECE OF ADVICE WE JUST GOT, EH, MISTER WANG? GWAHHA HA...
YOU'RE GOING TO HAVE THE WHOLE WORLD GUNNING FOR YOU. DO YOU REALIZE THAT?

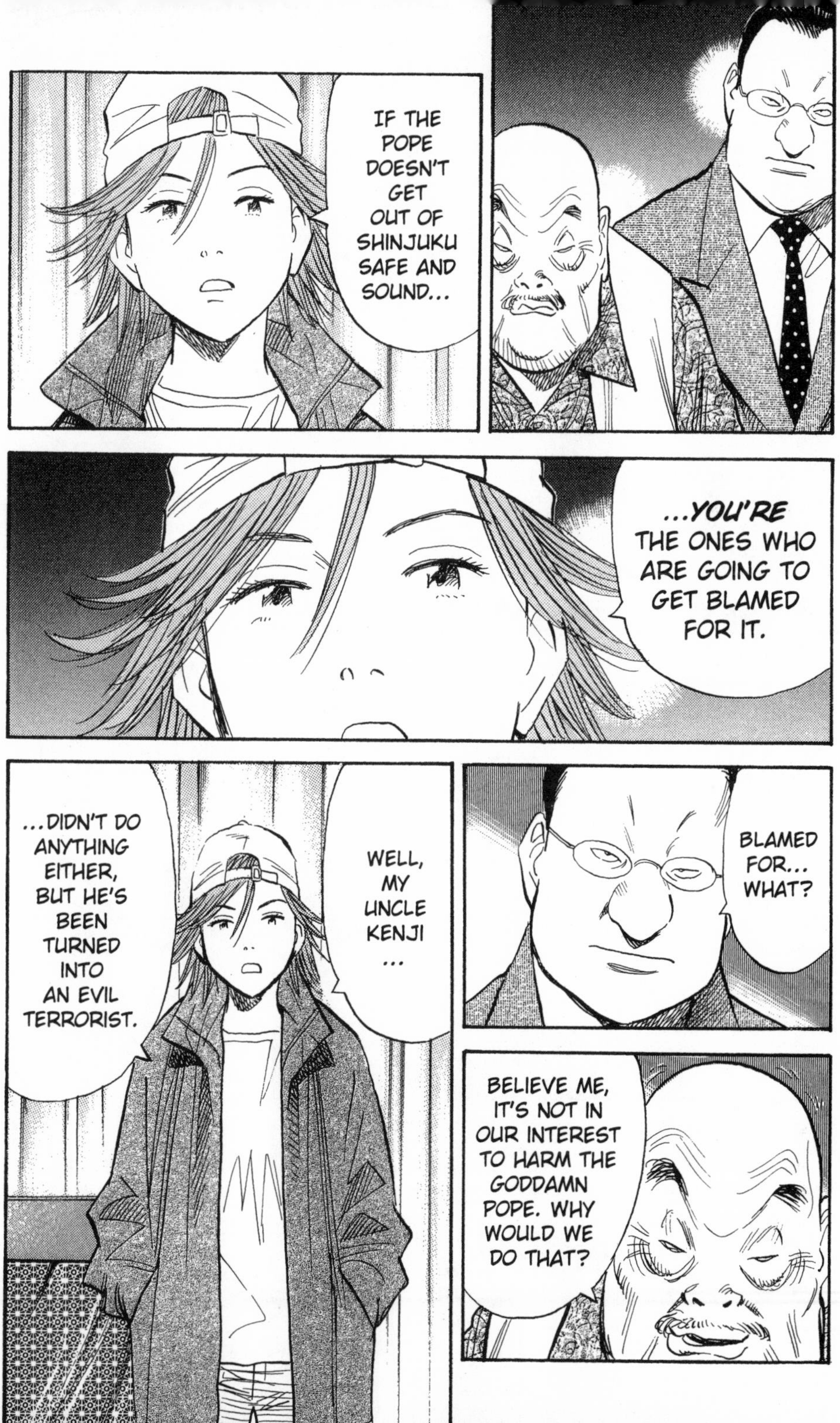
IF THE POPE DOESN'T GET OUT OF SHINJUKU SAFE AND SOUND...
...*YOU'RE* THE ONES WHO ARE GOING TO GET BLAMED FOR IT.
BLAMED FOR... WHAT?
BELIEVE ME, IT'S NOT IN OUR INTEREST TO HARM THE GODDAMN POPE. WHY WOULD WE DO THAT?
WELL, MY UNCLE KENJI ...
...DIDN'T DO ANYTHING EITHER, BUT HE'S BEEN TURNED INTO AN EVIL TERRORIST.

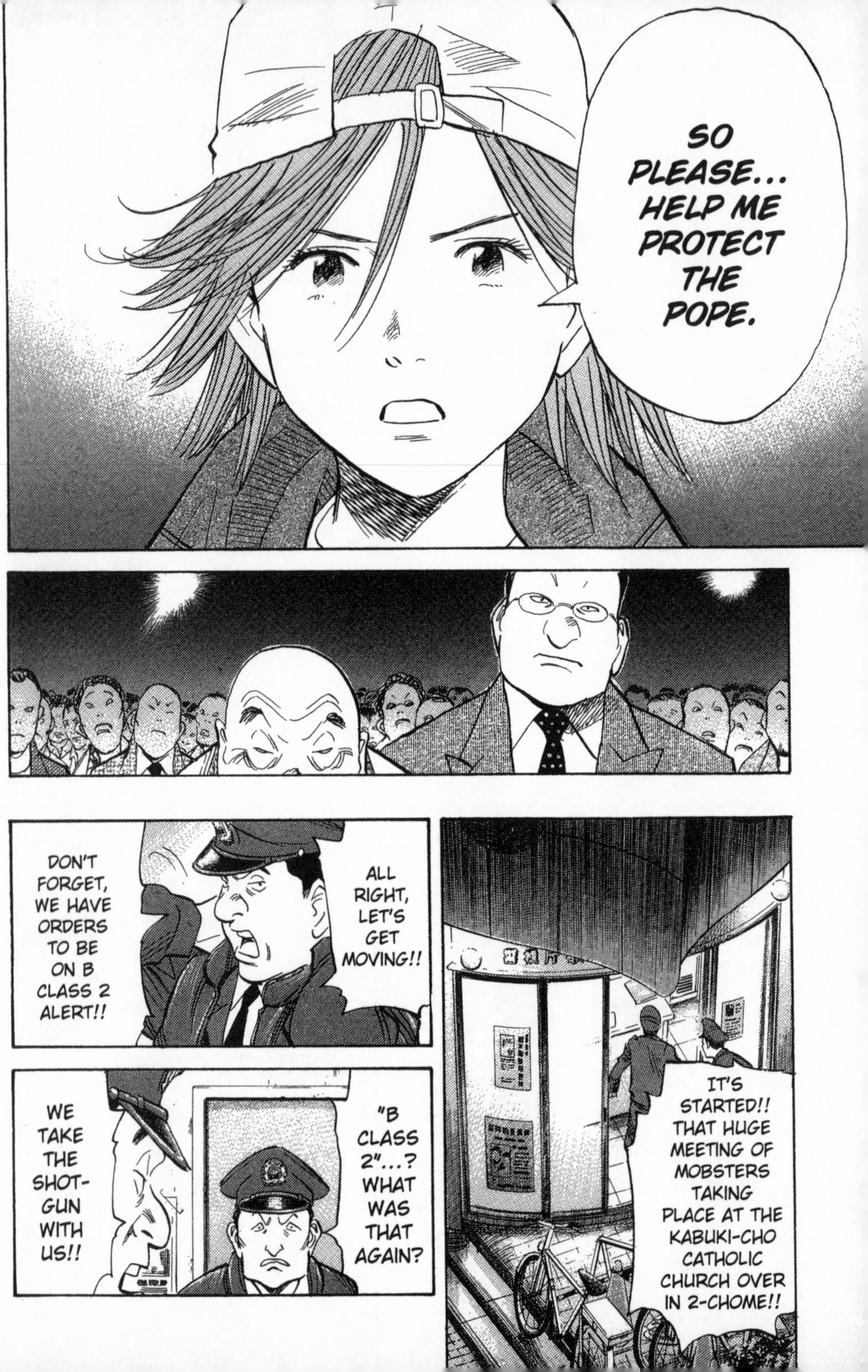
SO PLEASE... HELP ME PROTECT THE POPE.
IT'S STARTED!! THAT HUGE MEETING OF MOBSTERS TAKING PLACE AT THE KABUKI-CHO CATHOLIC CHURCH OVER IN 2-CHOME!!
ALL RIGHT, LET'S GET MOVING!!
DON'T FORGET, WE HAVE ORDERS TO BE ON B CLASS 2 ALERT!!
"B CLASS 2"...? WHAT WAS THAT AGAIN?
WE TAKE THE SHOT-GUN WITH US!!

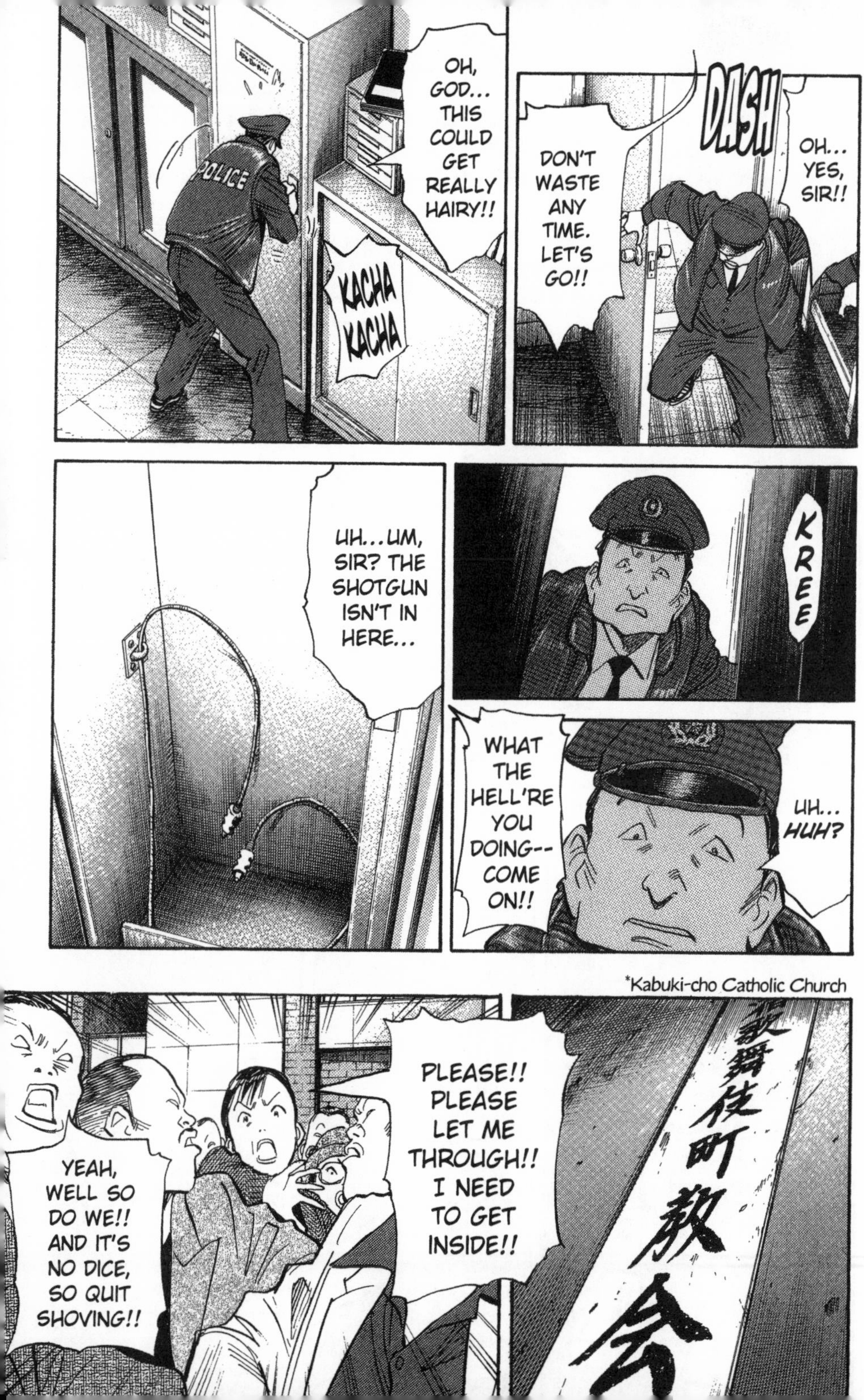
DASH
DON'T WASTE ANY TIME. LET'S GO!!
OH... YES, SIR!!
OH, GOD... THIS COULD GET REALLY HAIRY!!
KACHA KACHA
KREE
WHAT THE HELL'RE YOU DOING-- COME ON!!
UH... HUH?
UH...UM, SIR? THE SHOTGUN ISN'T IN HERE...
*Kabuki-cho Catholic Church
舞伎町教会
PLEASE!! PLEASE LET ME THROUGH!! I NEED TO GET INSIDE!!
YEAH, WELL SO DO WE!! AND IT'S NO DICE, SO QUIT SHOVING!!

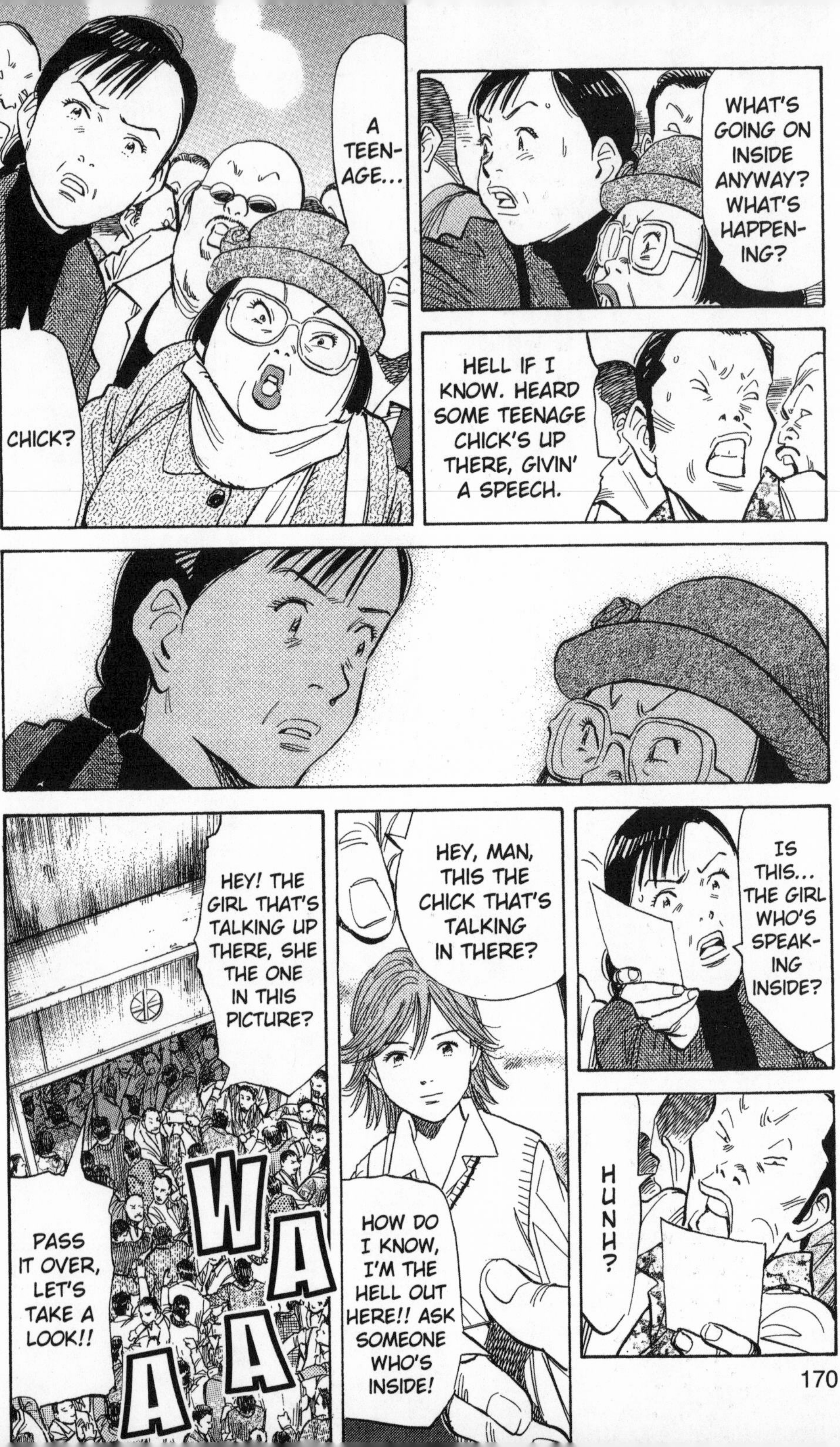
WHAT'S GOING ON INSIDE ANYWAY? WHAT'S HAPPEN-ING?
HELL IF I KNOW. HEARD SOME TEENAGE CHICK'S UP THERE, GIVIN' A SPEECH.
A TEEN-AGE...
CHICK?
IS THIS... THE GIRL WHO'S SPEAK-ING INSIDE?
HUNH?
HEY, MAN, THIS THE CHICK THAT'S TALKING IN THERE?
HOW DO I KNOW, I'M THE HELL OUT HERE!! ASK SOMEONE WHO'S INSIDE!
HEY! THE GIRL THAT'S TALKING UP THERE, SHE THE ONE IN THIS PICTURE?
PASS IT OVER, LET'S TAKE A LOOK!!
WAAAA

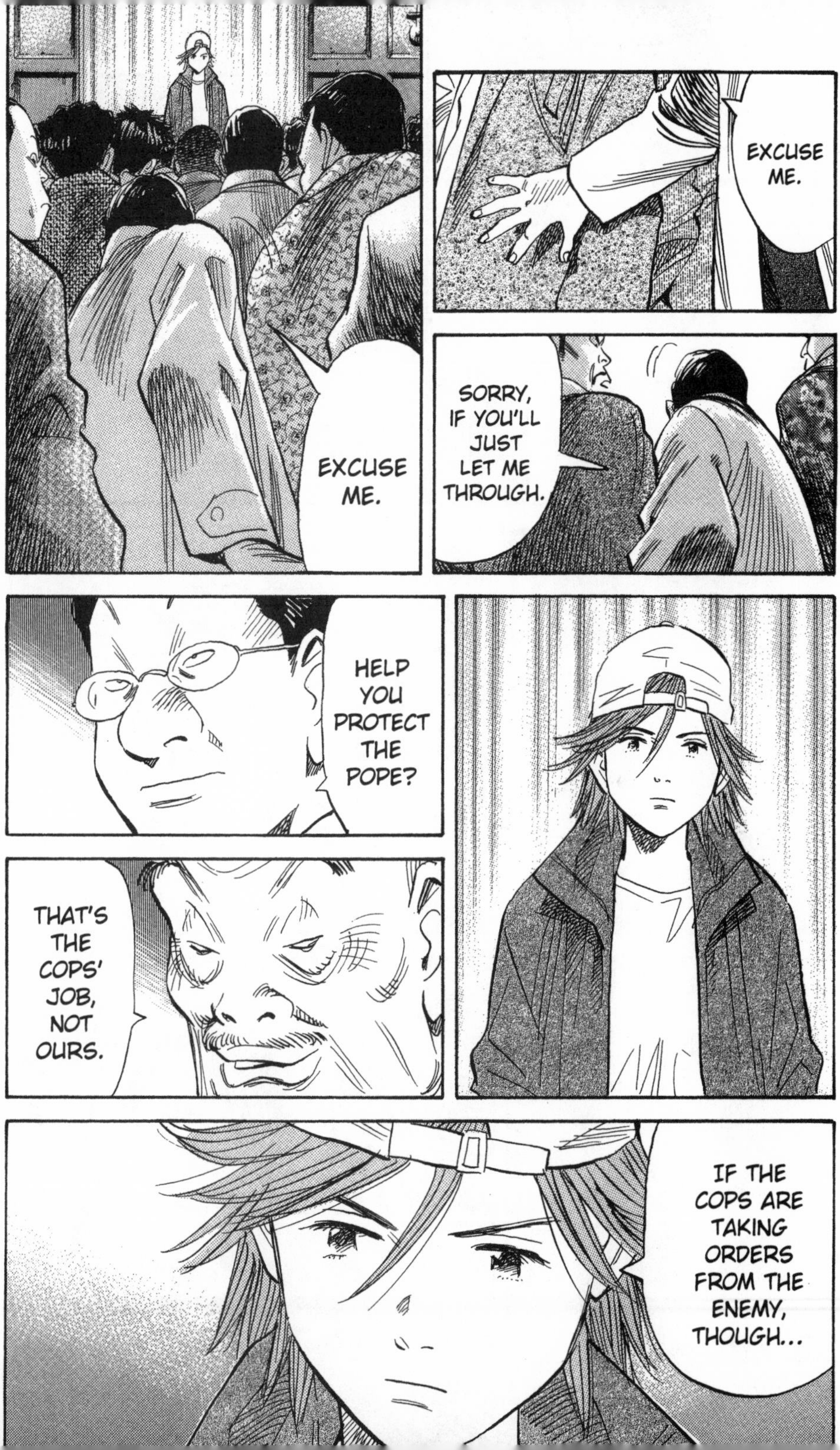
EXCUSE ME.
SORRY, IF YOU'LL JUST LET ME THROUGH.
EXCUSE ME.
HELP YOU PROTECT THE POPE?
THAT'S THE COPS' JOB, NOT OURS.
IF THE COPS ARE TAKING ORDERS FROM THE ENEMY, THOUGH...

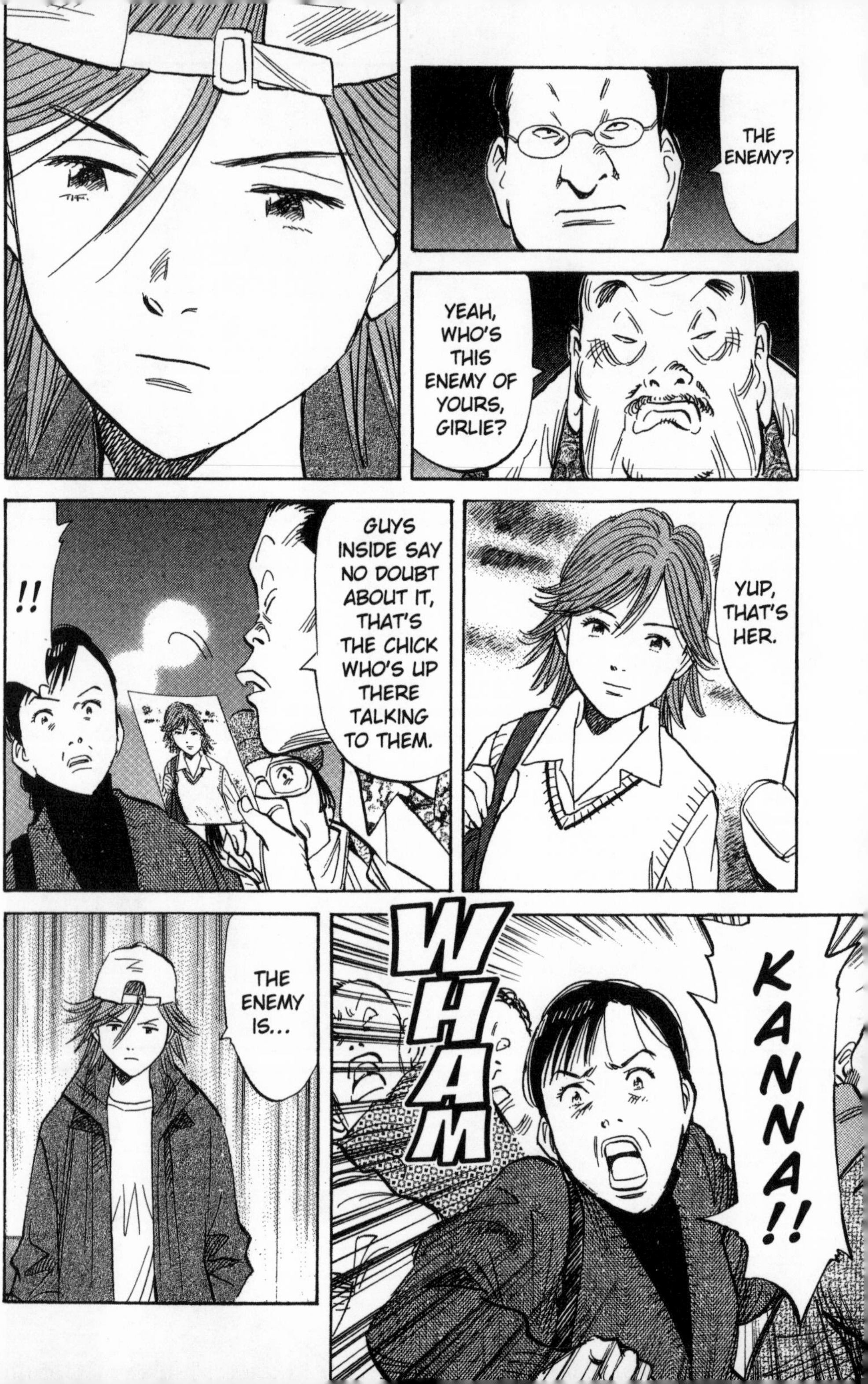
THE ENEMY?
YEAH, WHO'S THIS ENEMY OF YOURS, GIRLIE?
YUP, THAT'S HER.
GUYS INSIDE SAY NO DOUBT ABOUT IT, THAT'S THE CHICK WHO'S UP THERE TALKING TO THEM.
!!
KANNA!!
WHAM
THE ENEMY IS...

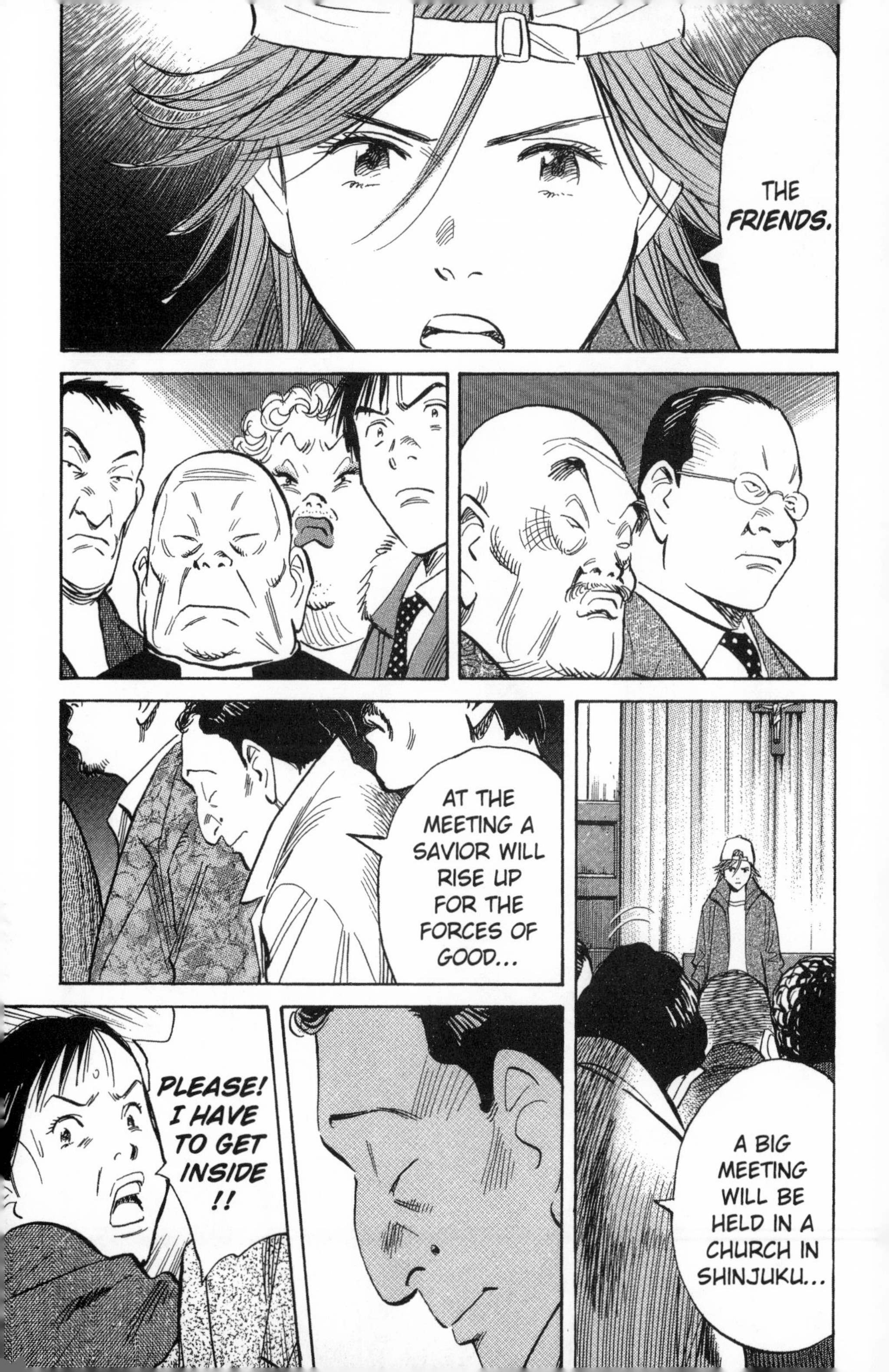
THE FRIENDS.
A BIG MEETING WILL BE HELD IN A CHURCH IN SHINJUKU...
AT THE MEETING A SAVIOR WILL RISE UP FOR THE FORCES OF GOOD...
PLEASE! I HAVE TO GET INSIDE !!

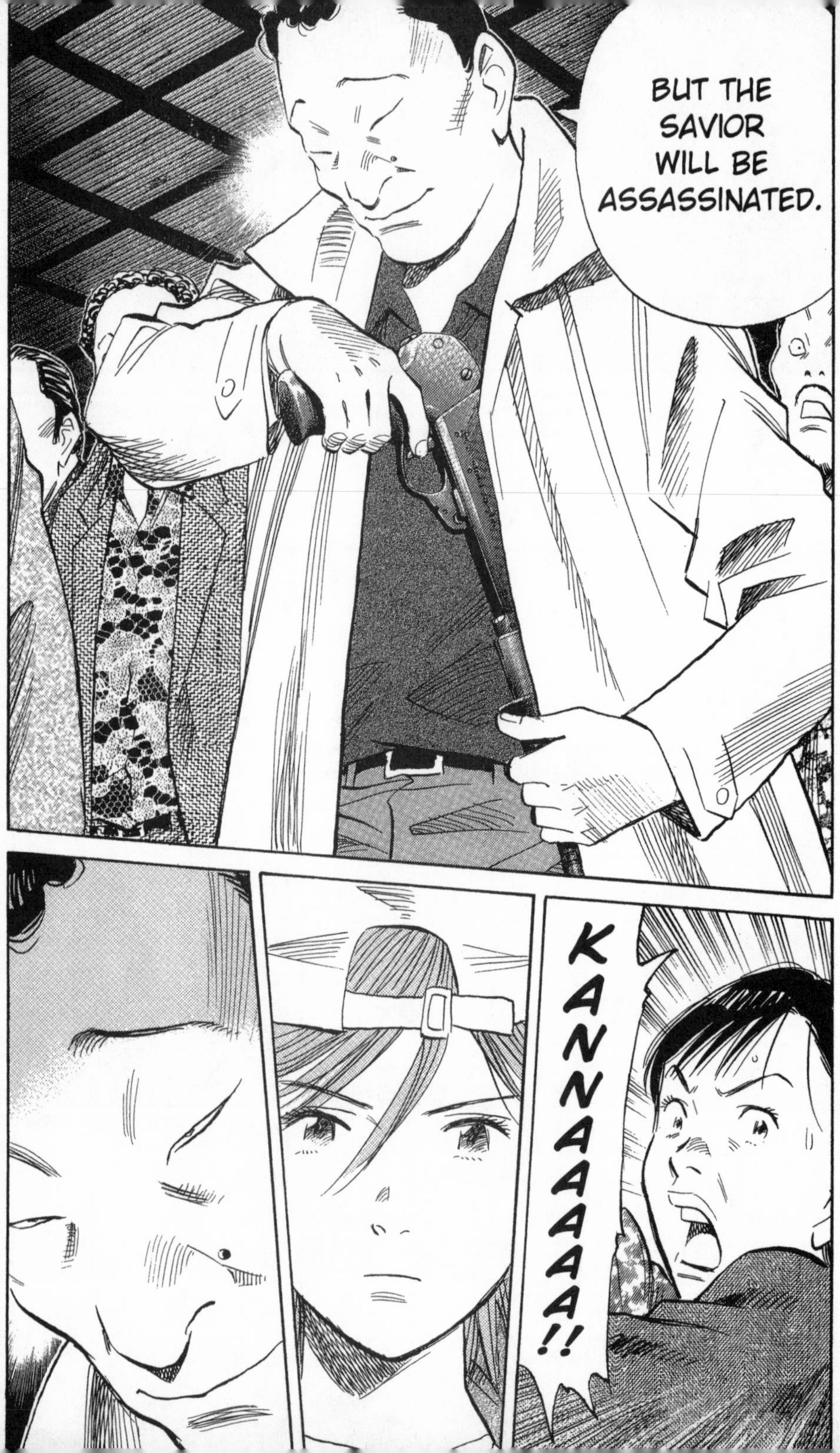
BUT THE SAVIOR WILL BE ASSASSINATED.
KANNAAAAAAA!!

Chapter 10 Assassination

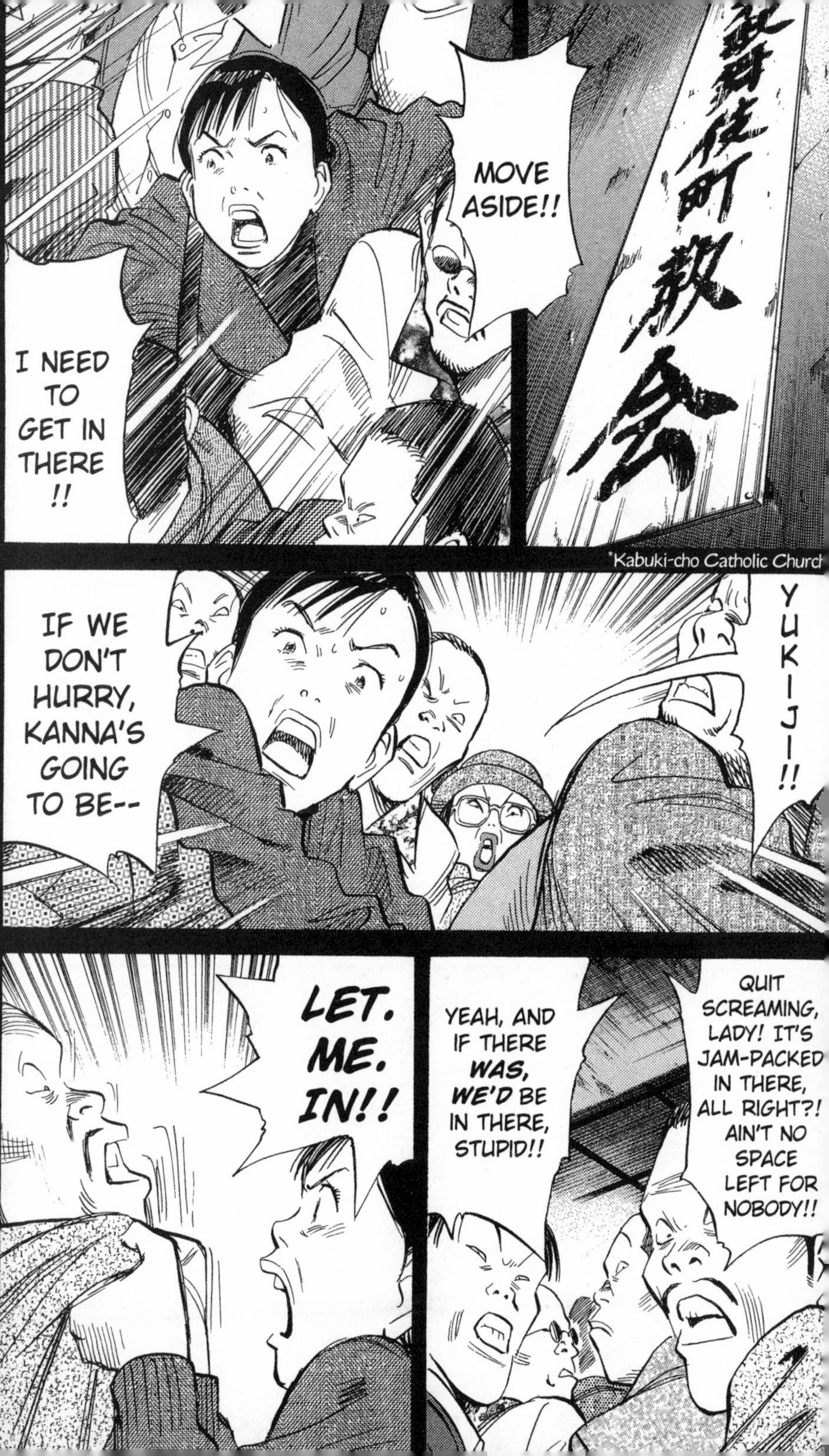
伎町教会
*Kabuki-cho Catholic Church
MOVE ASIDE!!
I NEED TO GET IN THERE!!
YUKIJI!!
IF WE DON'T HURRY, KANNA'S GOING TO BE--
QUIT SCREAMING, LADY! IT'S JAM-PACKED IN THERE, ALL RIGHT?! AIN'T NO SPACE LEFT FOR NOBODY!!
YEAH, AND IF THERE *WAS, WE'D* BE IN THERE, STUPID!!
LET. ME. IN!!

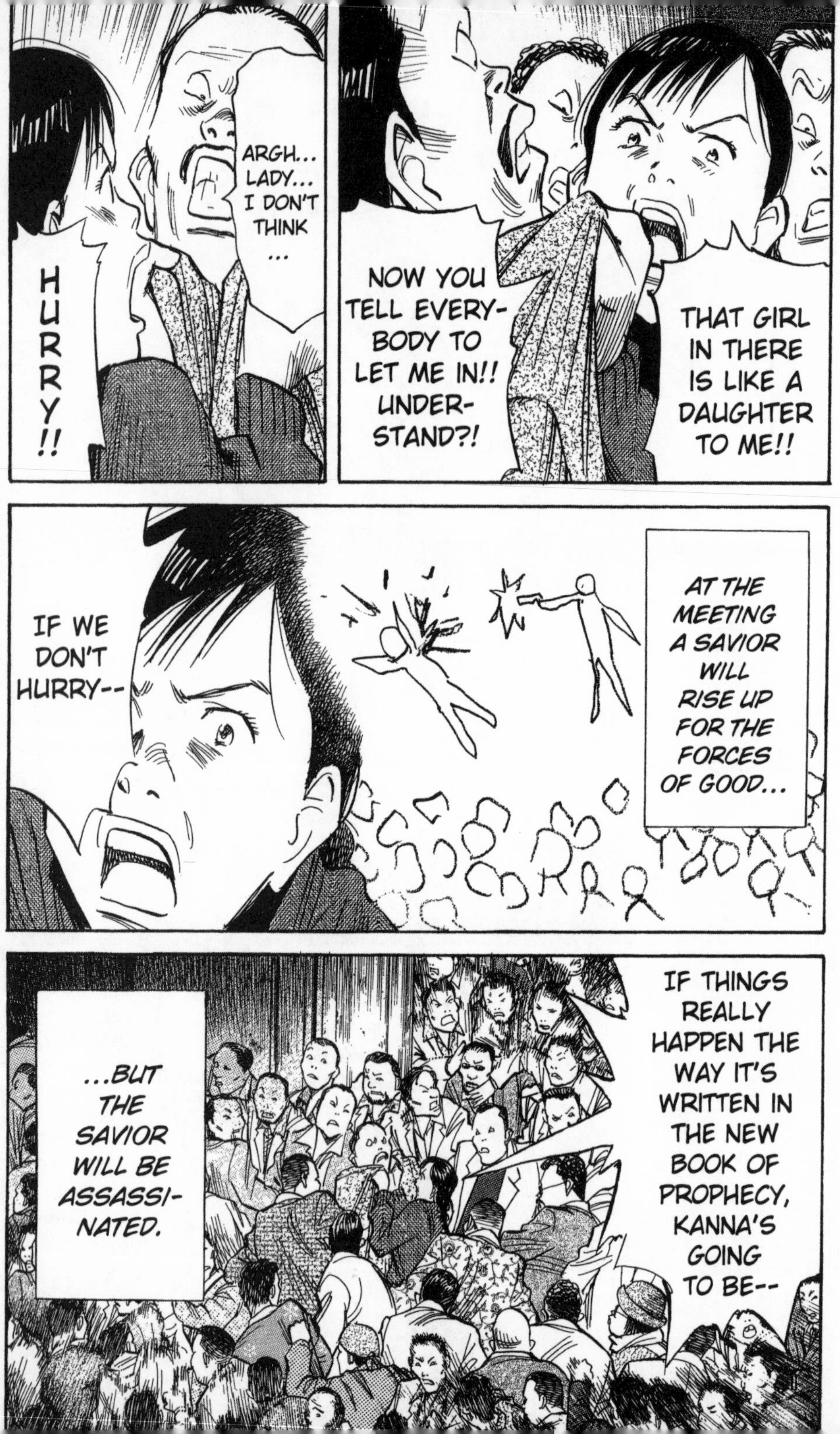
THAT GIRL IN THERE IS LIKE A DAUGHTER TO ME!!
NOW YOU TELL EVERY-BODY TO LET ME IN!! UNDER-STAND?!
ARGH... LADY... I DON'T THINK ...
HURRY!!
AT THE MEETING A SAVIOR WILL RISE UP FOR THE FORCES OF GOOD...
IF WE DON'T HURRY--
IF THINGS REALLY HAPPEN THE WAY IT'S WRITTEN IN THE NEW BOOK OF PROPHECY, KANNA'S GOING TO BE--
...BUT THE SAVIOR WILL BE ASSASSI-NATED.

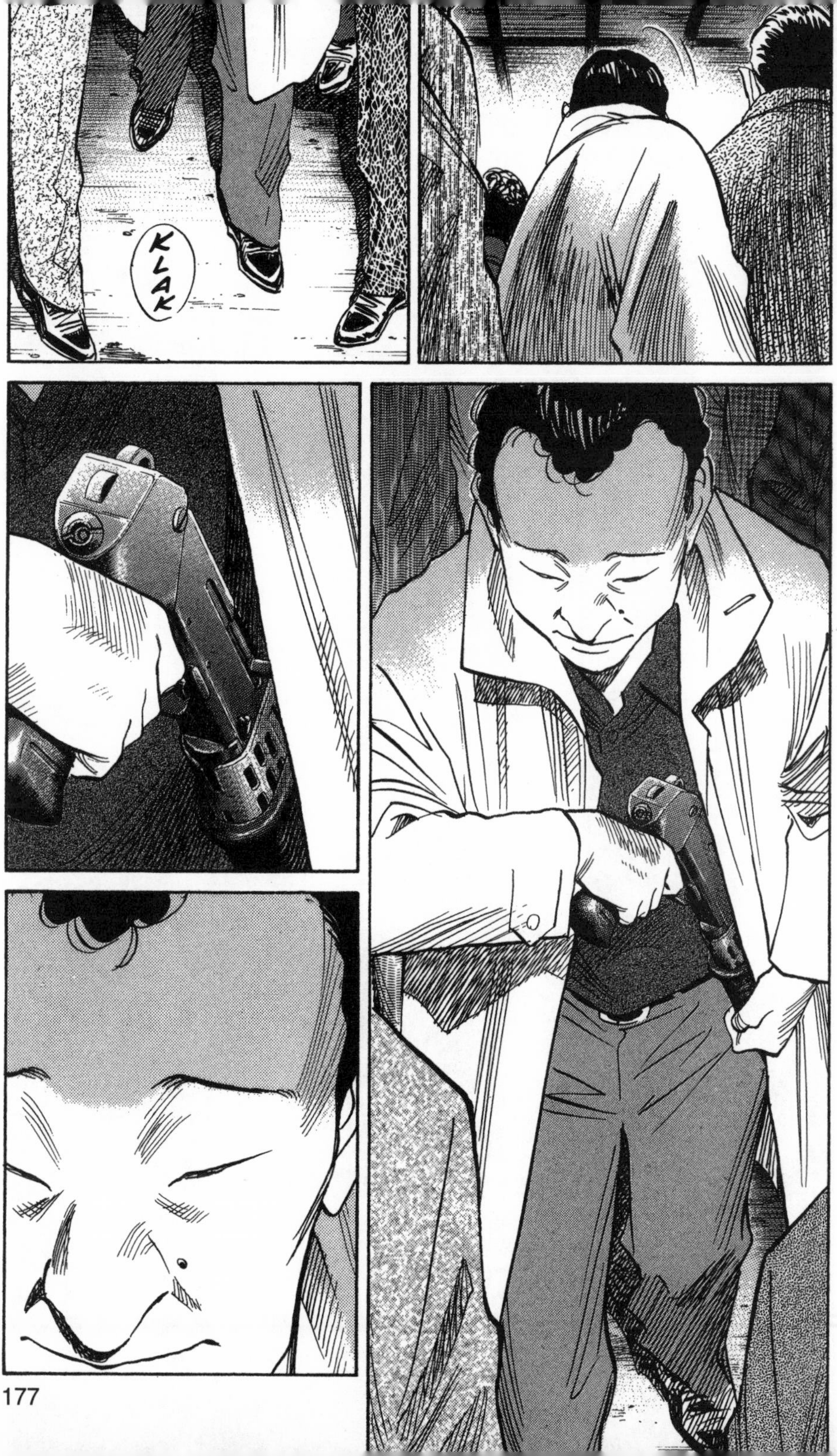
KLAK

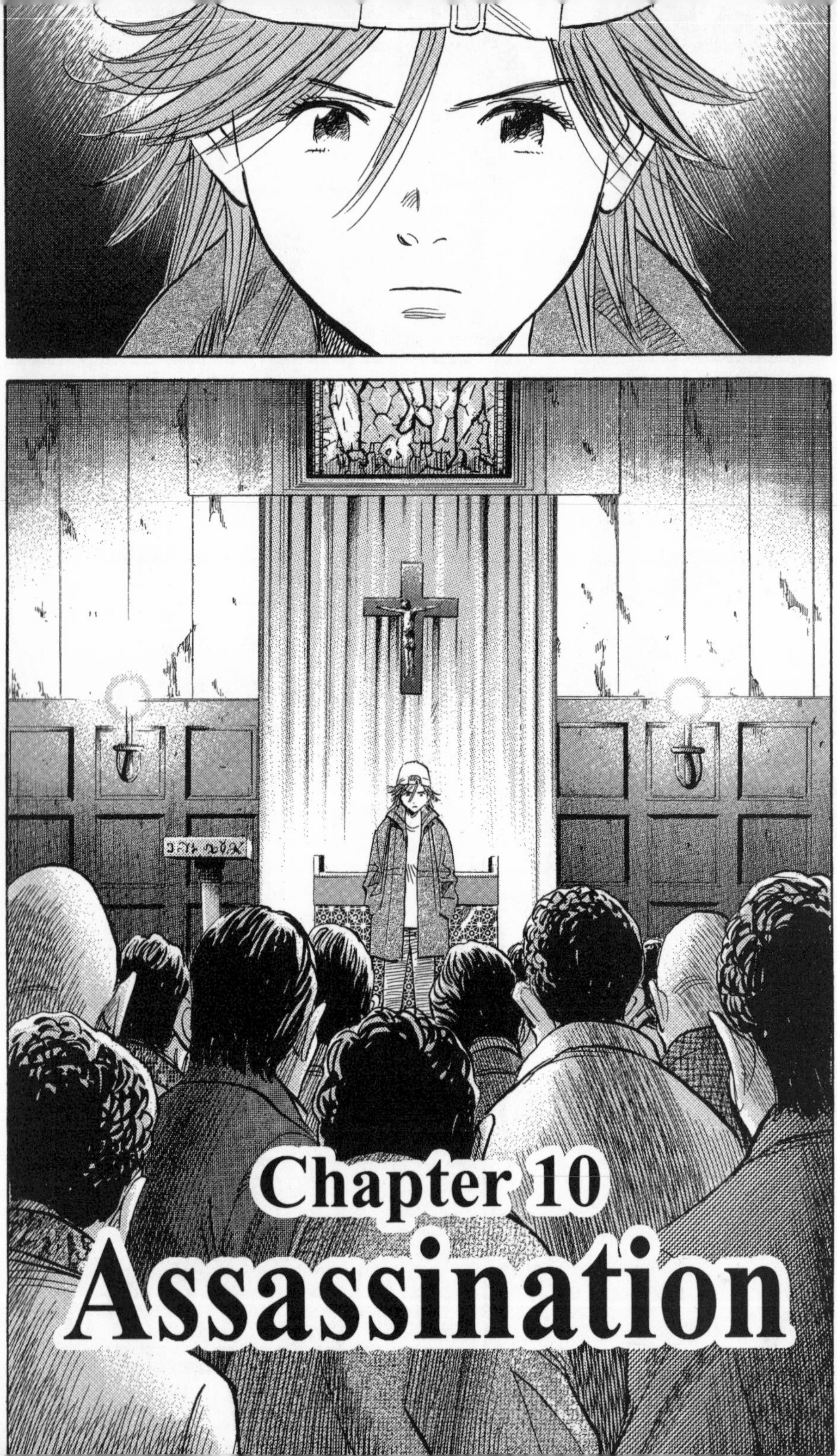
Chapter 10
Assassination

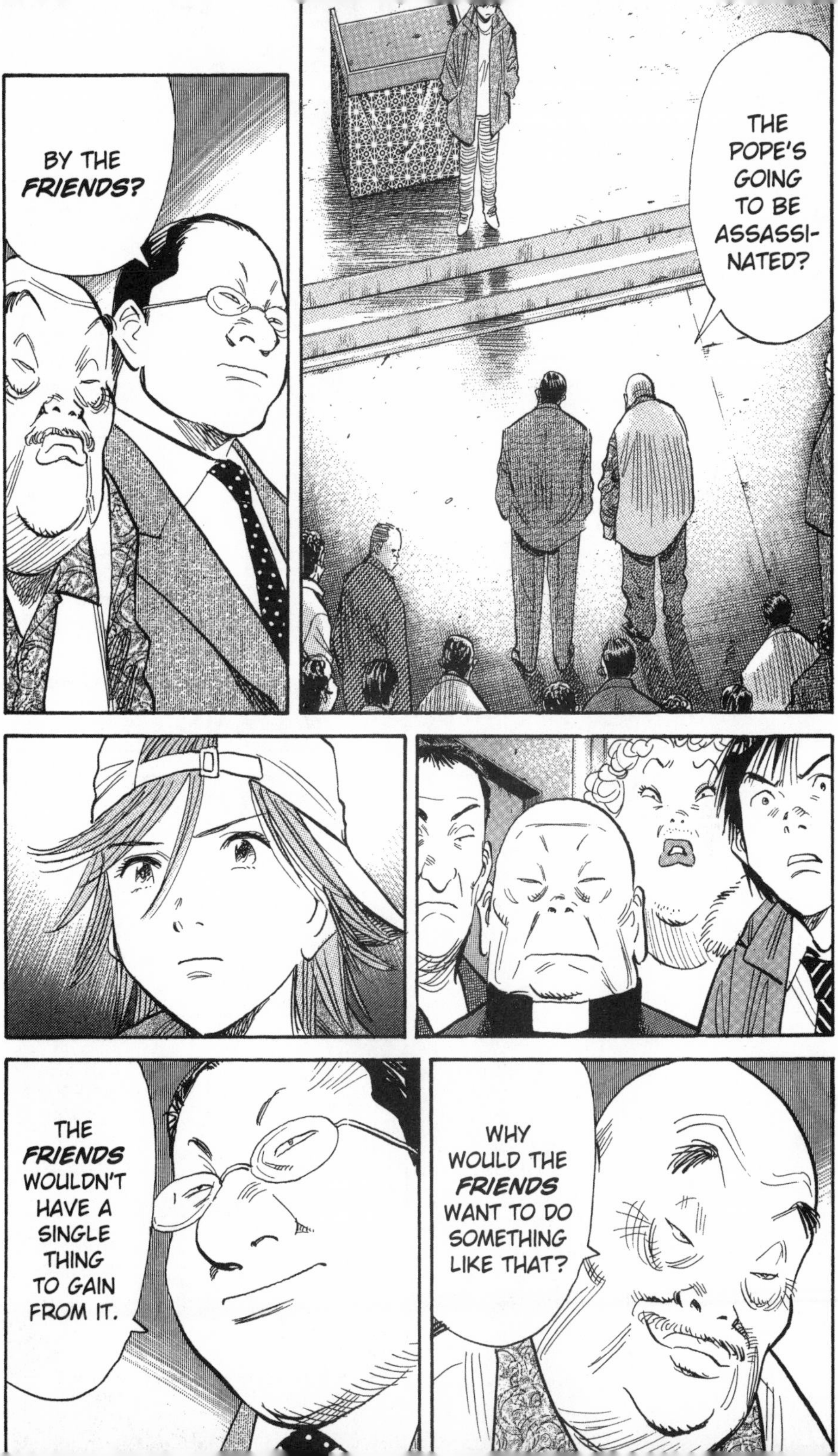
THE POPE'S GOING TO BE ASSASSI-NATED?
BY THE *FRIENDS?*
WHY WOULD THE *FRIENDS* WANT TO DO SOMETHING LIKE THAT?
THE *FRIENDS* WOULDN'T HAVE A SINGLE THING TO GAIN FROM IT.

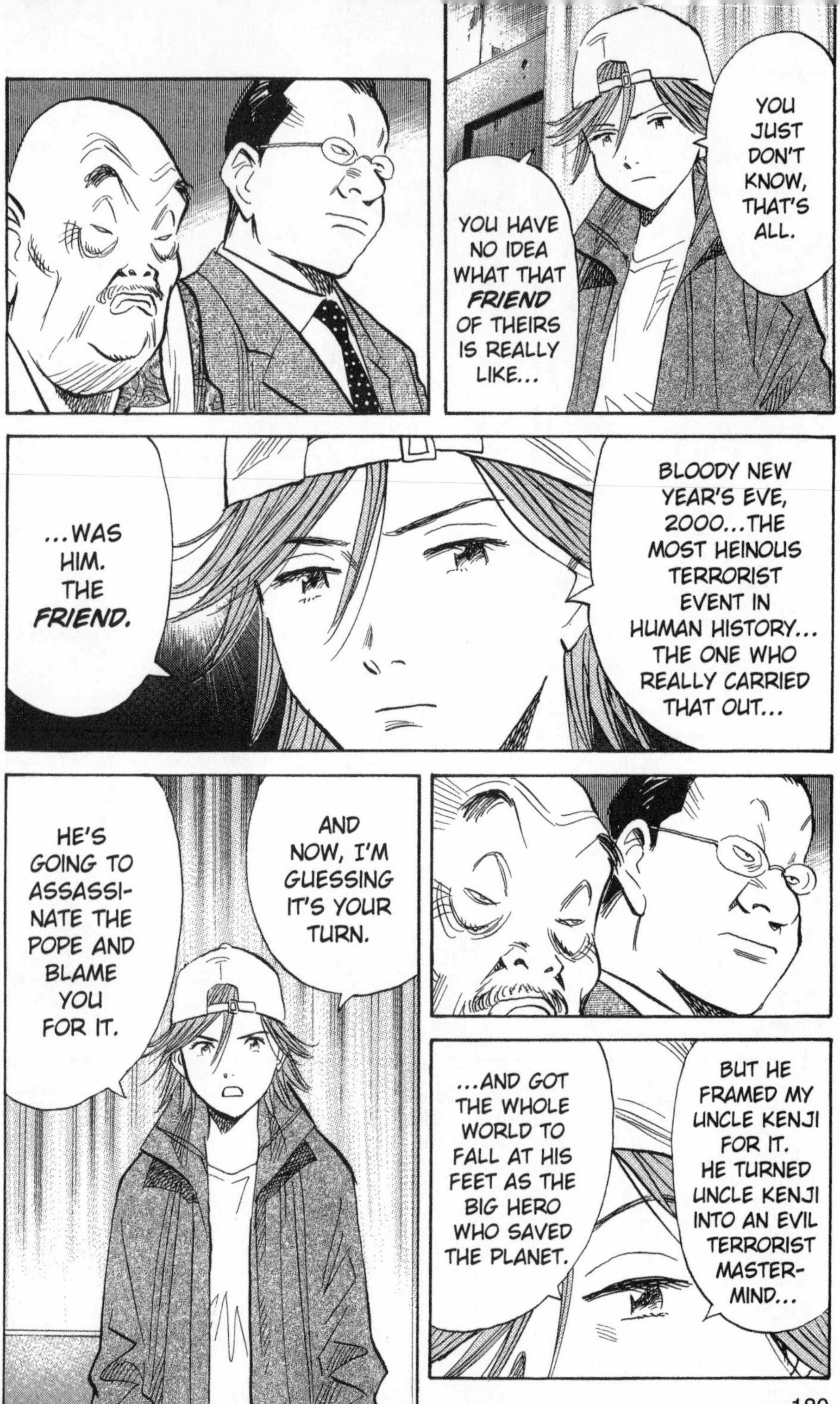
YOU JUST DON'T KNOW, THAT'S ALL.
YOU HAVE NO IDEA WHAT THAT FRIEND OF THEIRS IS REALLY LIKE...
BLOODY NEW YEAR'S EVE, 2000...THE MOST HEINOUS TERRORIST EVENT IN HUMAN HISTORY... THE ONE WHO REALLY CARRIED THAT OUT...
...WAS HIM. THE FRIEND.
BUT HE FRAMED MY UNCLE KENJI FOR IT. HE TURNED UNCLE KENJI INTO AN EVIL TERRORIST MASTER-MIND...
...AND GOT THE WHOLE WORLD TO FALL AT HIS FEET AS THE BIG HERO WHO SAVED THE PLANET.
AND NOW, I'M GUESSING IT'S YOUR TURN.
HE'S GOING TO ASSASSI-NATE THE POPE AND BLAME YOU FOR IT.

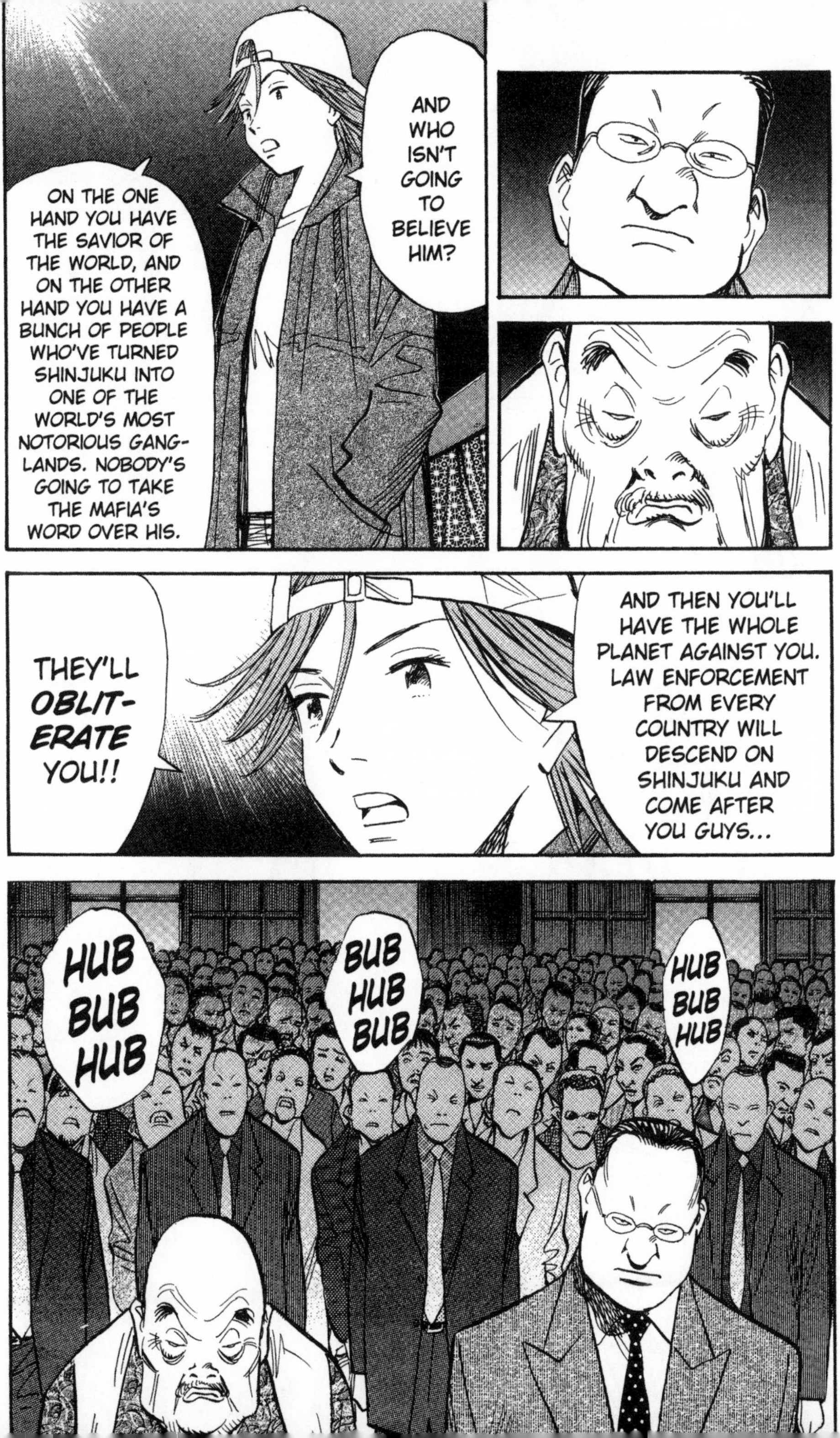
AND WHO ISN'T GOING TO BELIEVE HIM?
ON THE ONE HAND YOU HAVE THE SAVIOR OF THE WORLD, AND ON THE OTHER HAND YOU HAVE A BUNCH OF PEOPLE WHO'VE TURNED SHINJUKU INTO ONE OF THE WORLD'S MOST NOTORIOUS GANG-LANDS. NOBODY'S GOING TO TAKE THE MAFIA'S WORD OVER HIS.
AND THEN YOU'LL HAVE THE WHOLE PLANET AGAINST YOU. LAW ENFORCEMENT FROM EVERY COUNTRY WILL DESCEND ON SHINJUKU AND COME AFTER YOU GUYS...
THEY'LL *OBLIT-ERATE* YOU!!
HUB BUB HUB
BUB HUB BUB
HUB BUB HUB

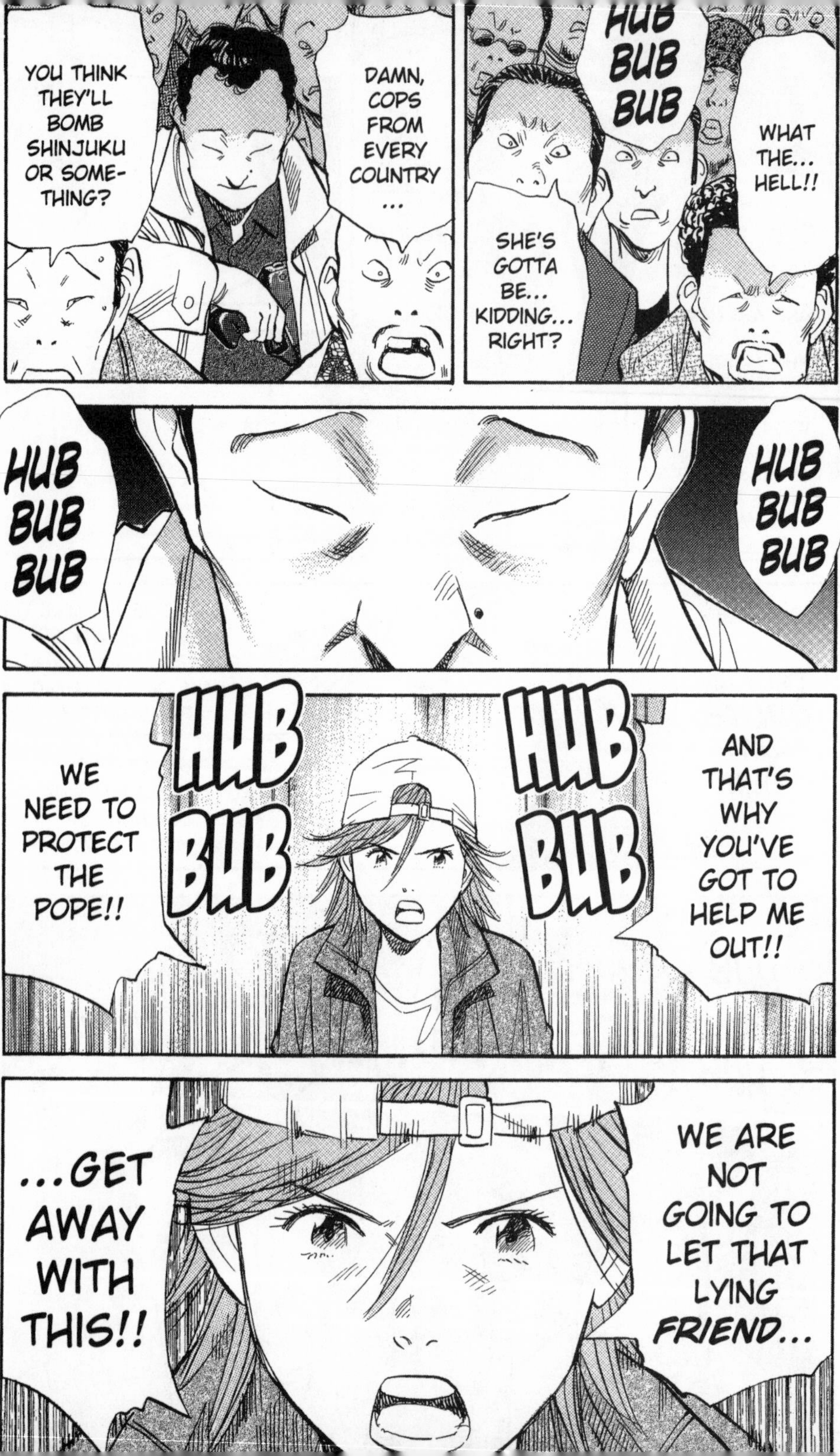
HUB BUB BUB
WHAT THE... HELL!!
SHE'S GOTTA BE... KIDDING... RIGHT?
DAMN, COPS FROM EVERY COUNTRY ...
YOU THINK THEY'LL BOMB SHINJUKU OR SOME-THING?
HUB BUB BUB
HUB BUB BUB
AND THAT'S WHY YOU'VE GOT TO HELP ME OUT!!
HUB BUB
HUB BUB
WE NEED TO PROTECT THE POPE!!
WE ARE NOT GOING TO LET THAT LYING *FRIEND*...
...GET AWAY WITH THIS!!

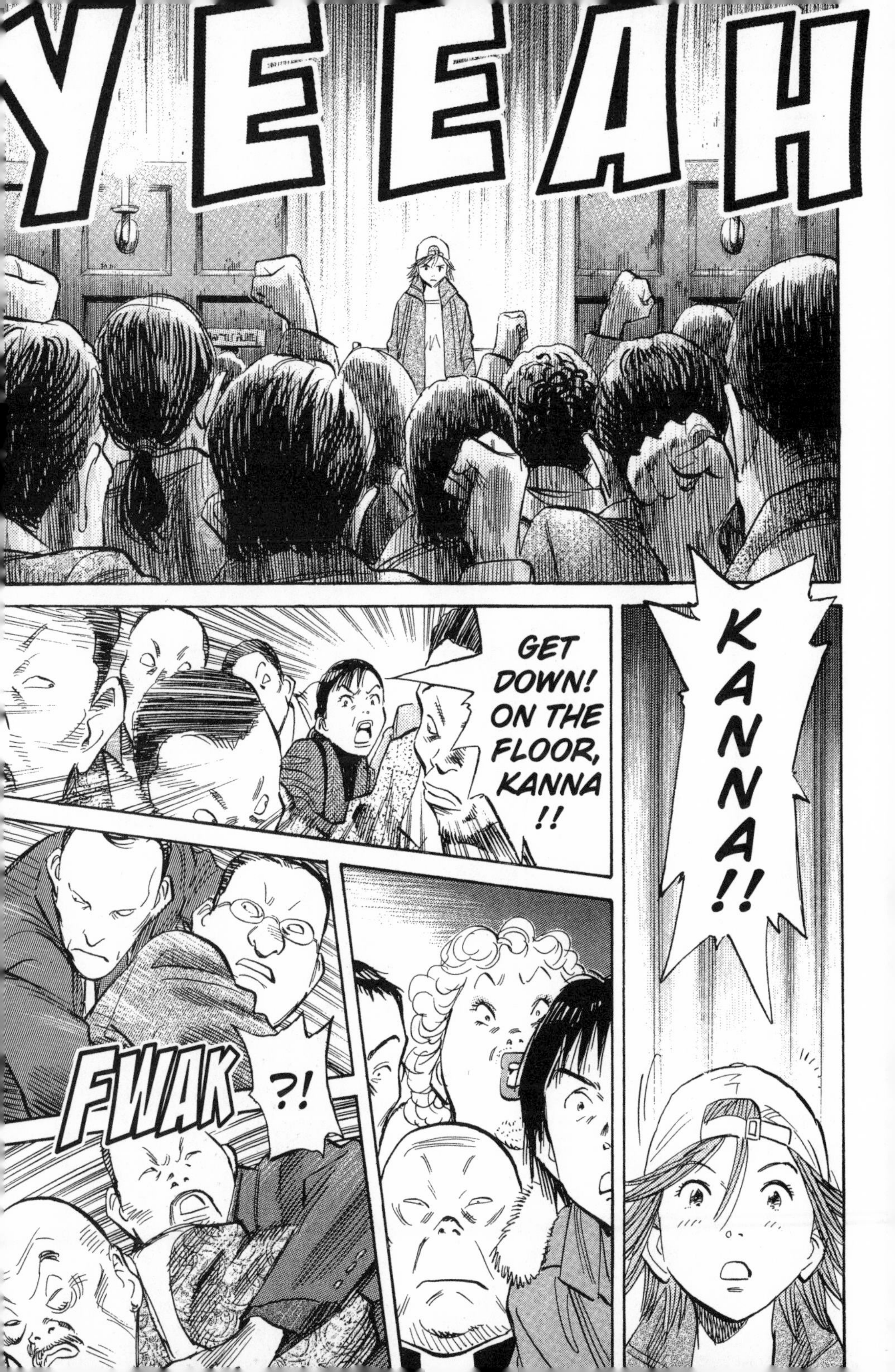
YEEAH
KANNA!!
GET DOWN! ON THE FLOOR, KANNA!!
?!
FWAK

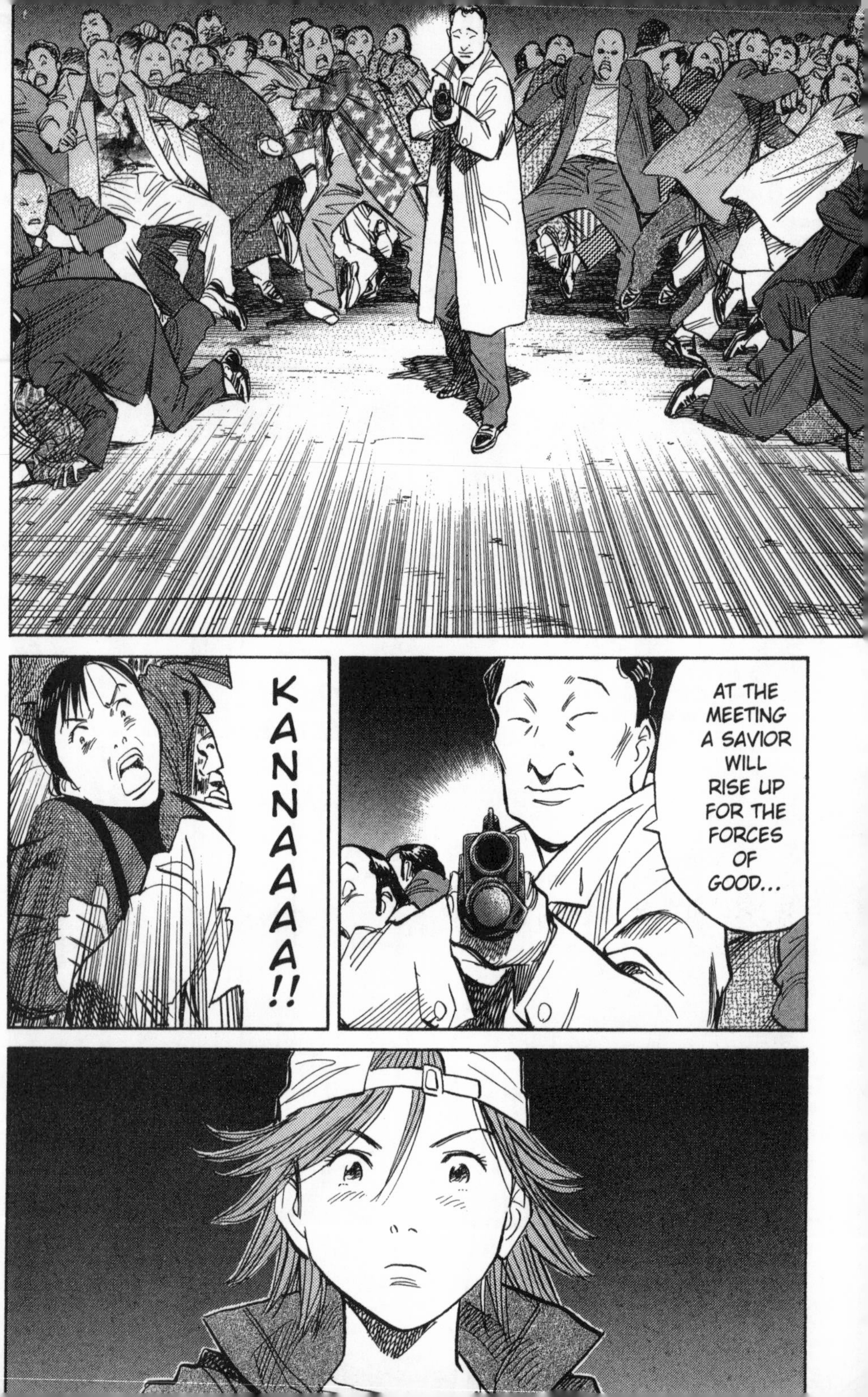
AT THE MEETING A SAVIOR WILL RISE UP FOR THE FORCES OF GOOD...
KANNAAAAAA!!

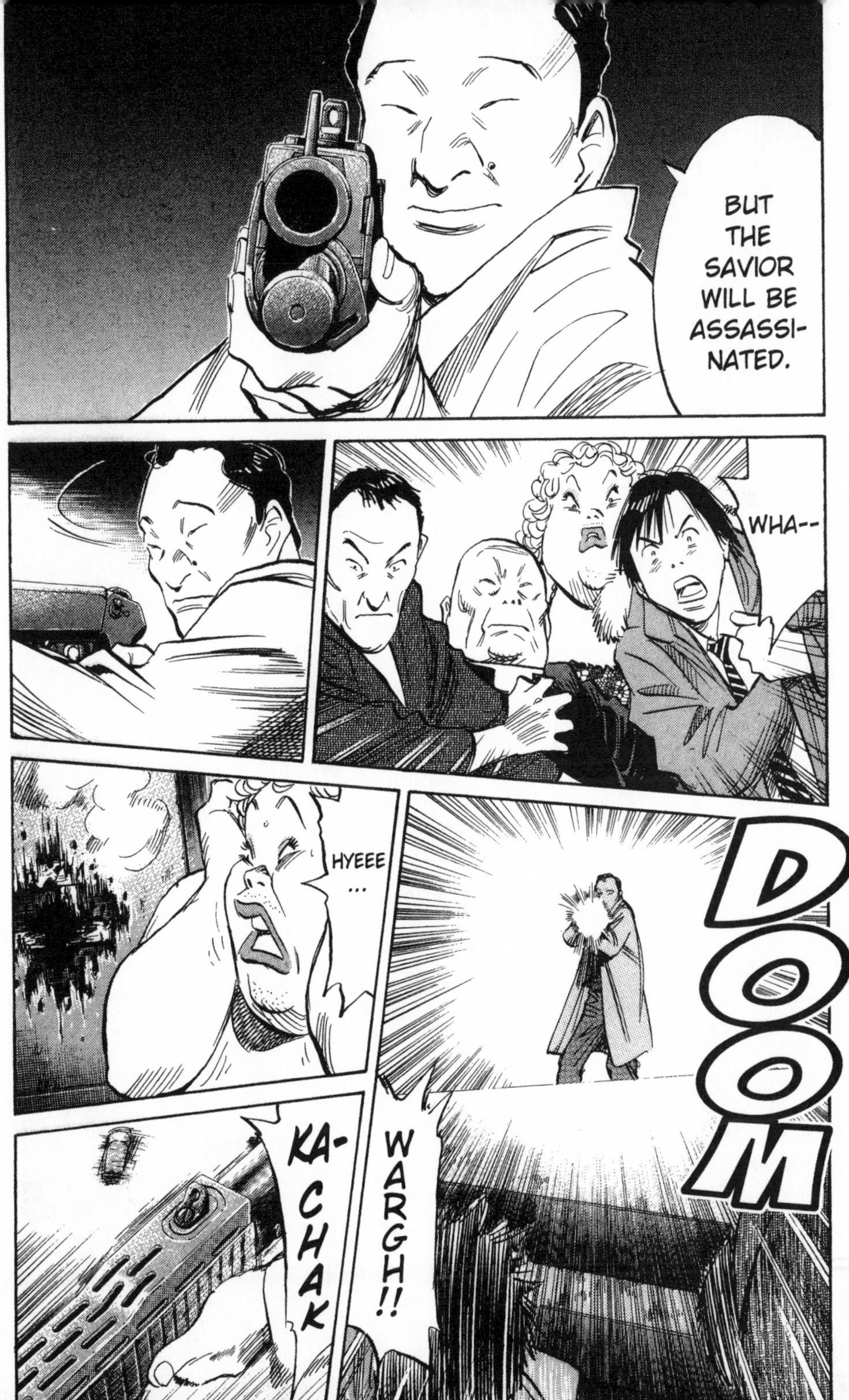
BUT THE SAVIOR WILL BE ASSASSI-NATED.
WHA--
DOOM
HYEEE ...
WARGH!!
KA-CHAK

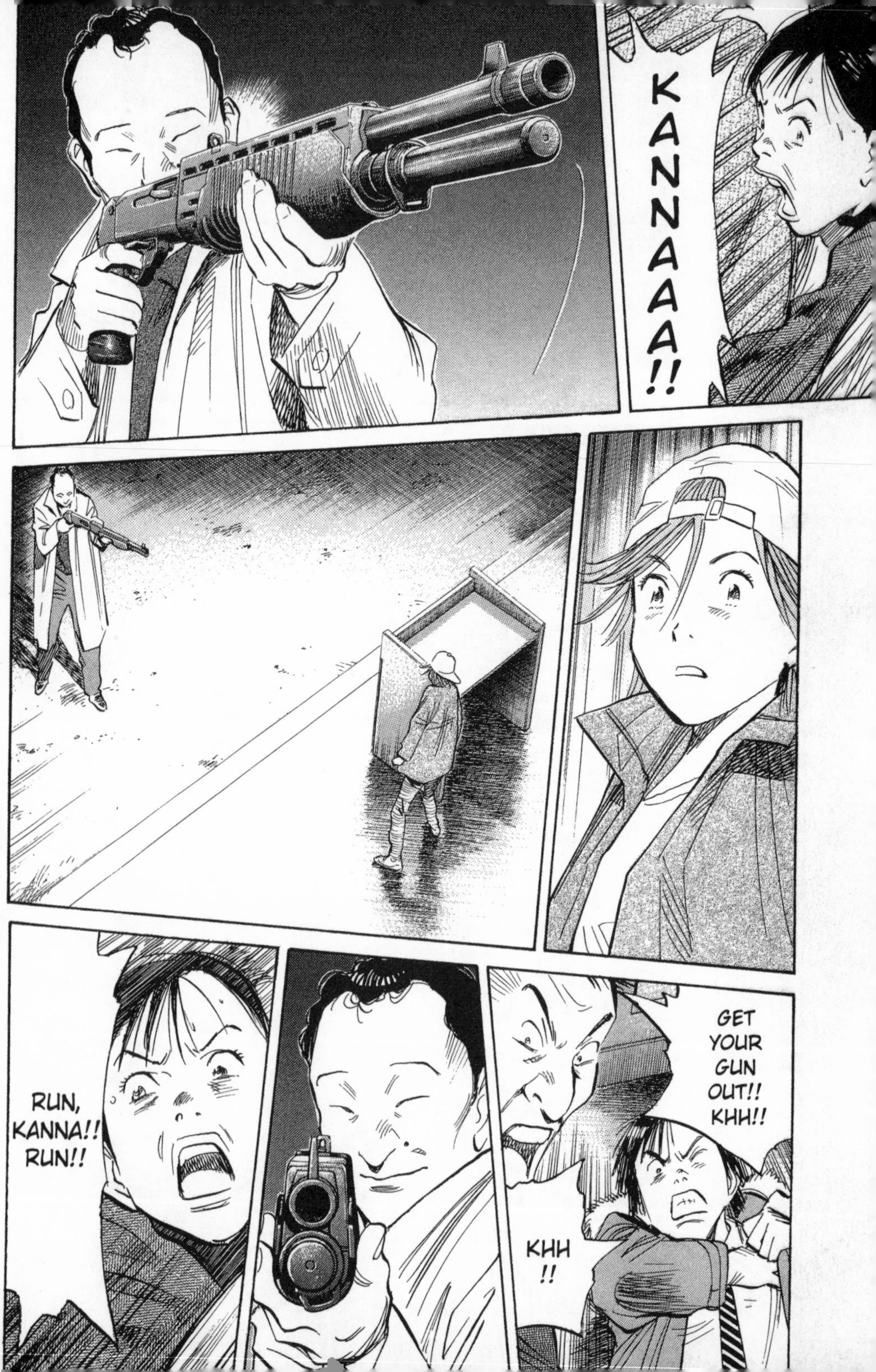
KANNAAAA!!
GET YOUR GUN OUT!! KHH!!
KHH !!
RUN, KANNA!! RUN!!

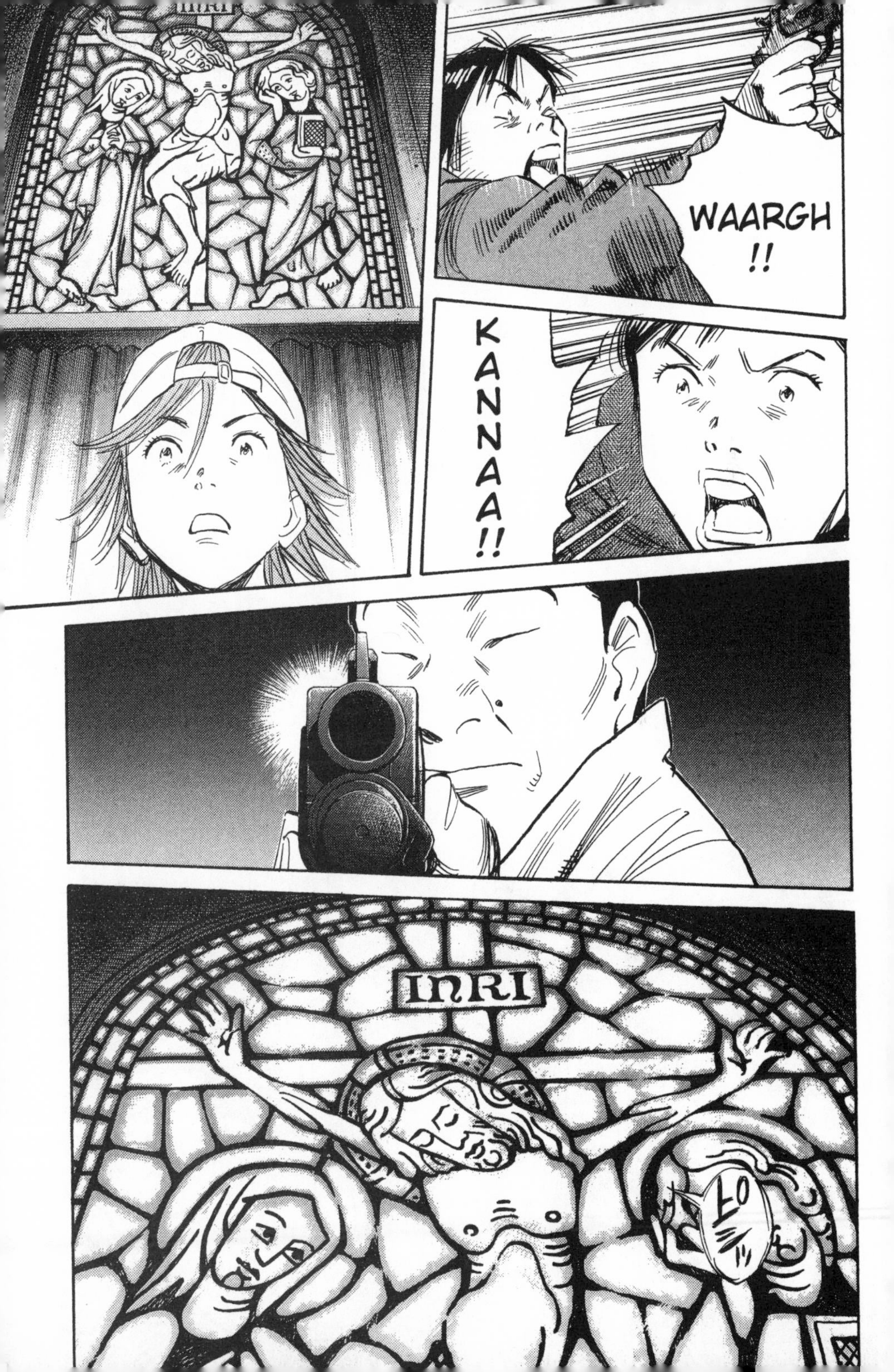
WAARGH !!
INRI
KANNAAA!!
INRI

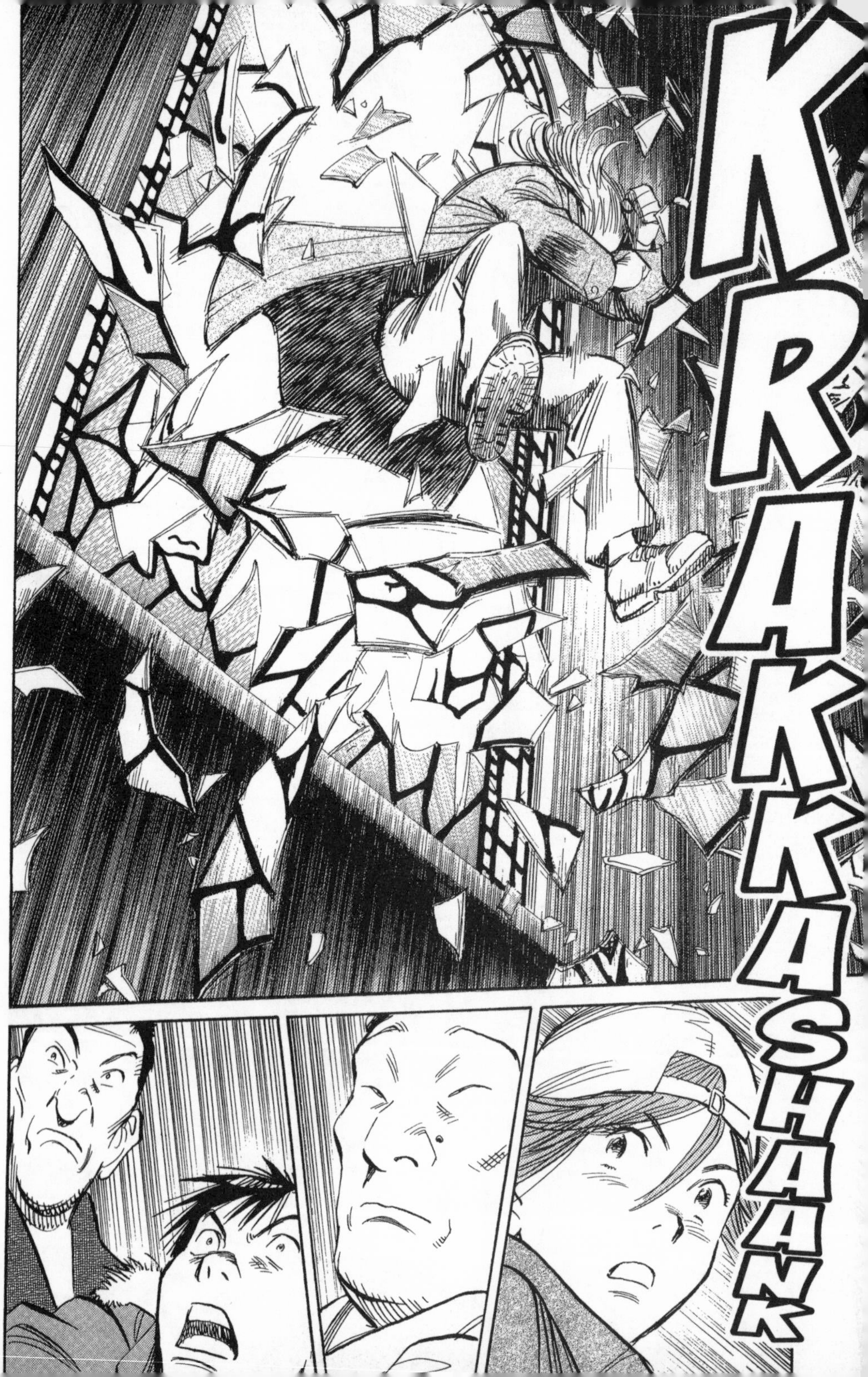
KRAKKASHANK

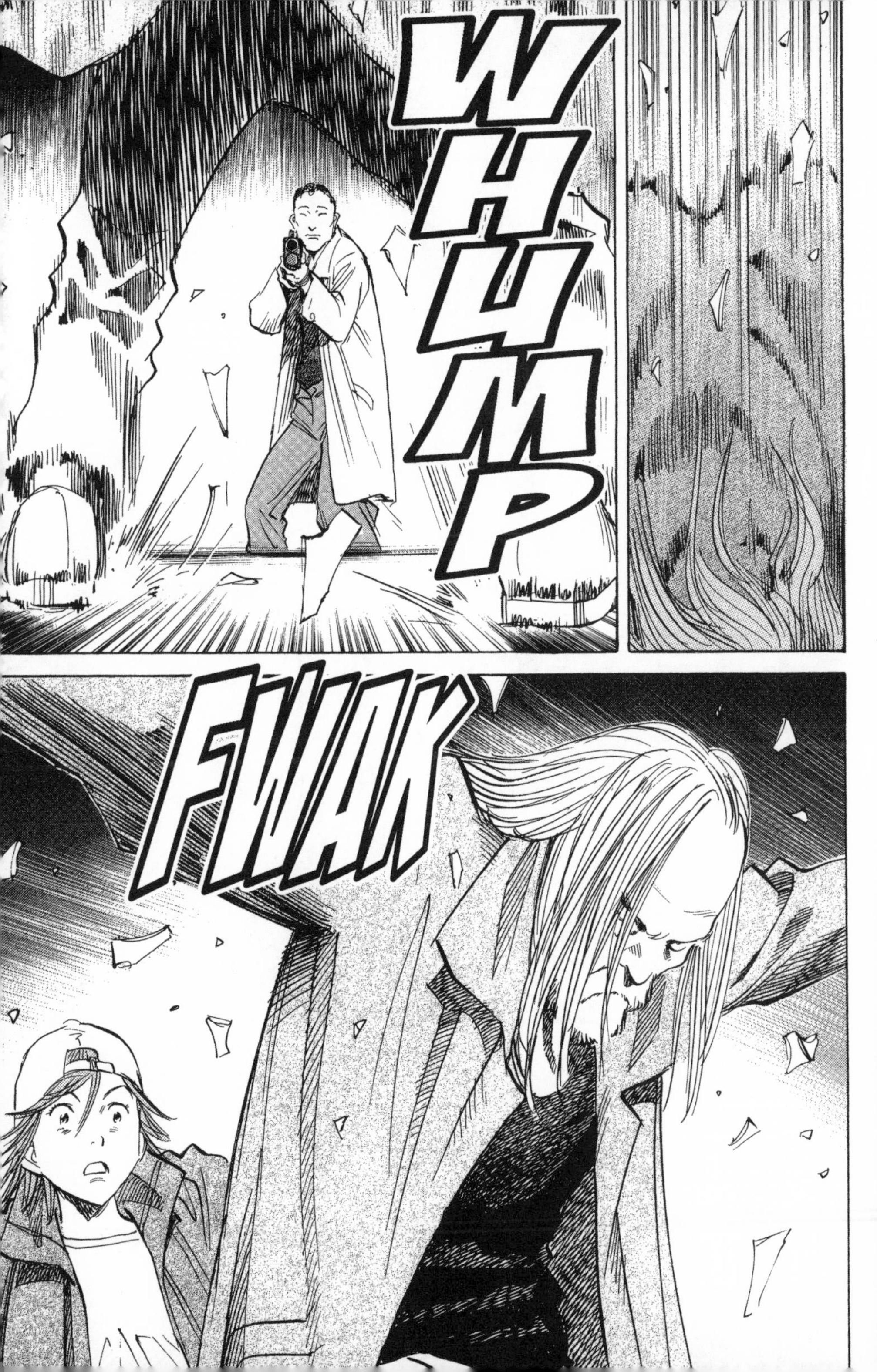
WHUMP
FWAK

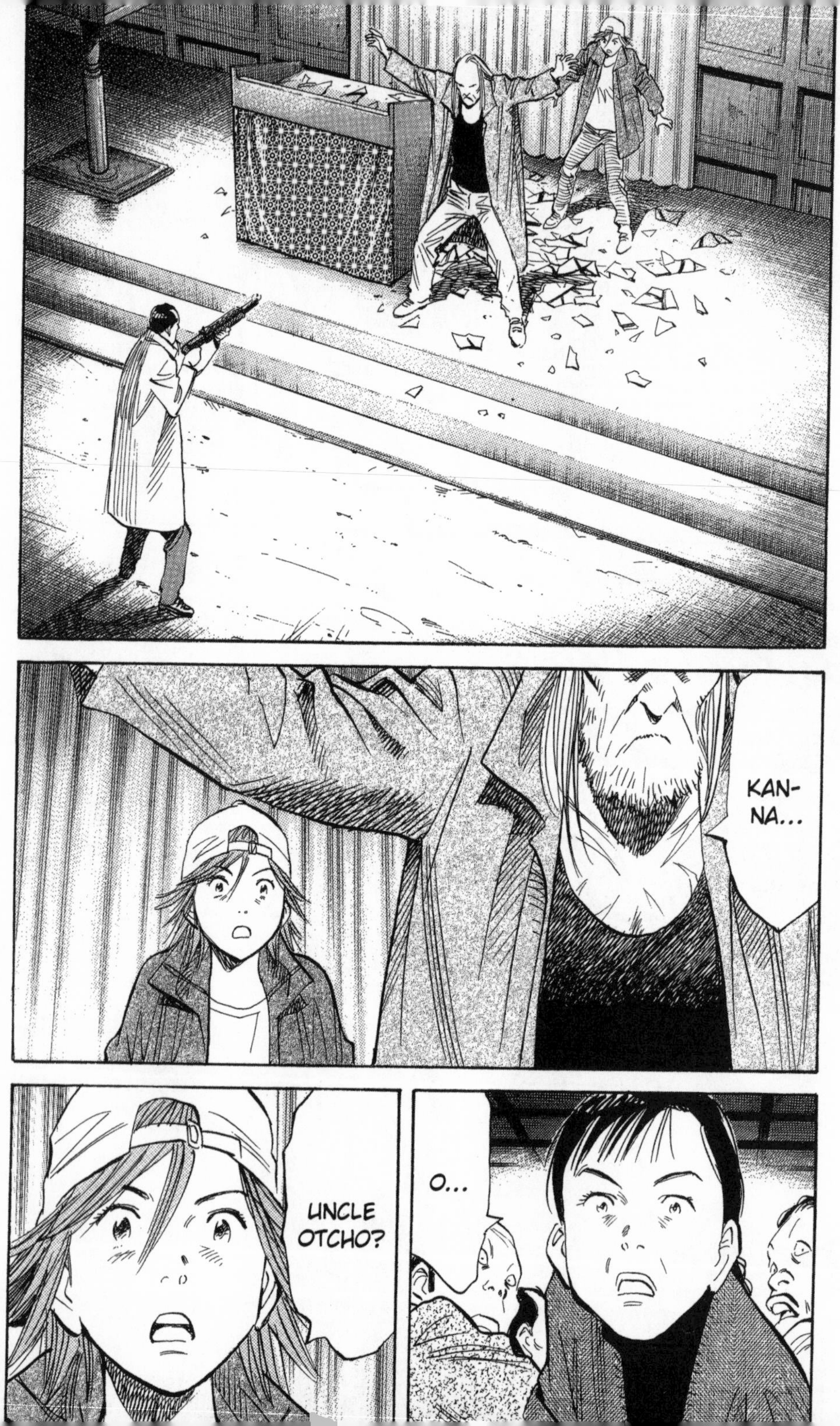
KAN-NA...
O...
UNCLE OTCHO?

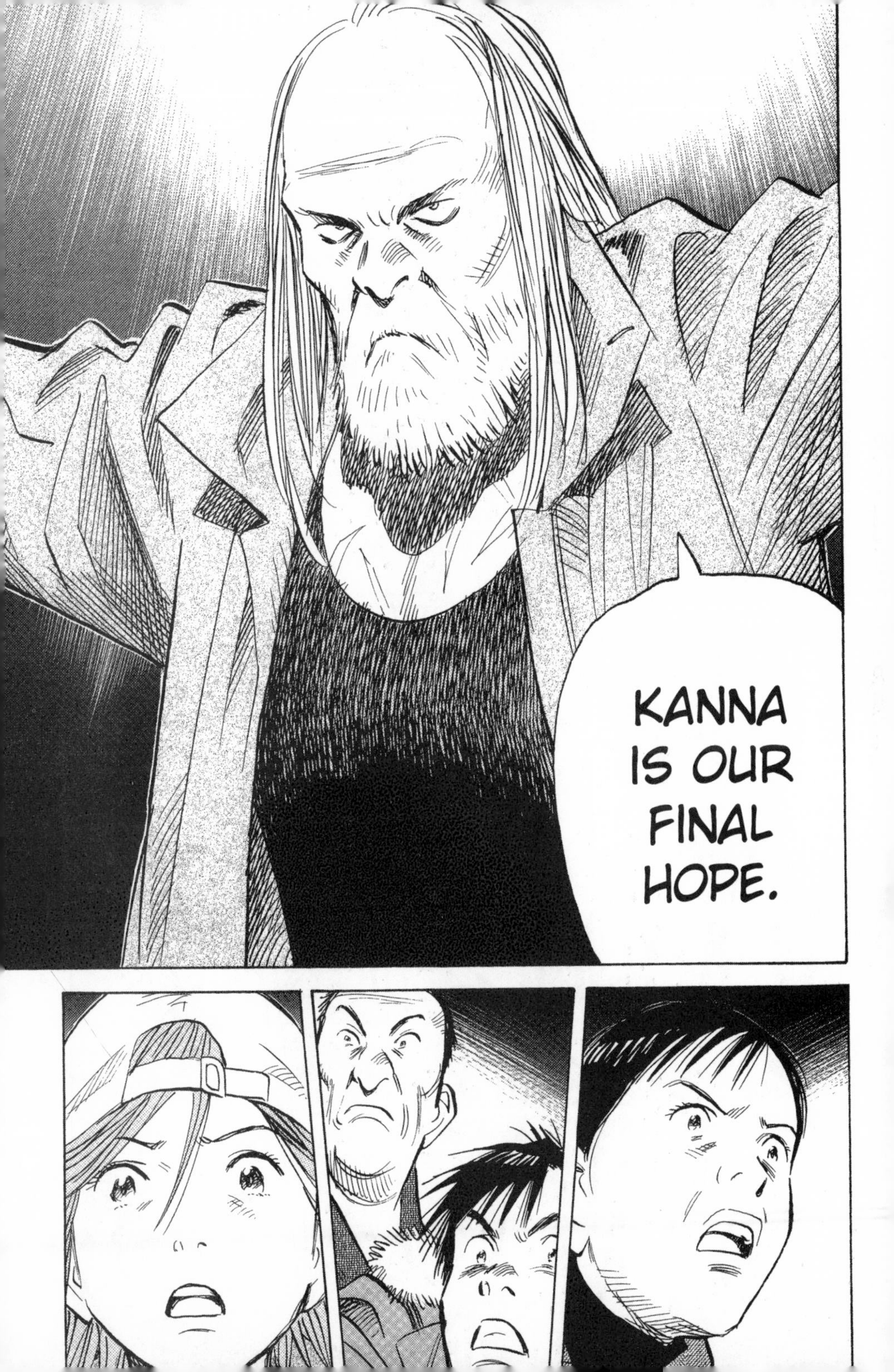
KANNA IS OUR FINAL HOPE.

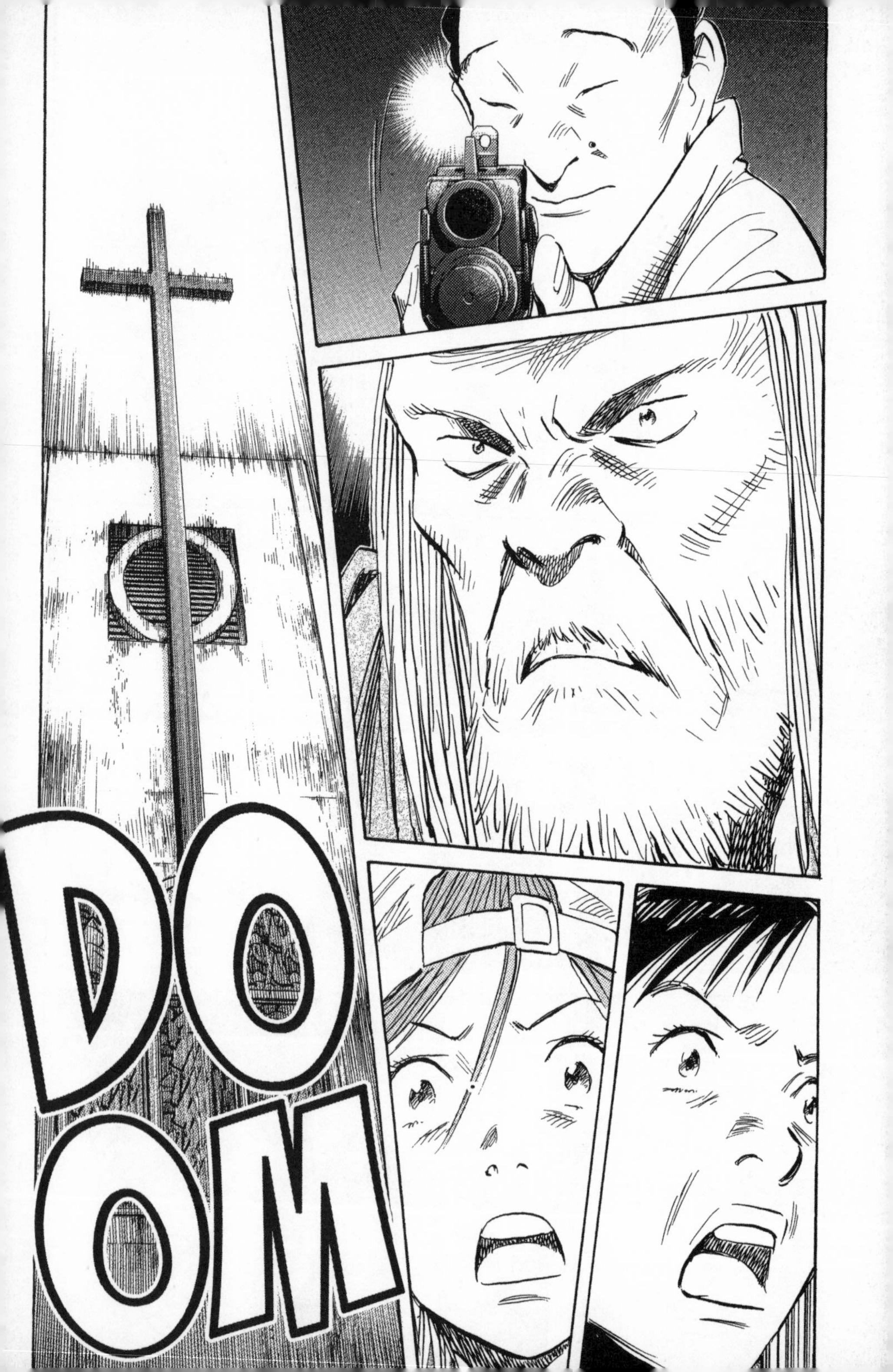
DOOM

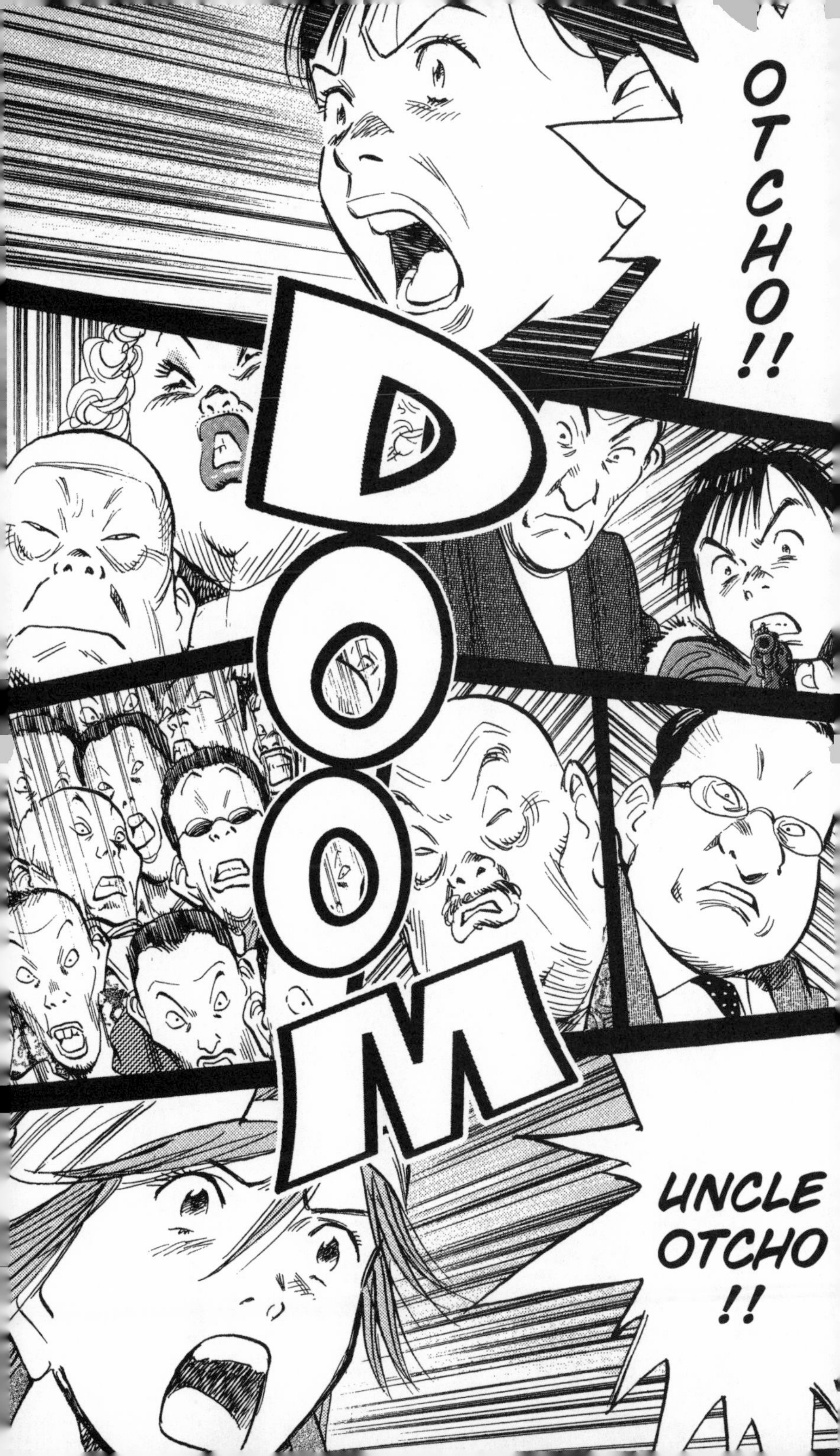
OTCHO!!
DOOOM
UNCLE OTCHO !!

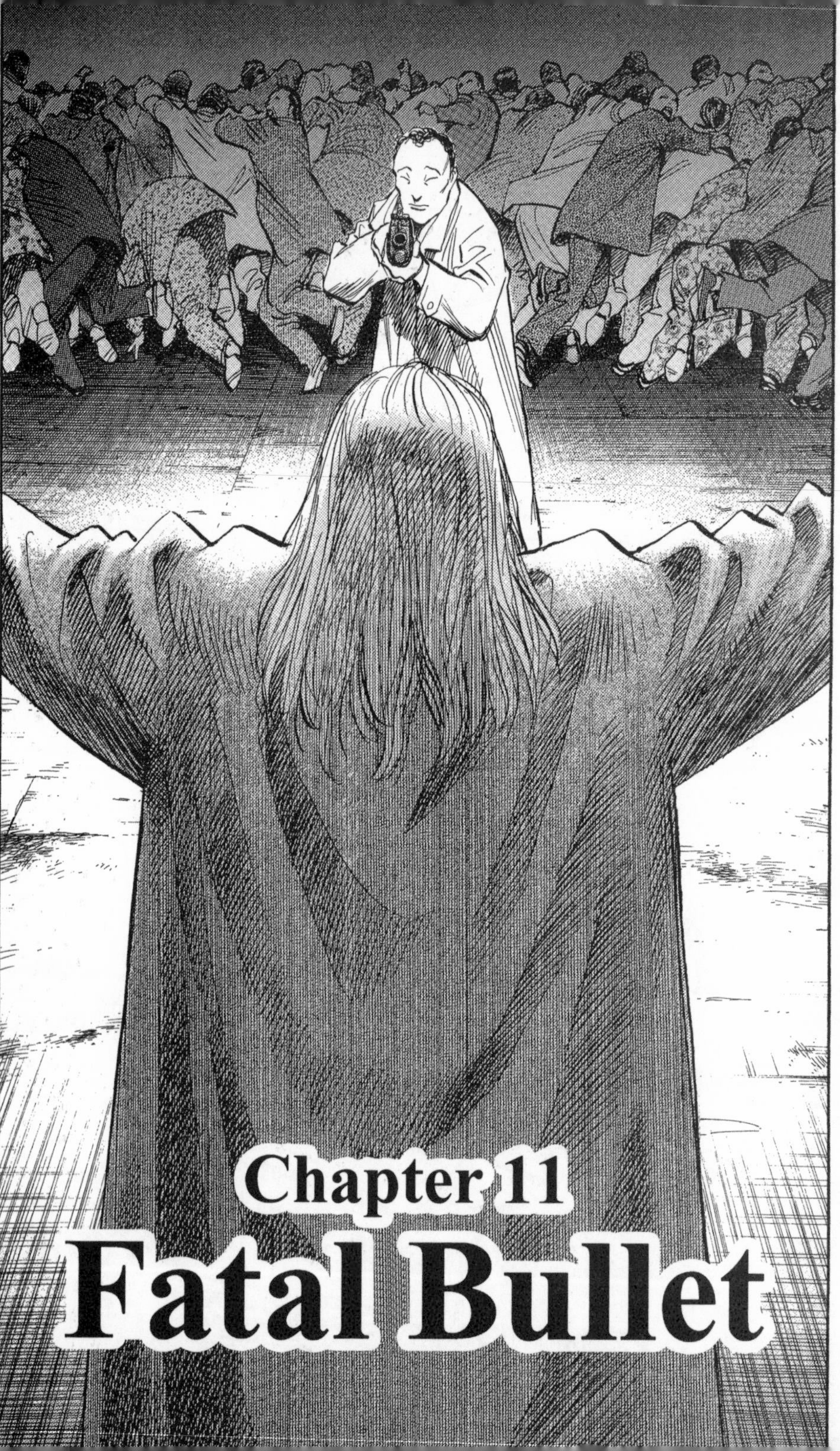
Chapter 11
Fatal Bullet

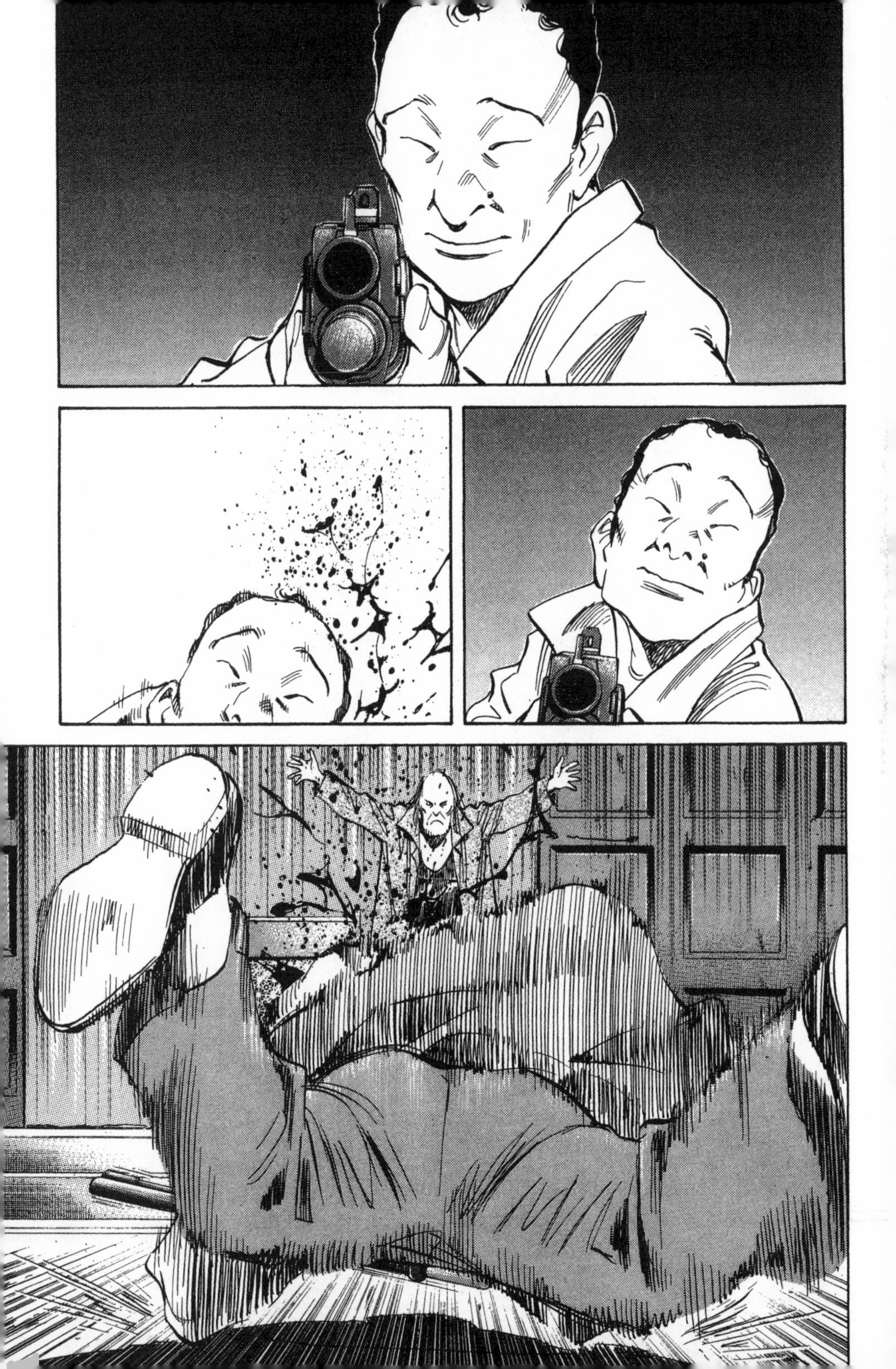

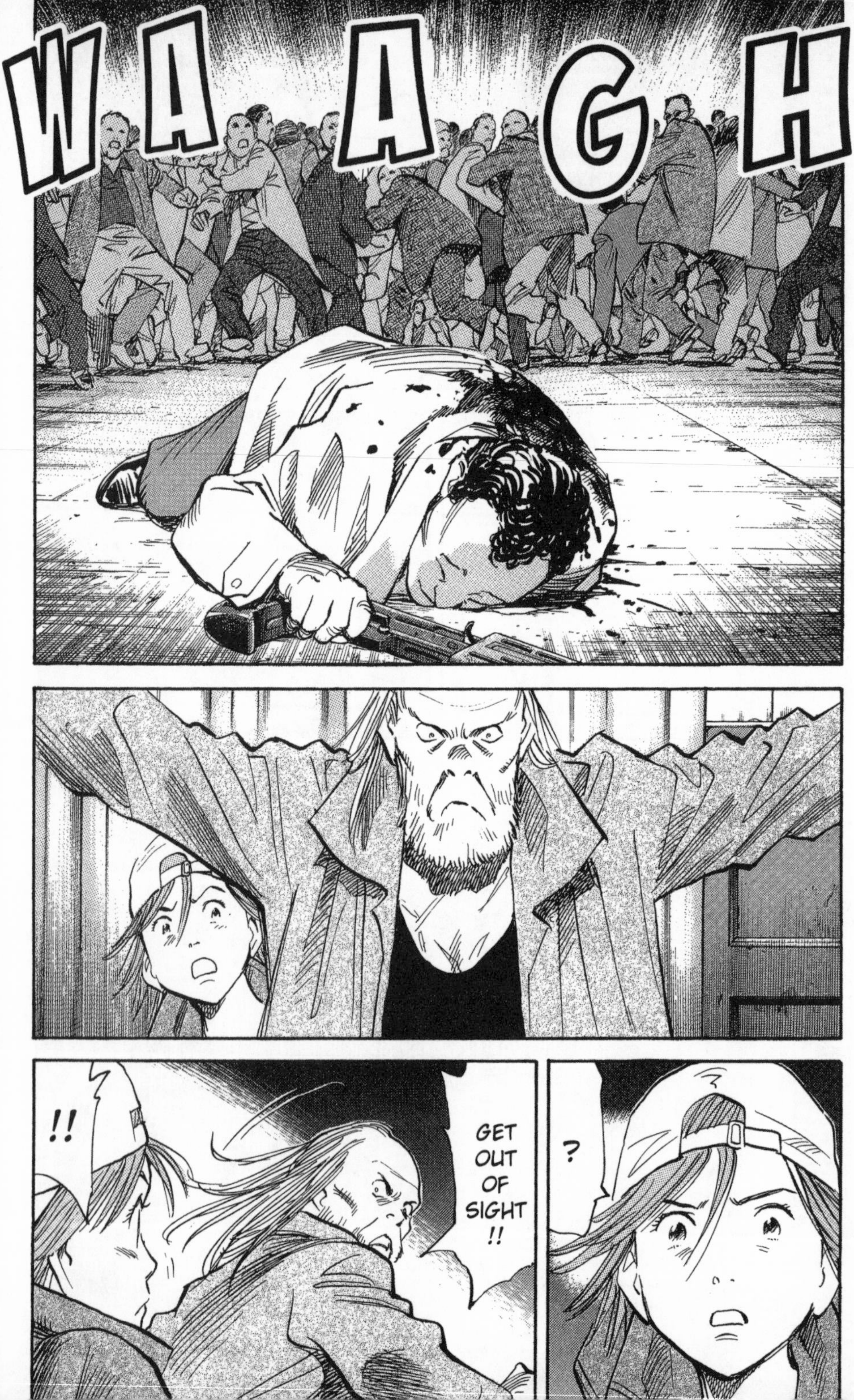
WAAGH
?
GET OUT OF SIGHT!!
!!

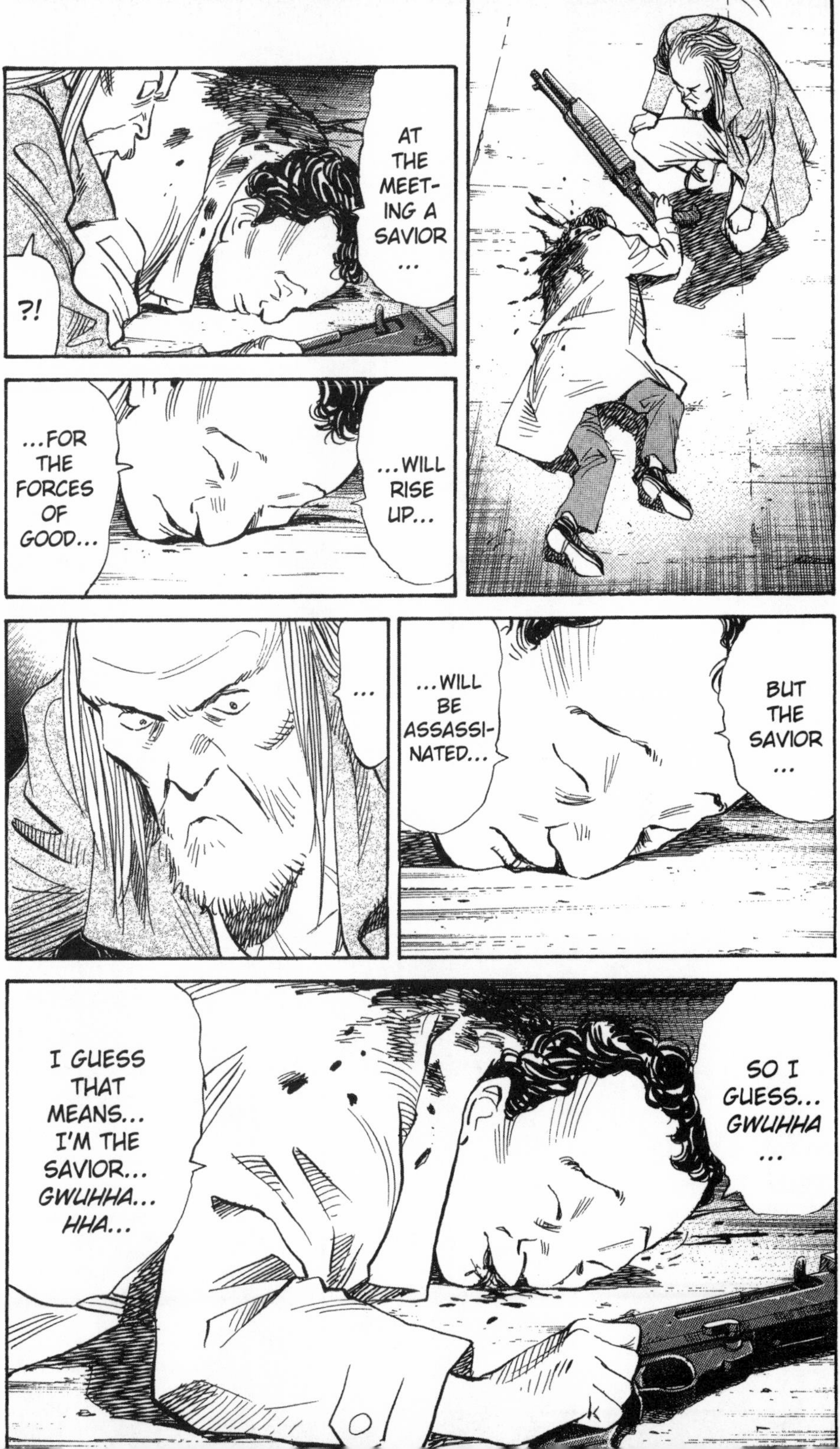
AT THE MEET-ING A SAVIOR...
?!
...WILL RISE UP...
...FOR THE FORCES OF GOOD...
BUT THE SAVIOR...
...WILL BE ASSASSI-NATED...
...
SO I GUESS... GWUHHA...
I GUESS THAT MEANS... I'M THE SAVIOR... GWUHHA... HHA...

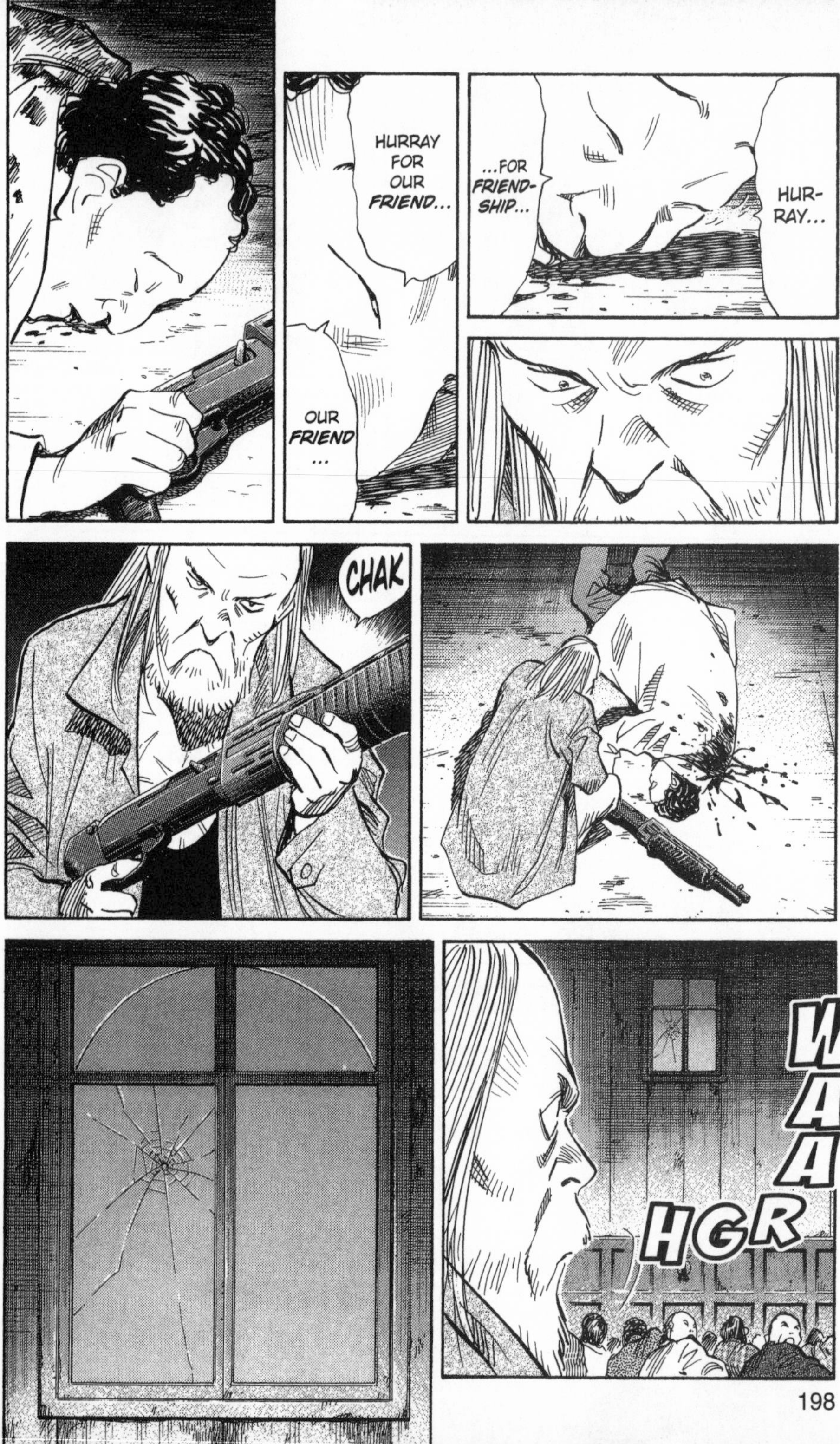
HUR-RAY...
...FOR FRIEND-SHIP...
HURRAY FOR OUR FRIEND...
OUR FRIEND ...
CHAK
WAAA HGR

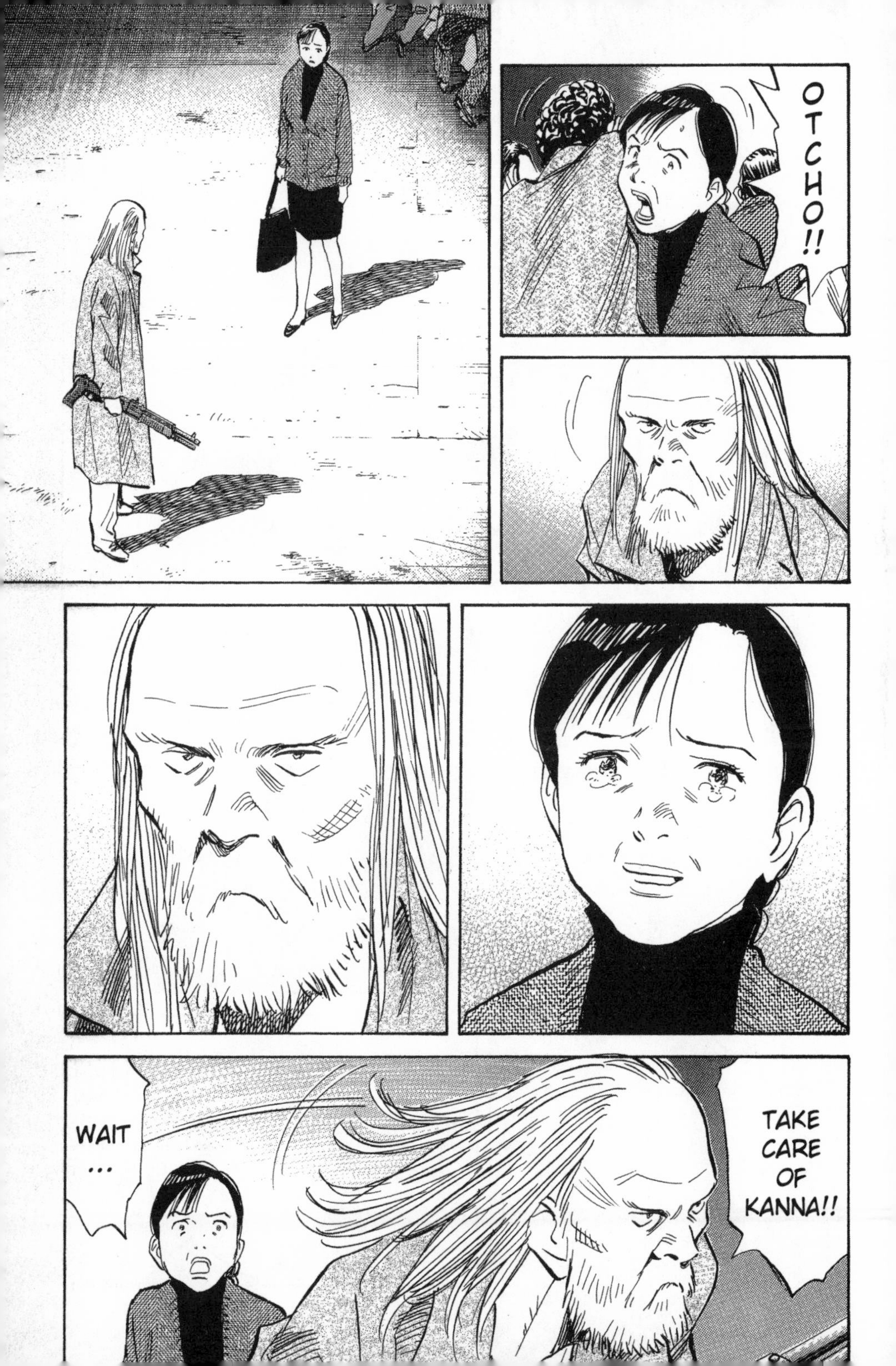
OTCHO!!
TAKE CARE OF KANNA!!
WAIT ...

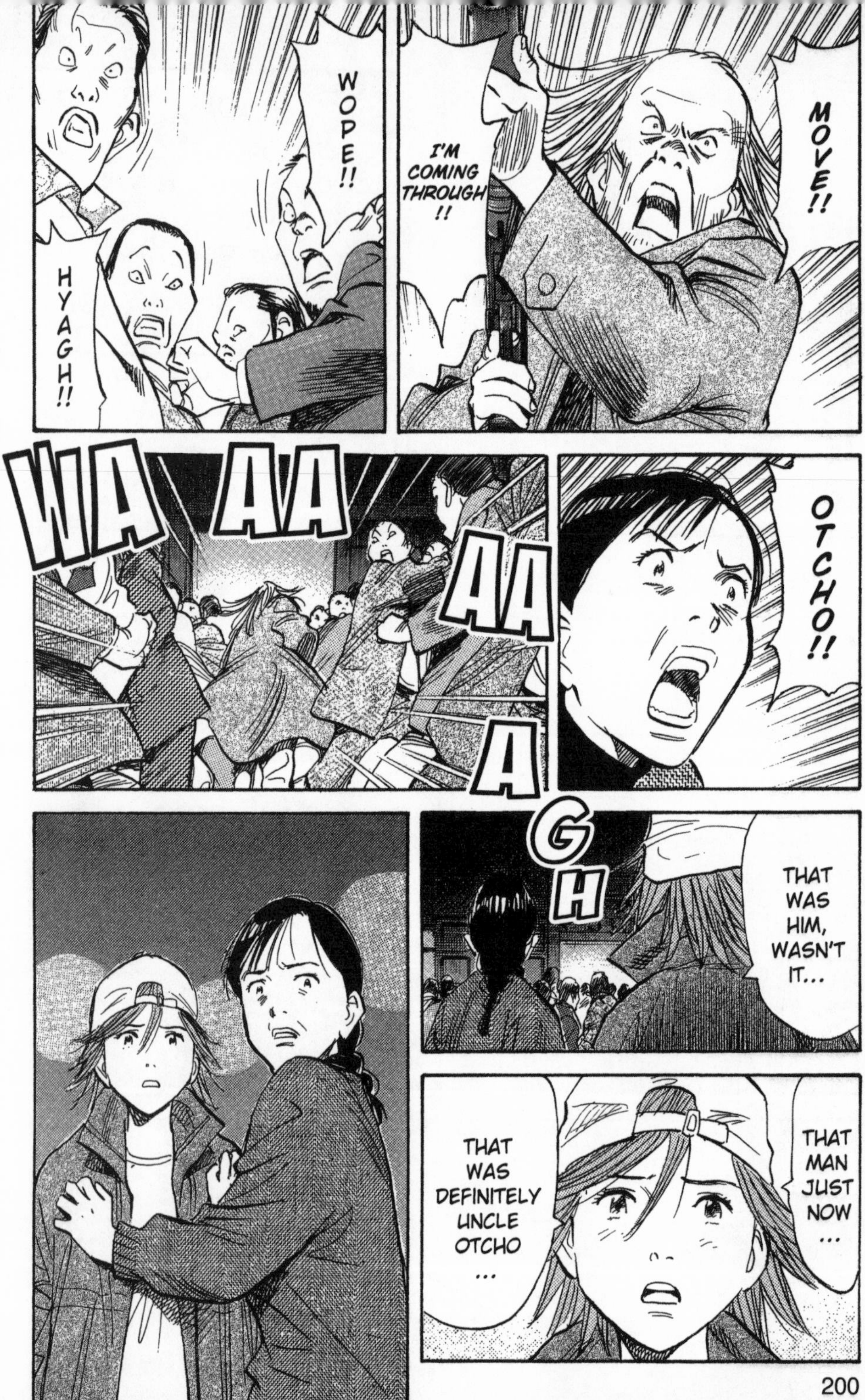
MOVE!!
I'M COMING THROUGH!!
WOPE!!
HYAGH!!
OTCHO!!
WA AA AA A GH
THAT WAS HIM, WASN'T IT...
THAT MAN JUST NOW...
THAT WAS DEFINITELY UNCLE OTCHO...

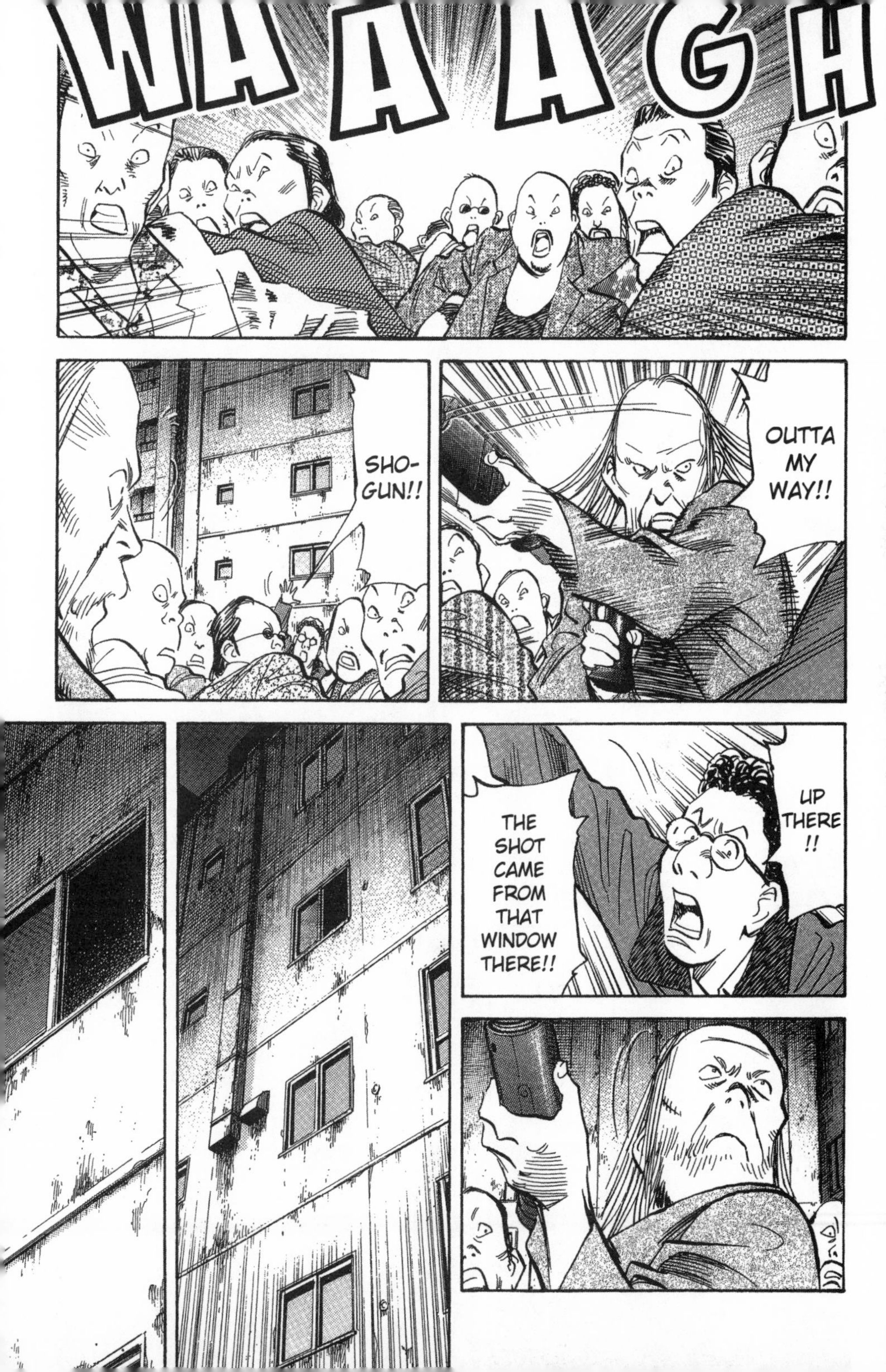
WAAAGH
OUTTA MY WAY!!
SHO-GUN!!
UP THERE!!
THE SHOT CAME FROM THAT WINDOW THERE!!

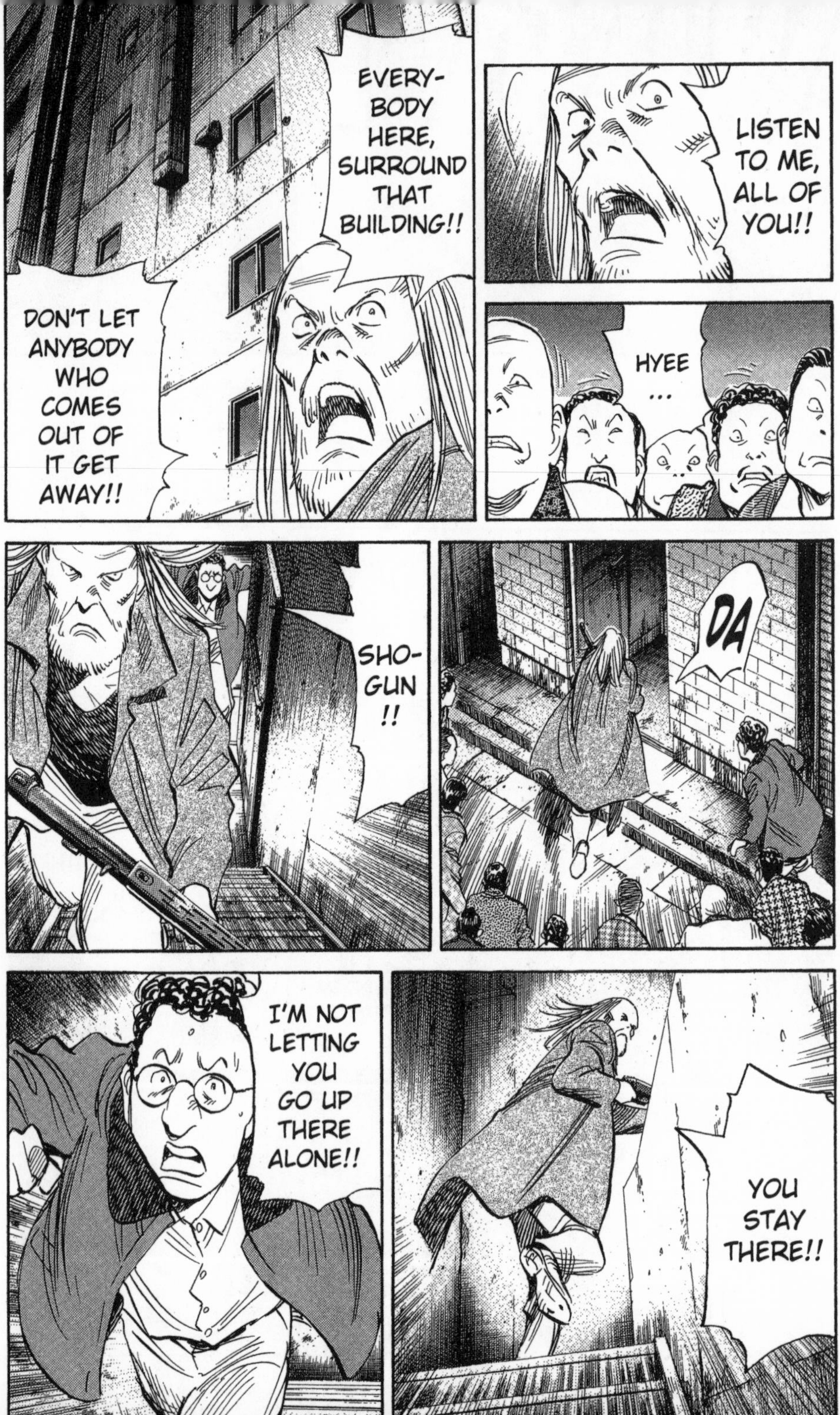
LISTEN TO ME, ALL OF YOU!!
HYEE ...
EVERY-BODY HERE, SURROUND THAT BUILDING!!
DON'T LET ANYBODY WHO COMES OUT OF IT GET AWAY!!
DA
SHO-GUN !!
YOU STAY THERE!!
I'M NOT LETTING YOU GO UP THERE ALONE!!

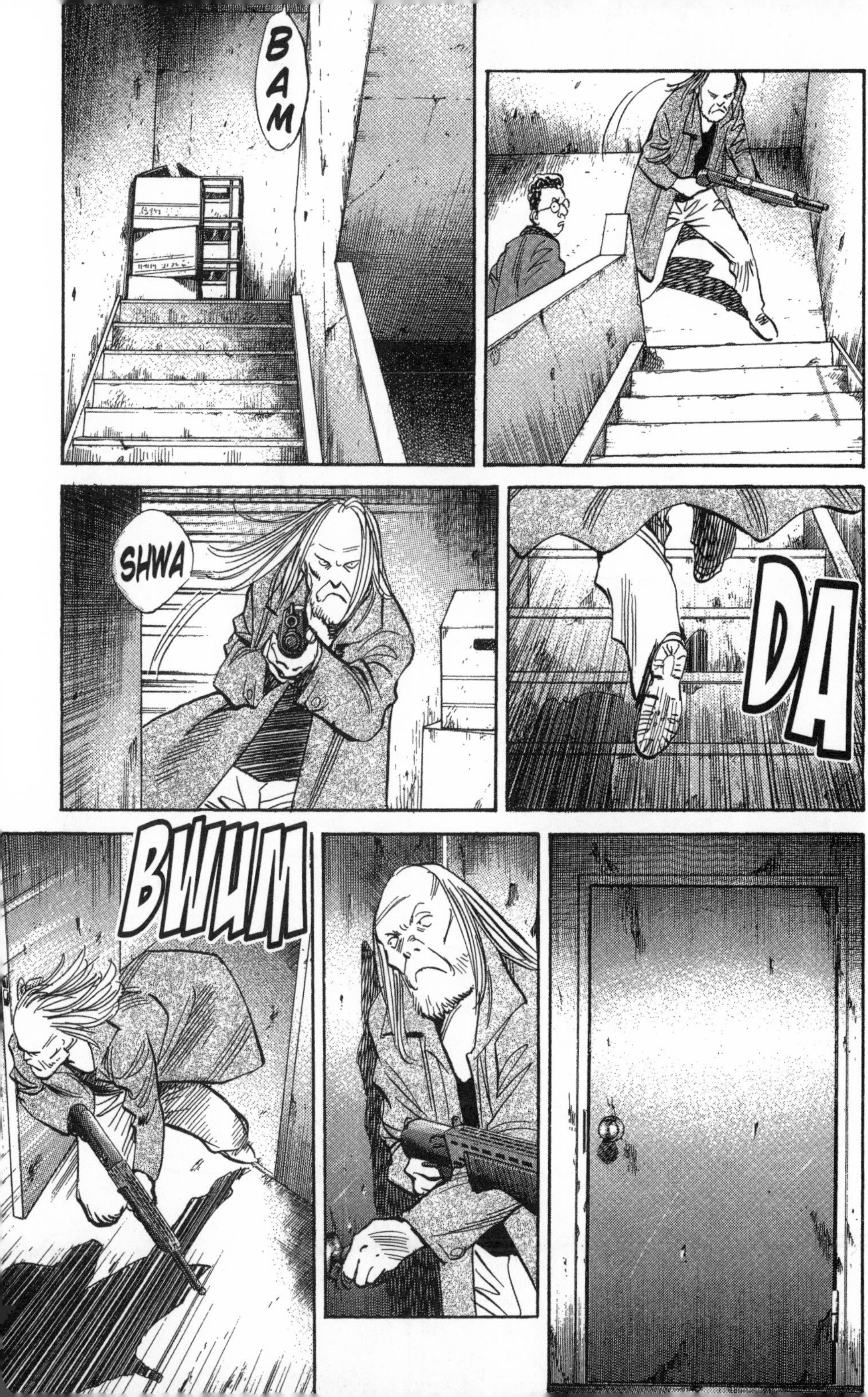
BAM
DA
SHWA
BWUM

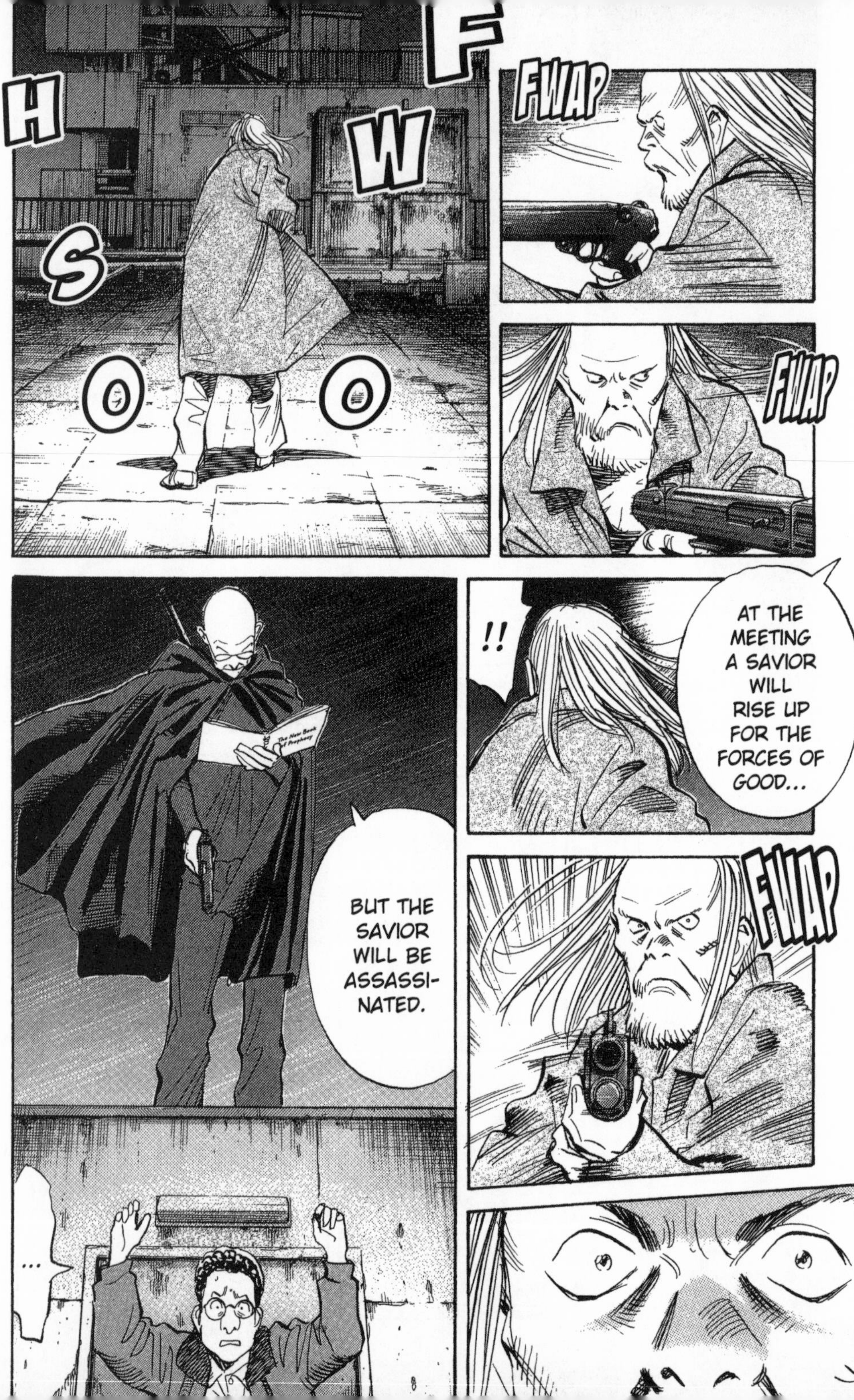
FWAP
FWAP
F
W
H
S
O
O
AT THE MEETING A SAVIOR WILL RISE UP FOR THE FORCES OF GOOD...
!!
FWAP
BUT THE SAVIOR WILL BE ASSASSI-NATED.
The New Book of Prophecy
...

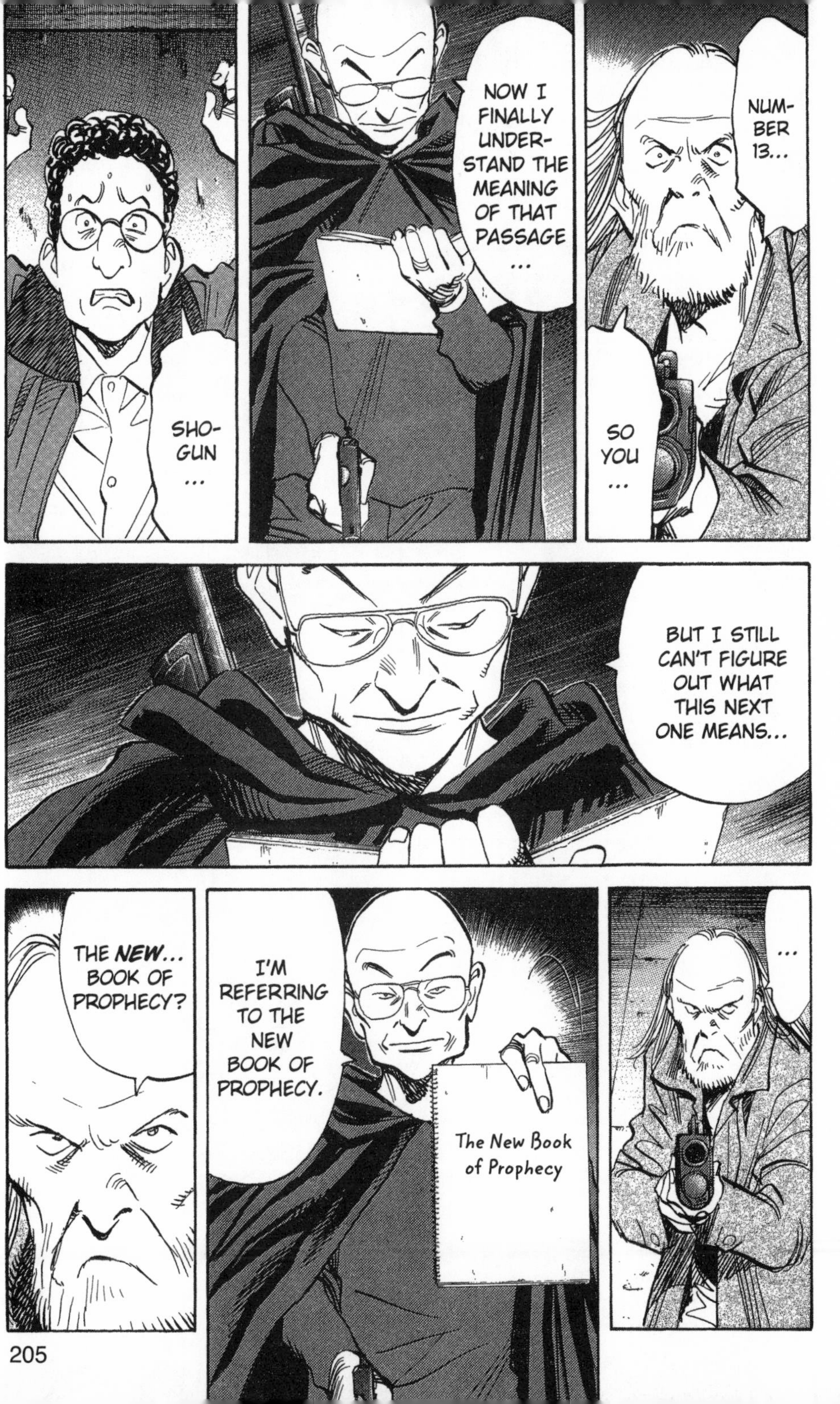

NUMBER 13...
SO YOU...
NOW I FINALLY UNDERSTAND THE MEANING OF THAT PASSAGE...
SHOGUN...
BUT I STILL CAN'T FIGURE OUT WHAT THIS NEXT ONE MEANS...
...
I'M REFERRING TO THE NEW BOOK OF PROPHECY.
The New Book of Prophecy
THE *NEW*... BOOK OF PROPHECY?

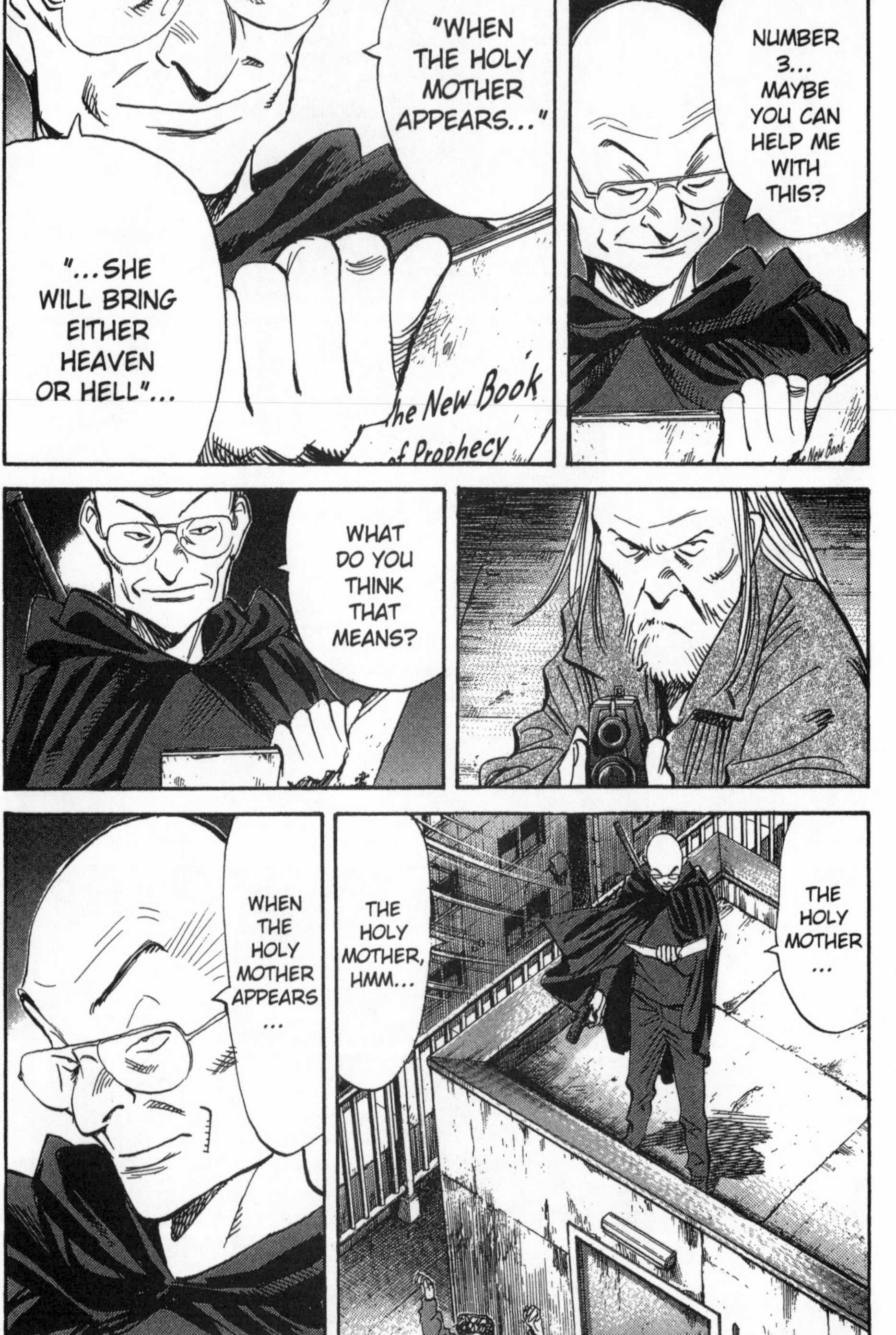
NUMBER 3... MAYBE YOU CAN HELP ME WITH THIS?
The New Book
"WHEN THE HOLY MOTHER APPEARS..."
"...SHE WILL BRING EITHER HEAVEN OR HELL"...
he New Book
of Prophecy
WHAT DO YOU THINK THAT MEANS?
THE HOLY MOTHER...
THE HOLY MOTHER, HMM...
WHEN THE HOLY MOTHER APPEARS...

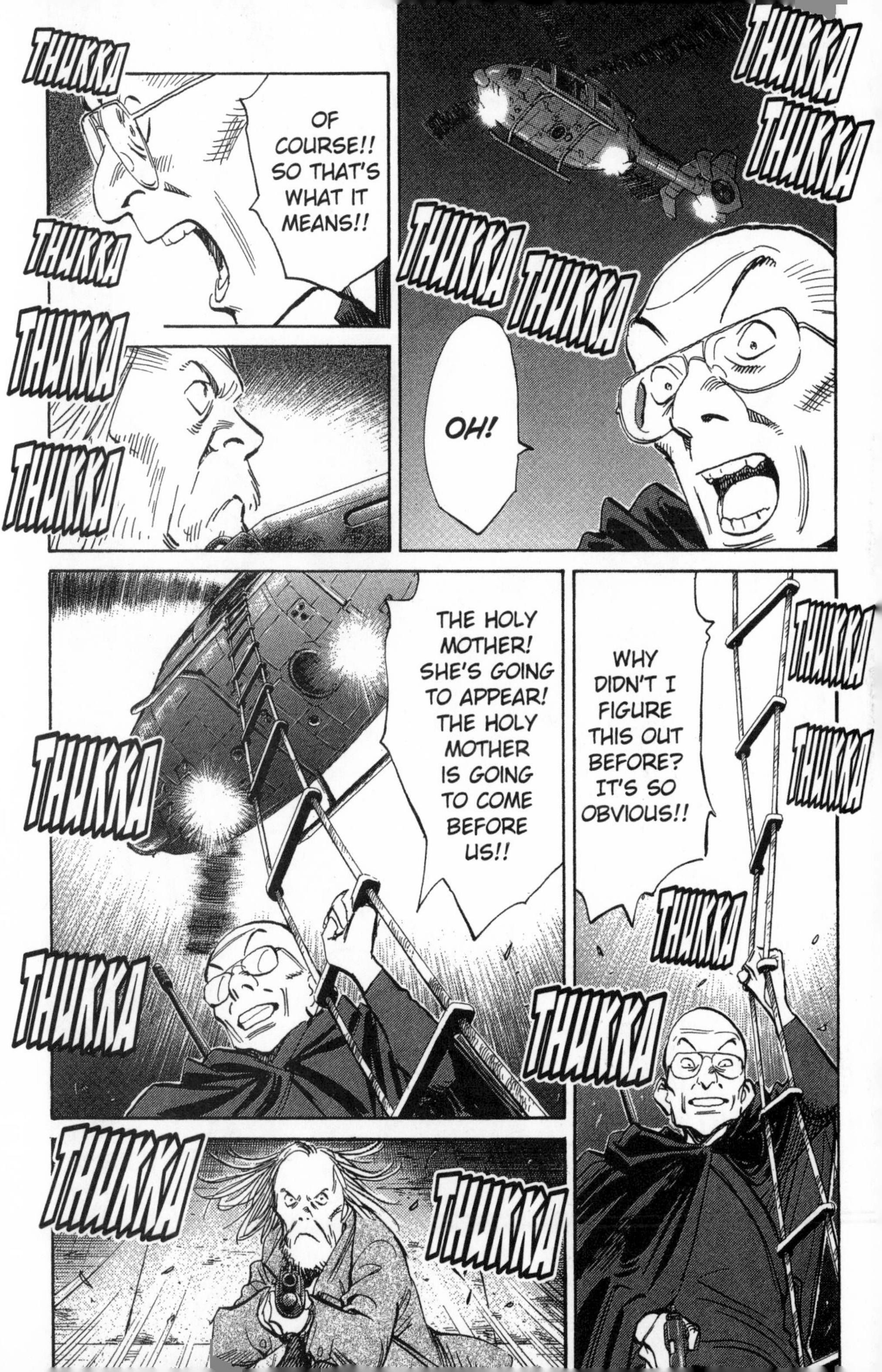
THUKKA
THUKKA
THUKKA
THUKKA
OH!
THUKKA
OF COURSE!! SO THAT'S WHAT IT MEANS!!
THUKKA
THUKKA
THUKKA
THUKKA
THUKKA
WHY DIDN'T I FIGURE THIS OUT BEFORE? IT'S SO OBVIOUS!!
THUKKA
THUKKA
THE HOLY MOTHER! SHE'S GOING TO APPEAR! THE HOLY MOTHER IS GOING TO COME BEFORE US!!
THUKKA
THUKKA
THUKKA
THUKKA

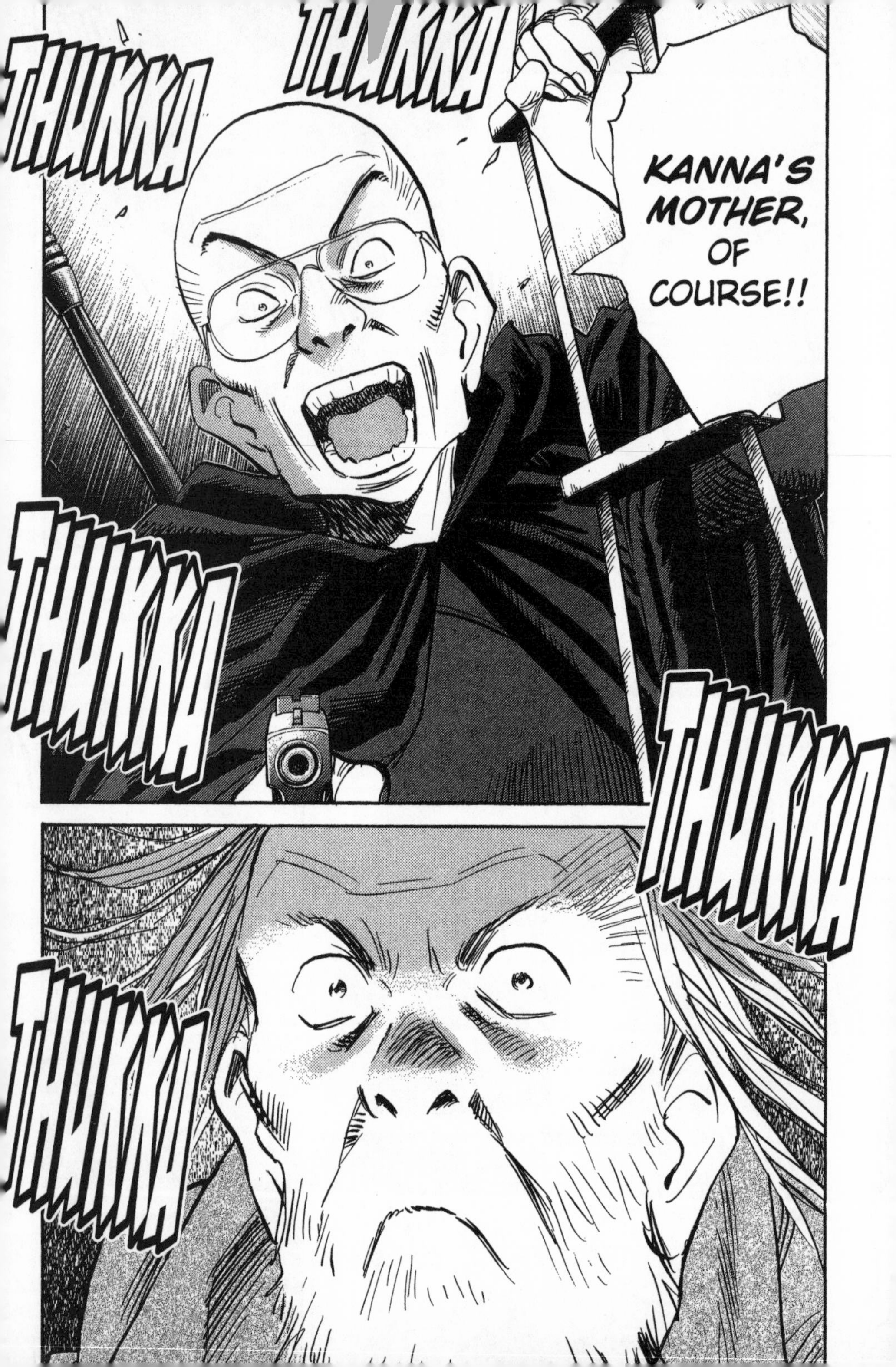
THUKKA
KANNA'S MOTHER, OF COURSE!!
THUKKA
THUKKA
THUKKA
THUKKA

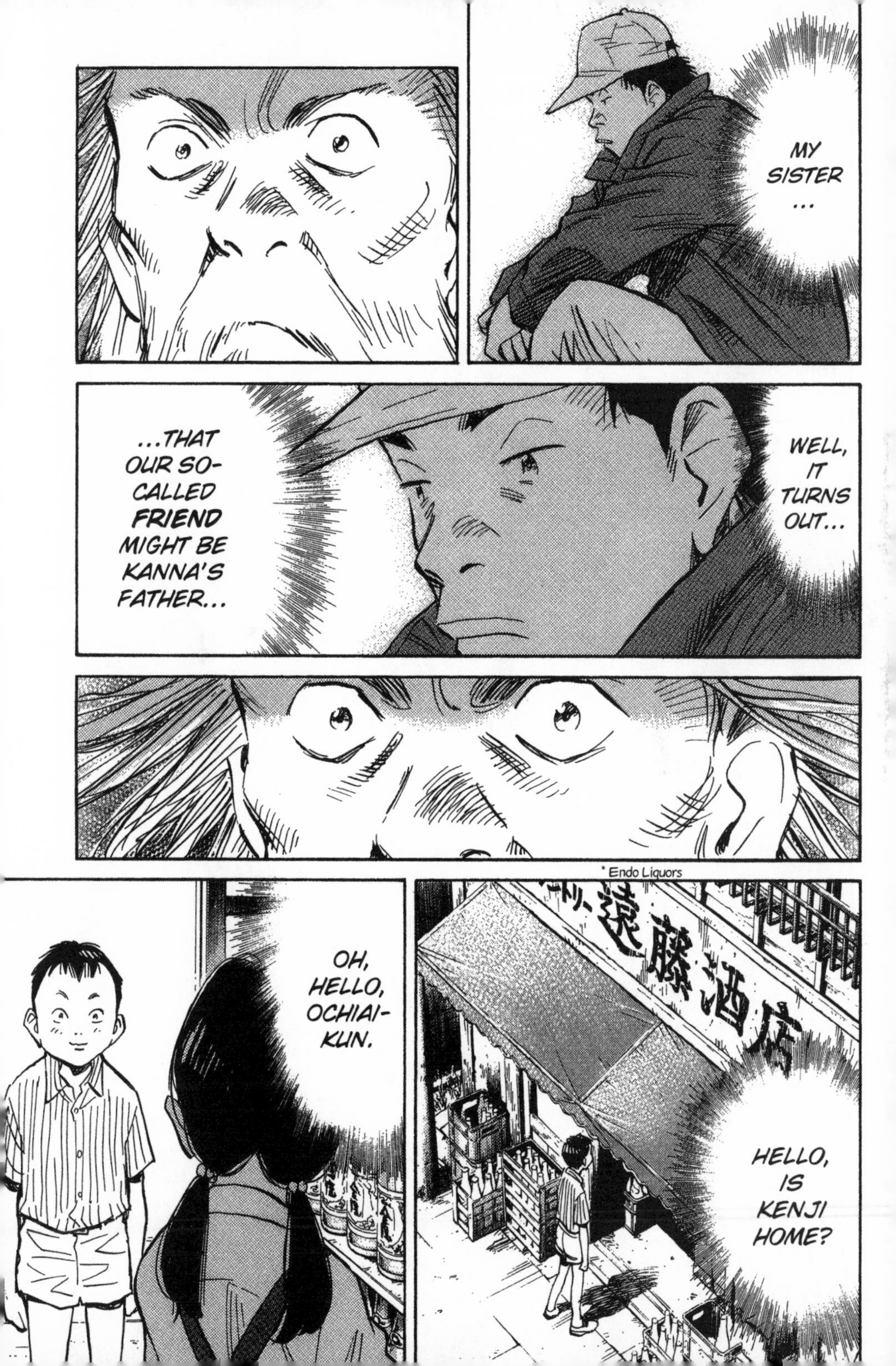
MY SISTER ...
WELL, IT TURNS OUT...
...THAT OUR SO-CALLED FRIEND MIGHT BE KANNA'S FATHER...
* Endo Liquors
遠藤酒店
HELLO, IS KENJI HOME?
OH, HELLO, OCHIAI-KUN.

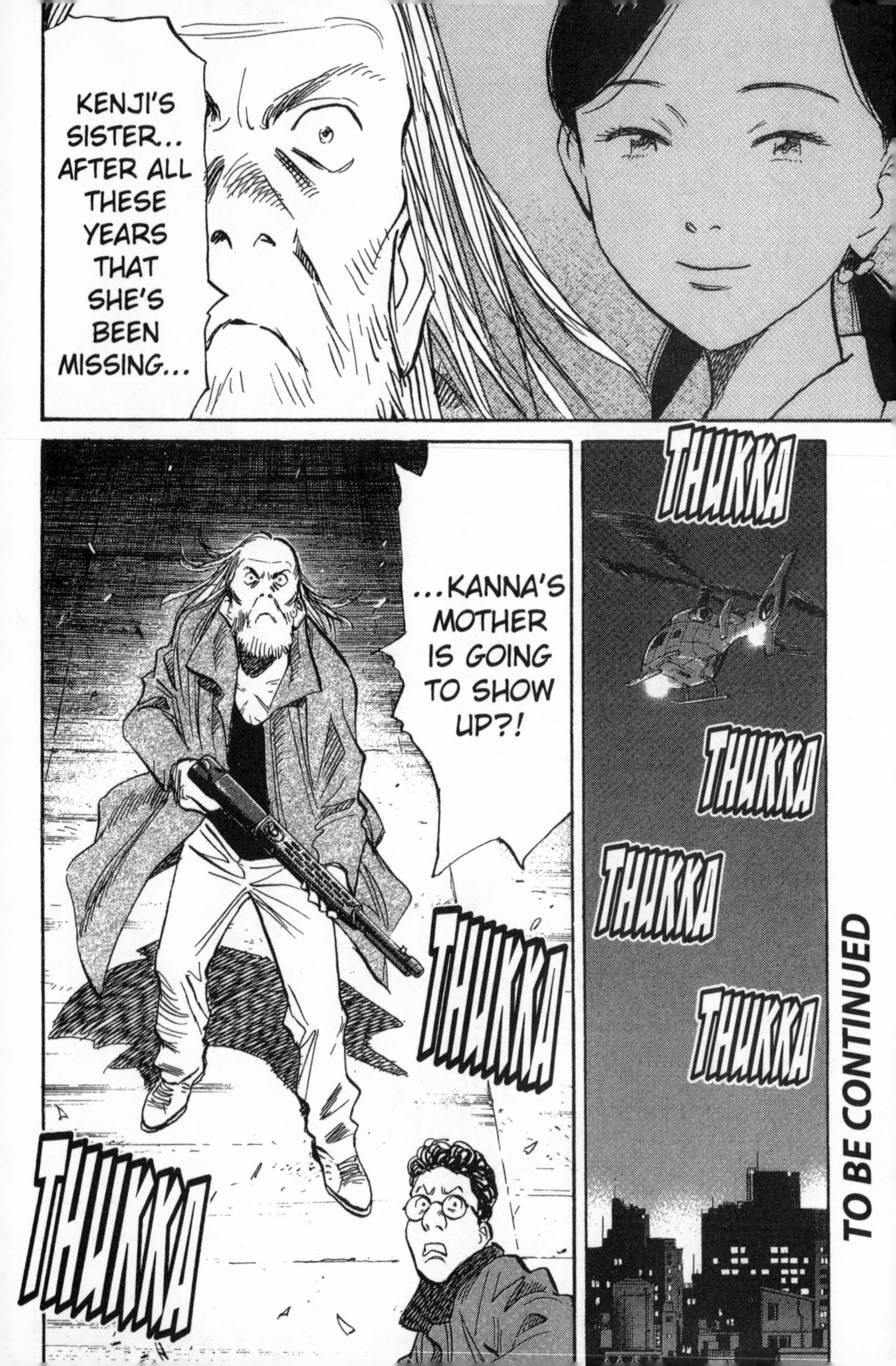
KENJI'S SISTER... AFTER ALL THESE YEARS THAT SHE'S BEEN MISSING...
THUKKA
THUKKA
THUKKA
THUKKA
...KANNA'S MOTHER IS GOING TO SHOW UP?!
THUKKA
THUKKA
TO BE CONTINUED

NOTES FROM THE TRANSLATOR

This series follows the Japanese naming convention, with a character's family name followed by their given name. Honorifics such as -san and -kun are also preserved.

Page 18: In Japanese schools, children change out of their street shoes into special indoor shoes when they get to school. There are shelves for these shoes in the entrance to the school, organized by grade and class, and each kid has his own cubbyhole with his shoes in it. This keeps the hallways and classroom floors clean, like the inside of a Japanese house, since it is the Japanese custom to take their shoes off to enter the house as well.

Page 92: The *Akai Hane Kyodo Bokin*, or "Red Feather Community Chest," is a nationwide charity drive all across Japan. In return for a donation, a person will receive a red feather to pin on their lapel.

Page 127: Takoyaki: "octopus balls," grilled balls of batter with a piece of octopus inside.

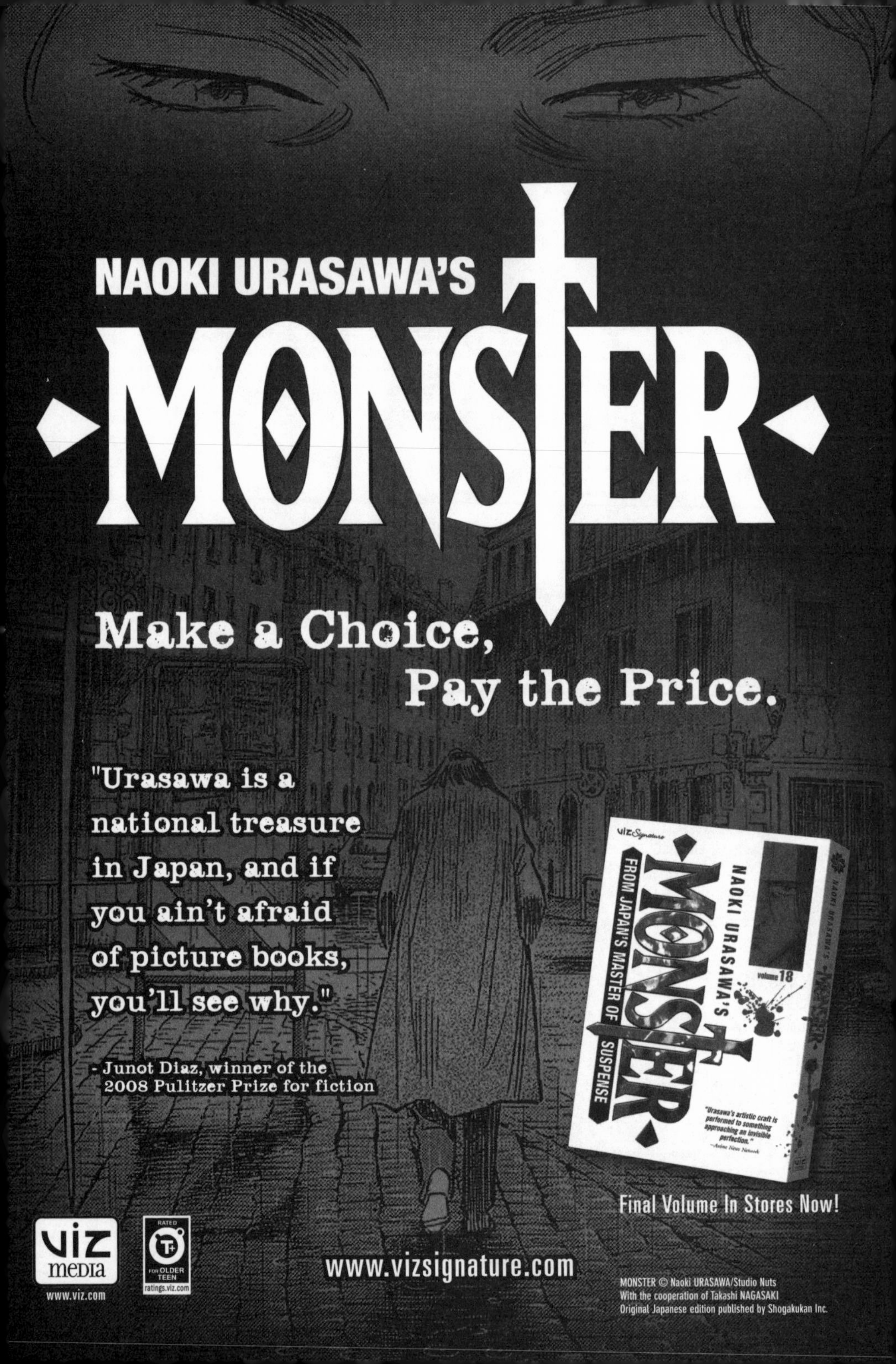
NAOKI URASAWA'S
MONSTER
Make a Choice,
Pay the Price.
"Urasawa is a national treasure in Japan, and if you ain't afraid of picture books, you'll see why."
- Junot Diaz, winner of the 2008 Pulitzer Prize for fiction
VIZ Signature
NAOKI URASAWA'S
MONSTER
FROM JAPAN'S MASTER OF SUSPENSE
volume 18
"Urasawa's artistic craft is performed to something approaching an invisible perfection."
—Anime News Network
Final Volume In Stores Now!
VIZ media
www.viz.com
RATED T+ FOR OLDER TEEN
ratings.viz.com
www.vizsignature.com
MONSTER © Naoki URASAWA/Studio Nuts
With the cooperation of Takashi NAGASAKI
Original Japanese edition published by Shogakukan Inc.

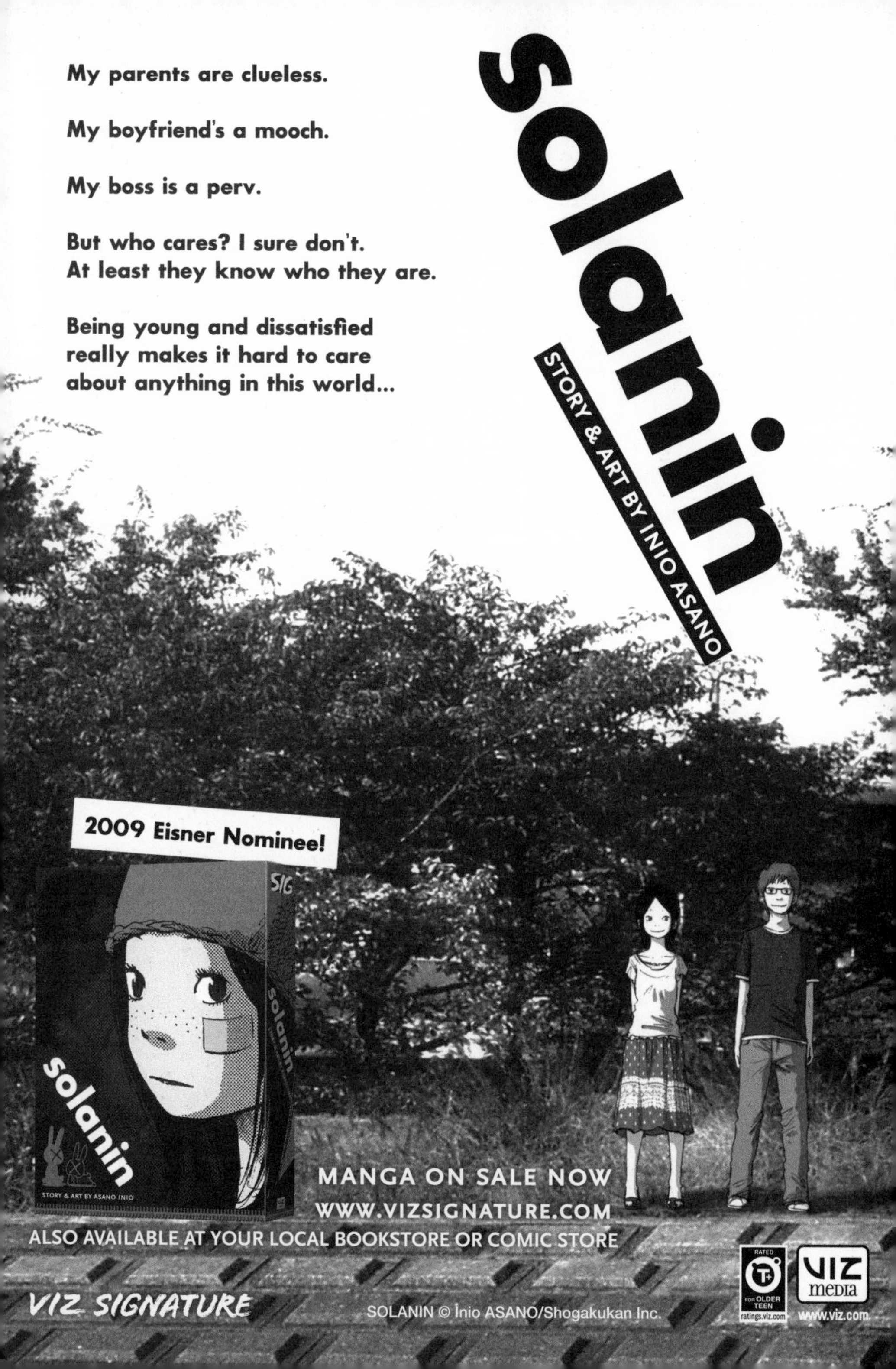
My parents are clueless.
My boyfriend's a mooch.
My boss is a perv.
But who cares? I sure don't.
At least they know who they are.
Being young and dissatisfied
really makes it hard to care
about anything in this world...
solanin
STORY & ART BY INIO ASANO
2009 Eisner Nominee!
SIG
solanin
solanin
STORY & ART BY ASANO INIO
MANGA ON SALE NOW
WWW.VIZSIGNATURE.COM
ALSO AVAILABLE AT YOUR LOCAL BOOKSTORE OR COMIC STORE
VIZ SIGNATURE
SOLANIN © Inio ASANO/Shogakukan Inc.
RATED
T+
FOR OLDER TEEN
ratings.viz.com
VIZ
media
www.viz.com